Teaching Children Science

A Discovery Approach

FIFTH
EDITION

Joseph Abruscato

University of Vermont

Allyn and Bacon

Boston   London   Toronto   Sydney   Tokyo   Singapore

To Anne Marie, Elizabeth, and Charlotte
who continue to give meaning to life

Vice President, Education: Paul A. Smith
Series Editor: Norris Harrell
Editorial Assistant: Bridget Keane
Marketing Manager: Brad Parkins
Editorial-Production Administrator: Annette Joseph
Editorial-Production Service: Susan Freese, Communicáto, Ltd.
Text Design and Electronic Composition: Denise Hoffman
Composition Buyer: Linda Cox
Manufacturing Buyer: Suzanne Lareau
Cover Designer: Jenny Hart

Copyright © 2000, 1996, 1992, 1988, 1982 by Allyn & Bacon
A Pearson Education Company
160 Gould Street
Needham Heights, MA 02494
Internet: www.abacon.com

Library of Congress Cataloging-in-Publication Data

Abruscato, Joseph.
    Teaching children science: a discovery approach / Joseph
Abruscato. — 5th ed.
      p.   cm.
    Includes bibliographical references and index.
    ISBN 0–205–28410–8
    1. Science—Study and teaching (Elementary).   I. Title.
LB1585.A29   1995
372.3'5—dc21   99–36512
                                              CIP

Printed in the United States of America
10 9 8 7 6 5 4 3 2 1   04 03 02 01 00 99

Contents

3   Science Process Skills   37

How can I use the science process skills as starting points for discovery-based units and lesson plans?

Part II Earth/Space Sciences and Technology

10 Unit, Lesson, and Enrichment Starter Ideas: The Earth/Space Sciences and Technology 165

Note: In the "B" chapters, the bracketed symbol that appears with each activity title identifies the corresponding NSE Content Standard. These symbols were created by the author.

Part III　Life Sciences and Technology

13　Unit, Lesson, and Enrichment Starter Ideas: The Life Sciences and Technology　269

15A   The Human Body: Content   331

15B   The Human Body: Attention Getters, Discovery Activities, and Demonstrations   345

Part IV   Physical Sciences and Technology

16   Unit, Lesson, and Enrichment Starter Ideas: The Physical Sciences and Technology   363

18A   Energies and Machines: Content   419

18B   Energies and Machines: Attention Getters, Discovery Activities, and Demonstrations   433

Preface

I continue to appreciate the kind words and helpful suggestions for *Teaching Children Science* that reach me from across North America and beyond. Its continuing success is due to many reasons, but I think two really stand out. First, the somewhat unique structure of the text provides great flexibility for both the instructors who teach with it and the undergraduate and graduate students who learn from it. And second, the friendly tone and informal style of writing in this book simply make it more enjoyable to read—certainly more so than the lifeless education texts I recall from my own college days. (In fact, there is no law that requires textbooks to be as flat as the paper they're printed on.)

So, a structure that provides flexibility and a writing style that speaks personally to you, the reader, characterize this fifth edition—the one that brings us into the twenty-first century.

Preparing for the New Millennium

Let's talk about children—those smiling, future adults looking at you from behind their desks and wondering what *you* are going to do next. What *will* you do next? As a teacher of the twenty-first century, your challenges are great but your tools are many.

As this new century begins, let me share some wonderful and long-overdue news that has shaped the content you will find within the familiar, flexible structure of *Teaching Children Science*. Actually, there are two pieces of good news. The first is that a truly incredible technology has reached the classroom—the Internet—and things will never be the same. And second, a group of respected educators and scientists, after laboring long and hard, have brought forth the National Science Education (NSE) standards.

Both these developments are important and will shape what we do next in teaching children science. You probably expect that I have built both into this new edition of *Teaching Children Science*—and I have. However, I must give you a small caution before I tell you how.

If a benevolent stranger ever rings your doorbell and gives you, at no cost, an amazing chicken that can talk and sing, don't be disappointed if you eventually discover that it can't tap dance, too. Just owning a talking and singing (but not presently tap-dancing) chicken could be your ticket to fame and fortune. And if you are very, very patient and an extremely good teacher, you might someday teach the chicken to tap dance. Just imagine the possibilities that would lie ahead for you and your feathered friend!

That's precisely how I feel about the NSE standards and the Internet. Neither is perfect, but in the hands of a patient, talented teacher, both are rather extraordinary resources.

The NSE Standards

The NSE standards provide some long-awaited direction for the development of state science curriculum frameworks, local school district curriculum guides, and even the efforts of text and resource book publishers. After others had spent so many years and so many hundreds of millions of dollars exploring possible curriculum directions, we finally have been given a compass.

In this book, I have presented the NSE Content Standards for grades K–8 in several ways. First, they are introduced in the opening chapter. Then their implications for curriculum scope and sequence are presented in Chapter 4, their recommendations for assessing understanding and inquiry are the focus of Chapter 5, their implications for WebQuest development are shown in Chapter 8, and later—in Chapters 10, 13, and 16—these standards are used as organizers for new lesson and unit plan starter ideas. All the activities and demonstrations in the "B" chapters also now correlate to the K–8 content standards. Finally, the entire NSE Content Standards are reprinted in the appendix.

Note that all materials related to the NSE standards are identified with this graphic:

And all those related to Project 2061 are identified with this graphic:

The Internet

The Internet has tiptoed into our classrooms and snuck in and around our dust-covered overhead projectors, erratically working videocassette players, years-old computers, and tired educational software. Nonetheless, it has arrived!

Today, virtually every teacher in every school can help children access a great portion of all the recorded information of humankind. Think about that for a minute! Being connected to the Internet is changing how we live, how we teach, and potentially how we learn. This technology is not risk free, considering the potential danger of children accessing inaccurate or inappropriate materials, but this danger can be overcome by providing guidance and using software filters. Without a doubt, the Internet is an extraordinary connection!

You and I, as teachers, must learn to use the Internet wisely or we will end up mere spectators in the extraordinary drama being played out on the human stage. We need to be *on* that stage, actively shaping the direction of the plot and the roles of the players. The alternative is to sit back and politely applaud as children and colleagues use this new technology, move on, and remember us as nothing more than dim faces in the crowd.

The Internet is present in this new edition in several different areas:

- Each of the nine chapters in Part I, dealing with science methods, has a new section called Internet Resources. In this section, you will find brief descriptions of important Internet sites related to the content of the chapter, including the URL (uniform resource locator), or address, for each site.

- I believe Chapter 8, Science WebQuests, is the first chapter in any science methods book to teach readers how to plan specific science-related Internet experiences for children. A master WebQuest is provided along with several completed examples.

- New to Chapters 10, 13, and 16 are sections that identify and briefly describe Internet sites that provide lesson plans, unit plans, and enrichment content for the earth/space, life, and physical sciences, respectively. Like those in Part I, these sections are called Internet Resources and include descriptions and URLs for all websites.

- All Internet-related materials in *Teaching Children Science* are identified with this graphic:

The addition of these new features related to the NSE standards and the Internet, along with the updating of science content and methodology throughout the book, will increase the flexibility you have come to expect in using *Teaching Children Science*. I hope you enjoy and learn from this new edition as well as a brand-new resource I have just completed for pre- and in-service teachers—*Whizbangers and Wonderments: Science Activities for Young People* (also published by Allyn and Bacon).

How This Book Is Organized

Part I: Strategies and Techniques

The first nine chapters of this book deal with major topics that will shape what you teach, how you teach, and how you interact with children. To help focus your reading and discussion in these chapters, keep in mind that each has a consistent format that includes these components:

- *A Look Ahead:* A list of the topics discussed in the chapter
- *Text:* A discussion of specific content-related topics
- *Real Teachers Talking:* Excerpts from conversations between teachers that will stimulate your own thinking and discussions with others
- *Make the Case:* A thought-provoking challenge for you to complete individually or as a member of a cooperative learning group
- *Internet Resources:* Brief descriptions of content-related Internet sites accompanied by their URLs
- *Summary:* A review of the main ideas in the chapter
- *Going Further:* Learning activities that you may do on your own or in a cooperative learning group
- *Suggested Readings:* A list of books and articles that will help extend your study of the chapter's main points

Parts II–IV: Methods, Content, and Activities for Teaching Science and Technology Units

Each of these parts begins with a chapter (10, 13, and 16, respectively) of practical starter ideas to help you plan and teach the science units and lessons related to the topic at hand. As noted earlier, two new sections have been added to these chapters: Internet Resources and Unit Plan Starter Ideas based on the NSE K–8 Content Standards.

These part-opening chapters are followed by "A" and "B" chapters:

- The "A" chapters present the science content for units and lessons (see 11A, 12A, 14A, 15A, 17A, 18A).
- The "B" chapters offer activities appropriate for the units and lessons (see 11B, 12B, 14B, 15B, 17B, 18B). These activities are grouped as Attention Getters, Discovery Activities, and Demonstrations. In this edition, the activity and demonstration ideas in the "B" chapters correlate to the NSE standards for grades K–8 listed in the appendix.

The chapters in Part II address the earth/space sciences and technology, those in Part III address the life sciences and technology, and those in Part IV address the physical sciences and technology.

For the Teacher's Desk

The materials in this section are provided as a resource for your use now and in the future. Divided into two sections, they include these materials:

- Your Classroom Enrichment Handbook
  - Keeping Living Things . . . Alive
  - Safety Management Helper
  - Materials to Keep in Your Science Closet
  - The Metric Helper
  - Content Coverage Checklists
  - Your Science Survival Bookshelf
- Your Science Source Address Book
  - Free and Inexpensive Materials
  - The "Wish Book" Companies
  - Bilingual Child Resources
  - Special-Needs Resources
  - Science Teachers Associations
  - NASA Teacher Resource Centers

Appendix: The NSE Content Standards, Grades K–8

Again, the entire standards are reprinted here for your reference. All the activities and demonstrations in the "B" chapters also are correlated to this list.

Acknowledgments

Although this book has only one author, many people have shaped its contents, directly and indirectly. I would like to thank my many colleagues for their continued support and encouragement, including Lowell J. Bethel at the University of Texas; Jack Hassard at Georgia State University; Russell Agne, Susan Baker, and Joyce Morris at the University of Vermont; Rod Peturson of the Windsor Schools, Ontario, Canada; Marlene Nachbar Hapai at the University of Hawaii, Hilo; William Ritz at California State University, Long Beach; and Larry Schaeffer at Syracuse University.

In addition, I would like to thank those individuals who reviewed this edition for Allyn and Bacon for their valuable suggestions: Thomas W. Giles, Cumberland College; Steve Gregorich, California State University, Sacramento; and Tom Howick, University of Southern Maine. I would also like to thank the reviewers and survey respondents from previous editions: Stan Chu, Bank Street College of Education; William Hughes, Ashland University; Raymond Jobin, Keene State College; Archibald Sia, California State University, Northridge; Rene Stofflett, University of Illinois; Barbara Kasten, Trinity College; Bonnie Kotvis, Alverno College; Margaret Mason, William Woods College; J. Philip McLaren, Eastern Nazarene College; Lucy J. Orfan, Kean College of New Jersey (now Kean University); and Harold Roberts, Hendrix College.

If you have used *Teaching Children Science* before, you are already aware of the feature in Chapters 1 through 9 called Real Teachers Talking: A Starting Point for Thinking, Talking, and Writing. I wish to acknowledge the "real teachers" who were kind enough to take the time to participate in conversations about the topics in each chapter: Chris Copes, Suzanne Fields, Susy Griffin, Wendi Harada, Suzy Ho, Nancy Hunter, Cheryl Ilnicki, Candice Nelson, Amy Okino, Debra Payne, Bonnie Petersen, Danette Quilausing, Kathlynn Tabandera, Chris Wakida, and Janet Weiss. I took a few editorial liberties to condense their conversations, so I have used pseudonyms in the text. I am sure their dialogues will provoke your thinking. Thank you, all.

Finally, may I once again say—as I have said in the prefaces to previous editions of *Teaching Children Science*—the order of the words in the title of this book is purposeful. *We* are teaching children science. It is not the other way around!

J. A.

— 1 —

Science and Technology

What are science and technology?
Why teach them?

A Look Ahead

Life barely clings to our small blue-and-white ball of a planet hurtling through space. To most of us, it seems like life is everywhere. It is not. If you think of Earth as a giant apple, life exists only in the peel—a thin film that in an instant could be stripped away.

In many ways, we teachers are the stewards of life. We are the cultivators, the caregivers, the eye-openers, the mind-stretchers. What and how we teach children today will race ahead of us as children grow and bloom in a harvest we can only imagine, in a time we will never see. *What* and *how* we teach will touch tomorrow. *You* will touch tomorrow.

You, Children, and Science: Some Fears, Some Hopes, Some Dreams

I think I know you. You are probably confident of your ability to teach children to read, to write, to do mathematics, and to learn social studies. Having grown up with e-mail and the World Wide Web, you are likely comfortable helping children use computers as tools and the Internet as a boundless reference shelf.

Now I may be wrong, but I don't think you are as confident about the prospect of teaching children science. You may fear that science is a subject that will be difficult for children to understand, provoking questions that are hard for you to answer. You may also fear that science time will be one of utter chaos and confusion, as strange liquids bubble out of beakers and chemicals flash, pop, and bang.

I know you have great hopes for your life as a teacher. You look forward to a future in which your own hard work, the advice of others, and the use of resource materials will help you create a classroom in which children not only learn science but *enjoy* learning science. You would like science time to become the favorite time of the day for you and your students. You would like to help them acquire the critical knowledge and skills that will carry them to a happy, productive, and prosperous adulthood in the twenty-first century.

I would like to help you start your journey toward that future—a journey in which you will overcome your fears, expand your hopes, and fulfill your dreams. Preparing every page in this resource book is my way of stretching out a helping hand. The very first step I will guide you to is learning what science really is.

What Is Science?

Science is the body of knowledge people build when they use a group of processes to make discoveries about the natural world. The people who produce this particular body of knowledge carry out work that is characterized by certain values and attitudes. We call these people *scientists*.

As a science teacher, you will teach children how to use this special group of processes to make their own discoveries and gather new knowledge. You will do this by creating an environment in which children discover and learn and then discover some more.

Together, these children and their teacher are discovering the wonders that surround them.

Science as Processes That Lead to Discovery

Just as a newborn reaches out to touch the new world, we continually explore the world around us. As humans, we wonder and discover, trying very hard to make sense of our surroundings.

In an effort to make sense of *their* surroundings, scientists use one or more *science process skills:* observing, classifying, using space/time relationships, using numbers, measuring, communicating, hypothesizing, experimenting, controlling variables, interpreting data, and defining operationally. These skills are explained in greater detail in Chapter 3 (see also Figure 1.1).

FIGURE 1.1
While these sample concepts and principles relate to the physical sciences, the sample science processes shown here also apply to the earth/space and life sciences.

Concepts

- Energy can be changed in form.
- Matter can be changed in form.
- The total amount of matter and energy in the universe never changes but is just changed in form.

Principles

- Objects that are dropped increase in velocity as they approach the earth's surface.
- Like poles of magnets will repel each other. Unlike poles of magnets will attract each other.
- For every action, there is an equal and opposite reaction.

Processes

• Observing	• Using numbers	• Experimenting
• Classifying	• Measuring	• Controlling variables
• Using space/time relationships	• Communicating	• Interpreting data
	• Hypothesizing	• Defining operationally

If you are going to teach children science, however, I hope that your curiosity drives you to ask why, what, when, and how, because you will be surrounded by children who ask those questions constantly. Your challenge will be to mesh your curiosity with theirs as they make discoveries about their world. The challenge is not that difficult because children bring tremendous energy and enthusiasm to their quest for answers. All children seem to be scientists at heart; they want to discover.

Science as Knowledge

The processes of science produce a body of knowledge that we usually call *content*. This body of knowledge includes the facts gathered, the generalizations or concepts that unify these facts, and a set of principles that can be used to make predictions. To a very large measure, science is a search for underlying principles, or *laws*, that predict how objects and organisms behave.

What do children think science is? Figure 1.2 offers the ideas of some fourth-graders. Most show some enthusiasm for science—it's fun! How can you nurture that feeling?

If, as a teacher, you only emphasize the facts of science, children will learn that science is an accumulation of factual knowledge. If you only emphasize the concepts of science, children will learn that science is a set of generalizations. If you only em-

FIGURE 1.2
A few fourth-grade children offer their definitions of *science*.

"Science is a class that we go to and learn about important things we have to know. I think science is the funnest class I've ever been to." —Jennifer

"Science is . . . I think that science is neat, fun. It is interesting you learn all kinds of neat stuff." —Renee

"Science is fun and it can be really hard to do. It is very hard to do some of the work sheets." —Mark

"Science is . . . Alot of fun we study Whales. We work in books and get more homework but science is fun learning experiment. We make maps and we blow them up." —Alan

"Science is the explanation for the way the things on earth work." —Nico

"Science is important to me. I will be an vet or animal scientist. I love science and when I'm sad or up set I try to be scietific and it cheers me up. It makes me happy when I make a dedution. Once I start trying to think up the answer to a problem and I won't i mean won't stop even for eating and sleeping even reading! So I love science a lot." —Mary Catherine

"Science is important to me couse we have alot of pages we have to do. I think it is easy to do." —Robbie

"Science is fun. I liked it when we used salt and flour to mold a map. Salt and flour is sticky. I like science." —Erik

phasize the principles of science, children will learn that science is a set of predictions. But science consists of more than process skills and more than content. Science manifests a set of *values*.

Science as a Set of Values

While there are many values you can emphasize as you help children experience science processes and learn content, there are six that you will find particularly useful:

1. Truth	4. Order
2. Freedom	5. Originality
3. Skepticism	6. Communication

Since science seeks to make sense out of our natural world, it has as its most basic value the search for *truth*. The scientist seeks to discover not what should be but what *is*. The high value placed on truth applies not only to the discovery of facts, concepts, and principles but also to the recording and reporting of such knowledge.

The search for truth relies on another important value—*freedom*. Real science can only occur when a scientist is able to operate in an environment that provides him or her with the freedom to follow paths wherever they lead. Fortunately, free societies rarely limit the work of scientists. When scientists are *not* allowed to act freely, the reason is not so much from the fear of what they may discover than the fear that freedom will cultivate another dangerous value—*skepticism*.

Skepticism—the unwillingness to accept many things at face value—moves scientists to ask difficult questions about the natural world, society, and even each other. Scienctists value skepticism, and skepticism sometimes causes nonscientists to doubt the results of scientific enterprise. In an article entitled "Uh-Oh, Here Comes the Mailman," James Gleick, a well-known science writer, describes excerpts from some of the letters he has received:

> Here is a lengthy single-spaced essay (painstakingly tied up with what looks like tooth floss) titled "Chaos and Rays." Apparently, one of these rays "impregnates the chaos" and "fructifies the forces."

> A Canadian reader has discovered (he encloses the calculations) that all spheres, including the Earth, are 20 percent larger than geometers have thought—"Perhaps the reason missiles keep crashing short of their course."[1]

While Professor Gleick may smile at these letters, he also notes:

> It's hard to remember, but it's surely true, that the instinct bubbling to the surface in these letters is the same instinct driving real scientists. There is a human curiosity about nature, a desire to peer through the chaos and find the order.[2]

There is, then, an underlying *order* to the processes and content of science. In their search for truth, scientists gather information and then organize it. It is this order that allows scientists to discover patterns in the natural world. Children need to develop this ability to organize information, which is why you will be helping children learn how to organize and keep track of their observations.

For all its order, however, science also values *originality.* Although some may view science as a linear activity—one in which people plod along, acquiring more and more detailed explanations of phenomena—in reality, science is fueled by original ideas and creative thinking. It is this kind of thinking that leads to discoveries.

Children love to talk with each other; so do scientists. The talk of scientists includes reports, articles, speeches, and lectures, as well as casual conversation. The ability to communicate results is vital if knowledge is to grow. Without extensive *communication,* progress would be greatly limited.

As a teacher, you will need to help children understand that science is more than a collection of facts and a group of processes. Science is a human activity that has as its framework a set of values that are important in day-to-day life.

What Is Technology?

 Technology is the use of science to solve human problems. There is certainly nothing difficult to grasp in this definition. It is simple and direct.

What is more difficult to understand and appreciate is the impact that technology has your life and the lives of the children you teach. Think for a moment about the almost mind-boggling technology that today's children will meet in their lifetimes—technology that, as one science writer has said, appears to be magic.

Although advanced technology is not magic, its effects are startling and life changing. Therefore, you will need to add technology to the ever-growing list of topics you must address with children.

Why Teach Children about Science and Technology?

 Why is a short word but such a powerful one. It represents the quest for a rationale or, as the French say, a *raison d'être,* or "reason for being." There are at least two good reasons why you should and must teach children about science and technology:

1. It will help children develop intellectually and socially.
2. It will help society develop and keep pace in a rapidly changing world.

As a teacher, you will need more than reasons for teaching science and technology. You will also need goals that focus and direct your work. The following sections will address two types of goals that will help organize your thinking:

1. Child development goals
2. Science, technology, and society (STS) goals

Child Development Goals

Developing Thinking Skills

> "Young man, you should know that an empty wagon
> makes the most rattle."

I will not divulge how often I heard this remark from one of my teachers. However, I will tell you that I think she was trying to impress upon me that my brain would serve me a lot better if it had something worthwhile in it. In her own quaint, repetitive way, she was telling me that if I was going to get anywhere, I had better gain some knowledge before voicing an opinion. She wanted me to use my full range of mental capacities. I know now that she was desperately trying to get me ready for an unknown future.

Are *you* ready to prepare children for the future? Science time will give you wonderful opportunities to help children become better thinkers, and that prospect has profound importance for today and tomorrow. The task may seem a bit overwhelming, but you have access to a valuable tool that will make teaching children how to think more manageable. Experts in human thinking have identified six levels of thinking, from simple to more complex:

1. Knowledge
2. Comprehension
3. Application
4. Analysis
5. Synthesis
6. Evaluation

Becoming aware of these levels will make your own thinking about thinking a lot easier. You can also apply this knowledge to help children improve on their own thinking skills during science time. You will make more and more progress as you gain knowledge about teaching children science and have more classroom experience.

Developing Positive Affect

For many teachers, a lesson about a caterpillar becoming a butterfly will only be about a caterpillar and a butterfly. But the same lesson in the hands of a master teacher—a great teacher, an extraordinary teacher, a truly gifted teacher—will be an experience in which children are thunderstruck with the realization that one living thing has become a completely different living thing right before their eyes.

The day on which that lesson occurs will be a day when those children's lives will be changed forever. They will leave school filled with a sense of wonder that has been sparked by brand-new knowledge as extraordinary as anything they will see on television that night. They will leave school wanting to know more, curious about what may lie around the corner. They will also leave school with new attitudes that will shape who they are and who they will become.

You can become that gifted teacher if you are willing to work toward the very noble goal of shaping children's lives. You will know you are getting close to achieving it when you notice that children are not only gaining science knowledge and skills but also developing positive affect about science, about school and about the won-

FIGURE 1.3
A child's environment has a powerful impact on his or her affective development.

> ### *Children Learn What They Live*
> *Dorothy Law Nolte*
>
> If a child lives with criticism,
>   he learns to condemn.
> If a child lives with hostility,
>   he learns to fight.
> If a child lives with fear,
>   he learns to be apprehensive.
> If a child lives with pity,
>   he learns to feel sorry for himself.
> If a child lives with ridicule,
>   he learns to be shy.
> If a child lives with shame,
>   he learns to feel guilty.
> If a child lives with encouragement,
>   he learns to be confident.
> If a child lives with praise,
>   he learns to be patient.
> If a child lives with praise,
>   he learns to be appreciative.
> If a child lives with acceptance,
>   he learns to love.
> If a child lives with approval,
>   he learns to like himself.
> If a child lives with recognition,
>   he learns that it is good to have a goal.
> If a child lives with sharing,
>   he learns generosity.
> If a child lives with honesty and fairness,
>   he learns what truth and justice are.
> If a child lives with security,
>   he learns to have faith in himself and in those about him.
> If a child lives with friendliness,
>   he learns that the world is a nice place in which to live.
> If you live with serenity,
>   your child will live with peace of mind.
>
> With what is your child living?

ders of the natural world. At that point, you will know you have done your part to help children grow toward the positive goals presented so beautifully in Dorothy Law Nolte's "Children Learn What They Live" (see Figure 1.3).

Developing Psychomotor Skills

I am envious of friends who have wonderful psychomotor abilities and insist on telling me tales of endless hours of jogging, bicycle riding, tennis playing, and skiing. When they are done with these tales, I not only feel envious but tired, as well. Nevertheless, I must admit that being able to lead a full and productive life depends in part on whether we acquired excellent motor skills at a young age and then successfully maintained them.

Surprisingly, science time can provide opportunities for children to learn to coordinate what their minds will with what their bodies are able to perform. Children must learn to operate their bodies to manipulate the environment in which they live. They need to develop gross motor abilities, which can happen through discovery-based activities such as assembling and using a simple lever, hoeing and raking a class vegetable garden, or carefully shaping sand on a sand table to make a land form. Children also need to develop fine motor skills, which can be refined through cutting out leaf shapes with scissors, drawing charts and graphs, and sorting seeds on the basis of physical characteristics. All these experiences will contribute to children's general psychomotor development, which will affect them throughout their lives.

Developing Responsible Citizenship

The children whose eyes will be on you during science time will not likely be concerned with issues such as raising taxes to pay for an underground sprinkler system in a city park or doing something about the smell coming from a local factory. However, they probably will be concerned with these and other issues at some time in their lives. The issues that will emerge in their twenty-first century adulthood will need to be addressed with wisdom—wisdom built on a foundation constructed many years earlier.

If you let children practice working in groups, teach them to gather facts before they reach conclusions, and help them learn to use natural resources responsibly, you will be putting in place the bricks and mortar that will support a life of good and active citizenship. During science time, children can gain the knowledge and skills that may someday help them make the world a better place for themselves and their children.

Science, Technology, and Society (STS) Goals: The National Science Education Standards and Project 2061

Add *STS* to the list of acronyms you store in your brain. As a person who will be teaching children science, you should know that these letters will appear in articles and books describing what you should teach and how you should teach it. But what do they mean?

STS stands for the interrelationship among science, technology, and society. In simple language, it represents the idea that you, as a teacher, are expected to teach children how science and technology affect society and how society affects the pursuit of science and technology.

You do not have to be concerned about developing your own STS materials right now. Many materials already exist and will be available to you as a teacher. What you should spend time and energy on is adapting available materials to fit the needs and interests of the children you will teach. To help you do so, two sources of guidance have been directly or indirectly sponsored by the federal government:

1. The National Science Education (NSE) Standards
2. Project 2061: Science for All Americans

The National Science Education (NSE) Standards

What you teach children in the twenty-first century will be shaped by a document called the *National Science Education Standards.*[3] The result of work by teachers, scientists, and others, this document identifies what it means to be a scientifically literate citizen and specifies what should be taught at various grade levels. The NSE standards also deal with a variety of other issues, including what knowledge and skills teachers should have, how students should be assessed, and how school districts should implement curriculum changes that will result in greater scientific literacy. Later in this book (in Chapters 4, 10, 13, and 16), you will learn what content the standards specify for your classroom.

Project 2061: Science for All Americans

Project 2061 identifies learning outcomes teachers should work toward in teaching children science and also provides direction for the content of science teaching. Various parts of Project 2061 will be treated more fully in Chapters 10, 13, and 16, but for now, you should be aware of its potential as a resource. Here is an overview of six content goals that you should strive toward achieving as a teacher:

1. The human presence on Earth affects the environment, and the environment affects the quality of human life.
2. Human survival requires having a continuing supply of clean food, water, and air.
3. The goods individuals need and use are manufactured using technology.
4. Earth's energy resources are limited and must be used wisely.
5. Technology can help individuals communicate with one another and locate sources of information.
6. Individuals can improve their health and that of others by using what they learn about science and technology.[4]

I hope that as a result of reading these goals, teaching STS-related issues will emerge as an important dimension of your work in the classroom. Doing so is one of the many ways that science can be the vehicle through which you expand children's awareness of issues that touch everyone's lives.

What Is Discovery Learning?

Children obviously can, do, and should learn *some* science through watching, listening, and reading. But if they learn *only* in this secondhand way, they may learn a lesson you did not intend to teach: that science is abstract, boring, and far removed from their lives.

REAL
TEACHERS
TALKING

A
Starting
Point
for
Thinking,
Talking,
and
Writing

Sean: My children this year are really something. They are super motivated for science time and a lot less motivated for the other subjects. It gets right to their curiosity. We are constantly searching for the "whys" and "hows."

Melanie: Do you get beyond the search for the clues and answers to dealing with the people who actually are the detectives in the mystery? I think it's important for children to understand what scientists and engineers do, since it's bound to affect their lives.

Sean: I don't think the traditional ideas for teaching about careers exactly fit younger children, but I do think we should build in some work on career awareness. You know, it's not so much for getting kids thinking about what they might do when they grow up but just giving more attention to what scientists really do.

Melanie: I don't think we should do units on career awareness. We just need to tie it in. If you are interested in giving more time for career awareness, I think the science process skills are the natural connection. They capitalize on the children's natural curiosity and easily lead to discussions and other activities on career awareness.

Sean: I guess I worry about us spending time and energy doing a lot with process skills and career awareness and then not having the follow-through at the upper-elementary and middle grades. That really frustrates me.

▶ *Point to Ponder:* *It may be easier to build career awareness into the science curriculum for the middle grades than into the science curriculum for the earlier grades. If you were teaching young children science, what activities or projects would you do to make them more aware of the work done by people involved in science and technology?*

The underlying premise of this book is that teachers must have children do far more than watch, listen, and read. Teachers must use their knowledge and classroom teaching skills to create an environment in which children explore, acquire new knowledge, and then use that knowledge in new situations. You will meet these three steps again in Chapter 3, which addresses the science process skills in detail.

Discovery learning is possible when children use science process skills in the context of scientific values that are as important in everyday life as they are in the classroom. Creating such a classroom environment will take dedication and hard work. You have already taken the first important step in understanding what science and technology really are and why they must be taught. The next step will take you even closer to becoming a teacher who creates a discovery-based classroom. You will learn how knowledge about human learning can be put to use in your classroom.

The Scientist: Who Is She?

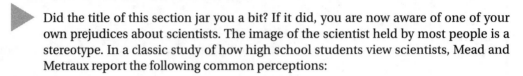

Did the title of this section jar you a bit? If it did, you are now aware of one of your own prejudices about scientists. The image of the scientist held by most people is a stereotype. In a classic study of how high school students view scientists, Mead and Metraux report the following common perceptions:

FIGURE 1.4   A sampling of "Draw a Scientist" illustrations by *college* students.

The scientist is a brain. He spends his days indoors, sitting in a laboratory, pouring things from one test tube into another. . . . He can only eat, breathe, and sleep science. . . . He has no social life, no other intellectual interests, no hobbies, or relaxations. . . . He is always reading a book. He brings home work and also brings home creepy things.[5]

Although students made these observations almost fifty years ago, their attitudes reflect, to a large degree, the views of society today. The students' choice of pronoun does not seem to reflect the purposeful use of *he* for *he or she* but rather the strength of the stereotype of the scientist as a male.

One of my favorite activities with children (and also with adults) is to ask each of them to draw a scientist (see Figure 1.4). In most cases, the scientist is represented as a bespectacled white male with a slightly mad glint in his eyes and a crop of straggly white hair. While it may seem amusing, the real harm of this stereotype lies in the

Make the Case

An Individual or Group Challenge

The Problem

The children in your classroom may be unaware of the many ways in which science and technology affect their daily lives.

Assess Your Prior Knowledge and Beliefs

To what extent are each of the following aspects of your life affected by science and technology?

Health	very little	little	somewhat	a great deal
Safety	very little	little	somewhat	a great deal
Nutrition	very little	little	somewhat	a great deal
Personal security	very little	little	somewhat	a great deal
Communication	very little	little	somewhat	a great deal
Transportation	very little	little	somewhat	a great deal
Recreation	very little	little	somewhat	a great deal

The Challenge

Your principal has asked you to give a five-minute talk at the next meeting of the Parents/Teachers Organization to encourage parents to cultivate their children's interest in science and technology. Identify five key points you would make in your presentation.

fact that it may dissuade children from considering science or science-related careers. Moreover, the sex-role stereotyping harms boys as much as girls: Girls learn that science is not for females, and boys learn that girls do not like science. The persistence of these falsehoods injures our future because in discouraging some individuals from pursuing careers in science and technology, we may lose great discoveries that would improve our lives.

Internet Resources

Websites for Science and Technology

General Science Skills

http://www.monroe2boces.org/shared/instruct/science78/gensk.htm

Although you will be learning about the science process skills in greater detail in Chapter 3, this page will give you a sense of how such skills are used in designing a science curriculum. Specific examples of various skills are presented.

Key Science Concepts

http://www.sasked.gov.sk.ca/docs/elemsci/menu_ksc.html

The authors identify 26 concepts that should be part of a science curriculum. As a person who teaches children science, you should be aware of the range of concepts that teaching units and plans should cover. Science content examples are linked to each concept shown.

The Values That Underlie Science

http://www.sasked.gov.sk.ca/docs/elemsci/menu_val.html

This site identifies seven values that should be part of any science curriculum. Each is linked to resource materials that provide specific examples of how that value can be fostered in the classroom.

NSE Standards On Line

http://www.nap.edu/readingroom/books/nses/html

This is the complete text of the *National Science Education Standards.* Since it is in hypertext format, you will find it easy to navigate from one part of the standards to another.

Project 2061 Home Page

http://project2061.aaas.org/about/index.html

As discussed earlier in this chapter, the focus of Project 2061 is to foster scientific literacy. This page is an overview of Project 2061 and the materials that have been developed to help educators develop curricula that ensure students attain scientific literacy. The entire text of *Benchmarks for Science Literacy* is online and can be reached from this site. *Benchmarks* expands the science literacy goals first stated in *Science for All Americans* into specific goals that should be achieved by the end of grades 2, 5, 8, and 12.

LatinoWeb

http://www.latinoweb.com/history.html

As you browse through this site, you will discover information related to strategies and techniques for encouraging youths from minority groups to pursue careers in science and engineering. You should be able to apply some of these ideas in developing career awareness activities for elementary-age children.

Society for the Advancement of Chicanos and Native Americans in Science (SACNAS)

http://www.sacnas.org/

This page has an extremely useful link to a resource you should find helpful in working to overcome scientist stereotypes. Search for the link to the "Biography Project," and then explore the helpful information included within the "By Scientist," "By Subject," "By Grade Level," and "Women Scientists" categories.

African Americans in the Sciences

http://www.lib.lsu.edu/lib/chem/display/faces.html

This site profiles African Americans who have made important contributions to the sciences and engineering. It is extremely well organized and lists individuals by category (e.g., biologists, chemists, physicists, inventors, etc.). Each name listed also serves as a link to biographical information. This site is another excellent resource for teachers who wish to demolish the scientist stereotype.

African American Scientists and Inventors

http://www.ll.georgetown.edu/os/blackhis.html

This site is an excellent resource for elementary and middle-level teachers who wish to expand their curricula by including the accomplishments of African American scientists and inventors. Many links are provided to other helpful Internet resources.

Women in Science and Technology

http://www.feminist.org/gateway/science.html

This site contains numerous links to Internet resources that provide examples of science and technology contributions made by women. It is also an excellent source of biographical information on well-known female scientists and females in technology-related careers. This site is very easy to use efficiently, since every link is accompanied by a brief description of the resource you will find at that destination.

4000 Years of Women in Science

http://www.astr.ua.edu/4000WS/4000WS.html

This is a "must see" Internet site. It is a truly extraordinary collection of biographies, photographs, and graphics about women scientists and the contributions they have made. There are approximately 150 separate, detailed entries.

Summary

Science is the body of knowledge people build when they use a group of processes to make discoveries about the natural world. This knowledge is shaped by the values and attitudes that underlie scientific enterprise. Children need to understand the knowledge, processes, and values of science and how this knowledge is applied within society. The use of science to solve human problems is *technology.*

Two sets of goals create a foundation for teaching children about science and technology: child development goals and STS goals. The first set views the knowledge and skills of science and technology as important elements of the process by which a child learns and develops. The second set deals with the advancement of society through the development of a scientifically literate population. The NSE Standards and Project 2061 provide guidance in setting STS-related goals.

Discovery learning is possible when children use science process skills in the context of scientific values that are as important in everyday life as they are in the classroom.

Stereotypes of scientists may discourage children from considering careers in science or science-related fields. Activities in career awareness may help eliminate the effects of these stereotypes.

Going Further

On Your Own

1. Consider your present feelings about teaching children science, and identify the factors that have influenced your attitudes.

2. If possible, interview an elementary school teacher to find out how he or she would answer such questions as How do you feel about teaching children science? What do children think science is? What science materials for learning science are available in your classroom or school? Do you feel well prepared to teach science?

3. Do some library research to determine the role that science and technology have played in shaping present-day society. Consider such questions as Would society be better served if science were pursued only for the sake of the technology that results from it? Does the scientist occupy a prestigious position in modern society? What responsibility do scientists have for communicating the results of their work in a way that is understandable to the public?

On Your Own or in a Cooperative Learning Group

4. Discuss the effects of the role models that your parents, teachers, textbooks, and the media offered you in elementary school. Can you recall your level of career awareness as an elementary student? What did you want to become? Why? If you are a woman, what factors tended to turn you toward or away from a scientific career? If you are a man, what stereotypes, if any, did you have about women and careers in science and technology?

5. Prepare a chart that lists the sample goals from Project 2061. Have members of your group offer examples of learning experiences from their own elementary, middle grade, high school, or college schooling that could be appropriately placed under each.

Notes

1. James Gleick, "Uh-Oh, Here Comes the Mailman," *The New York Times Review of Books* 4 (March 1990): 32.

2. Ibid.

3. National Research Council, *National Science Education Standards* (Washington, DC: National Academy Press, 1996), p. 13.

4. Based on *Project 2061: Science for All Americans* (Washington, DC: American Association for the Advancement of Science, 1989). See also *Benchmarks for Scientific Literacy* (New York: Oxford University Press, 1993).

5. M. Mead and R. Metraux, "Image of the Scientist among High School Students," *Science* 126, no. 3270 (August 30, 1957): 384–390.

Suggested Readings

American Association for the Advancement of Science. *Benchmarks for Science Literacy*. New York: Oxford University Press, 1993.

————. *Project 2061: Science for All Americans*. Washington, DC: American Association for the Advancement of Science, 1989.

————. *Resources for Science Literacy*. New York: Oxford University Press, 1998 (CD-ROM and book).

Barman, Charles R. "Completing the Study: High School Students' Views of Scientists and Science." *Science and Children* 36, no. 7 (April 1999): 16–21.

Calabrese Barton, Angela. *Feminist Science Education*. New York: Teachers College Press, 1998.

Calkins, Andrew. "National Science and Technology Week." *Science Scope* 22, no. 5 (February 1999): 28 (and attached poster).

Close, Denise, et al. "National Standards and Benchmarks in Science Education: A Primer." *ERIC Digest* (September 1996): EDO-SE-96-09 (2 pages).

Craig, Dorothy Valcarcel. "Science and Technology: A Great Combination." *Science and Children* 36, no. 4 (January 1999): 28–32.

Ferrell, Kathy. "What's My Line?" *Science Scope* 22, no. 5 (February 1999): 22–24.

Fiore, Catherine. "Awakening the Tech Bug in Girls." *Learning and Leading with Technology* 26, no. 5 (February 1999): 10–17.

Fones, Shelley White, and Lisa K. Wagner. "Addressing the Standards in the Garden." *Science Scope* 22, no. 6 (March 1999): 50–52.

Hurd, Paul DeHart. *Inventing Science Education for the New Millennium*. New York: Teachers College Press, 1997.

Lowery, Lawrence (ed.). *NSTA Pathways to the Science Standards*. Arlington, VA: National Science Teachers Association, 1997.

McCann, Wendy Sherman. "Teaching about Societal Issues in Science Classrooms." *ERIC Digest* (May 1997): EDO-SE-97-01 (2 pages).

National Research Council. *National Science Education Standards*. Washington, DC: National Academy Press, 1996.

Nix, Maria. "Stellar Women." *The Science Teacher* 65, no. 3 (March 1998): 28–31.

Rosser, Sue V. *Re-Engineering Female Friendly Science*. New York: Teachers College Press, 1997.

Sullenger, Karen. "How Do You Know Science Is Going On?" *Science and Children* 36, no. 7 (April 1999): 22–26.

Walsh, Carol S. "The *Life* of the Party." *Science Scope* 22, no. 5 (February 1999): 25.

2

Learning Science

How can I use key ideas from learning theory to create a discovery-based classroom?

A Look Ahead

Are You Learning Now?

Did you learn anything new today? Maybe a new name, an easier way to get from one place to another, a better way to clean your contact lenses? Did you discover how to jiggle your car door handle so you can climb into your vintage automobile easily or that a new kind of yogurt tastes just like velvety smooth vanilla ice cream?

Learning doesn't happen only for children, and it doesn't occur only in school. Learning is an ongoing process in which the learner finds new ways of thinking and acting. As you read these words, people everywhere are learning. As a matter of fact, right now, somewhere not far from you, someone is learning that it doesn't matter whether the corn seed is planted upside down or right side up because new shoots, just like young children, grow toward the light.

The Classic Learning Theories

There is still a great deal of work to be done regarding human learning. Perhaps in the future, experts will so understand the mysteries of the human brain that they will be able to tell teachers what they should do to help learning happen. For now, the best that we can do is review briefly some prominent learning theories. The insights we gain from these may direct us toward teaching so that learning happens for more children.

There are two broad ways of thinking about how children actually learn. One way is known as *behavioral theory,* and one is known as *cognitive theory.* The effective teacher must use elements of both theories to create an environment that stimulates sound thinking and acting and continually challenges, changes, and enriches a child's previous knowledge and perceptions.

The Behaviorists

The behaviorist approach suggests that what a child does, and consequently what a child learns, depends on what happens as a result of the child's behavior. From this perspective, your job as a teacher is to create a classroom in which good things happen when children work with science materials, interact with one another in cooperative group work, and complete science projects. If children enjoy these experiences, receive praise from peers and the teacher, and are successful, they will be learning and developing a positive attitude. In order to have more experiences and receive more praise, they will continue to work hard.

From the behavioral perspective, the teacher's job is to create a science learning environment in which certain behaviors and the acquisition of knowledge, concepts, and skills are increased and reinforced. *Tangible reinforcers* include receiving good grades, winning certificates or prizes in science fairs, earning points for free time, earning the privilege of taking care of the classroom animals for a week, and so forth. *Intangible reinforcers* include recognition of good work and praise from the teacher and the child's peers and parents. Figure 2.1 offers a list of some practical applications of behavioral principles.

PRACTICAL APPLICATIONS

Behavioral Principles for Your Science Classroom

1. *Reinforce positive behavior.*

   EXAMPLES • Praise children when they complete projects well.

   • Tell children who do a particularly good job of cleaning up after a particularly messy science activity that you appreciate their efforts.

2. *Reinforce effort.*

   EXAMPLES • Thank children for trying to answer questions during class discussions.

   • Praise children whose behavior improves with each field trip.

3. *After a behavior has been established, reinforce the behavior at irregular intervals.*

   EXAMPLES • Surprise the class with special visitors or field trips during particularly challenging units.

   • Take individual photographs (slides) of children at work on long-term (multiweek) science projects, and present slide shows unannounced at various times during the project.

FIGURE 2.1 You can find many ways to apply behavioral principles in your science classroom.

The Cognitivists

Cognitive theorists believe that what children learn depends on their mental processes and what they perceive about the world around them. In other words, learning depends on how children think and how their perceptions and thought patterns interact.

To understand the cognitivist view, try this: Look at the drawing on the right. What does it look like? Now ask other people to look at the drawing. What do they believe it is? If you ask a few people, you will soon discover that people perceive the world differently and that their solutions to questions depend on what they see and how they think. According to cognitive learning theorists, a teacher should try to understand what a child perceives and how a child thinks and then plan experiences that will capitalize on these.

Many learning theories have evolved from cognitivism. In the sections that follow, you will read about some of the most important of these theories.

Piaget's Theories

Jean Piaget spent his professional life searching for an understanding of how children view the world and make sense of it. His work led him to propose that children progress through stages of cognitive development. The list that follows gives the stages and a few examples of the characteristics of each stage. Figure 2.2 offers some practical applications of this theory.

1. *Sensorimotor knowledge (0 to 2 years).* Objects and people exist only if the child can see, feel, hear, touch, or taste their presence. Anything outside the child's perceptual field does not exist.

2. *Preoperational (representational) knowledge (2 to 7 years).* The ability to use symbols begins. Although the child is still focused on the "here and now" early in this stage, the child can use language to refer to objects and events that are not in his or her perceptual field. The child has difficulty understanding that objects have multiple properties. For instance, he or she is not completely aware that a block of wood has color, weight, height, and depth all at once. Concepts of space and time are difficult to grasp. The child does not *conserve* attributes such as mass, weight, or number. For example, the child views a drink placed in a tall, narrow glass as more than the same amount of drink placed in a short, wide glass.

3. *Concrete operations (7 to 11 years).* The child can group objects into classes and arrange the objects in a class into some appropriate order. The child understands that mass, weight, volume, area, and length are conserved. The child has some difficulty isolating the variables in a situation and determining their relationships. The concepts of space and time become clearer.

4. *Formal operations (12 years through adulthood).* The child is able to think in abstract terms, is able to isolate the variables in a situation, and is able to understand their relationship to one another. The child's ability to solve complex verbal and mathematical problems emerges as a consequence of being able to manipulate the meanings represented by symbols.

Ausubel's Theories

David Ausubel's work suggests that a child's learning comes as a result of his or her natural tendency to organize information into some meaningful whole. According to Ausubel, learning should be a *deductive* process—that is, children should first learn a general concept and then move toward specifics. The teacher's responsibility is to organize concepts and principles so that the child can continually fit new learnings into the learnings that came earlier. To help the child make sense out of the experiences that will come next, the teacher can use Ausubel's idea of *advance organizers,* which could include presenting vocabulary lists, pictures, and lists of topics to be studied. Figure 2.3 (page 24) offers some practical applications of Ausubel's work.

Bruner's Theories

Jerome Bruner's research revealed that teachers need to provide children with experiences to help them discover underlying ideas, concepts, or patterns. Bruner is a proponent of *inductive* thinking, or going from the specific to the general. You are

Piaget's Ideas for
Your Science Classroom

1. *Infants in the sensorimotor stage* (0 to 2 years)

   EXAMPLES • Provide a stimulating environment that includes eye-catching displays, pleasant sounds, human voices, and plenty of tender, loving care so the infant becomes motivated to interact with the people and things in his or her perceptual field.

   • Provide stuffed animals and other safe, pliable objects that the child can manipulate in order to acquire the psychomotor skills necessary for future cognitive development.

2. *Preschoolers and children in the primary grades* (2 to 7 years)

   EXAMPLES • Provide natural objects such as leaves, stones, and twigs for the child to manipulate.

   • Toward the end of this stage, provide opportunities for the child to begin grouping things into classes—that is, living/nonliving, animal/plant.

   • Toward the end of this stage, provide experiences that give children an opportunity to transcend some of their egocentrism. For example, have them listen to other children's stories about what they observed on a trip to the zoo.

3. *Children in the elementary grades* (7 to 11 years)

   EXAMPLES • Early in this stage, offer children many experiences to use their acquired abilities with respect to the observation, classification, and arrangement of objects according to some property. Any science activities that include observing, collecting, and sorting objects should be able to be done with some ease.

   • As this stage continues, you should be able to successfully introduce many physical science activities that include more abstract concepts such as space, time, and number. For example, children could measure the length, width, height, and weight of objects or count the number of swings of a pendulum in a given time.

4. *Children in middle school and beyond* (12 years through adulthood)

   EXAMPLES • Emphasize the general concepts and laws that govern observed phenomena. Possible projects and activities include predicting the characteristics of an object's motion based on Newton's laws and making generalizations about the outcomes of a potential imbalance among the producers, consumers, and decomposers in a natural community.

   • Encourage children to make hypotheses about the outcomes of experiments in absence of actively doing them. A key part of the process of doing activities might appropriately be pre-lab sessions in which the children write down hypotheses about outcomes.

FIGURE 2.2
Piaget's ideas have many practical classroom applications.

FIGURE 2.3
Ausubel's
theories, which
stress preparation
and organization,
have practical
applications
for science
classrooms.

Ausubel's Ideas for
Your Science Classroom

1. *Use advance organizers.*

   EXAMPLES • List, pronounce, and discuss science vocabulary words prior to
   lessons that use new science terms.

   • Role-play situations that may develop on a field trip.

2. *Use a number of examples.*

   EXAMPLES • Ask the children to give examples related to the science phenomena
   observed in class from their own experiences.

   • Use pictures and diagrams to show various examples of such things
   as constellations, animals, clouds, and plants.

3. *Focus on both similarities and differences.*

   EXAMPLES • Discuss how plants and animals are the same and different.

   • Explain what conventional and alternative energy sources do and do
   not have in common.

4. *Present materials in an organized fashion.*

   EXAMPLES • Outline the content of particularly complicated lessons.

   • Organize the materials needed for a science activity in ways that indicate whether they are to be used at the beginning, middle, or end of
   the activity.

5. *Discourage the rote learning of material that could be
   learned more meaningfully.*

   EXAMPLES • Have children give responses to questions in activities or textbooks in
   their own words.

   • Encourage children to explain the results of science activities to one
   another.

using inductive thinking when you get an idea from one experience that you use in
another situation. Bruner believes that children are able to grasp any concept, provided it is approached in a manner appropriate for their particular grade level.
Therefore, teachers should encourage children to handle increasingly complex challenges. See Figure 2.4 for some practical applications of Bruner's work.

Gagné's Theories

Robert Gagné's work led him to conclude that humans acquire five different capabilities as a result of their interactions with their surroundings:

Bruner's Ideas for
Your Science Classroom

1. *Emphasize the basic structure of new material.*

   EXAMPLES • Use demonstrations that reveal basic principles. For example, demonstrate the laws of magnetism by using similar and opposite poles of a set of bar magnets.

   • Encourage children to make outlines of basic points made in textbooks or discovered in activities.

2. *Present many examples of a concept.*

   EXAMPLES • When presenting an explanation of the phases of the moon, have the children observe the phases in a variety of ways, such as direct observations of the changing shape of the moon in the evenings, demonstrations of the changes using a flashlight and sphere, and diagrams.

   • Using magazine pictures to show the stages in a space shuttle mission, have the class make models that show the stages and list the stages on the chalkboard.

3. *Help children construct coding systems.*

   EXAMPLES • Invent a game that requires children to classify rocks.

   • Have children maintain scrapbooks in which they keep collected leaf specimens that are grouped according to observed characteristics.

4. *Apply new learnings to many different situations and kinds of problems.*

   EXAMPLE • Learn how scientists estimate the size of populations by having children count the number in a sample, and then estimate the numbers of grasshoppers in a lawn *and* in a meadow.

5. *Pose a problem to the children, and let them find the answer.*

   EXAMPLES • Ask questions that will lead naturally to activities—Why should we wear seatbelts? and What are some ingredients that most junk foods have?

   • Do a demonstration that raises a question in the children's minds. For example, levitate a washer using magnets or mix two colored solutions to produce a third color.

6. *Encourage children to make intuitive guesses.*

   EXAMPLES • Ask children to guess the amount of water that goes down the drain each time someone gets a drink of water from a water fountain.

   • Give children magazine photographs of the evening sky, and have them guess the locations of some major constellations.

FIGURE 2.4
Bruner's ideas
can be used
to encourage
children to make
their own science
discoveries.

1. Verbal information
2. Intellectual skills
3. Cognitive strategies
4. Attitudes
5. Motor skills[1]

If you view these five capabilities as outcomes or objectives, it will help you determine the kinds of experiences you need to offer your students. Figure 2.5 provides some specific examples of what you could do to help children move toward each outcome.

Gardner's Multiple Intelligences

 Do you consider yourself intelligent? Of course you do—but why? What is *intelligence?*
Introductory psychology books tell us that intelligence is measured by IQ tests, which is a less than satisfying answer. At the very minimum, *intelligence* relates to a capacity to learn as well as an ability to apply that learning. It is usually reported as a number called an *intelligence quotient,* or *IQ.* Someone of normal or average intelligence has an IQ of 100.

How will knowing that number for each of your students help you create a classroom where all children learn? For instance, would knowing that Maria has an IQ of 135 and Ricky has an IQ of 110 change how you teach Maria and Ricky? Probably not. In fact, this traditional way of measuring and reporting a child's theoretical capacity to learn will be of little help as you plan science experiences that are responsive to individual differences.

Gardner's Original Theory

Howard Gardner has suggested a radically new way of thinking about intelligence. Early in his work, he discovered seven different intelligences that he believes each of us has to various degrees:

1. Logical-mathematical
2. Linguistic
3. Musical
4. Spatial
5. Bodily-kinesthetic
6. Interpersonal
7. Intrapersonal[2]

According to Gardner's theory, each child can be viewed as having a greater or lesser capacity to learn in each specific area. This means, in turn, that you as a teacher can

Gagné's Ideas for Your Science Classroom

1. *Verbal information*

   EXAMPLES
   - Have children recall science facts and concepts orally or in writing.
   - Model the use of advance organizers such as diagrams and lists of key words prior to children reading science material or observing videotapes of science phenomena.

2. *Intellectual skills*

   EXAMPLES
   - Have children invent rules that govern processes, find similarities and differences, and predict outcomes.
   - Emphasize search patterns and regularities during hands-on experiences. Whenever possible have children not only compare organisms, objects, and phenomena but also contrast them.

3. *Cognitive strategies*

   EXAMPLES
   - Encourage children to find their own ways to remember information and ideas.
   - Model the use of mnemonic devices, diagrams, outlines, journaling, audiotaping, and other techniques for retaining ideas.

4. *Attitudes*

   EXAMPLE
   - Select content and experiences that are relevant to children's daily lives and intriguing to them so children develop positive attitudes toward science and choose science-related experiences during leisure time.

5. *Acquisition of motor skills*

   EXAMPLE
   - Through the use of discovery-oriented experiences, provide children with opportunities to use hand lenses, simple tools, measuring devices, and the like.

FIGURE 2.5 When applied in the classroom, Gagné's theories emphasize relevance to children's daily lives and the search for patterns and regularities during hands-on experiences.

focus on particular intelligences as you create science learning experiences. You can teach to each child's strengths and find appropriate ways to help him or her grow in weak areas.

Gardner's Addition: Naturalist Intelligence

In more recent years, Gardner's work has led to what he describes as *naturalist intelligence:* the ability to discern subtle characteristics and patterns and then easily group objects or events in appropriate categories.[3]

27

REAL
TEACHERS
TALKING

A
Starting
Point
for
Thinking,
Talking,
and
Writing

Robin: I've been reading a lot about Gardner's ideas in teacher magazines and discussing them in teacher workshops. I must admit that they have really caught my attention. They've broadened my vision of what we can accomplish with children.

Angela: Do you think they have actually affected your planning or your teaching or how you assess the children? I think his ideas could really affect all of them.

Robin: Oh, they really have affected all three. The idea that really stands out is that children have a wide variety of abilities beyond just the academic. So Gardner's ideas are affecting how I plan, teach, and assess. He is saying that we may be missing opportunities to capitalize on these multiple intelligences, and that really bothers me.

Angela: For me, the most important thing is that you use the theory in your actual teaching. Of course, some parts of his theory fit some people's teaching style better than others. Personally, I think most of it fits for me.

Robin: Even though teachers sometimes complain that their preservice or inservice courses are too theoretical, as professionals we need to have some framework to support what we do. Teaching is not incidental. We need to have a reason for doing what we do. Gardner's ideas about human abilities can help us clean up and straighten out basic assumptions and bring what we actually do with children in science more in line with what we believe about how all of us learn.

Angela: Especially if it's a theory that has such an optimistic view about the range of abilities that each child has. The flip side of all this is that I'm not sure that the general public is ready for the idea that we want to change the curriculum in ways that take it pretty far beyond the traditional academics they want us to teach.

▶ *Point to Ponder:* *If you were asked to present some of Gardner's ideas to a meeting of 50 elementary and middle grade teachers who were working on a rationale for a new science curriculum, what would you emphasize?*

As a science teacher, the possibility that this intelligence exists could be very important, since you might be able to identify how much individuals are "science prone" based on their measured naturalist intelligence. Knowing this could help you adjust your teaching to build on the abilities of children who have strong naturalist intelligence and to develop ways to be more responsive to children who have a more modest level of naturalist intelligence. Adjustments might include providing some children with more sophisticated observation and classification challenges and others with more time to complete work that requires high levels of naturalist intelligence.

See Figure 2.6 for a few real-world examples of how you can help children grow in all eight of Gardner's multiple intelligences.

Gardner's Theory of Multiple Intelligences for Your Science Classroom

FIGURE 2.6
Gardner's theory of multiple intelligences has exciting implications and many practical applications for the classroom.

1. *Logical-mathematical*

   EXAMPLES
   • Emphasize the underlying patterns children observe in science activities.
   • Have children list the steps they undertook in an activity and what they thought at each step.

2. *Linguistic*

   EXAMPLES
   • Emphasize writing down predictions, observations, and so on in science journals and the importance of using appropriate descriptive words and new terminology.
   • Encourage children to maintain their own science dictionaries, which will include new science terms and drawings to illustrate word meanings.

3. *Musical*

   EXAMPLES
   • Whenever possible, use vocal and instrumental music selections to accompany the introduction of new concepts. For example, use songs related to the seasons when carrying out a unit on climate.
   • When teaching a unit on sound, emphasize the connections to music, such as the effect of changing the thickness of a string or the length of the air column of an instrument.

4. *Spatial*

   EXAMPLE
   • Have children express what they have learned through drawings and models.

5. *Bodily-kinesthetic*

   EXAMPLES
   • Encourage children to use equipment that builds upon coordination skills, such as the microscope, balance, and hand lens.
   • Wherever possible, have children demonstrate new learnings through movement and dance. For example, children might create a dance to illustrate the expansion of a balloon resulting from increasing the energy of motion of the molecules contained within it.

6. *Interpersonal*

   EXAMPLES
   • Have children create simulated television advertising on issues investigated in class, such as the environment or proper nutrition.
   • When doing cooperative group work, provide time for children to process how well their group has worked on a science project.

7. *Intrapersonal*

   EXAMPLE
   • Provide opportunities for children to informally assess their interest in science, how well they are learning, and how they feel about matters related to science and technology.

8. *Naturalist*

   EXAMPLE
   • Early in the school year, give children sets of natural objects or pictures of natural objects or events they have not previously seen (e.g., rocks, leaves, pictures of various cloud types). Then ask them to observe and group members of each set.

Constructivism

If you heard the term *constructivism* in an education or psychology class and began to research it because you were unsure of what it meant, you would soon find that it is associated with the generative model of learning. *Generative* has the same root as the term *generate,* and this term is at the heart of constructivism. Constructivism, which has its roots in cognitive psychology, proposes that children learn as a result of their personal generation of meaning from experiences. The fundamental role of a teacher is to help children generate connections between what they are supposed to learn and what they already know or believe.

Three principles make up the theory of constructivism:

1. A person never really knows the world as it is. Each person constructs beliefs about what is real.
2. What a person already believes, what a person brings to new situations, filters out or changes the information that the person's senses deliver.
3. People create a reality based on their previous beliefs, their own abilities to reason, and their desire to reconcile what they believe and what they actually observe.

Naive Conceptions

The first of these three principles is very important to teachers. Your experience with children probably has already taught you that not everything a child believes or knows is true. For example, Tom may believe that sweaters keep him warm because sweaters are warm. Uncle Harry, who lives with Tom's family, has told him many times to wear a warm sweater on a cool day. The belief that a sweater is warm is an example of a *naive conception*—an idea that does not fit reality when its validity is checked. Children and adults have many naive conceptions, and it is extremely difficult for a teacher to help a child construct new understandings if the child's naive conceptions filter out new experiences.

Assimilating and Accommodating New Learnings

The last two principles come into play when planning hands-on experiences for children. What happens when you provide a child with a hands-on experience in which he or she learns something that fits into ideas that the child already has about how the natural world works? Suppose, for example, Susie already believes that sunlight and plant growth are related and her teacher provides an experience in which she observes firsthand that depriving plants of light is detrimental to their health. Cognitive psychologists use a term that aptly describes this situation—*assimilation.* Susie assimilates, or absorbs, her new learnings easily.

Suppose, however, that Susie's teacher has the class plant seeds in two containers. One container is exposed to sunlight and one is kept in darkness. What sense will Susie make of her observation when she sees that both sets of seeds have produced

Constructivism for Your Science Classroom

1. *A person never really knows the world as it is. Each person constructs beliefs about what is real.*

   EXAMPLE • When beginning a unit of study, have children write or talk about what they already know or believe about that topic. For example, if you are starting a unit on space, give children a chance to write or talk about whether the terms *solar system* and *universe* are the same or different.

2. *What a person believes filters out or changes the information delivered by his or her senses.*

   EXAMPLE • After children have had an opportunity to tell what they know and believe, ask them if they would be willing to change some of their ideas if a discovery activity gave them new information. For example, ask the children who think a seed will grow properly if it is planted upside down if they will be able to change their minds if the activity gives a result that is different from what they expect.

3. *Each person creates a reality based on his or her previous beliefs, ability to reason, and desire to reconcile what he or she believes and actually observes.*

   EXAMPLE • Early in the year and perhaps early in each unit, discuss with children how they learn science. Share and discuss ideas about the importance of making careful predictions and hypotheses before an activity and the importance of reporting actual results, not results that fit their earlier ideas.

FIGURE 2.7
When used in the classroom, the principles of constructivism will lead you to discover what children know and believe before beginning a new unit.

tiny, healthy plants with small, green leaves? With help from the teacher, she can accommodate this strange observation by broadening her beliefs about plant growth to include the possibility that in its earliest stages of development, a plant is not dependent on light for food production but rather on food stored in the seed.

Constructivism focuses on the interplay between what the child already knows and the experiences the teacher provides. The conceptions and naive conceptions that the child has before an experiment make a very real difference in what the child will learn. Figure 2.7 identifies some practical applications of constructivism.

Learning Styles

 Do you learn in the same way that your brother or sister or father or mother does? Do you learn in the same way that the stranger sitting next to you in a class or workshop does? If you have answered no to these questions, the implications for you as a teacher are enormous.

Learning Styles for
Your Science Classroom

1. *It is likely that children prefer to learn in different ways.*

   EXAMPLE • Study curriculum materials to ascertain whether they will accommodate differences in learning styles, and then develop some alternative teaching techniques. For example, if children are expected to name and describe the functions of the organs of the digestive system, study the unit carefully and try to come up with two or three different ways for children to learn this information.

2. *You can tell a great deal about how children learn by observing how they deal with new learning experiences.*

   EXAMPLE • Early in the year, provide activities that include studying a section in a reference book, doing hands-on activities, doing library research, and working with a computer program. Observe how various children approach each task and their relative success with each.

3. *Provide a range of experiences in the classroom so that all children have opportunities to put their preferred learning styles to use as often as possible.*

   EXAMPLE • Think about the extent to which the activities for each unit are the same or different in terms of what children actually do, and consider how you could build in variations in approach. For example, suppose you realize that all the activities for a unit on sound require the children to do the activity first, observe phenomena, and then report results. To accommodate children who have trouble with this approach, adapt a few of the activities so that early in the unit, children have the option of reading and talking about a concept before beginning an activity.

FIGURE 2.8
An understanding of individual learning styles can help you prepare science experiences that all children can learn from and enjoy.

People who believe that individuals learn in different ways use the term *learning style*. The term means exactly what it says: Each person has his or her own way of learning.

If you are an experienced teacher who has attended many in-service workshops or courses or you are a preservice teacher who has had a variety of courses concerning how to teach, you may have heard and learned about learning styles. This is an interesting area of study because so many experts have their own ideas about the learning styles that people may have. Some expound about convergent and divergent thinkers; some emphasize the idea that some people prefer concrete experiences and others prefer abstract discussions of ideas and principles; some suggest that people can be grouped on the basis of whether they respond quickly (impulsive) or think first and talk or act later (reflective). See Figure 2.8 for some practical applications of this theory.

Make the Case

The Problem Providing a rich learning environment for children may require the teacher to take them out of the traditional classroom occasionally and into the real world. Sometimes it is difficult for new teachers to identify real-world experiences that will really improve children's achievement in science.

Assess Your Prior Knowledge and Beliefs What do you presently believe about the way in which children learn both in and out of the classroom?

1. Children learn best from direct experience with natural objects and phenomena.

   _____ agree   _____ disagree

   Your evidence: _____

2. Hands-on science experiences automatically provide reinforcers for children.

   _____ agree   _____ disagree

   Your evidence: _____

3. A child's prior knowledge and beliefs should be assessed before new experiences are introduced to ensure that the experiences are meaningful.

   _____ agree   _____ disagree

   Your evidence: _____

4. Children have few misconceptions about the natural world.

   _____ agree   _____ disagree

   Your evidence: _____

5. For highly able children, it probably makes little difference whether direct or hands-on instruction is used in the classroom.

   _____ agree   _____ disagree

   Your evidence: _____

6. Because children progress through identifiable stages of development, teachers should provide only experiences that fit the stage of development indicated by the children's age.

   _____ agree   _____ disagree

   Your reasoning: _____

The Challenge Integrate your knowledge of how children learn into one paragraph that will provide a rationale for taking the children to locations beyond the school grounds. Your intention is to use this paragraph in a letter you will send (with your principal's permission) to community leaders who may be willing to donate funds for this curriculum enrichment project.

33

Multiple Intelligences Exploration Page

http://www.mrc.twsu.edu/education/faculty/gladhart/mi.html

This site provides links to a variety of Internet resources dealing with Howard Gardner's theory of multiple intelligences. Some of the articles are practical in nature and offer specific suggestions for assessing and teaching to particular intelligences. One category of links will even take you to schools that have made a schoolwide commitment to trying to use multiple intelligences as the basis for developing curriculum and instruction. It has three subsections: "Learning styles information," "Learning styles tests," and "For teachers."

Light Unit Based on Multiple Intelligences

http://www.rockyview.ab.ca/bpeak/edge/light/mi.html

You may find this one of the most helpful resources on the Internet if you are interested in applying the theory of multiple intelligences to teaching children science. This site shows a complete teaching unit on light in which multiple intelligences theory was emphasized during the unit and in its culminating experience. What is really special about the presentation is that this unit was actually used, so samples of student work are depicted.

Cognitive Learning Strategies

http://web.syr.edu/~maeltigi/Cognitive/index.htm

This page presents a chart that lists the essential features of three cognitive learning strategies. Each is linked to a fuller explanation, which includes a link that presents examples in context. This may help you apply cognitive learning theory in the classroom.

Learning Styles Links

http://www.oise.utoronto.ca/~ggay/lstylstd.htm

This is a very comprehensive site that offers many links to Internet pages dealing with the application of learning styles in the classroom.

Constructivism in Elementary Education

http://www.indiana.edu/~eric_rec/ieo/bibs/cons-ele.html

This site lists ERIC documents dealing with the application of constructivism in the elementary school classroom. It has links that will take you to ERIC bibliographies on topics presented alphabetically and by category. (The categorized list will obviously be most helpful.) The site also has links to other Internet sites dealing with constructivism in the classroom. Instructions are provided on how to receive the full text of any document for which an abstract is provided.

Summary

Questions such as What is learning? and How do children learn? have stimulated vigorous discussion and debate for many years. Some experts explain learning by emphasizing the important role that a child's environment plays in reinforcing behaviors associated with learning. This approach to understanding human learning is commonly known as *behaviorism*. Another perspective on learning, known as *cognitivism*, suggests that learning results from the unique ways in which a child perceives and makes sense of his or her environment. Each of these general classical theories has practical applications for you as a science teacher.

In recent years, additional interesting insights about learning have come from a variety of sources, including Gardner's work on multiple intelligences, a movement to develop teaching strategies based on constructivism, and educators who propose the assessment of children's learning styles as a critical first step in planning science instruction.

Going Further

On Your Own

1. Interview a primary, elementary, or middle grade teacher to determine what factors he or she believes affect how well a child learns science and what types of science experiences should occur in the classroom. Gather as much information as you can without guiding the interview toward any of the ideas brought forth in this chapter. After the interview, prepare a list that summarizes the key factors identified by the teacher, and try to group the items in the list with respect to the major ideas of this chapter.

2. Interview a school principal to determine what he or she believes are the key factors that affect the quality of science instruction in the school. After the interview, prepare a chart that relates key phrases from the interview to the major ideas of this chapter.

3. Based on your personal experiences as a student or teacher, to what extent are behaviorist principles applied when children have science experiences? Provide as many firsthand examples as you can.

4. Based on your personal experiences as a student or teacher, to what extent are cognitivist principles applied when children have science experiences? Provide as many firsthand examples as you can.

5. Based on your personal experiences as a student in science classrooms, would you say that you have a preferred style of learning that leads to success in such environments? If you would, identify the factors that contribute to your preference.

On Your Own or in a Cooperative Learning Group

6. Have each member of the group reflect on Gardner's theory of multiple intelligences, and then identify which intelligences each member feels he or she would score the highest and lowest in if they could be measured. Have members of the group comment on the nature of their science experiences in primary, elementary, or middle school and the extent to which these intelligences were applied.

7. Have each member of the group interview at least one child to ascertain his or her knowledge or beliefs about a key concept from life, earth/space, and physical science

and technology. In the course of each interview, be sure to encourage the child to respond to questions that might reveal some naive conceptions. Use questions such as Why doesn't the moon fall to the earth? Are whales fish? Does the sun move across the sky? Is a sweater warm?

8. As a group, reflect on the difference between *assimilation* and *accommodation*. Have group members identify one or two naive conceptions that they once had about life, earth/space, and physical science and technology. Have individuals indicate whether it was difficult or easy for them to revise these conceptions when they learned facts to the contrary or had direct experiences that produced results in conflict with their conceptions. Based on this group work, prepare a list of implications for teachers who wish to create science classroom environments in which children have experiences that reveal naive conceptions and lead to new learnings.

Notes

1. Guy R. Lefrançois, *Psychology for Teachers* (Belmont, CA: Wadsworth, 1994), p. 149.
2. Thomas Armstrong, *Multiple Intelligences in the Classroom* (Washington, DC: Association for Supervision and Curriculum Development, 1994), pp. 2–3.
3. Kathy Checkley, "The First Seven . . . and the Eighth: A Conversation with Howard Gardner," *Educational Leadership* 55, no. 1 (September 1997): 8, 9.

Suggested Readings

Bellanca, James. *Active Learning Handbook for the Multiple Intelligences Classroom.* Arlington Heights, IL: Skylight Professional Development, 1997.

Campbell, Bruce. *The Multiple Intelligences Handbook.* Tuscon, AZ: Zephyr Press, 1999.

Chaille, Christine, and Lory Britain. *The Young Child as Scientist: A Constructivist Approach to Early Childhood Science Education.* New York: Longman, 1997.

Chase, Kim. "The Other Intelligences (Oy Vey!)." *Educational Leadership* 56, no. 3 (November 1988): 72–73.

Checkley, Kathy. "The First Seven . . . and the Eighth: A Conversation with Howard Gardner." *Educational Leadership* 55, no.1 (September 1997): 8–13.

Dever, Martha T., and Deborah E. Hobbs. "The Learning Spiral: Taking the Lead from How Young Children Learn." *Childhood Education* 75, no. 1 (Fall 1998): 7–11.

Guild, Pat Burke, and Sandy Chock-Eng. "Multiple Intelligence, Learning Styles, Brain-Based Education: Where Do the Messages Overlap?" *Schools in the Middle* 6, no. 6 (March/April 1998): 38–43.

Kovalik, Susan, and Karen D. Olsen. "The Physiology of Learning—Just What Does Go On in There?" *Schools in the Middle* 6, no. 6 (March/April 1998): 32–37.

Minerich, Jim. "Elementary Science Study Groups." *Science and Children* 36, no. 7 (April 1999): 40–43.

Mintzes, Joel J., et al (eds.). *Teaching Science for Understanding: A Human Constructivist View.* San Diego, CA: Academic Press, 1998.

Phye, Gary D. (ed.). *Handbook of Academic Learning: The Construction of Knowledge.* San Diego, CA: Academic Press, 1996.

Schulte, Paige L. "Lessons in Cooperative Learning." *Science and Children* 36, no. 7 (April 1999): 44–47.

Sinclair, Anne, and Linda Coates. "Teaching Multiple Intelligences." *Science Scope* 22, no. 5 (February 1999): 17–21.

Smith, Bruce. "Constructive Connections." *Science Scope* 22, no. 6 (March 1999): 32–33.

Sweet, Sharon. "A Lesson Learned about Multiple Intelligences." *Educational Leadership* 56, no. 3 (November 1988): 50–51.

Tomlinson, Carol Ann. "Teach Me, Teach My Brain: A Call for Differentiated Classrooms." *Educational Leadership* 56, no. 3 (November 1988): 52–55.

Williamson, Ronald D. "Designing Diverse Learning Styles." *Schools in the Middle* 6, no. 6 (March/April 1998): 28–31, 44.

3

Science Process Skills

*How can I use the science process skills
as starting points for discovery-based
units and lesson plans?*

A Look Ahead

Discovery Learning

Imagine learning to drive a car without a car. Imagine learning to bake chocolate chip cookies without flour, eggs, sugar, fresh milk, and large, semisweet morsels of rich, dark chocolate. It's hard, isn't it? Now imagine teaching children science without having them touch leaves or shells or magnets or hand lenses or resource books or pieces of granite or mirrors or batteries or thermometers or a gerbil. Imagine teaching a unit on butterflies without offering children a chance to watch delicate butterflies dance across the last flowers of fall. I find it hard to imagine.

It's probably possible to *teach* science without the items listed above, but I doubt that children will *learn* science without them. Experience has been and continues to be the best teacher. In science, we have a special name for the learning that occurs when children, with our guidance, increase their cognitive, psychomotor, and affective development through direct experience. We call it *discovery learning*.

I know of no elementary or middle grade teachers who, as their *total approach* to discovery learning, dump boxes of leaves, shells, or magnets on a desk and cheerily announce, "Come on up, grab some stuff, have some fun, and discover." This is not discovery learning.

A Definition of Discovery Learning

Discovery learning is hands-on, experiential learning that requires a teacher's full knowledge of content, pedagogy, and child development to create an environment in which new learnings are related to what has come before and to that which will follow. It doesn't involve a teacher bringing a box of science stuff to a classroom and dumping it on a desk. A chimpanzee could be trained to do that! Learning through discovery is a personal, willful act on the part of the child that happens in an environment designed by a teacher. It is the teacher's professional responsibility to help children make discoveries that are important to their needs and interests and that will help them become more knowledgeable, literate, skilled, responsible human beings.

What exactly is the teacher's role in discovery learning? The teacher's responsibility is to help children move through a continuing series of experiences that include hands-on work with science materials and to challenge children to make sense out of their discoveries through writing, library research, mastery of science vocabulary, and a host of other activities that lead them to make still more discoveries.

A Learning Cycle for Discovery

The cyclical nature of the learning process has a long history of discussion in science education and developmental psychology. Over the years, various individuals and groups have named and defined the stages. Perhaps the most well-known elaboration is that which was used as the central organizing structure for science experiences developed by the Science Curriculum Improvement Study, a major curriculum development effort sponsored by the National Science Foundation. That cycle consisted of exploring, inventing, and discovering.

Barman's more recent refinement of the cycle is an important contribution to helping teachers think through the planning process for discovery learning. He suggests the following:

1. *Exploration.* During this phase, the teacher plays an indirect role as an observer who poses questions and assists individual students and small groups of students. The students' role at this time is very active. They manipulate materials distributed by the teacher.

2. *Concept introduction.* During this stage, the teacher assumes a more traditional role by gathering information from the students that relates to their experiences. This part of the lesson is the vocabulary-building time. Textbooks, audiovisual aids, and other written materials may be used to introduce terminology and information.

3. *Concept application.* At this time, the teacher poses a new situation or problem that can be solved on the basis of the previous exploration experience and the concept introduction. As in the exploration phase, the students engage in some type of activity.[1]

I believe we can build on this excellent exposition of the learning cycle by making one change in terminology to focus a bit more clearly on the acquisition of concepts in stage 2. Renaming this stage *concept acquisition* gives us a three-stage teaching/learning sequence with the following nomenclature:

1. Exploration
2. Concept acquisition
3. Concept application

You can use the three stages of this learning cycle to organize your thinking about how to teach and how to provide a good environment for discovery learning. This is not to suggest that you should always follow these three stages but that you should reflect upon the stages as you think through your approach to planning and teaching science lessons. What you actually do with the children will depend on a number of variables unique to you and your teaching environment.

The Science Process Skills: Individual Descriptions with Classroom Examples

 The discoveries that scientists make come from their ability to use a group of very different but very important skills formally known as *science process skills*. They are important skills that we can use to develop a classroom learning environment that has discovery learning as its central focus.

The process skills about to be discussed are reemphasized in Chapter 10, Unit, Lesson, and Enrichment Starter Ideas: The Earth/Space Sciences and Technology; Chapter 13, Unit, Lesson, and Enrichment Starter Ideas: The Life Sciences and Technology; and Chapter 16, Unit, Lesson, and Enrichment Starter Ideas: The Physical Sciences and Technology. Also be aware that the science activities described in the "B" chapters later in this book include an identification of the particular process skills emphasized in each activity.

The Basic Processes

Observing

▶ *What Does It Mean?*

Observing means using the senses to obtain information, or *data,* about objects and events. It is the most basic process of science. Casual observations spark almost every inquiry we make about our environment. Organized observations form the basis for more structured investigations. Acquiring the ability to make careful observations will create a foundation for making inferences or hypotheses that can be tested by further observations.

Sample Activities That Emphasize Observing

1. Children can observe that different animals have very different solutions to the problem of getting from place to place. By directly observing animals outdoors or displayed in the classroom, children can describe whether each animal walks, swims, or flies. You may wish to challenge children to identify animals that can do all three—for example, ducks.

2. Have children observe how the marked *N* and *S* poles of two bar magnets affect one another. They can suspend one magnet from its center and then observe the effects of bringing the *N* pole of the second magnet near the *N* pole and then the *S* pole of the hanging magnet. The children will observe the repulsion of like poles and the attraction of unlike poles.

Using Space/Time Relationships

▶ *What Does It Mean?*

All objects occupy a place in space. The process skill *using space/time relationships* involves the ability to discern and describe directions, spatial arrangements, motion and speed, symmetry, and rate of change.

What process skills are these children using?

Sample Activities That Emphasize Using Space/Time Relationships

1. One aspect of the property we call *symmetry* is the repetition in size and shape of one part of an object on the opposite side of a line or plane. Display circles, squares, and spheres and ask children to try to draw a line or plane through each object to show whether the parts on opposite sides are identical.

2. Provide children with a small metal mirror (metal instead of glass as a safety precaution) and half an apple or a pear made by a lengthwise cut through the fruit. Ask children to discover if the right and left sides of the half are symmetrical. They can put the mirror lengthwise down the middle of the fruit section to see if they can observe the image of a complete fruit.

Using Numbers

▶ *What Does It Mean?*

We need numbers to manipulate measurements, order objects, and classify objects. The amount of time spent on the activities devoted to *using numbers* should depend largely on the school's mathematics program. It is important for children to realize that the ability to use numbers is also a fundamental process of science.

Sample Activities That Emphasize Using Numbers

1. Help young children learn to compare sets with the use of natural objects such as rocks. Place a collection of rocks on a table. Pick out a set of six rocks, and ask various children to come to the collection and make a set containing one more element than your set. Encourage children to use language such as the following to describe their set: "My set has seven, which is more than your set of six rocks." Do this with other sets of rocks.

2. Young children enjoy practicing number concept acquisition skills using natural objects. Give them each nine leaves, and ask them to respond to directions such as "Show a member of the set of leaves"; "Show the members of a set of six leaves"; and "Show a set of two leaves joined to a set of six leaves."

Classifying

▶ *What Does It Mean?*

Classifying is the process scientists use to impose order on collections of objects or events. Classification schemes are used in science and other disciplines to identify objects or events and to show similarities, differences, and interrelationships.

Sample Activities That Emphasize Classifying

1. Have children construct a simple classification scheme and use it to classify the organisms in a classroom terrarium.

2. Ask children to bring pictures of plants and animals to school. Use the pictures from all the children to develop entries for a classification system.

A
Starting
Point
for
Thinking,
Talking,
and
Writing

Kelley: I really had an interesting experience this year with what our school calls the "special motivation class."

Nicole: You always seem to have interesting experiences with that class. What happened?

Kelley: Next to the school is a working farm where plants and animals are raised, so I thought it would be neat to take advantage of it.

Nicole: But your children come from a rural background. Don't they know all about working with plants and animals already?

Kelley: You'd be surprised. Even though they obviously have been in this kind of environment all their lives, they actually don't have real hands-on experience with much of it. I thought it was at least worth a try.

Nicole: So, what did you do? Field trips? Classroom visits by the farmer?

Kelley: Oh no. We went right over there early in the year, and each child was given some specific responsibilities for the year. They could choose to be involved with plants or animals or, if they had time, both.

Nicole: Did they enjoy it or get bored with it after awhile? You know how children sometimes react to a new pet. They are really interested for awhile, and then the interest can fade away.

Kelley: Oh, they enjoyed it a lot, but the most important part was that it gave them a chance to do some things that used the ideas we were trying to teach during our regular class time.

Nicole: You were really lucky to have access to a resource like the working farm. Teachers in urban schools don't have such things.

Kelley: I don't know about that. I think most teachers are in communities where there are resources that may be going to waste. It's just a question of finding them. I know from my experience that it really is worth the effort. You should have seen the pride in the faces of my students as they saw the changes in the plants or animals all through the year and realized that they actually had something to do with helping these living things grow.

▶ *Point to Ponder:* *Think for a moment about the community resources available to a teacher who teaches children science in an urban area. What resources might come close to or surpass the resource discussed by these teachers from a rural area?*

Measuring

▶ *What Does It Mean?*

Measuring is the way observations are quantified. Skill in measuring requires not only the ability to use measuring instruments properly but also the ability to carry out calculations with these instruments. The process involves judgment about which instrument to use and when approximate rather than precise measurements are

Be sure to have children use the metric system as they work on science activities.

acceptable. Children can learn to measure length, area, volume, mass, temperature, force, and speed as they work on this process skill.

Sample Activities That Emphasize Measuring

1. Have children estimate the linear dimensions of classroom objects using centimeters, decimeters, or meters, and then use metersticks to measure the objects.

2. Provide children with a drawing of an *Apatosaurus* and a drawing of a *Tyrannosaurus*. Have them estimate the sizes of these animals using background or foreground features as reference objects. Finally, tell them that the *Apatosaurus* was about 20 meters long and the *Tyrannosaurus* was about 6 meters high, and have them measure out these distances in the classroom.

Communicating

▶ *What Does It Mean?*

Clear, precise communication is essential to all human endeavors and fundamental to all scientific work, which makes *communicating* skills valuable. Scientists communicate orally, with written words, and through the use of diagrams, maps, graphs, mathematical equations, and other visual demonstrations.

Sample Activities That Emphasize Communicating

1. Encourage children to write concise accounts of natural phenomena such as the changes that occur when the caterpillar of the monarch butterfly creates its chrysalis and eventually emerges as a butterfly.

2. Display a small animal such as a gerbil, hamster, or water snail. Ask children to write descriptions of the organism that include such characteristics as size, shape, color, texture, and method of locomotion.

Predicting

▶ *What Does It Mean?*

A *prediction* is a specific forecast of a future observation or event. Predictions are based on observations, measurements, and inferences about relationships between observed variables. A prediction that is not based on observation is only a guess. Accurate predictions result from careful observations and precise measurements.

Sample Activities That Emphasize Predicting

1. Have children construct a questionnaire about breakfast cereal preference and gather data from all the classrooms in the school except one. Have students analyze their data and make a prediction about the outcome of the survey of the children in the last room before polling the children.

2. Have children predict what will occur when you invert Pyrex beakers of various sizes over a burning food-warming candle that has been placed in the center of an aluminum pie plate. The children can make estimates of burning times in seconds and compare their predictions to their direct observations.

Inferring

▶ *What Does It Mean?*

Inferring is using logic to draw conclusions from what we observe. Nothing is more fundamental to clear thinking than the ability to distinguish between an observation and an inference. An *observation* is an experience that is obtained through one of the senses. An *inference* is an explanation of an observation. The thought involved in making an inference can occur in a fraction of a second and is often strongly affected by past experiences.

Sample Activities That Emphasize Inferring

1. Provide a number of wrapped packages, and ask children what they can learn about the contents of a package by external examination. Have them list their conclusions about the contents of each package. Emphasize that a conclusion based on observations is an inference.

2. Take children on a mini–field trip to a tree on school property, and have them prepare a list of observations about the ground at the base of the tree, the tree bark, and the leaves. Ask children to make inferences from their observations about the animals that may live in or near the tree (e.g., birds, insects, squirrels).

The Integrated Processes

Controlling Variables

▶ *What Does It Mean?*

Controlling variables means managing the conditions of an investigation. A *variable* is an object or quantity that can change. In an investigation, best results are achieved when the variables are identified and carefully controlled. Students can develop skills in identifying variables and in describing how they have controlled variables during science activities.

These children are clearly involved in rather sophisticated experimentation that includes controlling variables.

Sample Activities That Emphasize Controlling Variables

1. Children can identify the variable that causes roots to grow downward in the following manner. Have them plant the same number and type of bean seeds at the sides of three sealed, clear containers. This will allow them to see the root systems develop. After the roots have grown about 2 centimeters, have children turn one container upside down and one sideways. They will observe over a few days that the roots of seeds in the two turned containers have changed their direction of growth and are now growing downward. Children should be able to identify the one variable that might have caused the roots to change direction—gravity.

2. Have each child measure another child's pulse for 30 seconds and then double it to find the pulse rate per minute. Have the class make a chart to record the data. Ask children to create a list of variables that might explain why pulse rates for different children vary (e.g., size, weight, sex, amount of exercise before class, accuracy of pulse takers). Now have them write a hypothesis about the effect of exercise on pulse rate. They can then invent an experiment to test the hypothesis and control all variables listed except exercise.

Interpreting Data

▶ *What Does It Mean?*

The process of *interpreting data* involves making predictions, inferences, and hypotheses from the data collected in an investigation. We are constantly interpreting data when we read weather maps, watch the news on television, and look at photographs in newspapers or magazines. Students should have had previous experience in observing, classifying, and measuring before the process of interpreting data is approached.

Sample Activities That Emphasize Interpreting Data

1. Through extended study of a population of mealworms, children can participate in many activities emphasizing the interpretation of data. Mealworms, the larvae stage of a common cereal beetle, can be easily maintained in a classroom. Students can count the number of mealworms that are in the culture each week and graph their data. The interpretation of these data can focus on such questions as "What reasons could explain an increase in population?" and "What reasons could explain a decrease in population?"

2. Provide children with graph paper and the following information about the human population of the world at various times. Have them graph and then interpret the data to answer the questions that follow the information.

Year	Estimated Population (millions)
1500	450
1600	500
1700	600
1800	900
1900	1,500
1950	2,500
1975	4,000
1985	5,000
2000	6,000
2015	?

a. What do you estimate the population will be in the year 2015?
b. Has the population grown at a faster rate in the last 100 years than it did in the 100 years between 1700 and 1800?
c. What factors might increase/decrease the rate of population change?

Formulating Hypotheses

▶ *What Does It Mean?*

A *hypothesis* is an "educated guess." *Formulating hypotheses* should be based on observations or inferences. For example, you may observe that a cube of sugar dissolves faster in hot water than in cold water. From this observation, you might formulate the hypothesis that all substances soluble in water dissolve faster in hot water than in cold water. A hypothesis may also be generalized from an inference. For example, if you invert a glass jar over a burning candle, the candle will go out in a short time. You might infer from this observation that the candle goes out because all of the oxygen in the jar is used up. You might then formulate the hypothesis that all burning candles covered with glass jars go out when the oxygen in the jar is used up.

Sample Activities That Emphasize Formulating Hypotheses

1. Provide children with the materials needed to make a simple lever. After they have made a lever, identify the fulcrum (the turning point) and explain that the force we apply to move an object is called *effort*. The object moved is the *load*. Have children make hypotheses about the amount of effort needed to move various loads. Then move the fulcrum closer and farther away from the load and have children make hypotheses about how these changes will affect the effort needed to move the load.

2. Based on their observations of objects and background color, children can make predictions about the likelihood of finding a higher proportion of "non-green" toothpicks on a lawn than green toothpicks. The children can check their predictions by dyeing the toothpicks various colors, including green. Equal numbers of the toothpicks can be randomly scattered on the lawn be-

fore the children are given a fixed amount of time to gather as many toothpicks as they can. The children can then formulate a hypothesis to explain the biological advantage of being a green-colored insect that lives in the lawn.

Defining Operationally

▶ *What Does It Mean?*

When students use the *defining operationally* process, they define terms in the context of their own experiences. That is, they work with a definition instead of memorizing it. A definition that limits the number of things to be considered and is experiential is more useful than one that encompasses all possible variations that might be encountered. In the physical sciences, an operational definition is based on what is done and what is observed. In the biological sciences, an operational definition is often descriptive.

Sample Activities That Emphasize Defining Operationally

1. Children can construct an operational definition of *mass* from observing that it requires more force to move a cart containing many books than one with few books. Children should write a definition that includes their experiences with trying to move both carts.

2. Have students invent operational definitions for plant parts based on the functions of the parts they observe. For example, part of an operational definition for a *stem* is that "water moves up it." This definition might be derived by observing that a carnation stem placed in colored water serves to conduct the coloring to the petals. Part of the operational definition for a *bud* might include a reference to it as a site where they have observed a flower or a leaf emerge.

Experimenting

▶ *What Does It Mean?*

Experimenting is the process that encompasses all of the basic and integrated processes. An exercise in experimenting usually begins with observations that suggest questions to be answered. Sometimes the student formulates a hypothesis from a question or questions. The succeeding steps in experimenting involve identifying the variables to be controlled, making operational definitions, constructing a test, carrying out the test, collecting and interpreting data, and sometimes modifying the hypothesis that was being tested.

Sample Activities That Emphasize Experimenting

1. Children can invent an experiment to test the effects of light on the growth of plants. Provide children with an assortment of sprouted corn and bean plants. Ask them to describe an experiment that would see how the availability of light affects how fast plants grow. Be sure to ask children to indicate what tools they may need to complete the experiment (e.g., lamp, meterstick, graph paper).

2. Children can design an experiment to investigate the effect of adding baker's yeast to a sugar/water solution. In the experiment, they can compare observations of a sugar-solution liquid without yeast (the control) and a sugar-solution liquid with yeast (the test). By counting the bubbles of carbon dioxide released per minute in the test solution after fermentation begins, they will have an indication of how rapidly the yeast cells are metabolizing (i.e., using sugar as an energy source and releasing carbon dioxide). *Note:* Alcohol and water are also by-products of the fermentation reaction.

Make the Case

An Individual or Group Challenge

The Problem   Children in discovery-based classrooms may become so involved in their explorations that they spend too much time *doing* and too little time *thinking.*

Assess Your Prior Knowledge and Beliefs

What are your present beliefs about each of the following?

1. Before engaging in an activity, children should establish a hypothesis.

   _____ agree   _____ disagree

   Your reasoning: _____

2. Even if there is an official recorder, all the children in a group should record their personal observations.

   _____ agree   _____ disagree

   Your reasoning: _____

3. As long as children have hands-on, discovery-based experiences, they will learn science process skills.

   _____ agree   _____ disagree

   Your reasoning: _____

The Challenge   Your state or province has awarded you a $500 grant for a single discovery-based science project that involves a simulation of life in a space colony on Mars. At the end of the year, you must write a report describing what the children have learned. Describe how you would incorporate the children's mastery of the basic science process skills as central elements of your report.

A Summary of Commonly Identified Science Process Skills

http://www.ag.ohio-state.edu/~youth4h/expedu/#appendixc

In addition to identifying and briefly discussing the science process skills, this site gives you alternate ways of assessing whether young people have achieved the skills. Another helpful feature is a checklist you can use to determine whether particular activities do, in fact, provide learners with experiences that will advance their learning.

Integrated Science Process Skills

http://www.ccet.ua.edu/process_skills.htm

If you are interested in curriculum for middle-level students, this site will be of interest to you. It presents a theme-based curriculum that integrates the life and physical sciences and also has a strong emphasis on the science process skills. This particular portion of the site identifies the specific process skills that students work on as they study various science topics. A link on this page will take you to the full curriculum.

Hypothesis Testing

http://www.thegateway.org/index2/hypothesistesting.html

This page will direct you to a variety of activities intended to foster the development of science process skills. Each activity clearly identifies the science process skills it emphasizes.

Scientific Inquiry

http://www.cyfernet.mes.umn.edu/scistandards.html#link3

This is a subsection of a larger site that deals with strategies and techniques that should be used in informal education. This portion of the site identifies the science process skills and lists the behaviors you should look for as you assess whether a student has mastered a skill.

Lower School Science Program

http://www.pinecrest.edu/lowerschool/science/

This site describes a school in which the science curriculum in the primary grades is strongly infused with experiences that foster what they refer to to as the *science-processing skills*. Browse through the curriculum descriptions of other subjects to note the extent to which hands-on experiences are used for skill acquisition throughout.

Growing the Scientific Method

http://www.unc.edu/depts/cmse/curriculum/growing.html

This site begins with a brief introduction to the science process skills, which is followed by an identification of resources that relate the science process skills to environmental education and gardening.

Greenwood School District 50 Kindergarten Science

http://www.gwd50.k12.sc.us/exp-web/Exp9801/ExprPage.htm

If you have a special interest in teaching young children, you should become aware of which science process skills and manipulative skills those children are expected to learn. This site presents an overview of the skills that one school district believes should be emphasized at the kindergarten level.

Science Proficiency Outcomes

http://seedsnet.stark.k12.oh.us/prof.html

This page specifies the science process skills that children are expected to learn at various grade levels. From this page, you can travel to the full curriculum and examine its scope and sequence, which identifies process skills, learning objectives, and suggested materials to deliver the curriculum in the classroom.

Intended Learning Outcomes

http://www.usoe.k12.ut.us/curr/science/ele_out.htm

Various states have prepared lists of expected outcomes for children's work in science. At this site, you will find Utah's state curriculum expectations for both the basic and integrated science process skills. You will also find a list of outcomes related to affective development and the social and historical impact of science as well as other key components of the science curriculum.

The Rhode Island Benchmarks: Science Process Skills

http://instruct.ride.ri.net/doehome/scope.html

This site provides a somewhat formal presentation of the rationale for Rhode Island's state science curriculum framework, which reveals a very strong emphasis on the science process skills. From this location, you can also travel to a presentation of the complete science framework so you can see how the science process skills are used with suggested content and experiences.

Summary

The science content that we teach is the result of discoveries that scientists have made about the natural world. One important approach to teaching children science is to develop a classroom environment that encourages them to make their own discoveries. While there are many ways to foster discovery learning in the classroom, one important strategy involves a three-stage learning cycle in which children explore, acquire concepts, and apply concepts. As children progress through these stages, they can learn and use a number of investigative procedures, commonly referred to as the *processes of science*.

Going Further

On Your Own

1. This chapter described a three-stage learning cycle that can be useful as you think about fostering discovery learning in the classroom. Pick a science topic that you might teach a group of children, and provide examples of specific things you might do to involve students in each stage of the cycle.

2. Some of the process skills discussed in this chapter are also used in the nonscience portions of the elementary/middle school (e.g., social studies, language arts, and so on) curriculum. Select three science process skills, and discuss how each might be used to integrate at least one other subject with science.

3. This chapter dealt with the inclusion of science process skills as an important aspect of hands-on science. What potential is there for an elementary or middle grade teacher to teach some of these skills through classroom demonstrations? Explain your response.

4. This book identifies the content domains of science as the life, earth/space, and physical sciences. Would you foresee a teacher having problems incorporating particular science process skills in any of the content fields? If so, which skills might pose difficulty with which content fields? Why?

5. Some resistance to including the science process skills comes from teachers not having had much personal experience with science activities or experiments in college. To what extent did your college-level experience include opportunities to utilize the science process skills?

On Your Own or in a Cooperative Learning Group

6. Draw a line on a sheet of paper or a chalkboard to represent the continuum from content-based science to process-based science. Challenge others to identify positions on the continuum that represent (1) the degree to which their own science experiences in elementary/middle grade science emphasized science process skills; (2) the extent to which their secondary school science experiences emphasized science process skills; (3) the extent to which their college-level science experiences emphasized science process skills; and (4) the extent to which they believe their own teaching of elementary/middle grade science will emphasize science process skills.

7. How might a week of classroom time (30 minutes per day) early in the school year be used to teach children in primary, elementary, or middle school that science is a way of doing things as well as an organizational collection of facts, concepts, and principles?

8. Select either a commercially available school science textbook series or a science curriculum prepared by a school district, and determine which science process skills are emphasized. Note whether particular skills are intended to be stressed at particular grade levels. Using examples from these materials, prepare a chart that illustrates the relationships between the science process skills and the stages of the learning cycle discussed in this chapter.

Note

1. Charles Barman, *A Procedure for Helping Prospective Elementary Teachers Integrate the Learning Cycle into Science Textbooks,* monograph 4 (Council for Elementary Science International, an affiliation of the National Science Teachers Association, Arlington, VA), p. 5.

Suggested Readings

Brendzel, Sharon. "Prints to Ponder." *Science Scope* 22, no. 7 (April 1999): 22–23.

Burruss, Jill D. "Problem-Based Learning." *Science Scope* 22, no. 6 (March 1999): 46–47.

Calkins, Andrew. "Find Out Why." *Science and Children* 36, no. 5 (February 1999): 32–33.

Curtis, Jeran. "Exploring Experimental Design." *Science and Children* 36, no. 4 (January 1999): 24–27, 60.

Evans, Jane H. "Sorting Out Seeds." *Science Scope* 22, no. 7 (April 1999): 18–21.

Gaylen, Nancy. "Encouraging Curiosity at Home." *Science and Children* 35, no. 4 (January 1998): 24–29.

Greene, S. Niane. "Take Off with Scientific Methodology." *Science and Children* 36, no. 3 (November/December 1998): 38–43, 71.

Keller, J. David, and Beth Brickman. "The Ball Olympics: Up and Down, All Around." *Science and Children* 36, no. 2 (October 1998): 26–31, 56.

Marek, Edmund A., and Ann M. L. Cavallo. *The Learning Cycle.* Westport, CT: Heinemann, 1997.

Meyer, Steve, et al. "Weather Detectives: Searching for Cool Clues." *Science and Children* 36, no. 4 (January 1999): 33–37.

Micklo, Stephen. "Estimation: It's More Than a Guess." *Childhood Education* 75, no. 3 (Spring 1999): 142–145.

Moscovici, Hedy, and Tamara Holmlund Nelson. "Shifting from Activitymania to Inquiry." *Science and Children* 35, no. 4 (January 1998): 14–17.

Pearce, Charles R. *Nurturing Inquiry.* Westport, CT: Heinemann, 1999.

Pratt, Harold, and Jay Hackett. "Teaching Science: The Inquiry Approach." *Principal* 78, no. 2 (November 1998): 20–22.

Silva, Patricia, and Paul Yamamoto. "M&M Mystery." *Science Scope* 22, no. 5 (February 1999): 26–27.

Smith, Robert. "Teaching Animal Classification with Beanie Babies." *Science and Children* 36, no. 3 (November/December 1998): 20–23.

4

Planning and Managing

How can I plan and manage discovery-based units and lessons?

A Look Ahead

The Water Rat and the Sea Horse

 How will you plan your teaching so that the children you teach will learn? One way to develop your response to this fundamental question is first to consider the extremes of planning styles that may be used. To show you these extremes, I would like to have two very interesting animals present their approaches to the teaching and learning process—the water rat and the sea horse. The water rat, who is explaining the joys of boating to his friend the mole, will speak first:

> "Believe me, my young friend, there is nothing—absolutely nothing—half so much worth doing as simply messing about in boats. Simply messing," he went on dreamily: "messing—about—in—boats; messing—."
>
> "Look ahead, Rat!" cried the Mole suddenly.
>
> It was too late. The boat struck the bank full tilt. The dreamer, the joyous oarsman, lay on his back at the bottom of the boat, his heels in the air.
>
> "—about in boats—or *with* boats," the Rat went on composedly, picking himself up with a pleasant laugh. "In or out of 'em, it doesn't matter. Nothing seems really to matter, that's the charm of it. Whether you get away, or whether you don't; whether you arrive at your destination or whether you reach somewhere else, or whether you never get any-where at all, you're always busy, and you never do anything in particular; and when you've done it there's always something else to do, and you can do it if you like, but you'd much better not. Look here! If you've really nothing else on hand this morning, suppos-ing we drop down the river together, and have a long day of it?"
>
> The Mole waggled his toes from sheer happiness, spread his chest with a sigh of full contentment, and leaned back blissfully into the soft cushions. "What a day I'm having!" he said. "Let us start at once!"[1]

Now, the sea horse:

> Once upon a time a Sea Horse gathered up his seven pieces of eight and cantered out to find his fortune. Before he had traveled very far he met an Eel, who said,
>
> "Pssst. Hey, bud. Where ya' going?"
>
> "I'm going out to find my fortune," replied the Sea Horse, proudly.
>
> "You're in luck," said the Eel. "For four pieces of eight you can have this speedy flip-per, and then you'll be able to get there a lot faster."
>
> "Gee, that's swell," said the Sea Horse, and paid the money and put on the flipper and slithered off at twice the speed. Soon he came upon a Sponge, who said,
>
> "Pssst. Hey, bud. Where ya' going?"
>
> "I'm going out to find my fortune," replied the Sea Horse.
>
> "You're in luck," said the Sponge. "For a small fee I will let you have this jet-propelled scooter so that you will be able to travel a lot faster."
>
> So the Sea Horse bought the scooter with his remaining money and went zooming through the sea five times as fast. Soon he came upon a shark, who said,
>
> "Pssst. Hey, bud. Where ya' going?"
>
> "I'm going out to find my fortune," replied the Sea Horse.
>
> "You're in luck. If you'll take this short cut," said the Shark, pointing to his open mouth, "you'll save yourself a lot of time."
>
> "Gee, thanks," said the Sea Horse, and zoomed off into the interior of the Shark, there to be devoured.
>
> The moral of this fable is that if you're not sure where you're going, you're liable to end up someplace else—and not even know it.[2]

As a teacher, you will face the same important choices—to rush ahead, to putter, to go in one direction only, or to let the stream carry you—that these animals faced, but your environment will not be a stream or an ocean. Your environment will be a classroom overflowing with hopes and dreams for the future.

As you begin the planning process, you will undoubtedly develop some learning experiences that are very open, informal, and consistent with the Water Rat's approach to life. You probably will also develop some learning experiences that are more directed. Even though the approach you take may vary from lesson to lesson and even within a lesson, at the end of the year, you will still have to answer for yourself this fundamental question: Have my children had sufficient opportunities to *explore, acquire concepts,* and *apply what they learned?* Discovery learning and planning go hand in hand—they are not a contradiction in terms and they don't happen by accident. Expert teachers plan in ways that foster discovery within a context that helps children acquire the knowledge, attitudes, and skills needed for success at school and in life.

The Scope of the Science Curriculum

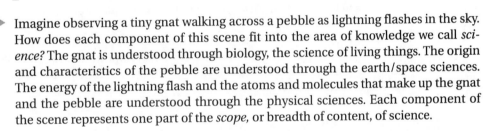 Imagine observing a tiny gnat walking across a pebble as lightning flashes in the sky. How does each component of this scene fit into the area of knowledge we call *science?* The gnat is understood through biology, the science of living things. The origin and characteristics of the pebble are understood through the earth/space sciences. The energy of the lightning flash and the atoms and molecules that make up the gnat and the pebble are understood through the physical sciences. Each component of the scene represents one part of the *scope,* or breadth of content, of science.

Determining the Scope of Your Curriculum

The *earth/space sciences* represent our knowledge of the origins of the universe and of our Earth in particular. They include astronomy, geology, meteorology, and other areas of study. The earth/space science topics commonly taught in elementary school include the following:

1. The stars, sun, and planets
2. The soil, rocks, and mountains
3. The weather

The *biological sciences* include botany, zoology, and ecology. These disciplines are usually represented in the elementary science curriculum as the following topics:

Good teaching requires advance preparation.

1. The study of plants
2. The study of animals
3. The study of the relationship between plants and animals
4. The study of the relationship between living things and the environment

The *physical sciences* include physics and chemistry. Physics is concerned with the relationship between matter and energy. Chemistry is concerned with the manner through which various types of matter combine and change. In the elementary school, the following topics would be considered part of the physical sciences component of a science curriculum:

1. The study of matter and energy
2. The study of the chemical changes that matter undergoes

Although these three areas of content would seem to be more than enough, there is another area of study not usually listed as a major content component: technology. As noted in Chapter 1, *technology* is the use of science to solve human problems. An infusion of technology into the three central areas of the curriculum can offer you many opportunities to raise and consider questions of great societal import with children.

Science, technology, and society (STS) is not a "cold" curriculum area to be dealt with reluctantly. It can, without question, be an important and relevant part of science instruction that touches the lives of children and helps them grow as people and as scientifically literate citizens.

The NSE Standards: Implications for Appropriate Scope

The NSE standards provide guidance for teachers and others on a variety of aspects of science education. The area of the standards that will probably be of most interest to you will be that dealing with what you should be teaching. If you wish to teach content that is sensitive to the NSE recommendations, then its scope should at least range across the following eight topics, or *standards:*

1. Unifying concepts and processes in science
2. Science as inquiry
3. Physical science
4. Life science
5. Earth and space sciences
6. Science and technology
7. Science in personal and social perspectives
8. History and nature of science[3]

The first standard—"Unifying concepts and processes in science"—identifies broad science concepts that are needed to tie the other content areas together:

1. Systems, order, and organization
2. Evidence, models, and explanation
3. Change, constancy, and measurement
4. Evolution and equilibrium
5. Form and function[4]

If you presently lack a strong science content background, you will need to study the explanations and examples of these unifying concepts presented in the full NSE report.

The second standard—"Science as inquiry"—essentially states that children should be expected to ask questions about objects, organisms, and events; plan and carry out investigations; gather data; explain what they have learned; and communicate what they have learned. Teachers are expected to help children understand that scientists continually engage in these aspects of inquiry themselves.[5]

Standards 3 through 8 are more straightforward than the first two. Study Figure 4.1 (pages 58–59) to get a clear picture of the intended scope for units and lessons based on the NSE standards. Also use this figure as a reference as you consider the appropriate sequence of topics for children. As you use these lists, however, please bear in mind that they are *recommendations* and should be treated as such.

The Sequence of the Science Curriculum

A knowledge of the scope of science will help you decide what topics can be reasonably included within the body of science experiences you present to children. However, one important question still remains: In what order should these topics be presented? For example, should children learn about the earth they live on before they learn about the structure and function of their bodies, or should the sequence be reversed?

Determining the Sequence of Your Curriculum

There is no definitive answer to the question of sequence. However, these three guidelines may help you consider the place of science in a child's school experience:

1. Since no learning can occur if the learner is inattentive to the experience, any decision you make should favor those topics that will generate the most learner involvement and interest.

2. As a general rule, organize learning experiences from the child outward. That is, select experiences that relate first to the child and then to the science content. In teaching electricity, for example, have children consider how they use electricity before they study its source.

3. In general, when deciding to expose children to a concept that can be considered concretely or abstractly, use the concrete approach first.

Unifying Concepts and Processes

Standard: As a result of activities in grades K–12, all students should develop understandings and abilities aligned with the following concepts and processes.

Systems, order, and organization
Evidence, models, and explanation
Constancy, change, and measurement

Evolution and equilibrium
Form and function

Content Standards: K–4

Science as Inquiry*

Content Standard A: As a result of activities in grades K–4, all students should develop
- Abilities necessary to do scientific inquiry
- Understanding about scientific inquiry

Physical Science [PS]**

Content Standard B: As a result of the activities in grades K–4, all students should develop an understanding of
- Properties of objects and materials [PS 1]
- Position and motion of objects [PS 2]
- Light, heat, electricity, and magnetism [PS 3]

Life Science [LS]

Content Standard C: As a result of the activities in grades K–4, all students should develop an understanding of
- The characteristics of organisms [LS 1]
- Life cycles of organisms [LS 2]
- Organisms and environments [LS 3]

Earth and Space Sciences [ESS]

Content Standard D: As a result of the activities in grades K–4, all students should develop an understanding of
- Properties of earth materials [ESS 1]
- Objects in the sky [ESS 2]
- Changes in earth and sky [ESS 3]

Science and Technology [S&T]

Content Standard E: As a result of the activities in grades K–4, all students should develop an understanding of
- Abilities of technological design [S&T 1]
- Understanding about science and technology [S&T 2]
- Ability to distinguish between natural objects and objects made by humans [S&T 3]

Science in Personal and Social Perspectives [SPSP]

Content Standard F: As a result of the activities in grades K–4, all students should develop an understanding of
- Personal health [SPSP 1]
- Characteristics and changes in populations [SPSP 2]
- Types of resources [SPSP 3]
- Changes in environments [SPSP 4]
- Science and technology in local challenges [SPSP 5]

*This general standard is the foundation of all the NSE standards. Since it is emphasized in all *Teaching Children Science* activities, it is not identified for each experience.

**The bracketed symbol to the right of each standard was prepared for this book by this author.

FIGURE 4.1
The *National Science Education Content Standards, Grades K–8*

History and Nature of Science [HNS]

Content Standard G: As a result of the activities in grades K–4, all students should develop an understanding of
- Science as a human endeavor [HNS 1]

Content Standards 5–8

Science as Inquiry

Content Standard A: As a result of their activities in grades 5–8, all students should develop
- Abilities necessary to do scientific inquiry
- Understandings about scientific inquiry

Physical Science [PS]

Content Standard B: As a result of their activities in grades 5–8, all students should develop an understanding of
- Properties and changes of properties in matter [PS 4]
- Motion and forces [PS 5]
- Transfer of energy [PS 6]

Life Science [LS]

Content Standard C: As a result of their activities in grades 5–8, all students should develop an understanding of
- Structure and function in living systems [LS 4]
- Reproduction and heredity [LS 5]
- Regulation and behavior [LS 6]
- Population and ecosystems [LS 7]
- Diversity and adaptations of organisms [LS 8]

Earth and Space Sciences [ESS]

Content Standard D: As a result of their activities in grades 5–8, all students should develop an understanding of
- Structure of the earth system [ESS 4]
- Earth's history [ESS 5]
- Earth in the solar system [ESS 6]

Science and Technology [S&T]

Content Standard E: As a result of the activities in grades 5–8, all students should develop an understanding of
- Abilities of technological design [S&T 4]
- Understanding about science and technologyy [S&T 5]

Science in Personal and Social Perspectives [SPSP]

Content Standard F: As a result of the activities in grades 5–8, all students should develop an understanding of
- Personal health [SPSP 6]
- Populations, resources, and environments [SPSP 7]
- Natural hazards [SPSP 8]
- Risks and benefits [SPSP 9]
- Changes in environments [SPSP 10]
- Science and technology in society [SPSP 11]

History and Nature of Science [HNS]

Content Standard G: As a result of the activities in grades 5–8, all students should develop an understanding of
- Science as a human endeavor [HNS 2]
- Nature of science [HNS 3]
- History of science [HNS 4]

The NSE Standards: Implications for Appropriate Sequence

One of the very best ways of starting spirited discussion in a teachers' meeting is to say something like "The butterfly life cycle is too complicated for second-graders." If you are silly enough to make such a statement, you should be prepared to immediately weave your own protective chrysalis!

Too often, interested parties tell us that first-graders should learn X, second-graders should learn Y, and so on. That approach is much too specific and assumes that children in certain grades are homogeneous in terms of their present knowledge of science as well as their interest and ability to pursue science concepts. They are not. What children are able to do at a given grade level largely depends on the particular children, the teacher, and the resources available.

The NSE standards take a more sensible and flexible approach to recommending the sequence in which science topics should be introduced. They identify the recommended content for grades K–4 and 5–8, as shown in Figure 4.1.

Unit Planning

 ### What Makes a Good Unit Plan?

When full-time teachers lack a sense of the "big picture," their students have, in effect, a substitute teacher every day of the school year. Each school day that children have learning experiences that are not part of any larger context is a day that relates neither to the past nor to the future.

Children need appropriate learning experiences in school—activities that will reflect their teacher's concern with goals and that will involve them cognitively, affectively, and physically. To accomplish this, teachers must plan experiences that encourage children to *explore;* to *acquire* new concepts, attitudes, and psychomotor skills; and to *apply* their new knowledge and abilities in new situations. Unit plans take a variety of forms. The list of possible components in Figure 4.2 may prove useful when you develop your own unit plans.

Will Unit Plans Work in Schools That Use Science Textbooks?

Many schools use textbooks or curriculum guides as organizing elements for the curriculum. With some creative planning on your part, such materials can offer a starting point for the development of meaningful science experiences for children. After diagnosing student needs and interests, you can use a portion of a textbook or curriculum guide as a basis for a unit plan. Indeed, the teachers' editions of many recent science textbooks can be important planning resources. Many contain lists of concepts to show scope and sequence; lists of emphasized process skills; ideas for beginning units and lessons; lesson plans; lists of science materials needed; science

Component	Purpose
• Rationale	Helps you think through the reasons for doing a unit on a particular topic
• Instructional objectives*	Help you focus on the intended outcomes of the unit
• Listing of science concepts and processes to be emphasized	Helps you focus on the major ideas and methods of science that should be stressed
• Content outline (for teachers)	Helps you review the content that will provide the foundation for the learning experience
• Daily lesson plans*	Help you think through learning activities and their relationship to exploration, concept acquisition, and concept application
• Materials list	Helps you make certain that you have all the materials needed for science activities that occur in daily lessons
• Audiovisual materials and list	Helps you make certain that you have such things as computer hardware and software, videotapes, and other required equipment
• Assessment strategies	Help you consider informal and formal ways to assess the extent to which children have achieved cognitive, psychomotor, and affective growth during the unit

*Considered in greater detail later in this chapter.

FIGURE 4.2
A science unit may have many components, but each component has a specific purpose.

content for the teacher; lesson enrichment ideas; bulletin board and field trip ideas; lists of related children's books; and computer software and audiovisual aids.

Although a teacher's edition can be an important resource, it is not a recipe book and should not be used in place of your own planning. After all, you are the only one who knows the children in your class.

Lesson Planning

What Makes a Good Learning Objective?

The central characteristic of a learning objective is the specification of the behavior that the child is likely to exhibit as a result of the learning process. When you write an objective, be sure to specify the action you wish the child to perform. Attempt to answer the question What will the child be able to do? Here are some key performance words that appear in instructional objectives. Notice how some of these are used in the sample objectives that follow this list:

Write	Plan	Explain orally	Select	Measure	Label
Bake	List	Construct (make)	Define	Solve	Name
Sing					

Unit Topic	Sample Objective
1. Force and Motion	Measure how high a tennis ball bounces when dropped from different heights.
2. Using Electrical Energy	List five safety rules for using electrical appliances.
3. The Nervous System	Name the five senses.
4. Good Nutrition	Bake a batch of cookies that do not require sugar.
5. Protecting Our Environment	Write a poem about preventing pollution.
6. The Changing Earth	Construct a model of a volcano.

The science activities presented in this book include learning objectives that specify expected student behaviors. These objectives will probably be specific enough for most schools. However, some school systems require teachers to establish objectives that are even more specific.

What Makes a Good Discovery-Based Lesson Plan?

If you were to lock three teachers in a room and ask them (under pain of losing their parking spaces) to reach a consensus about the best format for a lesson plan, you would probably end up with four formats (and three teachers walking to school). The fact is, there are many approaches to lesson planning, and it is difficult to know in advance which one will work best for you.

Be that as it may, you *do* need a starting point for lesson planning. The following key elements—enhanced with additional components suggested by veteran teachers, school administrators, and others—will serve you well:

1. Objectives
2. Process Skills Emphasized
3. Materials
4. Learning Cycle Procedures
5. Assessment
6. Assignment

Sample Discovery-Based Lesson Plans

Figures 4.3, 4.4, and 4.5 (pages 63–65) are sample lesson plans that all have a strong discovery emphasis. This should be evident as you note, in particular, the Learning Cycle Procedures component that is the foundation for each.

Will It Sink or Will It Float?

Objectives

Observe that some objects sink and some float.

Predict whether various small objects will sink or float.

Classify objects as "sinkers" and "floaters."

Process Skills Emphasized

Observing, predicting, classifying

Materials

Easel paper and marker

Empty aquarium

Plastic water jugs (filled)

Shell, pine cone, leaf, marble, coin, buttons, clothespin, cork, and spoon

Bath soap that floats and bath soap that doesn't

One paper bag containing assortment of different objects that sink or float, including a rubber duck (put a question mark on the bag)

Second paper bag containing additional three objects

Learning Cycle Procedures

1. *Exploration.* Ask children, "Do you play with toys when you take a bath? If you do, what toys do you play with?" As they answer, list their bath toys on the easel paper. Ask, "Do your toys sink or float on the water?" Write an "S" in front of each item that sinks and an "F" in front of each that floats. Display the collection of objects. Invite children to come to the front of the room or center of the learning circle to select an object and tell whether he or she thinks it will sink or float.

2. *Acquisition.* After all predictions have been made, ask children to classify the objects according to the predictions. Have a child help you pour water into the aquarium. Now have various children act as assistants and gently place each object in the water. Have the children reclassify the objects based on the results.

3. *Application.* Display the bag with the question mark. Tell the children that when they have free time, they can work at the table to classify the objects in the bag as to whether they will sink or float and then experiment to test their predictions.

Assessment

Observe whether any children offer to bring in objects from home to test. Note whether their predictions about sinking and floating are correct. Listen for children to bring experiences with floating objects into classroom conversations.

Assignment

Display the second paper bag. Show the objects and have children practice remembering what the objects are by putting them back in the bag and removing them again. Finally, tell the children to think about each object tonight and predict whether it will sink or float when tested tomorrow.

FIGURE 4.3
A sample discovery-based lesson for grade K or 1

Planting Popcorn

Objectives

Make careful observations of a popcorn kernel and pebble without using sight.

List the conditions needed for the kernel to become a plant and then plant the kernel.

Write a story telling how one of the twins in Tomie dePaola's *The Popcorn Book* gets into trouble by mixing a jar full of popcorn kernels into a gardener's flower seeds.

Develop a positive attitude about caring for living things, as demonstrated by the children's follow through on plant care responsibilities.

Process Skills Emphasized

Observing, measuring, inferring

Materials

Bag of popcorn kernels and bag of equal-sized pebbles
Paper cups, potting soil, and small sandwich bags
The Popcorn Book, by Tomie dePaola (Holiday House, 1978)
Access to water

Learning Cycle Procedures

Keep the seeds and pebbles out of the children's sight. Soak enough kernels in water for two days so each child can trade his or her dry kernel for a soaked one.

1. *Exploration.* Have children shut their eyes and outstretch both hands so they are ready to receive some mystery objects. Explain that they are to keep their eyes shut until you say to open them. Indicate that the mystery objects should be kept in their closed hands until you say to open them. Distribute the mystery objects so that each child gets one pebble and one kernel. Go to the board and record children's observations of the objects, classifying them as right- or left-hand objects. Have the children open their hands to reveal their objects.

2. *Acquisition.* Discuss the differences between living and nonliving things. Ask the children to describe what their kernel will need in order to grow into a popcorn plant. Read *The Popcorn Book* to the class.

3. *Application.* Form cooperative learning groups, three children per group. Distribute a few soaked kernels to each group. Explain the need to soak the kernels for a day or two before planting. Distribute the cups and the plastic bag with potting soil, and indicate that you will be asking them to record the growth of their plants on a large bulletin board chart for each of the following 8 weeks.

Assessment

Keep anecdotal records that show which groups are observing and attending to the needs of their planted kernels each day.

Assignment

Ask the children to think about two or three good ideas they learned that they can use in writing stories about what a seed in a cornfield needs in order to grow into a corn plant. Have them write their stories the next day.

FIGURE 4.4
A sample discovery-based lesson for grade 2 or 3

What Is a Healthy and Tasty Meal?

Objectives

Classify foods on the hot lunch menu and those from a typical fast-food lunch into the categories of the food pyramid.

State examples of foods from each food category.

Construct a menu for a balanced lunch.

Process Skills Emphasized

Classifying, interpreting data, formulating hypotheses

Materials

Today's hot lunch menu

Bag from fast-food restaurant containing wrappings or containers for the following: burger, salad, fries, cookies, soda, milk

Information pamphlet available from the major fast-food chain that details calorie and nutrient information for each product

Copy of food pyramid chart and chart paper for each group.

Transparency listing food items that would make a complete meal from a menu of a local fancy restaurant

FIGURE 4.5
A sample discovery-based lesson for the middle grades

Learning Cycle Procedures

1. *Exploration.* Show the closed bag from the fast-food restaurant to the class. Have children guess what's in it. Begin a discussion of why eating a well-balanced diet is important. Distribute copies of the food pyramid chart, and have children discuss where each part of their most recent fast-food meal would be placed within the pyramid.

2. *Acquisition.* Describe to the class how the digestive system processes foods from each portion of the pyramid. Encourage the children to take notes. Mention that sample foods from each group contribute to the functioning of other body systems—for instance, minerals from dairy products and vegetables are used in bone formation. Place the children in groups, and distribute chart paper to each group. Have them prepare a food pyramid chart with space for sample foods under each category. Reveal the contents of the bag, and have children classify the foods that the wrappings represent. Distribute copies of the nutrition pamphlet, and have students locate the information related to each item they put on their chart.

3. *Application.* Write today's hot lunch menu on the board. Have the groups classify the foods from the hot lunch menu and record them on a pyramid chart. Have each group write a hypothesis that explains why the school lunch menu includes an assortment of foods that do or do not meet the requirements of the food pyramid.

Assessment

Project a copy of the menu for a complete meal from a local fancy restaurant. Ask children to classify each food item into its proper location on the pyramid. Also ask if they think they will be improving their food choices as a result of this lesson.

Assignment

Ask children to design and bring in a hot lunch menu each day of the week that includes foods from each group on the pyramid.

As you review these plans, notice what they have in common and how they are different. Also assess how much children involved in the lesson will be able to:

1. Have an opportunity to explore—*Exploration*
2. Have an opportunity to acquire new knowledge, attitudes, and psychomotor skills—*Concept acquisition*
3. Apply what they learn to new situations—*Concept application*

Classroom Organization and Management for Discovery Learning

 I'm not going to provide an elaborate treatise on maintaining appropriate classroom behavior. I have seen more teachers produce discipline problems than I have seen children cause them. If you are able to maintain appropriate behavior when you teach social studies, reading, math, or any other subject, you will be able to when you teach science. If you have problems with classroom control, science activities will neither solve your problems nor make them worse. Even so, you can take some steps that will help things go more smoothly for everyone. Appropriate classroom behavior is not hard to achieve; it just requires attention to a few common-sense matters.

Distributing Materials

The attack of a school of piranha on a drowning monkey is a model of tranquillity when compared with a group of 20 children trying to acquire a magnet from a tote tray containing 10 of them.

In order to distribute materials effectively, you need to devise techniques that are appropriate for your setting. In some settings, for example, two or three children can distribute materials to all the groups. Another technique is to have one child from each group come forward to acquire needed materials. Regardless of the procedure you employ, try to avoid having all the children get what they need simultaneously.

Providing Work Space

"Please make him (her) stop bugging us, or I will wring his (her) neck."

This is a rather common classroom request (threat) among children involved in science activities. One way to diminish this type of problem is to give your learning groups some work space. This may be difficult if you have a small room, but you should try anyway. Movable bookcases, room dividers, and similar objects should be pressed into service to give groups of children semiprivate work spaces. Since science activities provide ample opportunities for social interaction among group

REAL
TEACHERS
TALKING

A
Starting
Point
for
Thinking,
Talking,
and
Writing

Terry: I think most of us feel that planning is much easier than management. Good management is what makes it work. It really is what creates success or failure with your lessons.

Marie: But it's good planning that leads to good management, and the key to planning is to try the lesson yourself beforehand. That is what really helps you get the steps in the best sequence and the timing right, especially if you are going to be doing a lot of hands-on science with children. It's only when I try each activity myself that I get the sequence and timing down. That's what makes the actual class management of everything easier.

Terry: But there is more to it than just getting the science activities worked out. You have to think about other things, also. Something as simple as allocating space in the classroom for cooperative groups working on science projects can make a real difference. Working and reworking the directions you are going to give to groups also seems like a small matter, but it makes all the difference in the world.

Marie: Sometimes when new teachers observe experienced teachers, it almost looks too easy. People shouldn't think a classroom, especially a science classroom, runs smoothly by accident. There is a lot to it, and most of the work that makes it happen is done before class even starts!

Terry: Well, there is a lot that happens during class, as well. I am always changing my plans during a lesson. I've noticed that I am making changes even in my cooperative group work.

Marie: What do you mean?

Terry: Sometimes you think that a science project might be too hard for a group, but as soon as the group gets started, you realize it's going to be too easy. As soon as you see this happening, you've got to intervene, to make changes right on the spot. If you don't, a management disaster is just a few minutes away.

Marie: I think the trick with cooperative group work is to be ready with alternatives so that each group gets projects that are so challenging that the group has to come up with alternative ways of working things out. If you can do this, you get the children a lot more focused. I think that is what makes the idea of assigning roles to different children in a group really work. If the project is too easy, the roles lose their meaning.

Terry: Nothing ties a group together like a real challenge—one where they really depend on one another for success.

▶ *Point to Ponder:*   *These teachers stressed the ability to take quick remedial action during class time as a critical component of good management. They also emphasized the need for challenging science projects to keep groups focused. What do you see as the possible management consequences of giving groups science projects that are too challenging? What could you do to be ready to deal with the management problems that might result from such a situation?*

members, there is little need for groups to interact with one another. Such contact is often counterproductive.

The most important element of a science work space is a flat surface. If you have the opportunity to select furniture for your classroom, choose tables and chairs rather than conventional desks. The typical classroom desk for children is designed for *writing*, not for doing science activities. If your classroom has desks with slanted tops, you will need to acquire tables, build your own tables, or use the floor as the place for science activities. Some teachers find that the inflexibility presented by traditional desks can be overcome by placing tables along the periphery of the room. Students can then carry out their science activities on the tables and use their desks during other instructional activities.

Make the Case

An Individual
or Group
Challenge

The Problem   Chaos can result if a teacher has not carefully thought out classroom management issues before children engage in hands-on, discovery-based science experiences.

Assess Your Prior Knowledge and Beliefs   Based on your classroom observations or teaching/tutoring experiences, consider the probable classroom management consequences of including each of the following in your classroom or curriculum:

An aquarium   _____

Small mammals in cages   _____

Reptiles in cages   _____

Insects in cages   _____

Rock, mineral, or shell collections on science tables or in learning centers   _____

Taking a nature walk along a stream or pond in a city park   _____

Taking a field trip to a hands-on science museum   _____

The Challenge   Create a Dos and Don'ts poster focused on appropriate classroom behavior that could be used at the beginning of the year to prepare children for a curriculum that includes experiences with all of the above. Be sure to give special attention to taking the class on field trips.

Providing Clear Directions

> *"I didn't know what I was supposed to do with the ice cubes,*
> *so I put them down her back."*

Children (and adults) seem to get into trouble when they don't understand what they are supposed to be doing. Problems arise in the classroom when children don't understand what your expectations are. If you learn to announce these expectations clearly and simply, you will find that misbehaviors decrease.

If the science activity the children are going to do requires procedures or materials they are unfamiliar with, you will need to model the use of these materials or procedures (except, of course, when the objective of the activity is the discovery of how to use them). *Children who do not know how to read a meterstick will use it as a baseball bat or sword rather than as a device for making linear measurements.* By taking a few minutes to teach children how to use materials and equipment properly, you can make the process of discovery more pleasant for you and them.

Internet Resources

Websites for Planning and Managing

Elementary Science Support Center

http://essc.calumet.purdue.edu/

If you are in the process of unit and lesson planning, visit this site to study its collection of hands-on science activities, science-related children's literature, and support software for lessons and units. The section "Useful Science Links" will take you to other planning resources on the Internet.

Science Lesson Plans

http://www.col-ed.org/cur/science.html#sci1

This site, sponsored by the Columbia Education Center in Oregon, provides a rather extraordinary collection of elementary/middle-level science lessons. You should be able to find a sample lesson on any topic commonly taught at the elementary or middle grades here.

New Teacher Resources

http://www.teachersfirst.com/new-tch.htm

This page contains links to articles written by new teachers who have faced or are facing the challenges of planning and managing a classroom. The links have been carefully selected so that most of the challenges a new teacher is likely to face are probably addressed. The resources are definitely practical in nature and cover many of the planning and management issues you are likely concerned about.

Science Resource Page

http://www.curtin.edu.au/curtin/dept/smec/web/science.htm

This page has an extraordinary collection of links to science education resources. Many will take you to sites containing sample science lessons at various grade levels.

Whales and Oceans

http://www.athena.ivv.nasa.gov/curric/oceans/whales/index.html

If you will be involved in planning a teaching unit on some topic in oceanography, this site will be of interest to you. It provides many suggestions for lessons and activities, with whales as the principal topic. You also will find links to other ocean resources for unit and lesson planning.

Curriculum Units

http://www.cis.yale.edu/ynhti/curriculum/units/

This extensive collection of teaching units covers every subject in the curriculum. When you reach this site, browse through it to locate science-related units. Then follow the links to determine if the content and suggested grade level are appropriate for your classroom. These are very thoroughly prepared units and as such should prove very helpful to you.

New York: Learning Standards

http://www.cnyric.org/cnyric/standards/standards.html

This site permits you to download a complete standards document, which will prove quite useful as you develop unit and lesson plans. The standards cover a wide range of science topics and are clearly identified as to the grade level for which the developers feel they are most appropriate. (When you reach the site, follow the directions to be sure you also download the software needed to read the standards on your computer.)

The National Science Standards

http://www.nap.edu/readingroom/books/intronses/

Every person who teaches children science should visit this site. As an official site for the National Science Standards, it presents the standards, their rationale, and suggestions to help teachers use them. If you are planning units and lessons and want to be sure they relate to the National Science Standards, this site is the resource to visit.

Summary

The success of a discovery-oriented classroom depends on your ability to both plan and manage. The science curriculum for children typically consists of a number of learning units. Unit plans are long-term plans for science experiences that focus on particular topics. Daily lesson plans are single components of unit plans. This chapter offers three sample lesson plans. A classroom that permits students to carry out science activities as part of group work undoubtedly will provide some class-room management challenges. Teachers can use various techniques to ensure that science time is rich in appropriate learning opportunities yet manageable, as well.

Going Further

On Your Own

1. How you plan for teaching will probably depend to a great extent upon your general out-look on the nature of teaching and how children learn. To bring these perceptions into focus, respond to each of the following statements:
   a. Careful planning is consistent with how I carry out life activities.
   b. Planning can restrict flexibility.
   c. I never had a teacher who planned.
   d. Children will learn regardless of how much teachers plan.

2. Review the sample lesson plans in this chapter. Then select a science topic appropriate for the grade level you are interested in and develop a lesson plan. If possible, teach the lesson to a group of children or peers who role-play children. Assess the extent to which your lesson emphasizes exploring, concept acquisition, and concept application.

3. Sketch your vision of the ideal classroom in which to teach science. Label the special areas in your classroom. Note, in particular, the location and arrangement of classroom seating and work space. What advantage does your ideal classroom have over a conven-tional elementary school classroom? How could you use your ideas for classroom orga-nization in a conventional classroom?

On Your Own or in a Cooperative Learning Group

4. Brainstorm a science activity for each of the following science units. Then try to place the activities in the most appropriate order in which they should be taught. Which do you think will cause the most management problems? Why?
   a. Indoor Gardening
   b. Animals with Pouches
   c. The Changes in the Seasons
   d. Earthquakes
   e. Friction

5. Role-play a job interview between a school principal and a teaching candidate for either a self-contained classroom or a departmentalized school. During the interview, the "principal" should ask about the following:

  a. The teacher's awareness of the NSE standards
  b. The science content and experiences appropriate for children at that grade
  c. The planning style the prospective teacher would use
  d. The management strategies the teacher would use
  e. Ideas the teacher has for giving children opportunities to explore
  f. Alternate techniques the teacher could use to introduce a concept
  g. Ideas that the teacher has for helping children apply concepts to new situations

Notes

1. Kenneth Grahame, *The Wind in the Willows* (New York: Macmillan, 1991).
2. Robert F. Mager, *Preparing Instructional Objectives*, 2nd ed. (Belmont, CA: Pitman Learning, 1975), pp. v, vi. Reprinted by permission of the publisher.
3. National Research Council, *National Science Education Standards* (Washington, DC: National Academy Press, 1996), p. 6. Reprinted with permission of National Academy Press.
4. Ibid., 104.
5. Ibid., 103.

Suggested Readings

Ahlness, Mark. "The Earth Day Groceries Project." *Science and Children* 36, no. 7 (April 1999): 32–35.

Althouse, Rosemary. *Investigating Science with Young Children*. New York: Teachers College Press, 1998.

Ames, Nancy. "Practices and Strategies." *Schools in the Middle* 8, no. 4 (Janauary/February 1999): 18–23, 44–45.

Belzer, Jan. "Bringing the Internet into Daily Lesson Plans." *Media & Methods* 34, no. 4 (March/April 1998): 20.

Bianchini, Julie. "What's the Big Idea?" *Science and Children* 36, no. 2 (October 1998): 40–41.

Cook, Helen, and Catherine E. Matthews. "Lessons from a 'Living Fossil.'" *Science and Children* 36, no. 3 (November/December 1998): 16–20.

Donovan, Susan E. "A Science Showdown." *Science Scope* 22, no. 6 (March 1999): 66–69.

Ebenezer, Jazlin, and Eddy Lau. *Science on the Internet: A Resource for K–12 Teachers*. Columbus, OH: Merrill Education, 1999.

Eick, Charles J. "Growing with the Standards." *Science Scope* 21, no. 7 (April 1998): 10–14.

Girod, Mark. "Riding the Dinosaur Wave." *Educational Leadership* 56, no. 1 (September 1998): 72–75.

Harim, Jean Love. "A *Tree*mendous Learning Experience." *Science and Children* 35, no. 8 (May 1998): 26–29.

Helde, Ann, and Linda Stilborne. *The Teacher's Complete and Easy Guide to the Internet*. New York: Teachers College Press, 1999.

Holler, Edward. "Standardizing Practices." *Schools in the Middle* 8, no. 4 (January/February 1999): 26–30.

Jacobsen, David A., et al. *Methods for Teaching: Promoting Student Learning*. Columbus, OH: Merrill Education, 1998.

O'Sullivan, Elaine. "Wings of Spring." *Science and Children* 35, no. 8 (May 1998): 35–37.

Scherer, Marge. "The Discipline of Hope: A Conversation with Herbert Kohl." *Educational Leadership* 56, no. 1 (September 1998): 8–13.

Snyder, Robert C. "'Scrounging' in Support of the Standards." *Science and Children* (January 1998): 18–20.

5

Strategies for Discovery Learning

How can I use cooperative learning, special questioning, active listening, and other strategies to foster discovery learning?

A Look Ahead

The Problem with Talk

My greatest challenge as a teacher is to refrain from telling my students everything—far more than they want to know. This problem seems to be a highly contagious ailment that can be transmitted from professor to student. I have reached this conclusion because I find that teachers in grades K–8 tell their students too much—usually more than the children really want to be told. A favorite story of mine concerns a first-grade child who asks a teacher to explain nuclear fusion. The teacher replies, "Why don't you ask your mother? She is a nuclear physicist." The child replies, "I don't want to know that much about it."

Perhaps it is just human nature to tell people more than they really want to know. In my case, it happens when I get excited about the content I am sharing; I want everyone to get the information quickly. When I work in science classrooms, I try to restrain myself from talking so much because I know that I will enjoy watching children discover something special on their own, and I know that will happen only if I talk less. That smile or screech of excitement from a child who makes a discovery is powerful medicine that stops my wagging tongue. How can we do more real science with children? Perhaps the first step is to talk less and to use more creative strategies that help children learn on their own—with our guidance, to be sure, but not with so much guidance that the smiles and screeches are lost.

Cooperative Learning Strategies

We science teachers are not perfect. We may not have the best-looking bulletin boards. We may do demonstrations that smell—literally. We may even be responsible for the terrorism of an entire school wing or learning center when a gerbil, rabbit, or boa constrictor makes an unexpected break for freedom during cage cleaning time. But we cannot be accused of doing insufficient group work.

Unless a school is so well equipped that children do science activities independently, most hands-on science experiences for children are group activities. There are few 20-child elementary classrooms with 20 flashlight lamps, 20 flashlight lamp receptacles, 20 dry cells, 20 switches, and 40 lengths of wire available for the construction of simple electrical circuits. Consequently, for most elementary teachers who emphasize discovery learning in science, group work occurs every day.

When you observe a group of children at work, do you sense that they are working toward some common shared purpose and learning from one another, or do comments like the following tell you that something very different is really going on?

"You get the magnets, you get the nails, I'll do the speriment, and you write it down since you've got a pencil."

"Mrs. McGuire, why do I always wind up with a group of dummies?"

"I don't believe it. He ate the tomato slice we were supposed to use for the seed counting."

A
Starting
Point
for
Thinking,
Talking,
and
Writing

Nadine: One of the problems I notice with cooperative learning is that some-times one member of the group gets left out. So, it's really important for the teacher to create a science learning experience that really is going to involve everyone on the team.

Pat: I think part of the answer is trying to choose a task that has many sub-tasks. This way, there will be enough work to go around. Of course, one problem with this approach is that it makes it tempting for children to just work on their subtask, which flies in the face of the big ideas about cooperative learning.

Nadine: Well, you have to keep in mind that during an entire school year, you might use a number of different models of cooperative learning, al-though the emphasis is always on the team product. For example, there is a strategy called "think, pair, share" in which the students pair up, study, and discuss the topic or complete their projects. Then they share what they learn with the class. This type of cooperative project really fits science nicely.

Pat: What about the use of roles? Does the idea work for you? What roles and responsibilities make most sense to you as a science teacher?

Nadine: Each member of the team has a name that tells the type of task he or she must perform. The "materials manager" picks up and returns materials and leads the clean-up work. The "tracker" helps record and maintain information for the team. The "communicator" helps resolve problems and is the only member who can leave the team to seek help. The "checker" acts like the team captain, keeping everyone on task.

Pat: So, I guess the challenge is to have a task or project that is sufficiently challenging and, where appropriate, to give children roles that will keep them involved. Of course, even if we are able to do both, we still have to keep a sharp eye out for children who are left out. I think some teachers call these children "hitchhikers"—meaning that they are just along for the ride. I guess that's a role we don't have to create in advance!

▶ ***Point to Ponder:*** *In this conversation, Nadine discussed four possible roles for chil-dren in science groups. Teachers of young children might find the names for these roles are a bit complicated for their students. Suppose you are a teacher of young children. What names would you suggest for these roles?*

Just putting children in groups and having them engage in a project may teach some lessons about working with others that you would rather not teach. On the other hand, when done well, group work offers enormous opportunities for helping children learn science and discover ways of working together.

What Is a Cooperative Learning Group?

Each stage of the discovery learning cycle of exploration, concept acquisition, and concept application can be enriched by the use of well-thought-out group work. One promising approach to group work that is becoming widely used is known as *cooperative learning*. A cooperative learning group consists of a group of children who are, in fact, working together on a project, supportive of one another, and accountable for their individual learning as well as the learning of every other person in the group. A variety of characteristics distinguish cooperative learning groups from the traditional groups that operate in a classroom. Figure 5.1 displays nine characteristics that you can use to distinguish cooperative learning groups from traditional learning groups.

Finding a Focus for Your Groups

If you want your students to discover and carry out their explorations in cooperative learning groups, *you* must answer a very basic question before the children even get to your classroom: What challenges or problems will attract and hold the attention of a cooperative learning group? Answering this question may be the hardest part of your work day. Even so, you must answer it before the children arrive!

You can identify appropriate science and technology-related problems for cooperative groups to explore in several ways. To start, look over your local science curriculum, the NSE content standards, and Project 2061 goals. List those topics, standards, or goals that will attract and hold student interest.

If you really are motivated to get your groups functioning in a positive way, think about your students' real-life experience to find topics that will fuel their interest. One teacher did this by providing students with a list of household products and

FIGURE 5.1
What is the difference between a cooperative learning group and a traditional learning group?

Cooperative Learning Groups	Traditional Learning Groups
• Positive interdependence	• No interdependence
• Individual accountability	• No individual accountability
• Heterogeneous	• Homogeneous
• Shared leadership	• One appointed leader
• Shared responsibility for each other	• Responsibility only for self
• Task and maintenance emphasized	• Only task emphasized
• Social skills directly taught	• Social skills assumed and ignored
• Teacher observes and intervenes	• Teacher ignores group functioning
• Groups process their effectiveness	• No group processing

asking them to form teams to test how well each product worked.[1] The teacher expected the students to identify at least three product characteristics to test. One group selected antibacterial soap and identified cost, smell, and germ-killing power. Another investigated the carbon dioxide content of leading brands of soda, and a third tested how long the fragrance lasts with certain perfumes.

Locating a good problem for group work is only the first critical step. You must also narrow and focus the topic so it will lead students to productive explorations. The teacher in the previous example reported his experiences with getting the groups moving forward this way:

> *But the challenge was just beginning. The teams were then expected to devise and carry out tests for all three variables. Cost and smell are relatively easy, but how about germ-killing power? The boys set up cultures of chicken broth, added soap and, a few days later, used a microscope to examine the cultures for bacterial growth."* . . .
>
> - *A team investigating the carbon dioxide content of leading brands of soda put balloons over the tops of cans, shook the cans which released the gas and noted the size of the balloons.*
> - *A team investigating the staying power of perfume, sprayed three colored balloons with perfume, hung them on a tree outside the school for six hours and then polled other students to see which perfume was the strongest.*[2]

This teacher's report reinforces the key strategies discussed for getting cooperative learning groups started in the proper manner. You must locate, develop, and focus study problems to give student groups a sense of purpose and direction. If you study the curriculum, think about the children's real world, and formulate interesting problems, you will have laid the foundation for successful cooperative group work in the classroom.

Three Steps to Successful Cooperative Learning Groups

Although Figure 5.1 displays nine characteristics of cooperative learning groups, these characteristics emerge from three more fundamental elements, or strategies, of cooperative learning. If you can build these strategies into your work with children before, during, and even after group work, you will increase the chances for successful group work. Here is a brief discussion of each:

1. *Teach for positive interdependence.* Help all members of each group understand that their success depends on the extent to which they agree on goals, objectives, and the roles each member is expected to carry out. They also need to agree in advance on an acceptable way to share available resources and information.

2. *Teach for individual accountability.* Help all members of each group understand that they are not only accountable for their own learning and behavior but also responsible for helping other group members learn and work productively.

The success of a cooperative learning group depends on the success of each of its individuals.

3. *Teach interpersonal and small-group skills.* If you expect children to work together and display appropriate group process skills, you will have to take the time to teach them those skills. Before group work, discuss group process skills such as sharing leadership, praising good work done by others, and active listening. Also teach children how to analyze how well the group process itself is going and how to modify the process to improve it.

To make these three elements easier to observe or implement in an actual science classroom, Figure 5.2 identifies each element and provides examples of the teacher behaviors and statements that characterize its implementation.

Questioning Strategies

 Sometimes when I visit a classroom, I get the feeling that I have stepped into the Spanish Inquisition. In some classrooms, the number of questions asked and the amount of time that question asking and answering takes up is unsettling. Educational researchers have long been concerned about the quantity and quality of teacher questions. It takes a great deal of self-discipline to ask only those questions needed to keep children moving as they explore, acquire, and apply what they learn. If, however, you can control the number of questions you ask, you can focus on the *quality* of questions you ask.

Improving the Questions You Ask

Over the years, many educators have devised "lenses" you can use to analyze the questions you ask of children. These lenses, or classification systems, which can be used with videotapes or audiotapes of your lessons, will allow you to assess, more or less objectively, your question-asking abilities. One very valuable classification system for questions relates the cognitive levels (knowledge, comprehension, application, analysis, synthesis, and evaluation) you read about in Chapter 1.

After some careful thought about the six cognitive levels, Orlich and others have proposed an easy three-category system for classifying questions. They suggest that you think in terms of just three types of questions. As you listen to or watch tapes of your own teaching or as you observe other teachers, see if you can classify each question you hear into one of these three categories:

1. *Convergent questions.* Get children to think in ways that focus on basic knowledge or comprehension. Examples: How did the yeast help our dough rise? What did the three-horned dinosaur eat? How was the plant cell different from the animal cell? How many planets go around the sun?

2. *Divergent questions.* Get children to think about a number of alternative answers. Examples: What are some ideas about what caused the dinosaurs to become extinct? If you were a prey animal in a jungle, what could you do to keep safe from predators?

FIGURE 5.2 These examples will help you implement successful cooperative learning groups in your classroom.

Cooperative Goal	What the Teacher Does	What the Teacher Says
Positive Interdependence	Helps a group write its goals on poster paper.	"You seem to be having trouble agreeing on a topic. Have you thought about 'Meat-Eating Plants' or 'Do dolphins really talk'?"
	Writes "Sink or swim together" on the chalkboard.	"I'll be expecting all of you to know how the inner planets and outer planets are different."
Individual Accountability	Gestures to child who seems to be daydreaming to get her on task.	
	Notices a mess on the floor near a group working with baking powder, carries a trash pail to the group, and informs members that some of them are forgetting good clean-up habits.	"I thought your group's name was 'Science All Stars' not 'Science Mess Makers!'"
Developing Group Process Skills	Helps a group rearrange its desks so children are all facing each other.	"Sarah, I don't think Jason can see those gorilla pictures you brought in."
	Gives feedback about a leadership problem.	"Marsha, I keep hearing your voice. It's a beautiful voice, but I never hear any of the other beautiful voices in your group."
	Gives feedback about a positive change in group behavior.	"Didn't cleaning Snowball's cage go much faster when you all worked together? I sure think it did."

3. *Evaluative questions.* Get students to give answers that show that they are offering a judgment that is based on some criteria. Examples: Of the sources of energy that we have studied, which one would you be willing to have used in an electrical power plant that was built right next to your house? Some people say that we could have cleaner air to breathe if we made it illegal to own a car; what do you think about that idea?[3]

Clearly, if you wish to create a classroom environment in which children discover science concepts, you will want to balance the types of questions you ask. As the children grasp important science concepts, consider asking more divergent and evaluative questions than convergent questions. This will make the classroom a more productive and interesting place for you and the children.

Using Wait-Time

Have you ever heard of *wait-time?* It is one way to increase the effectiveness of the open questions (as well as all other questions) that you ask. Wait-time simply means giving children sufficient time to think about questions before answering them and before receiving your response to their answers. Our questioning behavior tends to follow a certain pattern: We ask a question, receive a response from a child, and then immediately react to the response.

Tobin and Capie have compiled and analyzed the wait-time research carried out by numerous educational researchers over the years. One researcher, Mary Budd Rowe, discovered the following about the pauses separating speakers in a classroom:

> *When the average length of pauses was greater than approximately three seconds, desirable characteristics of student behavior were evident. Two types of pauses were identified: wait-time I was defined as the length of time a teacher pauses after asking a question; wait-time II was defined as the time a teacher waits after a pupil response before a comment is made or another question is asked.*[4]

Three seconds doesn't seem like a very long time to wait after a child responds, but most of us have trouble waiting even that long. Tobin and Capie report that studies show that the average wait-time is 0.9 seconds![5]

An increase in wait-time can help transform a traditional classroom into an environment in which discovery learning can occur. Tobin and Capie highlight the following important consequences of Rowe's exploration of the effect of extending wait-time beyond 3 seconds:

1. The length of student responses increased.
2. The number of unsolicited but appropriate responses increased.
3. Failure to respond decreased.
4. Confidence, as reflected by a decrease in the number of inflected responses, increased.
5. The incidence of speculative responses increased.
6. The incidence of child-child comparisons of data increased.
7. The incidence of evidence-inference statements increased.

8. The incidence of questions asked by students increased.
9. There was an increase in the incidence of responses emanating from students rated by the teacher as relatively slow learners.
10. The variety in the type of verbal behavior of students increased.

Rowe also reported that a prolonged wait-time schedule produced desirable changes on three teacher variables:

1. The teacher demonstrated a greater response flexibility.
2. The teacher's expectations for the performance of students rated as relatively slow learners changed.
3. The number and type of questions asked by the teacher changed.[6]

Wait-time seems to be the pause that both refreshes the learning process and improves teacher classroom behavior. Think about extending your own wait-time each time you work with children.

Active Listening Strategies

"For the third time, you draw the food chain arrows so the arrow heads point to the living things that get the energy. Why do I keep seeing people draw the arrows from the killer whale to the sea lions? Was anyone listening when we talked about the food chains?"

Active listening is the conscious effort to focus on what people are saying when they speak. It is a skill that you need to teach children and a skill you may have to teach yourself.

You can take some practical steps to increase active listening in your classroom:

1. Restructure your physical setting to minimize distractions. A classroom in which children are involved with materials and organisms will not be as quiet as a library or a tomb. As you speak, there will be the screeching sounds of the gerbil's exercise wheel, the bubbling sounds of the fish tank air pump, the background noise of shifting chairs or desks, and so on. The first step in providing an environment in which active listening can occur is to compensate for background noise. You can do this by having the children asking or answering questions speak louder, by moving classroom furniture so that you and the children can see the speaker, and by having the children look directly at and speak directly to the group or person they are addressing.

2. Have children listen for key science words. One way to keep their attention on the speaker is to listen for words such as *up, down, under,* and *above* that signal what is to follow. As a person teaching children science, you will need to teach the children to use such terms as *observe, classify, graph, measure,* and *predict* and reinforce the use of these words through your praise. On a regular basis after a child has spoken or you have spoken, ask a question such as "Did you hear any key words when Emilio told us about last night's storm?" By

teaching the children to listen for key words and what follows them, you and they will become listeners who hear more of what actually is being said.

3. Have children create questions for the speaker. Challenge them to become such good listeners that you and they are able to ask the speaker a question that uses some of the speaker's words and ideas. For example, if Nadine is reporting the results of her group's work on a rock classifying activity to the full class, ask the class at the end of the report if they have any questions for Nadine or her group. By doing this, you will help the children realize that they should be so attentive to the speaker that they can ask good questions about what was said when the speaker is finished. This is, of course, active listening.

4. Practice summarizing what the speaker has said. When children speak or ask questions, you should listen so attentively that you can restate in summary form what they said. To do this, the listener has to use the natural gaps in a speaker's speech patterns to mentally summarize the key ideas as they emerge. Model this by occasionally restating or rephrasing a child's question in a shorter form and then checking with the speaker to see if you have captured the point or question.

I'm sure you will be able to develop additional techniques for encouraging active listening in your classroom. These techniques will round out your strategy for creating a classroom in which children benefit as fully as possible from the words spoken by you and their classmates.

Demonstrations

"Do it again!"

This exclamation should bring joy to your heart after you do a science demonstration for children. These three little words are a clear message that you have made contact with a child's mind.

In recent years, I have observed a deemphasis on the use of demonstrations in elementary science classrooms. It seems that a long-overdue reemphasis on having children do activities has taken an important job away from the teacher—that job of showing children phenomena they cannot efficiently, effectively, or *safely* discover for themselves. Because it has enormous potential for focusing attention upon a phenomenon, the science demonstration can be an important tool for promoting inquiry in children. A demonstration can raise many questions for children that can then be addressed in greater detail by individual science activities.

Of course, demonstrations can be misused in the classroom. They should never replace the child's involvement in science activities. Moreover, they should not be used solely to reproduce phenomena that children have already read about. Demonstrations should be used to intensify children's curiosity about a unit to be studied; to clarify confusion resulting from the attainment of contrary results by children who have carried out identical science activities; and to tie together various cognitive, affective, and psychomotor learnings at the end of a learning unit.

FIGURE 5.3
Use this checklist
before and after
you observe or
perform a science
demonstration for
children.

A Demonstration Checklist

____ 1. Did the teacher begin the demonstration promptly, or did the children have to wait an excessive amount of time while the teacher got prepared?

____ 2. Was the demonstration essentially simple and straightforward, or was it elaborate and complex?

____ 3. Could *all* the children in the class observe the demonstration?

____ 4. Did it seem as if the teacher had pretested the demonstration, or was there evidence that this was the first time it had been tried—for example, missing equipment, confusion in the sequence of steps?

____ 5. Was the teacher able to create a bit of drama with the demonstration as a result of purposely puzzling situations or outcomes that were unexpected to the children?

____ 6. Did the demonstration endanger the health or safety of the children?

____ 7. Did the demonstration seem to fit the topic under study?

____ 8. Was the demonstration appropriately introduced, carried out, and concluded?

____ 9. Did the children have an opportunity to ask questions, make statements, and give reactions?

____ 10. Did the demonstration provide a significant learning experience for children?

This book includes elementary school demonstrations for the life, physical, and earth/space sciences. Other sources of science demonstrations are found in the resources at the end of this book. Bear in mind that by using larger equipment or materials, you can transform virtually any science activity into a demonstration you feel the children should experience as a class.

There are a number of considerations in presenting an effective demonstration. Figure 5.3 is a demonstration checklist for assessing the effectiveness of the science demonstrations that you or others do.

Science Textbooks

The year was 1489. The city was Florence, Italy. A young man, just 14 years old, was walking through the work yard next to a cathedral that was being built. He came upon an enormous old block of poorly shaped marble resting in the weeds, which was called "the Giant" by marble workers and sculptors. Many had tried to make some use of it and failed. "It had lain for 35 years in the cathedral's work yard, an awesome ghostly reminder to all young sculptors of the challenge of their craft."[7]

Twelve years later, the same man rediscovered and very carefully studied the sleeping, malformed Giant. Now, at 26, he saw something in the marble that only he could release. That something would become known as *David,* and the man who stripped away the excess marble to reveal perhaps the most extraordinary sculpture known to humankind was Michelangelo. Within the imperfect he saw what few others could see—potential.

Your science classroom will be filled with imperfect resources: computers with Internet access that may lock up just as your children reach the best part of your Internet assignment, stacks of videotapes of nature adventures that really don't fit your curriculum, and bookshelves of textbooks that seem far too dull for your active children. You can spend a great deal of time wishing that you had better resources, but doing so will make no difference at all.

Science textbooks, bought with taxpayer money and intended as useful resources, will probably be flawed in one way or another. Their limitations will be obvious to all, but their potential will be unseen by many. Jones tells us that "U.S. textbooks are about twice the size of textbooks in other countries, and this is one situation where bigger is definitely not better."[8] She goes on to cite another expert who comments on the fact that textbooks seem unfocused, repetitive, and lacking coherence.

Although modern textbooks have definite weaknesses, they also contain some resources that you, a discovery-oriented teacher, can make good use of—*if* you are creative. They contain science content written at particular grade levels and provide many hands-on science activities. In addition, they usually come with teachers' guides that include enrichment ideas.

The activities in a textbook series, of course, reflect a particular scope and sequence of science content. If you have the freedom and the desire to create your own science curriculum, the textbook can still be quite useful. By omitting some of the structure present in the textbook's directions to the children, you can modify the activities so that they place more emphasis on discovery learning.

Textbooks are typically divided into a number of *units,* or groups of chapters. If you look over the units and the teacher's guide that accompanies the book, you will find many helpful teaching ideas. You will also find that many of the suggestions can be applied to learning units that you devise on your own. Many teachers' guides for textbooks provide bulletin board ideas, suggestions for field trips, lists of audiovisual materials, lists of children's books, and other helpful information that you can use to enrich your learning units.

Many teachers like to include *learning centers* in their classrooms, and the content and activities in textbooks can provide you with ideas for learning centers that foster discovery. Indeed, you could probably prepare a science curriculum that had learning centers as the principal medium of instruction and textbooks as supplementary resources. If you are unfamiliar with the construction of in-class learning centers, see Chapters 10, 13, and 16 of this book, which contain numerous ideas and plans for learning centers.

In order for children to pursue their curiosity about the phenomena that they have learned about through hands-on activities, they need reading materials. With advance planning, you can identify units and chapters in available textbooks that relate to your curriculum. By reading this material, the children can acquire some fundamental terms and definitions that will give them the background they need to use other reference books to find answers to questions that come to mind. Children who are reading about science and learning vocabulary while carrying out hands-on activities will be in a good position to follow their interests.

The Problem A large class may make so many demands on a teacher's time and attention that some children who have a special aptitude for science may go unnoticed.

Assess Your Prior Knowledge and Beliefs Based on your personal experiences, comment on the extent to which each of the following may increase the likelihood of a teacher recognizing children with a special aptitude for science:

1. The group leader shares the results of a science activity with the class as a whole.

   _____

2. The teacher leads a discussion about a field trip the class has recently taken.

   _____

3. The teacher asks questions that will reveal the children's knowledge of a topic.

   _____

4. The teacher discusses demonstration results.

   _____

5. The teacher helps a cooperative learning group summarize its findings.

   _____

6. The teacher praises a group that has completed its science activity before other groups.

   _____

7. The teacher asks groups to select their own leaders.

   _____

The Challenge It has become clear that you must find some way to reach children who are not working to their full potential in science. You have decided to teach a few students in higher grades some basic questioning and cooperative group skills and then use these students as assistants. You have already decided to call the project "Science Buddies." What factors should you consider in the early stages of planning for this project?

Textbooks can give you and the children an underlying structure of content and experiences that provides continuity during the school year and from year to year within a school. Textbooks can help build a solid foundation from which children can be encouraged to reach out and learn more and more. Keep in mind, however, that while textbooks can be a meaningful aid to you and the children, the extent to which they lead to discovery learning will, in the final analysis, depend on you.

Internet Resources

Websites for Discovery Learning

Problem Solving in Elementary Schools

http://www.indiana.edu/~eric_rec/ieo/bibs/prob-ele.html

One of the goals in creating a classroom environment that emphasizes discovery learning includes having children learn problem-solving skills. This site identifies ERIC resources that address problem solving and also provides useful links to other Internet resources.

An Inquiring Idea

http://sln.fi.edu/planets/tips.html

This elaborate site provides users with a model for a one-week study of astronomy in the context of what the designers call *inquiry*. The emphasis here is clearly on providing teachers with very specific ideas that will help them create a classroom environment that capitalizes on children's natural curiosity about astronomy-related content. Another aspect of this site is the use of activities that integrate subjects such as art and mathematics with science.

Institute for Inquiry Activities

http://www.exploratorium.edu/IFI/activities/index.html

This page is part of a site prepared and maintained by the Exploratorium and dedicated to helping teachers develop inquiry-oriented classrooms. Although other parts of the site discuss in-service training opportunities, this part shares specific activities that foster the best elements of what is referred to as *inquiry teaching*.

Principles and Models of Teaching and Learning

http://www.rcc.ryerson.ca/learnontario/idnm/mod2/mod2.htm

This page provides an in-depth presentation of the strategies and techniques required to have children learn by making their own discoveries. Although it does not focus on the specific needs of the elementary school teacher, this page does provide a foundation of problem-based learning. It is, in fact, a course on the Internet that has problem-based learning as one of its key components. When you reach this site, select the lessons dealing with the topic "Problem Based Learning."

Young Inventors Educational Resource

http://inventors.miningco.com/msub11er.htm

This site is an excellent source of lesson ideas that bring children face to face with the challenge of creating inventions and learning from the discoveries they make as they engage in inventing. The lesson plans provided should give many opportunities to utilize cooperative group work as children create their inventions.

Summary

Classroom teachers have access to a variety of strategies that can be used to teach children science creatively. Cooperative learning groups can be used as an important part of any learning environment that encourages discovery learning. Teachers' use of questions, ability to teach children to become active listeners, inclusion of science demonstrations along with hands-on activities, and creative use of textbooks can all serve to enhance and enrich the learning environment they create for children.

Going Further

On Your Own

1. Reflect upon the science activities you experienced as an elementary schoolchild:
   a. Specifically, what activities do you remember? Why do you think you remember them?
   b. If you do remember activities, were they carried out by individual children or by groups? What do you think motivated the teacher's decision in this respect?
   c. While the activities were underway, were there any specific problems with work space, classroom behavior, or the availability of science materials?
   d. Would you say that your teacher or teachers encouraged discovery learning?

2. Select a chapter from a conventional elementary school science textbook that contains some science activities. Develop a strategy for using the activities and text materials as the basis for a group of discovery-based lessons. How does your strategy compare with the more conventional use of chapters in science textbooks? Would your approach offer any cooperative learning possibilities?

3. How could you use some of the ideas in this chapter to create an ideal curriculum for children at the grade level you are most interested in? Be specific and focus upon:
   a. The content you would stress
   b. The concepts you would stress
   c. How the curriculum would reflect the teaching style you would use
   d. How cooperative learning groups could be used
   e. The use of teacher and student demonstrations
   f. Examples of convergent, divergent, and evaluative questions

On Your Own or in a Cooperative Learning Group

4. With others, role-play the best and worst science demonstrations you have ever observed. What factors contributed to the quality (or lack thereof) of each? If you are doing this activity by yourself, respond in writing.

5. Select a topic commonly covered in elementary school science, and create five questions the teacher could use to help children make discoveries in this field of study. Also try to think of a demonstration that the teacher could use to raise questions among the children that might lead to discoveries.

6. Formulate your position on each of the following statements. You may wish to have a minidebate in which various members of the group adopt extreme positions.
   a. Discovery learning uses up valuable classroom time.
   b. Textbooks cannot be used with discovery-learning techniques.
   c. By asking questions, you can slow down a child's thought processes.

Notes

1. Ian Elliot, "Do-It-Yourself Science," *Teaching K–8* 28, no. 4 (January 1998): 34.
2. Ibid.
3. Donald Orlich et al., *Teaching Strategies: A Guide to Better Instruction* (Lexington, MA: D.C. Heath, 1994), pp. 186–193.
4. Kenneth G. Tobin and William Capie, *Wait-Time and Learning in Science* (Burlington, NC: Carolina Biological Supply, n.d.), p. 2.
5. Ibid.
6. Ibid., 5–6.
7. Robert Coughlan, *The World of Michelangelo* (New York: Time, 1966), p. 85.
8. Rebecca Jones, "Solving Problems in Math and Science Education," *The American School Board Journal* 185, no. 7 (July 1998): 18.

Suggested Readings

Cohen, Elizabeth. "Making Cooperative Learning Equitable." *Educational Leadership* 56, no. 1 (September 1998): 18–21.

Galas, Cathleen. "Questioning Strategies for the Information Age." *Learning and Leading with Technology* 26, no. 7 (April 1999): 10–13.

Johnson, David W., and Roger Johnson. *Learning Together and Alone*. Boston: Allyn and Bacon, 1999.

Kardos, Thomas. *75 Easy Earth Science Demonstrations*. Portland, OR: J. Weston Walch, 1997.

Maxim, George. "When to Answer the Question 'Why?'" *Science and Children* 35, no. 3 (November/December 1997): 41–45.

Misulis, Katherine. "Textbook Comprehension Strategies." *Science Scope* 20, no. 1 (September 1997): 39–43.

National Center on Education and the Economy and the University of Pittsburgh. *Performance Standards: Volume 1 Elementary School*. Washington, DC: New Standards, 1997.

———. *Performance Standards: Volume 2 Middle School*. Washington, DC: New Standards, 1997.

Sapon-Shevin, Maria. *Because We Can Change the World: A Practical Guide to Building Cooperative, Inclusive Classroom Communities*. Boston: Allyn and Bacon, 1999.

Schulte, Paige L. "Lessons in Cooperative Learning." *Science and Children* 36, no. 7 (April 1999): 44–47.

Tolman, Marvin N., et al. "Current Science Textbook Use in the United States." *Science and Children* 35, no. 8 (May 1998): 22–25, 44.

Traver, Rob. "What Is a Good Guiding Question?" *Educational Leadership* 55, no. 6 (March 1998): 70–73.

Ward, Charlotte. "Never Give 'Em a Straight Answer." *Science and Children* 20, no. 3 (November/December 1997): 46–49.

6

Assessment for Understanding and Inquiry

How can I move toward using authentic assessment and the assessment recommendations of the NSE standards?

A Look Ahead

"What D'ja Git?"

"What d'ja git?"
"She gave me a C!"

The words of children are very revealing. How would you feel if you heard this conversation after teaching a unit that took you weeks to plan, a unit so full of discovery-oriented science activities that you spent five afternoons trudging down the aisles of discount stores in search of inexpensive materials? Perhaps it was a unit that required one hour of after-school negotiations with the learning center director to liberate books on the topic. What if you heard it on a morning when your eyes were still bleary from reading science journals the night before? Would it get your attention?

I think it would and should for at least two reasons. First of all, it clearly tells you that the test you gave at the end of the unit probably didn't measure the children's success with the important aspects of the unit. Second, it tells you that the children have the extraordinary idea that the teacher *gives* a grade. Notice the phrasing "she gave." Do you detect even the slightest suggestion that the child *earned* a grade?

Fortunately, recent thinking and much hard work by teachers who want to improve the quality of science instruction have generated some promising ideas for improving the ways we assess children's progress in science. The goal is to help children think more about what they have learned and less about the gifts they think teachers give.

Traditional Assessment, Authentic Assessment, and the NSE Standards Approach

Are you ready for your two greatest challenges in the classroom? Well, here they are:

1. You must teach science content in an effective and interesting way.
2. You must determine whether the children have learned and, if so, what?

The previous chapters dealt with the first challenge—how to teach children science. This chapter deals with the second challenge, which is critically important if your goal is to become an excellent teacher. After all, none of us can do a better job tomorrow if we don't know how well we did today.

In this chapter, you will first learn about or review the *traditional* ways of assessing children in science class. This should be easy reading, since you've been a student in various science classes and been assessed in most or all of these traditional ways. Then you will learn about two modern approaches to assessment that are more consistent with the goals of developing scientifically literate citizens and using a teaching style that emphasizes hands-on discovery learning.

The first of these new approaches—*authentic assessment*—suggests that we should assess children on experiences that resemble their present and future real-life experiences with science. The second modern approach, which is advocated by the National Science Education (NSE) standards project, incorporates much of contemporary thought about authentic assessment into a useable framework. The NSE recommendations will help you create assessment techniques to assess both children's *understanding* and their ability to conduct their own *inquiry* (i.e., experiments).

We will begin with the traditional techniques and then move toward the more contemporary approaches.

Traditional Assessment Techniques

 ## End-of-Chapter Homework

> "... and then do numbers 1 through 5 on the last page."

Does this bring back a few classroom memories? Giving children an end-of-chapter homework assignment is a common way for teachers to discover whether the children remember what they have read. When you make such an assignment, you believe that children will read the chapter first and then answer the questions. Perhaps in elementary and middle school, you read your science chapters before you did your homework. If so, I congratulate you. If you didn't, this is a good opportunity to consider what traditional end-of-chapter homework does and doesn't accomplish.

▶ What Does It Accomplish?

Giving an end-of-chapter assignment does increase the probability that children will take their science books home, if your class happens to use a science book. Such an assignment tells the children that you are serious about the content you are teaching. It forces them to look at and, if you are fortunate, read text material if only to find answers to the questions they were assigned. This type of assignment provides you with one small indicator of how serious a child is about his or her schooling. The actual appearance of a textbook in the home tells parents that the child is doing something in science class. Finally, homework assignments that are not done provide you with a reason for talking with a child and the child's parents about his or her effort.

▶ What Doesn't It Accomplish?

End-of-chapter homework does not tell you much about what children know, and it doesn't tell you if they like science. Completed homework seldom reveals any understanding of information beyond the recall level of the cognitive domain. End-of-chapter homework will probably not so pique children's interest that they will want to learn more about the topic.

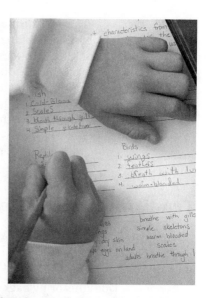

Traditional assessment may not reflect all of the learning that occurs in a discovery-based science classroom.

Using End-of-Chapter Homework Effectively

Before making the assignment, talk with children about the purpose of the homework and the reading they have done. Use statements such as "You know this first chapter on living things told us about the differences between living and nonliving things. The questions at the end will help you find out if you remember and understand some of the big ideas." After this introduction, give children a few minutes of class time to begin the assignment. At the minimum, have them prepare their papers for the assignment by writing down their names, the date, and the chapter assignment. All of these techniques will increase the probability of homework getting done and possibly make the experience somewhat more meaningful.

Quizzes

Do you still live in fear of the "pop" quiz? Does your heart flutter a bit just hearing the term *quiz?* Quizzes are a part of the classroom assessment process from elementary school through graduate school, and their effect on students seems to remain rather constant. A quiz takes little time and is usually used as a quick assessment of whether students remember or understand factual information or concepts.

▶ What Do They Accomplish?

Quizzes tell teachers whether children can think fast and have a sufficient command of writing to get their responses on paper before time is up. They are easy to grade and provide a snapshot of the student's recall of information. They also serve to keep children "on their toes," but they should not divert teachers from the science experiences that should be taking place in the classroom.

▶ What Don't They Accomplish?

Quizzes do not tell teachers much about in-depth understanding. Children's lack of success on a quiz may not reveal a deficit in knowledge or understanding but rather a deficit in being able to express themselves quickly.

Using Quizzes More Effectively

Quizzes should be used in moderation. If you wish to find out whether children are learning, giving a quiz now and then that is focused on the important ideas of a science unit can provide some information about student progress. Doing so can also help you discover that you need to modify your teaching or help a particular child before a unit is completed.

Tests

Given the large numbers of children in most classrooms, most teacher-developed tests are composed of short-answer questions and some multiple-choice items. At the end of the test, there may be a few so-called essay questions. In discovery-oriented classrooms, teachers who use tests are likely to include some questions dealing with how science activities were conducted and what was learned from them.

▶ *What Do They Accomplish?*

Test results tell children, parents, and you how well the children answered the questions that were asked. Test results give children a way to assess their own progress and a way to compare themselves to others. They give you a neat and tidy way to get information to use for grading. They also tell you which children in the class are good test takers. That information is important if you want to teach children skills that will be useful in later life.

If you have the time and energy to invest in creating a test with questions that discover more than children's recall abilities, you may get more useful information. The test results may reveal whether children have comprehended concepts, been able to apply what was learned, and are able to analyze the science phenomena studied. If, however, the test consists of recall questions, only the children's memories will be assessed.

▶ *What Don't They Accomplish?*

Tests only tell you what children know and understand about the particular questions you asked. Due to the limited time that teachers have to read and grade tests, very few tests assess how well children can express their thoughts. Questions that elicit this information are challenging to create, require many minutes for children to complete, and demand that the teacher spend a considerable amount of time outside class carefully reading each response, reflecting on the work, offering written feedback, and assigning grades.

Tests probably do little to motivate children to think about science as an interesting subject area or to increase their career awareness. Success on science tests does not indicate that children like science, are interested in science, will engage in free reading about science topics, will watch televised science programs, or even will become interested observers of the events in the world of nature.

Using Tests More Effectively

You may find a helpful test-making resource in the children themselves. If you ask "What would be some good questions for the test?" you may get some interesting ideas from the children and turn the test-giving process into more of a learning experience. You may be surprised to hear the children suggest questions that require far more thought than the questions you normally ask.

As you prepare the test, try to cross-reference each item to the cognitive, affective, or psychomotor objectives of the teaching unit. By doing this, you can measure student progress over all of the unit's objectives. To help you assess student achievement on the objectives of the unit and the quality of the questions you have asked, after the test, prepare a chart on which you will record the number of children who answer each question correctly. The numbers on the chart will show which items were the most and least challenging for the class and give some idea of what the children learned about the unit objectives.

Library Reports

Can you recall going to the school library or learning center to do research on a topic for a science report? Perhaps you remember pouring through encyclopedias and other reference books to find information on such topics as whales, volcanoes, tornadoes, and rockets. A great deal can be learned through library work that is related to the science experiences that occur in the classroom.

▶ What Do They Accomplish?

Science reports are common assignments in elementary and middle school and provide students with information and ideas that can round out what they have learned through hands-on activities, demonstrations, and class discussions. Library reports can lead children to think about topics and questions that were not considered during class. They can also help a child's grade for a marking period by making up for low quiz or test grades.

▶ What Don't They Accomplish?

When used in the traditional manner, library reports do little to extend and enrich the basic knowledge, skills, and attitudes emphasized in a discovery-oriented classroom. They do not present children with an opportunity to touch science materials or move through the full cycle of concept exploration, acquisition, and application. In the best circumstances, library reports tell you whether children can look up information in reference books and summarize what they have learned.

Using Library Reports More Effectively

To make library reports meaningful, they should engage children in a quest that resolves some issue or problem. Therefore, if the children are having discovery science experiences related to the life cycle of insects, you might say, "I would like you to do work in the learning center that will help you answer the question 'Why don't we ever see baby butterflies?'" This type of assignment captures the same curiosity that you are hoping to capitalize on with hands-on discovery science. Children should be going to the library or learning center to use books and media as *tools* that are as essential to the pursuit of science as microscopes and metersticks.

Activity Write-Ups

Science activities should do more than entertain children. Such activities should teach children, as well. But how will you know that children are learning, fitting new learnings into previous knowledge, and constructing new meanings? You can discover this by observing them, by listening to them, and by reading what they have written in their activity write-ups.

▶ *What Do They Accomplish?*

Having children synthesize and share what they have learned in activity write-ups tells them that you believe thinking, talking, and writing about what they have experienced is important. Listening to a child's observations of water droplets forming on an ice-filled glass or reading a list of written observations gives you valuable information about the learning that is occurring in your classroom.

▶ *What Don't They Accomplish?*

A variety of problems can arise when you use activity write-ups. The most obvious one is that a child may have completed an activity successfully but not be a good writer. Under these circumstances, a poor report may tell you more about language arts abilities than science abilities. Children with language difficulties will be unable to express what they have learned if you rely only on activity write-ups.

By necessity, the activity write-up is a very brief sketch of the work the child has done. While it will tell you a good deal about the results of a child's experimentation, it will tell you little about all the experiences he or she may have had as the activity was carried out.

Using Activity Write-Ups Effectively

When you look at or listen to a child's activity write-up, you need to be able to assess whether the efforts reflect the child's or the group's work on the activity. To help you do this, take some time to explain to the children the importance of clearly identifying all the group members involved in preparing the report.

Another component of assessing the quality of a write-up is determining whether an incomplete report shows a lack of effort on the child's part or a limitation in his or her ability to use language. The only way to make this distinction is to ask the child clarifying questions.

Standardized Tests

If you walk down a school hallway and notice that it is strangely quiet, that the children are seated quietly at their desks, and that the public address system is not blaring messages, chances are the children are taking a standardized test. For some reason, standardized tests create a time of quiet and anxiety.

In addition to the usual battery of IQ tests and personality inventories, some school districts have children take achievement tests in a variety of subjects. If you teach in a school that requires a standardized science achievement test, you may find that *you* are more concerned about the results than the children are.

▶ *What Do They Accomplish?*

The standardized achievement test in science compares how much the children in your class know compared to children nationwide, as reflected in norms. If the children in your class do well, it can make you feel very successful. If they do poorly, you may feel obliged to rethink what and how you are teaching. The results provide teachers, administrators, and members of the community with an opportunity to compare the success of their children to that of children around the country.

▶ *What Don't They Accomplish?*

If you have been teaching science using a hands-on, discovery-oriented approach, you may have good reason to be anxious when the children in your class are expected to display a command of the basic subject matter on standardized tests. After all, teaching science in a hands-on fashion may not provide the background in science knowledge that children from more traditional textbook-oriented classrooms have. On the other hand, the children in your class will probably have acquired many science process skills and have developed a favorable attitude toward science. Standardized achievement tests will not reveal your success in helping children grasp central science concepts through hands-on experimentation.

Using Standardized Achievement Tests More Effectively

It is possible to turn the use of standardized science tests into a positive experience. First of all, you can help the children understand that the test results will not measure all that they have learned. If, for example, your class has carried out a hands-on unit on the use and waste of water in your school, explain to the children that they should not expect to see questions about it on their tests. Point out that some of the science units they have studied have given them a lot of information that will not be measured. Emphasize that they should not feel bad if many of the things they have learned are not on the test.

Second, take some class time before the test to teach basic standardized test-taking strategies. The children likely will take many standardized tests while they are students and when they pursue employment. Investing time and energy to improve test-taking skills may annoy you because of your own feelings about testing, but it may help children become more successful test takers.

Finally, you have some responsibility for helping parents understand that many of the topics you teach go far beyond the expectations of the test makers. As you communicate with parents throughout the year, highlight the units you are doing and will do. Help them understand that many of the important things their children will be learning can only be revealed through assessments that require children to think, synthesize their thoughts, and then express their thoughts orally and in writing.

Authentic Assessment Techniques

 When modern teachers speak of authentic assessment, they are speaking of assessment that measures what students have actually *learned*. This is far more than what is measured on a test, quiz, or end-of-chapter list of questions. The strategies and techniques of authentic assessment are much more challenging to implement than the traditional techniques described earlier.

Authentic assessment is a goal for teachers. I have chosen the term *goal* purposefully. The defining quality of authentic assessment is the completion or demonstration of the desired behavior in a real-life context. Exceptional teachers are able to create classrooms in which children's experiences feel like real life! These rooms overflow with experiences that draw children in and involve them so fully that they forget they are children in a classroom and begin to act like scientists. In such environments, we can move very close to authentic assessment.

Let me further clarify this authentic assessment goal. Imagine for a moment that you have finished teaching a unit on green plants and are interested in discovering what the children have learned. If you ask a child to demonstrate his or her knowledge of the role of sunlight in plant growth, your assessment of that child's knowledge and skills will be authentic to the extent that the classroom models real life. If you provide the child with a tray of materials to carry out the demonstration, you have removed some real-life qualities. How could you make the assessment more authentic or give it more of a real-life feel?

You could ask the child to acquire all of the things that would be needed to discover whether the classroom geranium will live as well in the dark as it does in the light. When you can observe how a child approaches a problem without help, you can get a better indication of his or her knowledge, skills, and attitudes.

Portfolios

The use of portfolios is an exciting educational innovation that can help round out traditional assessment techniques. A *portfolio* is an organized collection of a person's work that shows the very best that he or she can do. At present, most teachers who use portfolios have children organize and display work in language arts, mathematics, and art. However, more and more teachers are considering the use of science portfolios as one way to get a fuller picture of children's progress. While each piece placed in a portfolio can be assessed with respect to the degree to which the student achieved specific unit objectives, the portfolio as a whole will illustrate the child's progress.

You may be wondering what specific examples of a child's science work should go in a science portfolio. Here are some products that could be included:

- Written observations and science reports
- Drawings, charts, and graphs that are the products of hands-on discovery activities
- Thank-you letters to resource people who have visited the classroom (e.g., beekeepers, veterinarians, health care providers)
- Reaction pieces, such as prepared written responses to science software, videos, discovery experiences, and field trips
- Media products, such as student-produced science work in audio, video, or digitized form

REAL TEACHERS TALKING

A Starting Point for Thinking, Talking, and Writing

Wendi: Lately, I've been reading more and more about authentic assessment. It really makes sense to me.

Suzanne: Does it all make sense or just parts of it?

Wendi: Well, I like the idea that students have access to their portfolios. It gives them a feeling of real ownership about their work.

Suzanne: I like that, too. It kind of does away with the idea of the magical, elusive grade book. If you know that your work is going to be seen by others besides the teacher, then you are going to be a little more careful in how you keep some things, such as a science journal. If it's going to wind up in your portfolio, then it has much more meaning than if the teacher is just going to give it a grade, put the grade in the grade book, and give you back the journal.

Wendi: There is another advantage for the teacher that is just as important. With so many children, it's hard to remember how they were doing in September when you are at the end of May. I mean, you have grades or some anecdotal records from September, but it would be really useful to actually have those September work samples around.

Suzanne: I think that would give us all, teachers and students alike, more of a sense of accomplishment at the end of the school year. I'm not sure where we would store all these work products, though. Could I use your room? Just kidding.

▶ ***Point to Ponder:*** *If you were teaching, what kinds of work products from science activities would show the development of a child's work over the course of a year? Which of these products could be kept in a portfolio?*

Anecdotal Records

> *Name: Jimmy Green*   *Age: 8*
> *Grade: 2*   *Date: May 5*
>
> *This week Jimmy's group, the Science Stars, which was responsible for taking care of the aquarium, found a dead guppy. Jimmy volunteered to bury it in the school lawn. He told the group, "Even though it's dead, it'll help the grass grow."*

A teacher's brief notes about a child's behavior can reveal a great deal about what the child has or has not learned. The notes, called *anecdotal records,* can help you assess how well individual children are doing. They can be particularly helpful when you wish to reflect upon and assess how well individual children are mastering science process skills or developing desirable attitudes and values.

Use these techniques to improve your ability to gather and reflect upon anecdotal records:

1. Consider focusing your observations on cognitive, affective, and psychomotor progress, and think about the situations in which children may demonstrate these abilities during the class period. You may wish to organize your notebook in the form of a daily chart, with a column for each learning component.
2. Remember to write down the student's name, the date, and the time when you make an observation.
3. Indicate to the children that you will be writing notes to yourself about how things are going. You may even suggest that they do the same.
4. Review your anecdotal records in detail at the end of a unit. This will help you assess the effectiveness of each activity in the unit.

You can learn a great deal by observing a child at work.

Affective Development Checklists

"Boy, do I hate science!"

If you heard one of your students say this, what would you conclude about his or her affective development? Your only basis for assessing changes in affect is your observation of the affect-laden behaviors students exhibit. Their comments, smiles, frowns, in-class behavior, and out-of-class behavior reveal a great deal about how much they are developing favorable attitudes toward science and your teaching.

There are some tools that can help you assess affective development. Figure 6.1 consists of a list of items that you may wish to draw upon to create an affective development checklist. Add your personal observations of student behaviors to create a more comprehensive list. Refer to your list as you think about each child in the classroom. Consider whether each boy and girl is acquiring science knowledge, demonstrating the process skills, and perhaps more importantly, moving in the direction of enjoying science and science-related issues.

FIGURE 6.1 Draw from these behaviors to create an affective development checklist.

- Makes drawings and diagrams of science-related objects and events
- Is curious about new objects, organisms, and materials added to the classroom
- Talks about surprising things he or she notices in the environment
- Spends free time at the in-class science learning center
- Questions but is tolerant of the ideas of others
- Enters science fairs and school science expositions
- Brings science-related magazine pictures to class
- Checks science-related books out of the class or school library
- Reads science fiction
- Collects natural objects as a hobby
- Comments on science-related programs seen on TV
- Comments on science-related films
- Asks for class field trips to museums, planetariums, and so on
- Invents things
- Builds models
- Asks questions about science-related news stories
- Asks to do more science activities
- Asks to make or fix science equipment
- Volunteers to carry out demonstrations
- Asks to work on science-related bulletin boards
- Asks to distribute materials and equipment for activities
- Questions superstitions
- Asks to take care of classroom animals or plants

Science Conferences with Children

The words we speak tell a great deal about what we know and how we feel. The quickest and possibly most reliable way to find out if children in a discovery-oriented classroom are learning is to give them an opportunity to talk to you. If you learn to listen carefully and gently probe around the edges of a child's talk, you will discover whether he or she has grasped the real meaning of a food web, has had anything to do with creating the group's drawings showing the movement of the continents, or is becoming increasingly curious about the natural world.

Science Journals

Have you ever watched a child fish around in his or her desk to locate a bologna-stained sheet of paper that contains yesterday's science notes? Some teachers have found that a journal or notebook devoted only to science can be a great asset for children as well as a useful tool for assessing how well individuals are doing. Here are some suggestions for implementing the use of science journals:

1. At the start of the year, ask each child to get a notebook he or she will devote exclusively to science. You may wish to have the children construct their own science journals.

2. Encourage the children to design covers for their science journals. One way to do this is to have a general discussion about the major themes or units they will do during the year.

3. Discuss with the class the use of science journals and your expectations related to them. Indicate where children should keep the journals and how often you will review them.

4. Encourage the children to write in their journals each day, and provide time for them to do so. Offer some guide questions, such as "What did you do? What did you learn? How do you feel about what you have learned?"

5. Schedule time at the end of each teaching unit for children to discuss some of the things they have written.

6. Keep your own science journal. Be sure that the children are aware that you are also keeping track of what you are learning.

7. Consider using the science journals during parent-teacher conferences. Also consider putting the journals on display for Parents' Night or Back-to-School Night.

Children's Self-Assessment

As teachers, we may forget that children naturally reflect on how well they do on each activity that is a part of their science experience. It seems logical to capitalize on self-reflection when you incorporate authentic assessment into your classroom.

There are many ways to stimulate children's self-assessment. For example, before the children begin to write in their science journals, you might say, "So far this month, you have worked on two projects. One was building a flashlight, and the other was using a flashlight and mirrors to study how light behaves. What did you learn in each project?" The children's responses will represent their efforts to assess what they have done. This is important information to you as a teacher.

The NSE Standards Recommendations for Assessing Understanding and Inquiry

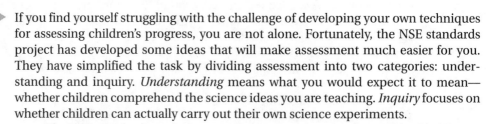 If you find yourself struggling with the challenge of developing your own techniques for assessing children's progress, you are not alone. Fortunately, the NSE standards project has developed some ideas that will make assessment much easier for you. They have simplified the task by dividing assessment into two categories: understanding and inquiry. *Understanding* means what you would expect it to mean—whether children comprehend the science ideas you are teaching. *Inquiry* focuses on whether children can actually carry out their own science experiments.

The NSE standards project assessment suggestions are summarized in Figures 6.2 and 6.3 (pages 103 and 104). And the following sections will provide some clarification of the intent of the standards along with some practical examples.

Assessing Students' Understanding

Definitions

▶ *What is a prompt?*

A *prompt* is a question or group of questions that includes a statement of a task to be done and directions on how to do it.

▶ *What is a scoring rubric?*

The term *rubric* (pronounced "roo-brick") is an overly fancy word for which most dictionaries provide many different definitions—none of which perfectly defines its use in modern educational jargon. As a teacher, you should think of a *scoring rubric* as the standard you would use when assessing a child's performance.[1]

Practical Examples

Here are ideas for using prompts and scoring rubrics in your classroom:

▶ *Sound (for young learners)*

The big idea children are to grasp: Sounds and vibrations are associated with one another.

Does the Child Understand?

Assessment

To assess whether a child understands a concept, law, principle, theory, or other "big idea," identify what you want him or her to assess and then:

1. Invent a *prompt* for the child to respond to.

    EXAMPLES   Puzzling demonstration, thought problem, natural phenomenon (such as a plant that has insect holes in leaves)

2A. Tell the child what *performance* you expect him or her to carry out.

    EXAMPLES   Oral report, class discussion, discovery activity, demonstration for classmates

2B. Tell the child what *product* you expect him or her to prepare.

    EXAMPLES   Model, labeled drawing, collection, photograph

Measurement

To measure success:

For most children:

1. Compare the performance or product to what the child could do earlier in the year.*
2. Compare the child's performance or product to what you would expect of most children at this grade/age.

For very able children:

Compare the child's performance or product to what you would expect of a scientifically literate adult.**

*This is this author's suggestion. It does not appear in the NSE standards.

**This does not mean you should assign a grade on this basis. The comparison is made to get a sense of how good the performance or product actually is.

FIGURE 6.2
Implementing the NSE assessment standards

Prompt: This little drum is made by stretching plastic wrap over a jar. I'd like you to tap the drum with the eraser, look at the plastic, and tell me what you see and what you hear. Then sprinkle some rice grains on the plastic and look at it as you tap it again.

Scoring rubric: The teacher will listen to the child's responses and then ask him or her to guess at what might be causing the sound. If the child refers to the up and down movement of the plastic wrap (as evidenced by the bouncing of the rice grains) as being related to the sound, he or she will be considered to have made a correct response.

Can the Child Carry Out
an Inquiry?

Assessment

To assess whether a child can carry out an *inquiry:*

1. Ask the child to identify a *researchable question*.

   EXAMPLE   What color of clothing is coolest on a hot, sunny day?

2. Ask the child to prepare a *research plan*.

   EXAMPLE   The child designs a plan to collect samples of cloth of different colors,
   invent an apparatus to hold cloth samples over thermometers, and
   measure temperature changes on a sunny day.

3. Have the child *carry out the plan*.

   EXAMPLE   The child follows through on item 2 above.

4. Ask the child to prepare a *report* on the inquiry.

   EXAMPLE   The child prepares a written and illustrated report.

Measurement

To measure success:

1. Assess the quality of the *research question*.
2. Assess the quality of the *research plan*.
3. Assess the quality of the *research*.
4. Assess the quality of the *report*.

FIGURE 6.3
Implementing
the NSE
assessment
standards

▶ *Density*

The big idea children are to grasp: You can find the densities of objects using simple equipment.

Prompt: Here are all the things you need to find the densities of these mystery objects on the tray. I would like you to find the density of each of the three objects.

Scoring rubric: A chart is used that lists the mystery objects and the densities the teacher discovered when he or she calculated them. If the child gets answers within 10% of the teacher's results, they will be considered correct.

▶ *Relationship between living and nonliving things*

The big idea children are to grasp: Living things depend on some of the nonliving things in their habitat.

Prompt: I would like you to use at least two books from the learning center to find at least three nonliving things that rain forest plants need.

Scoring rubric: The teacher has a checklist that includes sun, soil, water, and oxygen. If the child's report includes at least three of these items, his or her work will be considered successfully done.

Assessing Students' Ability to Conduct Inquiry

Wouldn't you be delighted if your children learned so much and acquired so many skills that they could actually invent and carry out their own experiments? It's happened to me on occasion, and it's a wonderful feeling.

Steps in Assessing Inquiry

The NSE Standards encourage teachers to have children design and carry out their own experiments (which the NSE standards refer to as *inquiry*) and then assess how well the children have done. The standards recommend that teachers assess achievement with a focus on whether children can actually function as young scientists. The following steps in the process *and* the final product should be evaluated:

1. Identifying a worthwhile and researchable question
2. Planning the investigation
3. Executing the research plan
4. Drafting the research report[2]

Practical Examples

Here are some ideas to help you develop your own techniques for assessing inquiry in the classroom:

▶ *Light and plants (for young learners)*

Identifying an inquiry question: Does the plant on Ms. Riley's desk really need sunlight to live?

Planning the inquiry: The children make a set of four drawings showing what they intend do. They depict how the plant looks today, including the colors they see; how it will look in the closet; how they will water the plant in the closet; and how they will draw the plant once a week for four weeks (at the end of each week).

Executing the plan: The children carry out the steps listed under "Planning the inquiry."

Drafting the report: The children show all their drawings and tell their conclusions.

Assessing the inquiry: The teacher makes an anecdotal record of the children's progress, noting whether all steps were followed and actual color changes were captured in the drawings.

Make the Case

The Problem   Teachers may devote so much classroom time and personal energy to providing hands-on, discovery-based science experiences that the children do not have opportunities to display what they have learned.

*Assess
Your Prior
Knowledge
and Beliefs*

Think for a moment about a science process skill that you feel you understand well. For that topic or skill, respond to the following:

1. State the topic or skill.

   _____

2. Where did you first learn about it?

   _____

3. When did you learn about it?

   _____

4. Did you learn it on your own, or did someone else help you?

   _____

5. How did you know that you had learned it?

   _____

6. How could you show that you have learned it?

   _____

The Challenge   To have the children demonstrate that they are learning, you have decided to ask each child to create an invention that uses what he or she has learned. You would like to stage a Convention of Inventions for parents on Back-to-School Night. What five key points about the importance of children demonstrating their knowledge in this manner could you use to convince your school principal to provide financial support for the materials children will need?

▶ *Melting a solid*

Identifying an inquiry question: What besides heat can make ice cubes melt faster?

Planning the inquiry: The children develop a plan that includes observing ice cubes (before and after their experiments), using a paper fan, crushing ice cubes, and adding salt to the cubes. The plan also calls for them to use a chart to record their observations and diagrams showing what changes they observed.

Executing the plan: The children carry out the steps in "Planning the inquiry."

Drafting the report: The children record their data on their chart and also write paragraphs that answer the research question.

Assessing the inquiry: The teacher uses a three-point scale to assess children's work. A 3 means "extremely well planned and carried out," a 2 means "readable and complete," and a 1 means "incomplete or hard to follow."

As your teaching career unfolds, you will develop your own approaches to assessing how well children understand science and can propose and carry out inquiry. I hope that the examples just given will help you develop those strategies. Also keep in mind that assessment may not be the most enjoyable part of your school day, but it is one of the most important. As a true professional, you must assess whether learning is happening while children are in your classroom.

Internet Resources

Websites Related to Assessment

Assessment Ideas for the Elementary Science Classroom

http://www.sasked.gov.sk.ca/docs/elemsci/ideass.html

This is one of few sites on the Internet that deals specifically with the needs of elementary-/middle-level science teachers. In addition to discussing conferences, interviews, contracts, and portfolios, this site provides *templates,* or guide sheets for creating and using various assessment techniques. This site has a very practical focus and should be of great use to you.

Performance Assessment

http://inet.ed.gov/pubs/OR/ConsumerGuides/perfasse.html

This *Consumer Guide,* sponsored by the U.S. Department of Education, is a publication for teachers, parents, and others who are interested in alternative techniques for student assessment. It not only discusses techniques but also lists the addresses of organizations that can provide additional information about the topic.

Alternative Assessment Techniques

http://www.indiana.edu/~eric_rec/ieo/bibs/altasses.html

This site provides a bibliography of ERIC documents dealing with alternative ways of assessing students as well as a procedure to help you acquire full text copies of those documents. The available documents are organized both alphabetically and by category. The "Category" choice is particularly helpful.

ERIC Clearinghouse on Assessment and Evaluation

http://ericae.net/

This site provides access to a wide range of ERIC documents dealing with assessment and testing. It also provides an extremely well-organized list of Internet sites that deal with topics of interest to teachers and others. The links range from specific resources for elementary teachers, such as ways of improving test construction, to general resources on how people in other countries deal with issues related to assessment and testing.

Project Zero

http://pzweb.harvard.edu/Research/Research.htm

This portion of the Project Zero site includes a section called "Recent Research Projects." Within it, you will find discussions of a variety of projects, including alternative and imaginative ways of assessing student progress in several disciplines, such as science. Most of the projects have an interdisciplinary focus, which makes issues of assessment rather interesting.

The National Assessment of Educational Progress

http://nces.ed.gov/NAEP/

You may have heard of the *The Nation's Report Card,* a continuing assessment of what American students know and can do in a variety of subjects, including science. The testing program itself is called the *National Assessment of Educational Progress,* or *NAEP.* It samples student achievement at grades 4, 8, and 12. A very interesting feature of this site is that it allows you to see science achievement levels in every state as well as how those results change from year to year. You can also look over sample test questions to judge whether they reveal important indicators of science achievement.

Summary

Teachers need to know what children are learning. For a variety of reasons, quizzes, tests, and teacher evaluations of homework, reports, and projects are often used to assess children's progress in science. These traditional assessment devices should be used with an awareness of what they do and do not accomplish. In recent years, there has been increasing interest in finding methods of assessment that go beyond the traditional ones. These newer methods include *authentic assessment* and a two-pronged approach to assessing understanding and inquiry proposed by the NSE standards project. Authentic assessment includes the use of portfolios, direct observations, and science journals. This approach helps teachers learn what children understand and can do, which can influence what and how teachers teach. The NSE standards approach applies many authentic assessment techniques as well as prompts and rubrics to assess children's understanding and ability to carry out inquiry projects.

Going Further

On Your Own

1. Imagine that you are an elementary or middle grade science teacher who has just received a $1,000 grant to improve the strategies and techniques used to assess children in science. What would you spend the money on? Explain your rationale.

2. Consider the traditional book conference. Then describe how a ten-minute *science* conference with a child might be similar and different from a book conference in terms of purpose and the types of questions asked by the teacher.

3. Select a science topic you might teach to childen at a grade level of your choice. For that topic, suggest a specific subject for an age-appropriate inquiry project. Then briefly describe how you would apply the five steps suggested by the NSE standards to determine whether the children were successful in completing the project.

On Your Own or in a Cooperative Group

4. Create a poster listing five techniques children should use to prepare for a traditional science unit test. Highlight techniques that you or members of your group have learned through direct experience as students.

5. Imagine that you and some other teachers have decided to give a Back-to-School Night presentation that will provide the rationale for using science portfolios in place of traditional assessment techniques. Prepare three overhead transparencies that you could use as part of the presentation.

6. On a sheet of newsprint, have your group identify one science topic at a grade level of interest. Under that topic, list three or four "big ideas" that children sould understand by the time the unit has been completed. Show that you can implement the techniques suggested by the NSE standards for gauging how well children understand the big ideas. Identify a prompt and a scoring rubric that a teacher could implement to assess understanding.

Notes

1. For a detailed discussion of the use of prompts and scoring rubrics, see National Research Council, *National Science Education Standards* (Washington, DC: National Academy Press, 1996), pp. 91–98.

2. From National Research Council, *National Science Education Standards* (Washington, DC: National Academy Press, 1996), pp. 98–100.

Suggested Readings

Angaran, Joseph. "Reflection in an Age of Assessment." *Educational Leadership* 56, no. 6 (March 1999): 71–72.

Baron, Rosemary W., et al. "Portfolio Assessments: Involving Students in Their Journey to Success." *Schools in the Middle* 6, no. 5 (January/February 1998): 32–35.

Benedict, Brenda. "Achievement Challenges for All Students." *Schools in the Middle* 8, no. 4 (January/February 1999): 31–33.

Clark, Sally N., and Donald C. Clark. "Authentic Assessments—Key Issues, Concerns, Guidelines." *Schools in the Middle* 6, no. 5 (January/February 1998): 50–51.

Colby, Susan A. "Grading in a Standards Based System." *Educational Leadership* 56, no. 6 (March 1999): 52–55.

Culbertson, Linda Doutt, and Mary Renck Jalongo. "But What's Wrong with Letter Grades?" *Childhood Education* 75, no. 3 (Spring 1999).

Mann, Larry. "Matching Assessment with Curriculum." *ASCD: Education Update* 40, no. 4 (June 1998): 1, 4–5.

McCullen, Caroline. "Taking Aim: Tips for Evaluating Students in a Digital Age." *Technology and Learning* 19, no. 7 (March 1999): 48–50.

National Research Council. *National Science Education Standards.* Washington, DC: National Academy Press, 1996.

NSTA Pathways to the Science Standards: Guidelines for Moving the Vision into Practice, edited by Lawrence F. Lowery. Arlington, VA: National Science Teachers Association, 1997.

Owens, Katharine D., and Richard L. Sanders. "Earth Science Assessments." *Science Scope* 22, no. 1 (September 1998): 44–47.

Owens, Lina L., Fanny E. Love, and Jean M. Shaw. "How Big Is Big? How Small Is Small?" *Science and Children* 36, no. 7 (April 1999): 36–39.

Potter, Ellen F. "What Should I Put in My Portfolio?" *Childhood Education* 75, no. 4 (Summer 1999): 210–214.

Richardson, Ann. "Changing Direction through Assessment." *Schools in the Middle* 8, no. 4 (January/February 1999): 34–36.

Schur, Sandra L. "Teaching, Enlightening: A Guide to Student Assessment." *Schools in the Middle* 6, no. 5 (January/February 1998): 22–31.

Smith, Mary Z., and Mary Pipal. "Mystery Assessment." *Science Scope* 22, no. 3 (November/December 1998): 30–33.

Sullenger, Karen. "How Do You Know Science Is Going On?" *Science and Children* 36, no. 7 (April 1999): 22–26.

7

Integrating Science

How can I integrate science with other subjects during the school day?

Making Connections

"You can't take off for spelling. This is science."

 The above comment can cause even the calmest, most thoughtful, patient, easy-going teacher to move to the edge of rationality with a high-volume, impromptu, arm-waving exposition on the subject of "taking pride in your work." If the comment comes near the end of a feet-hurting, head-throbbing day, you might even be tempted to say, "Yes, I do and you better get used to it."

When you hear "Why do we have to do math in science?" or "Do I have to write in complete sentences?" you should try to remain calm and remind yourself that children and adults often perceive the world as an unending sequence of disjointed experiences. This is unfortunate because such perceptions diminish the quality of each experience and contribute to a life of few connections, with minimal appreciation of how knowledge and human experience fit together to form a larger, more meaningful whole. Perhaps we inadvertently teach children to see a disjointed world. Each time we say "Well, it's 1:30; let's put the science materials away and get our paint brushes out for art," an accidental lesson is taught.

If we really care about the fullest development of every child, we must find creative ways to help our children learn that knowledge, experience, and most important, life itself is not characterized by experiencing "a" and then "b," with "a" and "b" unaffected by one another. Science time can provide us with extraordinary opportunities to help children see that human knowledge, like human beings, exists within a web of interactions.

Science and the Language Arts

 Even though you may see yourself as a science teacher, you also have a broader responsibility to extend and enrich children's language arts skills as they learn science. Here are some things you can do to make sure that children are developing their language arts skills as you teach them science.

Three Integrating Techniques

As the children entered the classroom on Monday morning, their exclamations could be heard the length of the hallway. "Wow!" "What happened here?" "It's beautiful!"

Over the weekend, their fourth-grade teacher had transformed the classroom into a tropical rain forest. The children knew that this was going to be no ordinary day. But their teacher was no ordinary teacher.[1]

Indeed, any teacher who finds creative ways to cross subject matter barriers using language arts as the bridge is special. You can be such a teacher if you focus on actively finding techniques to tie science and language arts together. Rakow and Vasquez, who described the fourth-grade teacher in the preceding excerpt, suggest three ways to do this:

1. *Literature-based integration* is simply the use of modern nonfiction science books dealing with earth/space, life, and physical science to help children acquire science-related information. Additionally, for those children who might benefit from getting science information through a story line, many fictional books by authors such as Eric Carle and Tomie dePaola have science information and concepts threaded through them.

2. *Theme-based integration* is instruction in which a major theme or concept becomes the foundation for a learning unit that cuts across subject lines. Think in creative ways as you identify a theme such as "The Rain Forest," "Space Neighbors" for astronomy, or "Animals with Pouches" for life sciences. Look for themes that will give children opportunities to learn science as they read, discuss, carry out discovery-based activities, and share what they learn.

3. *Project-based integration* involves children in actually carrying out a long-term activity in which they investigate a real-world problem. Here are a few examples of science-related projects that provide excellent opportunities to tie language arts development to science content:

   - Discovering the amount of paper wasted each day in a classroom or school and communicating ideas to others that will help solve the problem

   - Discovering how much water is wasted at school water fountains each day or week and communicating ideas to others that will help stop the waste

   - Discovering how well school hot lunch offerings and student choices match proper nutrition guidelines and communicating ideas to others that will help children choose better lunches[2]

Weaving It Together with Whole Language Instruction

The term *whole language* should mean something to you. The foundation for the popular whole language approach to teaching the language arts rests on the belief that we become good readers and good language users as a result of our personal experiences with language.

Teachers who emphasize the whole language approach draw on the real-life experiences of children and use children's speaking vocabulary as an important starting point for developing language arts skills. Class time overflows with children dictating stories, chanting, singing, speaking, writing, constructing "big books," and the like. These experiences help children develop and improve their language arts skills.

The teaching strategies of the whole language approach can be easily adapted to enrich and extend children's science experiences. Writing stories about butterflies and rockets, making "big books" about insects, and writing and singing songs about saving the earth's natural resources are activities that involve children in a variety of science topics and help develop their language arts skills.

Whether you use the whole language approach or another approach, I hope that you will create appropriate ways to develop each component of the language arts through science. In the sections that follow, you will find some very specific ways to achieve a science/language arts synergy.

Lynn: I know you have been doing a lot of curriculum integration in your classroom. Has it been worth the time and energy?

Toni: Oh, definitely! One of the hurdles teachers face is the amount of material that needs to be covered in the school year. With a more integrated curriculum, I can combine lots of things, save a lot of time that used to be spent teaching the same type of content within the separate subjects (I think making charts and graphs is a good example of this), and get more depth of coverage than I had before.

Lynn: That sure makes good sense to me in practical terms, but I think there is something bigger going on when you integrate. You know, in Eastern cultures, the focus of learning is more on the whole and less on the parts. Western education is more focused on the parts—the segmented disciplines. I think the Eastern idea of how we think and learn makes a great deal of sense since the mind seems to retain information when it is placed in a larger context. For your classroom, the larger context is the theme.

Toni: I agree completely, and I find that the more I integrate my curriculum, the easier it gets to tie it to real-life experiences. The learning seems to take on more meaning for the student. Life isn't departmentalized!

Lynn: I totally agree. I teach thematically, and I accept the student's evaluations through multiple assessment because I realize they have multiple intelligences that need to be addressed in different ways.

Toni: I'm glad curriculum is moving toward the seamless state. The topics we cover now have a purpose and focus and are not done just because I have said we have to study them.

Lynn: Another plus that I have found is that sometimes students get so involved with integrated science projects that they forget they are learning. I work with students who are at risk, so integrating has been a great bonus for the children and for me.

▶ **Point to Ponder:** *Based on your personal experiences in classrooms, do you see the integration possibilities as rich and promising as these two teachers see them? Are these teachers the exception to the rule, or do you sense a movement toward more integrated approaches to teaching children science?*

Extending the Basics:
Vocabulary, Comprehension, and Writing

Vocabulary

Someday, somewhere, some child will come up to you, look you straight in the eyes, and ask with a giggle, "What part of a fish weighs the most?" or "What grows down while growing up?"

Unfortunately, for many children, words and word meanings are not sources of jokes and riddles. For these children, words are mysterious combinations of ink marks that make little sense and create little pleasure. If you are not alert to the need to teach and reinforce reading skill development, the printed page of a science book can serve as a source of frustration for a child with limited vocabulary skills.

Here are some specific strategies you can use to help children learn new vocabulary words during science time:

1. Look through science trade books and elementary science textbooks before the children work with them to *identify terms that may be too difficult* to learn from the context and then preteach those words.

2. *Pronounce science vocabulary words with children* before they reach them in their science materials.

3. *Have each child develop a personal word card file* that lists and defines each new science word. Each card should include the word, the sentence in which the word was found, a phonetic respelling of the word, and, if appropriate, a drawing or diagram showing the object or concept that the word defines.

Comprehension

You can help children build their comprehension skills in science by focusing their attention on prereading experiences. Before the children begin reading a specific text, trade book, or Internet article, focus your discussion of the material around three magic words:

1. *What?* When you distribute trade books, text material, or resource material on a science topic, take the time to discuss exactly what you expect the children to do with the material. Describe how much time they will have and what they are expected to produce as a result of the reading.

2. *Why?* Take the time to explain to children why they are going to do the assignment. Do your best to describe how it will relate to work they have done before and work that will follow.

3. *How?* Describe how you expect children to learn from the material they are reading. You might say something like this: "Here are some topics you can use to organize the information you get about the planets from your reading—What is the planet's size compared to Earth? What is the surface like? How long is a day on the planet? Why don't you list them in your science notebook before you start reading. This way you will have specific places to put the information that you find in the book."

Writing

Writing is like talking to your best friend. —Eric, a first-grader

Writing is a dance in the sun. —Christi Ann, a second-grader

Writing is meeting the person in me I never knew. —Mike, a seventh-grader[3]

This excerpt from *Reading and Learning to Read* tells a lot about the power you give children when you help them learn how to move their thoughts to a page. Science classrooms that provide children with opportunities to explore the natural world are places that provoke thought and thus create unending possibilities for communication through the powerful medium of the written word. When you are teaching science, you are offering the possibility of many "dances in the sun."

You are quite fortunate when you teach children science because the breadth of content, processes, and affect that you teach is well matched by the range of writing forms that elementary school children need to practice. In *Language Arts: Learning Processes and Teaching Practices,* Temple and Gillet suggest that there are six basic writing forms:[4]

Description	Expression	Persuasion
Exposition	Narration	Poetry

Here are some examples of how you can help children develop their abilities with each writing form. I am sure that you can suggest many others.[5]

- *Description.* Have the children describe in detail an animal they observe on a class trip to a zoo.
- *Exposition.* Have the children explain how to make a flashlight lamp light using just one battery, one wire, and one bulb.
- *Expression.* Have the children write thank-you letters to a park ranger who visited the class to talk about protecting the natural environment.
- *Narration.* Have the children write stories about an incident in the life of a young girl who decides to be the first astronaut to set foot on the planet Mars.
- *Persuasion.* Have the children write scripts for a children's television commercial that will convince others to eat more green, leafy vegetables.
- *Poetry.* Have the children observe and draw a seashell and then write poems that use at least three of the observations they made about the shell.

Science and Mathematics

"Whose mine is it?" asked Milo, stepping around two of the loaded wagons.

"BY THE FOUR MILLION EIGHT HUNDRED AND TWENTY-SEVEN THOUSAND SIX HUNDRED AND FIFTY-NINE HAIRS ON MY HEAD, IT'S MINE, OF COURSE," bellowed a voice from across the cavern. And striding toward them came a figure who could only have been the Mathemagician.

He was dressed in a long flowing robe covered entirely with complex mathematical equations and a tall pointed cap that made him look very wise. In his left hand he carried a long staff with a pencil point at one end and a large rubber eraser at the other.[6]

This excerpt from *The Phantom Tollbooth* comes from the part of the book in which Milo, the watchdog Tock, and the Dodecahedron are about to find out where numbers come from.

"So that's where they come from," said Milo, looking in awe at the glittering collection of numbers. He returned them to the Dodecahedron as carefully as possible but, as he did, one dropped to the floor with a smash and broke in two. The Humbug winced and Milo looked terribly concerned.

"Oh, don't worry about that," said the Mathemagician as he scooped up the pieces. "We use the broken ones for fractions."[7]

The journey of Milo and his friends to the numbers mine has always struck me as an excellent frame of reference for both understanding the difficulties children may have with mathematics and helping them overcome those difficulties. Some children view numbers as squiggly lines on paper that have no basis in reality. For all they know, numbers come from number mines! Although there are many aspects of elementary school mathematics that can be reinforced, extended, and enriched as children do science, three are particularly important: computational skills; data collection and expression; and logical reasoning.[8]

Computational Skills

Figure 7.1 provides examples of various ways in which computational skills can be practiced and put to real work during science. As you look over the figure, see if you can think of other ways to have children work on computation as they carry out science activities and projects.

FIGURE 7.1
A variety of science activities will improve math computational skills.

Computational Skill	Science Teaching Example
• Counting	Determine the number of pieces of litter on the school lawn.
• Addition	Keep track of the number of birds that visit a feeder.
• Subtraction	Measure children's heights at the beginning and end of the year and calculate growth.
• Multiplication	Estimate the number of birds in a flock on the school lawn by first counting a small group and multiplying by the number of groups.
• Division	Do a school survey of animals in classrooms and find the average number in each.
• Working with fractions	Place half a collection of seeds in moist soil and half in dry soil and compare their relative growth.
• Working with decimals and percents	Study the list of ingredients and the nutrition chart on a sweetened cereal box and find what part of the weight of the cereal is sugar.

Data Collection and Expression

Zing! Another rubber band flies across the science classroom. Is this a sign of unmotivated students in an undisciplined classroom? Not this time. This otherwise unruly behavior is actually part of a hands-on activity that teaches students the basics of graphing and experimental design.[9]

Although I definitely don't suggest this particular activity for either brand-new or veteran teachers with limited classroom management skills, I share it with you to focus attention on what a creative science teacher can do to build a child's science/math skills. Even though shooting rubber bands will not be your first choice as an activity to use when your school principal is observing your magnificent teaching talents, it does provide a good data collection and expression experience. Notice the true sophistication of the activity:

In this experiment the independent (or manipulated) variable is the width of the rubber bands and the dependent (or responding) variable is the distance they fly. Does the width of a rubber band affect the distance it travels? Ask students to write a hypothesis using an if-then sentence format that states how the independent variable will affect the dependent variable. Once they have constructed a hypothesis, let the rubber bands fly![10]

Even if you are not quite ready (or will never be ready) to extend science through rubber band shooting, you can do equally interesting, if not equally exciting, activities that lead to data collection and expression. For example, you can have the children observe changes in the level of water in an open container. Begin by having a child place a mark on the container to show the present water level. The children can then mark the level each day for several days. At the end of the time, the children can measure the distance from the first mark to the new marks and make graphs to show the changes.

Can very young children express data through graphs and charts? They certainly can. By cutting paper strips that represent the distance from the water level to the original mark in the preceding example, each day's measurement can be recorded. The paper strips can then be placed in sequence to produce a rudimentary graph of changes in water level.

Following the data gathering process, the children can be led through a discussion of the

Children can create graphs using cutouts to represent their data.

lengths of their paper strips. Their understanding of math concepts can be probed and developed with questions such these as:

1. Can you explain why the strips are different lengths?
2. How much longer is the longest strip than the shortest?
3. How do the changes shown by your strips compare with those shown by other children's strips?

Logical Reasoning

An important goal of mathematics education for children is to develop an understanding of the logical structure of mathematics. In practice, this means a child is able to look at collections of items and make statements about collections and the outcomes of grouping and regrouping them. This is the mathematics of sets and subsets, open sentences, and the commutative, associative, and distributive properties. Science experiences can provide children with opportunities to put their understanding of mathematical concepts to work. You could, for example, have the children in your class do these activities:

1. Group collections of plants into sets and subsets.
2. Devise a system for classifying organisms into the set of all plants and the set of all animals.
3. Identify the similarities and differences of various elements of the set of all birds and fish.
4. Use a list of characteristics to determine whether an organism is part of such subsets as fish, birds, and reptiles.

Science and the Social Studies

"Whack it again . . . HARDER!"

The breaking of a piñata to shower goodies on loudly cheering classmates during a unit on "Our Neighbors North and South" represents my *total* recollection of elementary school social studies. Social studies and science too often share a low curriculum priority in the elementary child's school day. Fortunately, many of the topics taught in a modern social studies curriculum can be extended and enriched during science time. Figure 7.2 (page 120) provides some examples of how such topics can be integrated with science.

Attitude and value development are important dimensions of social studies that can easily be integrated with science. Children who learn that value questions cut across content fields are more apt to appreciate the significance of such topics. Here is a sampling of the type of questions you can use to stimulate attitude- and

Social Studies Topic	Related Science Concept
• The natural resources of a country	The sun as the original energy source in the solar system
	The protection of air and water resources
	The use of alternative energy sources
• The history and development of a country or part of the world	Contributions made by specific scientists and inventors
• The employment of North Americans in diverse occupations	Career awareness for occupations in science and technology
• The structure of the family and other social groups; the interaction of group members	The effect of improved technology on providing increased leisure, or free, time
• The production, transportation, and consumption of goods and services	The improvement of the quality and quantity of agricultural products through selective breeding and improved food preservation technology

FIGURE 7.2
Many social studies topics can be extended through science activities.

value-based science discussions and to generate ideas for activities and projects that relate science and social studies:

1. Should animals be kept in zoos?
2. Should cities and towns have animal control officers?
3. Should a factory that provides many jobs for people but also pollutes the town's air and water be closed down?
4. Should people be required to wear seat belts?
5. Should commercials for sugar-sweetened cereals be shown during Saturday morning children's shows?

Science and Art

In weak moments, I sometimes think that I have heard and seen everything there is to hear and see in a science classroom, but then I discover I haven't. The following excerpt is a wonderful example of the surprises that await anyone interested in gathering ideas for creative ways to relate science and art. I must say that I can't wait to try it myself!

> *Recently, I began to plan a unit on the human body. In an art unit that I had done a few years ago, the class used fabric crayons to make a wall mural for display in the hall. So I decided to use these crayons to make ourselves walking, anatomically correct models of the digestive and respiratory systems.*[11]

*Almost all children enjoy illustrating
the science topics they are studying.*

Jackie Moore, the teacher who came up with this clever idea, goes on to explain that first she had each child bring in a white, cotton-blend T-shirt. The fabric crayons were used to draw the systems and organ labels on paper, and the drawings were then ironed on the shirts. She describes the culminating activity this way:

> *To show off our beautiful bodies all my 125 students wore their shirts on the same day. Quite a sight to behold! Interestingly enough, the students do better on questions dealing with these two systems than on any of the other systems that we study.*[12]

This activity shows how you can easily encourage children to use art with science and thereby help them see the relationship between art and science. There are many other activities that you can use to accomplish this. Figure 7.3 is a starting point for you to develop your own strategies for relating science and art.

FIGURE 7.3
These sample activities integrate art and science.

Tree Stump Rubbings	Place paper on a smooth, recently cut tree stump and rub the paper with a pencil. Follow-up activities may include discussions about climatic changes, as reflected in changes in the annual ring pattern, or how to find the age of the tree.
Leaf Rubbings	Place paper over a variety of leaves and rub with the side of a crayon. Follow-up activities can include observation of leaf veins in the print or discussions of the variety of leaves found or defects in leaf surfaces as a result of insect activity.
Native Crafts	Use natural objects to make sculptures, including mobiles or stabiles, and pictures. Examples include stone people, acorn people, apple-head dolls, fruit and vegetable prints, dried flowers, and shell sculptures.
Sand Painting	After studying where sand comes from and its characteristics, dye the sand to use in sand paintings. This can be integrated with social studies, since it is an activity that comes from the heritage of native North Americans.
Moving Sculpture	Build simple circuits to operate sculptures that have moving parts as well as blinking lights.

Science and Music

 Music has become so much a part of our daily lives that we are sometimes oblivious to it, but the children that you teach are not. Even very young children are able to hum, dance, whistle, and sing a multitude of breakfast cereal commercials and know some of the words and phrases of the most popular songs on MTV. Music has had a profound impact upon our culture, and we should be able to take advantage of its ability to attract and hold a child's attention when we teach science.

Hapai and Burton have prepared a helpful resource book called *BugPlay* that offers many strategies for integrating one common science topic—insects—with the rest of the school curriculum. One of my favorite songs from this book, and a favorite of children for obvious reasons, is "Cock-a-Roaches." I have included the words and music in Figure 7.4 as an example of a creative way to integrate science and music.[13]

Another strategy for relating music and science is to locate music that was composed to express feelings about topics that you are covering in science. For example, if you teach the four seasons, you can fill your classroom with selections from Vivaldi's Concerto in F Minor, op. 8, no. 4, "Winter," from *The Four Seasons.*

FIGURE 7.4
Music and science can make an irresistible combination for a child.

Science and Health and Physical Education

The sun is shining. Feel its warm glow on your seed bodies. Now it's raining . . . a gentle rain. You are beginning to grow ever so slowly. Feel your sides enlarge. What are you growing into? A dandelion? A flower? A blade of grass? A young sapling? Feel your arms and fingers stretch into leaves, petals, or branches. S-T-R-E-T-C-H. Reach for the sky. Reach for the sun. Now there's a wind, a gentle breeze. Now there's a rainstorm. Move as a flower, plant, or tree would move in a rainstorm. Now the sun is peeking out from behind a cloud. Fill your body with its wonderful warmth. Breathe in the air . . . in and out . . . in and out.[14]

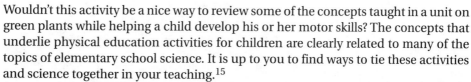 Wouldn't this activity be a nice way to review some of the concepts taught in a unit on green plants while helping a child develop his or her motor skills? The concepts that underlie physical education activities for children are clearly related to many of the topics of elementary school science. It is up to you to find ways to tie these activities and science together in your teaching.[15]

The physical education component of a child's day focuses upon such matters as recreational activities, the fullest development of the human body, and helping a child progress along a continuum of movement experiences.[16] In describing these movement experiences, Nichols includes many topics that provide opportunities for science/physical education connections:

In the body aspect the teacher helps the children to understand the actions of the body— curl, stretch, and twist; the actions of body parts in supporting body weight, leading the movement, and applying force; the types of body movement—locomotor, nonlocomotor, and manipulative; and the shape the body may assume in performing various movements. In space the child explores self (personal) and general space, direction, level, pathway, planes, and extensions (range). In studying effort the child learns about time, sudden or sustained; weight, firm or fine; space, direct or indirect; and flow, free or bound. The relationships explored are the relationship of body parts in performing various movements, the relationship of individuals or groups as they move in space, and the relationship of individuals or groups as they move with equipment or apparatus.[17]

Notice the use of the terms *time, space,* and *force* in the description of the content of movement education. Indeed, much of physical education incorporates concepts that may be learned by children in elementary science. Whether children become aware of this relationship is certainly a debatable question. To build a bridge across the content areas, you will need to establish a professional working relationship with the physical education teacher in your school. If you teach in a self-contained classroom, you should be able to develop each curriculum in a way that can emphasize and extend concepts that are common to both areas.

Make the Case

The Problem   As a result of school and real-world experiences, children may conclude that science is an isolated and complex branch of human knowledge.

Assess Your Prior Knowledge and Beliefs   Check your beliefs and knowledge about the following:

1. Children in the elementary grades learn that science is separate and different from other subjects.

   strongly disagree   disagree   agree   strongly agree

2. Children in the elementary grades learn that science is difficult.

   strongly disagree   disagree   agree   strongly agree

3. In the middle grades, children experience science as a separate subject.

   strongly disagree   disagree   agree   strongly agree

4. In the middle grades, children learn that science is a difficult subject.

   strongly disagree   disagree   agree   strongly agree

5. Science activities in most elementary and middle grade textbooks and resource books connect science to other school subjects.

   strongly disagree   disagree   agree   strongly agree

The Challenge   Prior to an interview for a teaching position, you review the science curriculum and notice that it includes sample science activities. At the end of each activity is the side heading *Connections,* which suggests how to relate the activity to other subjects. During the interview, the interviewer tells you: "We are so excited about our new curriculum. It is really interdisciplinary. I think you've had a chance to look it over. What do you think of it?" How would you respond?

Internet Resources

Websites for Integrating Science and Other Subjects

Integrated Thematic Learning Units

http://www.ps144global.org/UNITS.html

This site provides an example of a science teaching unit for elementary school called "Planet Earth: Water, Land and Space" that is designed to cross subject matter boundaries. The teachers who developed the unit were interested in creating learning materials that would help students become responsible citizens of planet Earth by studying various topics, including environmental issues.

Writing in the Science Classroom

http://www.indiana.edu/~eric_rec/ieo/bibs/writesci.html

This site by the ERIC Clearinghouse on Reading, English, and Communication at Indiana University provides links to resources related to science and writing. It has links to sites within the ERIC system as well as to other Internet resources.

Links

http://www.ssec.org/idis/cohasset/lessonlinks2.html

This site is a compilation of links to units and lesson plans that have a cross-disciplinary focus. As you scan the links, locate those that have terms such as *interdisciplinary* and *thematic*. They will take you to sites that will prove helpful in your own planning for integrated science teaching.

Elementary Education Energy Audit Kit

http://www.cvps.com/cvpage/enaudit.html

This site presents a very detailed unit that teaches children the value of energy conservation as they carry out an energy audit for their classroom. The lessons require children to put their skills in mathematics, science, and language arts to work.

Interdisciplinary Lesson and Unit Plans

http://www.stark.k12.oh.us/Docs/units/

The lessons and units at this site were developed by a group of teachers for middle-grade and upper-grade students. All emphasize technology, and many have a clear science focus, such as "Ecology," "Cycles," and "Wetlands." All units also follow a consistent format, which makes it easy to use them as resources. Additionally, the connections made between the science or technology content and other subjects, such as language arts or fine arts, are very clearly shown.

CRPC GirlTECH Lesson Plans

http://www.crpc.rice.edu/CRPC/Women/GirlTECH/Lessons/

The excellent units and lessons at this site are focused on integrating mathematics with science and technology. An additional feature is the strong emphasis on ensuring gender equity by providing examples that have appeal for girls as well as boys. The units and lessons range across grade levels, so you will have to identify those most appropriate for your grade level of interest.

Science, Technology, and Society

http://serp.la.asu.edu/sts_dir/sts_idx.html

This page is a compilation of lessons prepared by elementary and middle school teachers that are intended to integrate science, technology, and society-related concepts. The units are clearly marked with respect to grade level and, in fact, cut across more subject areas than the three that are their principal focus. You will find interdisciplinary units at this site dealing with weather, planetary survival, the environment, energy conservation, and other topics.

Summary

Too often, our experiences in school mirror the disjointed nature of contemporary life. Teachers need to continue their efforts to bring some level of integration to the content and experiences of a school day. Science provides an excellent arena for such integration. Science experiences offer many opportunities to build and extend language skills, whether these are taught through the whole language approach or through other methods. Math experiences for children, including computation, data collection and expression, and logical reasoning, can be easily tied to science work. Subjects such as social studies, art, music, and health and physical education also offer great potential for the teacher who is willing to invest the energy in helping children become aware of the connections between human knowledge and skills and engage in work that makes the integration of these two things real.

Going Further

On Your Own

1. Identify a reading or language arts activity that you could have children do when they are learning about each of these topics:
   a. The seasons
   b. Sound energy
   c. Endangered animal species
   d. Rocks and minerals
   e. "Technology Touches You"

   For each activity, suggest whether you would do it at the beginning, middle, or end of a unit of study.

2. What special techniques might you use to help poor readers read science materials successfully? How could you help children with writing problems improve their written communication skills while they learn science? Be specific in your responses, citing techniques that could be used with a wide variety of science content.

3. Can you recall any science experiences that you had as an elementary school child that integrated at least one other content field? If you don't recall such an experience, try to recall a science activity that could have been related to another content field with minimal teacher effort. What benefits could result from such an integrated activity?

4. The study of current events can provide you with many opportunities to relate science and social studies. Identify a recent news story that had a significant scientific or techno-

logic dimension. For this current event, describe a series of classroom activities that would provide children with experiences that highlight the relationship of science and social studies.

On Your Own or in a Cooperative Learning Group

5. Select a topic in science that could be used as a theme in a variety of subject areas. If you are working with a group, have each person play the role of a teacher of a specific subject in a departmentalized elementary or middle school. Discuss how a group of teachers at the same grade level might plan a teaching unit that integrates the subject areas. (If you are doing this on your own, prepare a written statement that highlights possible comments each teacher might make.)

6. Interview a teacher who works in a self-contained classroom. During the interview, determine:
   a. The major science topics emphasized during the year
   b. The science processes that are emphasized
   c. The extent to which the topics are enriched as a result of his or her efforts to relate other subjects to science

7. Interview a teacher in a departmentalized elementary or middle school. During your discussion, determine:
   a. The major topics and processes emphasized during the year
   b. The approximate length of a science period
   c. Whether other teachers at the grade level are aware of the topics dealt with in science class
   d. Whether all the teachers at the grade level ever work together to plan and teach any units with interdisciplinary themes

Notes

1. Steven J. Rakow and Jo Anne Vasquez, "Integrated Instruction: A Trio of Strategies," *Science and Children* 35, no. 6 (March 1998): 18.

2. Ibid., 19.

3. Jo Anne L. Vacca, Richard T. Vacca, and Mary K. Gove, *Reading and Learning to Read* (Boston: Little Brown, rpt. 1991), p. 127.

4. Charles Temple and Jean Wallace Gillet, *Language Arts: Learning Processes and Teaching Practices* (Glenview, IL: Scott, Foresman, 1989), p. 231.

5. You may wish to refer to the presentation of a sample unit on space exploration, which shows a detailed integration of the language arts with a science topic, in Susan I. Barcher, *Teaching Language Arts: An Integrated Approach* (New York: West, 1994), pp. 351–367.

6. Norton Juster, *The Phantom Tollbooth* (New York: Alfred A. Knopf, 1989), p. 179. © 1989 Norton Juster. Used with permission.

7. Ibid., 180.

8. AIMS Activities that Integrate Math and Science and GEMS (Great Explorations in Math and Science) are two interesting curriculum development projects involved in the preparation of teaching materials that cut across the traditional boundaries of mathematics and science. To receive overviews of available integrated activities from these projects, write to AIMS Education Foundation, P.O. Box 8120, Fresno, CA 93747 and GEMS, Lawrence Hall of Science, University of California, Berkeley, CA 94720.

9. Richard J. Rezba, Ronald N. Giese, and Julia H. Cothron, "Graphing Is a Snap," *Science Scope* 21, no. 4 (Janaury 1998): 20.

10. Ibid.

11. Jackie Moore, "Iron-On Respiratory System," *Science and Children* 28, no. 1 (September 1990): 36.

12. Ibid.

13. Marlene Nachbar Hapai and Leon Burton, *BugPlay* (Menlo Park, CA: Addison-Wesley, 1990).

14. Milton E. Polsky, "Straight from the Arts," *Instructor* 99, no. 7 (March 1990): 57.

15. You may think that movement activities to enrich science experiences can only be done with young children. To dispel this idea, refer to the rather interesting use of movement to teach older children some rather advanced ideas about bee communication in Jo Beth Agostino et al., "Dancing for Food: The Language of the Honeybees," *Science and Children* 31, no. 8 (May 1994): 14–17, 50.

16. For an in-depth and practical presentation of how the movement component of physical education can be woven into all aspects of your teaching, see Susan Griss, "Creative Movement: A Language for Learning," *Educational Leadership* 51, no. 5 (February 1994): 78–80.

17. Beverly Nichols, *Moving and Learning* (St. Louis: Times Mirror/Mosby, 1990), p. 31.

Suggested Readings

Barclay, Kathy, et al. "Making the Connection! Science and Literacy." *Childhood Education* 75, no. 3 (Spring 1999): 146–152.

Bracikowski, Christopher, et al. "Getting a Feel for Newton's Laws of Motion." *Science and Children* 35, no. 7 (April 1998): 26–30, 58.

Decker, Kelly A. "Meeting State Standards through Integration." *Science and Children* 36, no. 6 (March 1999): 28–32, 69.

DiBiase, Warren J. "Writing a Letter . . . to a Scientist." *Science and Children* 35, no. 6 (March 1998): 14–17, 66.

Eckhaus, Anita, and Rona Wolfe. "Gathering and Interpreting Data: An Interdisciplinary Approach." *Science Scope* 20, no. 1 (September 1997): 44–46.

Edgett, Ken. "The Legend of Joe the Martian." *Science and Children* 35, no. 5 (February 1998): 14–17.

Eisner, Elliot. "Does Experience in the Arts Boost Academic Achievement?" *The Clearing House* 72, no. 3 (January/February 1999): 143–149.

Hamm, Mary, and Dennis Adams. "Reaching across Disciplines." *Science and Children* 36, no. 1 (September 1998): 45–49.

Kalchman, Mindy. "Storytelling and Astronomy." *Science and Children* 36, no. 3 (November/December 1998): 28–31, 71.

Kirkwood, Tony Fuss. "Integrating an Interdisciplinary Unit in Middle School." *The Clearing House* 72, no. 3 (January/February 1999): 160–163.

Needham, Bobbe. *Ecology Crafts for Kids: 50 Great Ways to Make Friends with Planet Earth*. New York: Sterling, 1998.

Parlett, Karen. "What's the Connection?" *Science Scope* 22, no. 2 (October 1998): 30–32.

Rakow, Steven J., and Jo Anne Vasquez. "Integrated Instruction: A Trio of Strategies." *Science and Children* 35, no. 6 (March 1998): 18–22.

Rasmussen, Karen. "Visual Arts for All Students: Making Connections between Art and Life." *ASCD: Education Update* 40, no. 4 (June 1998): 1, 6–7.

Rezba, Richard J., et al. "Graphing Is a Snap." *Science Scope* 21, no. 4 (January 1998): 20–23.

Shelley, Anne Crout. "The Write Approach." *Science Scope* 22, no. 1 (September 1998): 36–39.

Thompson, Wendy. "A Moving Science Lesson." *Science and Children* 36, no. 3 (November/December 1998): 24–27, 70.

8

Science WebQuests

How can I plan and manage discovery-based projects for my plugged-in classroom?

A Look Ahead

A Strange Thing Happened on My Way to School One Day

What Is a Science WebQuest?

Relationship to the Process Skills

Relationship to the Discovery-Learning Cycle

Relationship to the NSE Standards, Project 2061, and Local Curriculum Guides

Alternative Strategies for Using Science WebQuests in Your Classroom

How to Plan and Prepare a Science WebQuest

Planning Challenges That Fit Your Students

Planning Journeys That Fit Your Students

Assessing the Report

Real Teachers Talking: A Starting Point for Thinking, Talking, and Writing

Make the Case: An Individual or Group Challenge

Internet Resources: Websites for Integrating Technology

A Strange Thing Happened on My Way to School One Day

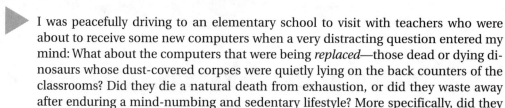 I was peacefully driving to an elementary school to visit with teachers who were about to receive some new computers when a very distracting question entered my mind: What about the computers that were being *replaced*—those dead or dying dinosaurs whose dust-covered corpses were quietly lying on the back counters of the classrooms? Did they die a natural death from exhaustion, or did they waste away after enduring a mind-numbing and sedentary lifestyle? More specifically, did they spend most of their time presenting arcade-type fact games, tired cross-country simulations, and diversions intended to teach the dates of obscure historical events?

As I drove along, pondering these questions, the real reasons for the computers' demise emerged: Perhaps they succumbed because most of the so-called educational software in use had little to do with the curriculum teachers were expected to teach. Perhaps the computers died of dust inhalation from being surrounded by software packages that were only rarely disturbed when the children or teacher sought educational diversions. Or perhaps the computers were bored to death!

Whatever the case, if teachers and students had real reasons to use computers, they would be used more often and much more appropriately. Then the computers would eventually die of exhaustion but happy in knowing they had led full and productive lives.

The most real and exciting reason I can think of for using computers is to explore the Internet. The odds are terrific that you will be teaching in a so-called plugged in classroom, so you need to develop ways to use computers to their full potential. Imagine the possibilities! Your children will be able to access all the online resources known to humankind!

Productive use of the Internet requires planning. I will share a planning technique that you may wish to use as it stands or to adapt it to fit your professional needs. It is called a *Science WebQuest* and is based in part on ideas originally put forth by Bernie Dodge and Tom March at San Diego State University and other experts in the field of educational technology.[1] I suggest an approach that focuses on the discipline of science and is geared toward elementary and middle grade teachers. My WebQuest approach has three components whose names are understandable to children: *challenge, journey,* and *report.* Finally, my approach requires teachers to correlate children's Internet explorations with the science process skills as well as the NSE standards, Project 2061, and/or local science curriculum guides.

What Is a Science WebQuest?

 A Science WebQuest is a discovery project for children that requires the use of Internet resources. The final product may take a variety of forms as a response to a specific *challenge.*

Computers with Internet access open unlimited learning possibilities for children. Science WebQuests can guide children to find and use appropriate resources as they respond to "challenges."

Although I will describe the Science WebQuest as being teacher prepared, you may wish to consider whether some of your students could prepare WebQuests for themselves or to challenge peers. Additionally, the Science WebQuest can serve as an opportunity for cooperative learning when a team of children engage in a WebQuest together.

So, what is a Science WebQuest? It's a sheet of paper—but also much more. Specifically, it's a three-step guide for students that will bring them into direct, focused contact with the Internet as a way to acquire knowledge, concepts, and skills. As indicated earlier, it's usually teacher prepared and consists of these components:

1. The challenge
2. The journey
3. The report

Figure 8.1 (pages 132–133) illustrates the three-part Science WebQuest form. Parts 1 and 2 should be completed by the teacher and given to the student or cooperative group. These parts structure and give direction to the quest. The student or cooperative group should complete Part 3 and prepare the WebQuest final report, which can take a variety of formats—a written summary, a set of answers to questions, a story, a skit, a piece of art, a poem, or a multimedia presentation in which the children use computers and related technology.

Relationship to the Process Skills

Using Science WebQuests with students is a teaching strategy that can effectively give individuals and groups practice with some of the key science process skills (discussed earlier in Chapter 3). Using these skills also provides experiences that are con-

FIGURE 8.1
A master science WebQuest form

WEBQUEST

Title: ____________________

Your Name or Cooperative Group's Name ______________________________

Start Date ______________ Completion Date ______________

1. Your Challenge

A. Introduction

B. The Challenge

2. Your Journey: Starting Your Search

A. To get more information, visit these sites:

Site	*URL*

B. To get even more information, use these key words with search engines:

3. Your Report: Sharing Your Results

A The report *must* be your answer to the Science WebQuest challenge.

B. Which of these words best describes your report? (You may check more than one.)

___ Written summary of what I (we) learned

___ Story   ___ Play   ___ Poetry   ___ Art

___ Music   ___ Chart   ___ Graph   ___ Multimedia

___ Other: _____

C. In two or three sentences, describe your Science WebQuest report. In other words, tell what the reader or viewer will observe in your report.

_____

_____

_____

Please attach your report to this Science WebQuest form.

Teacher Space

• Intended Grade Level(s) _____   Is adult help/supervision needed? _____

• Science Process Skill(s) Emphasized

___ Observing   ___ Using space/time relationships   ___ Using numbers

___ Classifying   ___ Defining operationally   ___ Communicating

___ Predicting   ___ Controlling variables   ___ Inferring

___ Interpreting data   ___ Formulating hypotheses   ___ Measuring

___ Experimenting

• NSE standards content area(s) to which this Science WebQuest is most closely related:

___ Physical science   ___ Life science   ___ Earth and space sciences

___ Science and technology   ___ Personal and social perspectives

___ History and nature of science

• Specific NSE standard or Project 2061 goal to which this Science WebQuest is most closely related:

_____

_____

• Local science curriculum guide topic to which this Science WebQuest is most closely related:

_____

_____

sistent with and supportive of discovery learning. In order to grasp how Science Web-Quests and the science process skills are related, look at a few examples:

Basic Science Process Skills	Possible Science WebQuest Experiences
Observing	Viewing recent Hubble telescope photos of planets and star clusters
Classifying	Compiling lists of rain forest animals, and grouping them into categories
Predicting	Studying weather maps over a three- or four-day period, and preparing weather forecasts

Integrated Science Process Skills	Possible Science WebQuest Experiences
Interpreting data	Gathering earthquake location data, plotting them on a map, and observing the emergence of the "ring of fire" pattern
Formulating hypotheses	Studying information gathered about the characteristics and locations of asteroids, and making a hypothesis to explain their origins
Experimenting	Gathering data from other schools who report their experiences with Oobleck, and using that information in combination with locally obtained data to prepare experiments for further hands-on explorations

Relationship to the Discovery-Learning Cycle

You may recall that earlier in the book (Chapter 3), I presented a model for discovery learning known as the *learning cycle.* That cycle has three components that can easily be incorporated in lesson and unit plans:

1. Exploration
2. Concept acquisition
3. Concept application

By creating a well-crafted Science WebQuest and providing strong teacher guidance, you can support the learning cycle in at least two ways. You could prepare three small Science WebQuests that each focus on one stage, *or* you could prepare a larger Science WebQuest that moves a student through all three stages.

Relationship to the NSE Standards, Project 2061, and Local Curriculum Guides

Why should you add Science WebQuests to your repertoire of teaching skills? What will doing so help you accomplish?

Consider how a child or cooperative group carrying out a Science WebQuest will achieve meaningful local or national curriculum goals as a result of the experience. Also consider the boundless variety of information, ideas, and opportunities for skill development that exist on the Internet and how learning or acquiring them will help students achieve curriculum goals. Let me be more explicit by listing a few goals from various curriculum sources and identifying some possible Science WebQuest challenges you could develop:

▶ *From the NSE Standards*

Goal or objective: "As a result of activities in grades K–4, all students should develop understanding of personal health." (Content Standard F)[2]

Possible Science WebQuest challenge: Use the Internet to find and creatively present four examples of how smoking cigarettes and using alcohol can harm a person's health.

▶ *From Project 2061*

Goal or objective: "The living environment, emphasizing the rich diversity of the earth's organisms and the surprising similarity in the structure and function of their cells; the dependence of species on each other and the physical environment; and the flow of matter and energy through the cycles of life."[3]

Possible Science WebQuest challenge: Using the Internet, create a list of five mammals you are likely to find in each of the following places on our planet: the Arctic, the desert, and the ocean. Also find out what each mammal feeds on and what feeds on it.

▶ *From a Local Science Curriculum*

Goal or objective: Students should understand the advantages and disadvantages of using each of the following energy sources to make electricity: coal, oil, and nuclear energy.

Possible Science WebQuest challenge: Use the Internet to locate information about the advantages and disadvantages of using each of these energy sources to make electricity: coal, oil, and nuclear energy.

Alternative Strategies for Using Science WebQuests in Your Classroom

The Science WebQuest planning model will support many different teaching styles, many different curriculum approaches, and the needs of diverse groups of children.

The following examples will help you see the range of possibilities for you and your classroom:

- Make multiple copies of the same Science WebQuest, and have all children or cooperative groups pursue the same challenge. When the individuals or groups have completed their work, all will benefit from observing the various reports. Bear in mind that the *forms* that the individual and group reports will take will vary greatly, including writing pieces, graphs and charts, poetry, art, skits, and multimedia presentations.

- Prepare two or three Science WebQuests that all deal with one general topic. Assemble the WebQuests to create a packet, and have individuals or groups select the one of most interest to them. (***Note:*** If you use cooperative groups as part of your overall instructional strategy, the within-group negotiations that go on as students select a WebQuest will reveal each group's social interaction skills.)

- Individually or in cooperative groups, have students do Internet research to prepare Science WebQuests for others. If you happen to teach science to more than one class (a typical pattern in middle grade settings), have each class prepare Science WebQuests to challenge the other classes. You will, of course, need to be deeply involved to make sure the WebQuests are not so difficult as to be impossible for a given class to complete.

- Use Science WebQuests as long-term assignments that students do at home or in association with free time at computers connected in the classroom or school learning center.

How to Plan and Prepare a Science WebQuest

 As you read this section, you may find it helpful to refer to the completed Science WebQuests shown in Figures 8.2, The Whale Deal—It's a Killer, and 8.3, The Space Warp Weather Network Gives You a Chance (pages 138 and 139).

Planning Challenges That Fit Your Students

Your success in getting children to carry out an Internet-related learning experience will depend on how well *you* carry out the essential first step—*motivation*. To successfully motivate children, you must establish a context or frame of reference for the actions you want them to take. This may mean, for instance, spinning a science-related tale that engages children's minds and builds their interest in accomplishing the Internet research task.

Your opportunity to motivate children's pursuit of a Science WebQuest comes in Part 1, "Your Challenge." Notice in Figure 8.2 that you need to prepare an *introduction* to set the context and then state the *challenge*. The *context*, or introduction, as a comedy writer will tell you, is equivalent to the setup for the punchline. It draws the reader's or listener's attention away from whatever he or she is thinking about to your topic. It serves to pique the reader's or listener's curiosity about the topic and builds some positive psychological tension that begs to be resolved. The *challenge*, on the other hand, is a clear statement of the process and product that will channel the child's motivation in a direction that will resolve the problem or issue raised in the introduction.

To help you understand these points more completely, here are a few examples of introductions and challenges for Part 1 of the Science WebQuest document:

Early Grade Samples

▶ *Animals in Danger*

Introduction: Tashia and Nathan's grandmother, Mrs. Nancy Nicelady, wants to take them on a trip to see animals that might soon disappear from the earth. She gives money every month to a group that tries to protect the animals and also takes people to see them in their natural environments. The trips are designed so they don't disturb the animals or their environments. If Mrs. Nicelady was willing to take you along on such a trip, which animals would you like to see?

The Challenge: Make a drawing of North and South America. Add the animals you want to see, drawing each where it actually lives. Also draw the plants and animals that each animal needs for food.

▶ *Is There a Volcano Near Your House?*

Introduction: While running to catch your school bus, you almost trip over a morning newspaper someone left on the sidewalk. You look down before you, kick it out of the way, and notice this headline: "Volcano Explodes, Killing 50 People." On the school bus, you look out the windows and notice some nearby mountains. You begin to wonder if there are any volcanoes in those mountains.

The Challenge: Using the Internet, find the locations of at least 10 volcanoes on the earth's surface. Make a map that shows where each volcano is. Also write the date that tells the last time each erupted. Circle the five that are closest to your state or province.

Middle Grade Samples

▶ *Atom Crushers*

Introduction: Most people think that atoms are the smallest pieces of matter, but they are wrong! Scientists have been smashing atoms for many years and discovered that there are smaller parts. There are even some parts that are smaller than protons and neutrons. Would you like to surprise some adults by telling them about these tiny pieces of matter?

The Whale Deal—It's a Killer

Your Name or Cooperative Group's Name _____

Start Date _____   Completion Date _____

1. Your Challenge

A. Introduction

You are paying some book fines when Mr. Bookman complains that not many of your friends take books home to read. "Hmmmmm," you think for a moment and then say that you would like to make a deal with him. If you can get more kids to check out books, then he will let you take home as many books as you want for as long as you want—with no fines. He agrees! Then you tell him you will cover the school walls with posters that advertise books. He likes it! You also tell him you'll start with the theme "Killer Whales," since he has a shelf of whale books that are covered with a thick layer of dust. Amazingly, Mr. Bookman agrees again, shakes your hand, reaches under the counter to get out his feather duster, and walks toward the whale books.

B. The Challenge

Do research on the Internet to find information about the size, shape, and life of killer whales. Try to discover what they eat, what tries to eat them, and where they live. Then make a poster for each topic that includes drawings, information, and questions that will get other children interested enough to check out killer whale books.

2. Your Journey: Starting Your Search

A. To get more information, visit these sites:

Site	URL
Sea World	http://www.seaworld.org/killer_whale/killerwhales.html
I Like Killer Whales	http://www.itek.chalmers.se/homepage/i4behe/killerwhale/
The Whale Information Network	http://www.webmedia.com.au/whales/whales6.html
The Orca Adoption Program	http://www.pacificrim.net/~bydesign/adopt.html
An Orca Primer	http://www.ohwy.com/or/q/qkprimer.htm

B. To get even more information, use these key words with search engines:

Marine Mammal   Orca   Shamu

FIGURE 8.2
A sample science
WebQuest

Note: See Part 3, Your Report, on page 133.

The Space Warp Weather Network Gives You a Chance

Your Name or Cooperative Group's Name _____

Start Date _____   Completion Date _____

1. Your Challenge

A. Introduction

You have just been selected by the SWWN (Space Warp Weather Network) as one of three finalists for the job of SWWN's first Solar System Weather Person. If you get the job, your forecasts will be used by space travelers to decide where they will take their vacations. Unfortunately, there is a small problem. To get the job, you will have to prepare and present a script that announces tomorrow's weather on each planet. If SWWN likes the script, you might get the job. If they don't, you will keep your present job serving french fry pills at Jason's Hyperfast Food Restaurant.

_____

_____

B. The Challenge

Locate information on the Internet about the weather and climate on each of the nine planets. Use the information to write a sample script for the weather forecast. You may audiotape or videotape yourself giving the actual forecast. You may also create weather maps to use during your presentation. If you are doing this Science WebQuest as a member of a group, each group member should be involved.

2. Your Journey: Starting Your Search

A. To get more information, visit these sites:

Site	URL
View of the Solar System	http://www.hawastsoc.org/solar/eng/homepage.htm
The Nine Planets	http://seds.lpl.arizona.edu/nineplanets/nineplanets/nineplanets.html
Solar System Journey through the Galaxy	http://www.stwing.upenn.edu/~jparker/astronomy/index.shtml
Planets and Moons	http://library.advanced.org/12713/noframes/planmoon.html
Astronomy for Kids: The Planets	http://www.dustbunny.com/afk/planets/planets.h

B. To get even more information, use these key words with search engines:

Planets _____   Solar System _____   Astronomy _____

FIGURE 8.3
A sample science WebQuest

Note: See Part 3, Your Report, on page 133.

The Challenge: Go to the Internet to find out about five pieces of matter that are smaller than protons and neutrons. Write down the name of each small piece of matter, and list two of its characteristics. Also tell the names of atom smashers used to break apart atoms and produce these tiny parts and where these atom smashers are located.

▶ *Be a Dino Detective*

Introduction: Are any dinosaur fossils buried under your school playground? How do you know for sure? This may sound like a strange question, but the answer might surprise you. This Science WebQuest will help you discover whether dinosaur fossils might be buried under your playground.

The Challenge: Make a map of your country that includes your state or province. On the map, show five places where dinosaur fossils have been found. If no fossils have been found in your state or province, show the nearest locations of dinosaur fossils. Name the dinosaurs discovered at these places, describe their characteristics, and make a hypothesis about whether dinosaur fossils are under your playground.

Notice that some of the introductions are written in a more fanciful way than others. Keep in mind that the tone and content of the introductions and challenges should fit the sophistication of the children you teach and your own creativity, too!

Planning Journeys That Fit Your Students

None of us has enough time to discover everything we need to know completely on our own. If we expected students to discover everything for themselves, there would be no time left for them to use their newly gathered information and concepts. Therefore, even discovery-based experiences require teacher guidance to ensure that children will achieve success in a reasonable amount of time.

The same is true for Science WebQuests. Guiding discovery during these experiences occurs naturally, since individual children or cooperative groups carry out their explorations in response to teacher-created challenges. The "road map" for children's journeys is actually quite simple to prepare. In fact, it's just a list of websites on the Internet with their accompanying *universal resource locators,* or *URLs.*

Before sending children on the journey, plot the course. To do so, you must have access to the Internet and conduct your own searches to locate suitable websites. Keep in mind that you are compiling a short list of prime sites that will help your students meet the challenge you gave them in Part 1.

As you prepare the journey, keep track of key words that students might use to go beyond the specific sites you identify with search engines. By identifying these key words, you will provide additional guidance but in a manner that's true to the basic concept of guided discovery. Figure 8.4 will help you think through the key word identification process.

FIGURE 8.4 One way to identify key words for Internet searches is first to prepare possible questions you might use in a challenge. The questions should lead you to appropriate key words.

WebQuest Topic	Questions about the Topic	Possible Key Words
Manatees	What is a manatee? Is a manatee a mammal? Where would you find a manatee? What do manatees look like? Are manatees a threat to people? Are people a threat to manatees? Are manatees an endangered species?	manatee manatee picture manatee drawing mammal endangered species
Elephants	Are all elephants endangered species? Are Indian elephants the same as African elephants? What problems do wild elephants cause people? Are people a threat to elephants? What is a poacher?	Elephants Indian elephants African elephants endangered species poacher
Planets in Other Solar Systems	How many planets have been found in orbit around stars besides our Sun? Do all astronomers agree that other planets have been found? Are any of the objects in orbit around stars like any of our planets? How can astronomers know that there are other planets if they can't see them? What is a radio telescope?	planets astronomy new planets other solar systems telescopes nearby stars radio telescope planet hunters

Assessing the Report

Students summarize the work they do in pursuit of the challenge in Part 3 of the Science WebQuest, the report. The final product of the Science WebQuest is then either attached (if it is a written document) or presented (if it is produced in another medium).

You should assess the report through simple observation, comparison with the original challenge, conferences with students in which they self-assess their work, and other strategies and techniques (see Chapter 6 on assessment techniques).

REAL
TEACHERS
TALKING

A
Starting
Point
for
Thinking,
Talking,
and
Writing

Marti: One of my favorite pieces of new technology is the digital camera. I was able to use one last year, and I really loved it.

Eileen: I've seen them, but I always thought they looked complicated. Was it easy to take and print the pictures you took? I know that no film is involved.

Marti: Oh, it's not hard at all. You just use the camera like an ordinary camera—point, click, and you've got the picture. Then I plug the camera into the computer, and the computer stores all the pictures on its hard disk. I just move the picture into a desktop-publishing program, so the pictures that we take of children doing science, pictures of objects and equipment we use, and pictures of children in costume doing science-related dramatics all become part of reports children write. Some teachers create science newsletters to send home. You can imagine the impact on parents of seeing pictures of their children in a newsletter that the class creates. It really isn't very hard to do.

Eileen: It must make your newsletters really interesting. Besides the use for the science newsletter, are you using the camera with student science portfolios?

Marti: You know, I've been thinking about that. It would be wonderful to have the children keep their science journals, or parts of them, as computer files and include digitized pictures of their work. If a child did a project on plant growth, he or she could take digital pictures of the plants to include in a science portfolio.

Eileen: I'm still amazed that we can now have a camera in the classroom that uses no film. It almost sounds too good to be true. We don't have to send film out to be developed, since it's all recorded as digital information, and if the picture doesn't turn out well, we just take another. We can take pictures, put them in a computer file, and then immediately print them on a laser printer, and it all happens right in our classroom. Who could ask for anything more?

Marti: Well, I could. I was thinking about how nice it would be to have a laser printer that prints in color. Now, that would really be something!

▶ *Point to Ponder:*   *The digital camera is only one example of a technological innovation that is changing what we do in science time and how we do it. Have you observed teachers use new technology to carry out interesting science projects with children? Would your science experiences in the elementary and middle grades have been much different if your teachers had some of the technology that today's teachers have?*

Make the Case

The Problem   It is difficult, if not impossible, for the busy science teacher to keep up with advances in instructional technology and to integrate them into day-to-day instruction.

Assess Your Prior Knowledge and Beliefs   As a person who will be or is now teaching children science, rate yourself on each of the following:

	Minimal knowledge and skill	Some knowledge and skill	Confident in knowledge and skill
1. General computer ability	_____	_____	_____
2. Ability to select hardware for classroom use	_____	_____	_____
3. Ability to select software for classroom use	_____	_____	_____
4. Knowledge of available software	_____	_____	_____
5. Ability to locate teaching/ learning resources on the Internet	_____	_____	_____
6. Ability to edit videos made by children	_____	_____	_____
7. Ability to create a multi-media presentation	_____	_____	_____
8. Knowledge of available videotaped programs	_____	_____	_____

The Challenge   While thinking about how you teach children science, consider how your role will change as new technologies find their way into the classroom. Based on your present level of knowledge and skills, predict how teaching children a unit on volcanoes and earthquakes may be different 10 years from now.

Internet Resources

Websites for Integrating Technology

WebQuests

http://www.lfelem.lfc.edu/tech/DuBose/webquest/wq.html

This collection of WebQuests cuts across many disciplines; however, science-related topics predominate. You will have to assess the appropriate grade level for each.

143

Hughes Academy of Science and Technology: WebQuests for the School Year

http://academynet.hughesacad.state.sc.us/web.html

This is a collection of WebQuests dealing with living things, earth and space, and matter and energy. Interdisciplinary WebQuests also are available at this site. The WebQuests presented have been developed for middle grade youngsters

"Some Thoughts about WebQuests" by Bernie Dodge

http://edweb.sdsu.edu/courses/EdTec596/About_WebQuests.html

This page on the Internet presents one of Professor Bernie Dodge's early articles on the nature and purposes of inquiry experiences using the Internet and other resources. Dodge also differentiates between short-term and long-term WebQuests. Within the article, you will find links to resources that will help you develop your own WebQuests.

The WebQuest Page

http://edweb.sdsu.edu/webquest/webquest.html

This site has links to collections of WebQuests, training materials for teachers interested in learning how to create WebQuests, and even fan mail about the use of WebQuests. The "What's New" link will keep you up to date on the locations of new WebQuests collections and training opportunities in WebQuest development.

WebQuests in Our Future

http://www.discoveryschool.com/schrockguide/webquest/webquest.html

This beautifully presented site includes a slide show that will help you think about the purposes and design of WebQuests. You can even print out the slide show for later reference.

Summary

The computer and its related technologies have become more important to teachers as the potential of the World Wide Web has been recognized in classrooms and schools around the world. The Science WebQuest is one practical technique teachers can use to guide students' work on the Internet. The challenge, journey, and report components of the Science WebQuest channel students' attention to focus on local, state, or national science curriculum goals, including those of the NSE standards and Project 2061.

Going Further

On Your Own

1. Using curriculum resources, identify five science-related topics commonly dealt with at a grade level of your choice. Select one topic for which a Science WebQuest might be an appropriate project for a child or cooperative group. Then actually prepare a Science WebQuest. Be sure to create a Part 1, Challenge, and Part 2, Journey, that are appropriate for the grade level you chose. If possible, field test part or all of your Science WebQuest with a child or group of children at that grade level. In a few paragraphs, reflect on the success of the WebQuest.

2. Based on your previous experience as a child in elementary or middle school, your observations of classrooms, and any personal teaching experience you might have, identify the major classroom management problems you feel might result from having computers in the classroom. Briefly describe what preventive steps a teacher might take to minimize one problem.

On Your Own or in a Cooperative Group

3. Try to achieve consensus among your group members as you prepare one response to each of the following questions:

   a. What are the long-term benefits of having a classroom in which children are able to link to the outside world through computer networking?

   b. Are there any negatives for children and teachers who use this networking capability?

4. Imagine that you are teaching in a school in a community that is the corporate headquarters of a well-known global telecommunications company. As part of its effort to support local education, the company has agreed to provide five long distance phone lines for Internet connection with no monthly charges to the school. The only requirement is that the teachers agree to use this service to support the networking of their classrooms with other classrooms around the country and around the world. You already have a computer and printer in your classroom, and the parents of one of the children are willing to donate a new high-speed modem to the class. On large sheets of newsprint, prepare a list of Science WebQuests you could use to convince the school principal to have one of the lines connected to your classroom.

5. Visit an elementary or middle school, and observe the extent to which individual classrooms use computers and related technology. If possible, interview the teachers to determine how each computer is used by children. Try to learn whether any science software is used and whether computers are used to keep track of science observations or prepare science journals. Without identifying individual classrooms or teachers, prepare a chart that summarizes your observations of the number of computers, their placement, the availability of related technology (e.g., printer, modem), the principal uses of the computer in support of the science curriculum, and the percentage of computers that are connected to the Internet.

6. Conduct an in-depth interview with an elementary or middle grade teacher or someone who has recently had a student-teaching internship in an elementary or middle school to discover what he or she feels is his or her present level of personal computer literacy (e.g., word processing, telecommunications), the extent to which he or she presently uses a computer and related technology in support of the science curriculum, and the extent to which children access the Internet in support of assignments.

Notes

1. I greatly appreciate the work of Bernie Dodge and Tom March at San Diego State University, whose exploration of this general area has helped many educators develop strategies for helping students access the Internet for instructional purposes. As reported in "Some Thoughts about WebQuests" (available at http://edweb.sdsu.edu/courses/EdTec596/About_WebQuests.html), Dodge's model suggests a six-component approach to WebQuests: introduction, the task, resources, the process, learning advice, and conclusion. My three-step model focuses specifically on the exploration of Internet science-related resources by elementary- and middle-level science students.

2. From the National Research Council, *National Science Education Standards* (Washington, DC: National Academy Press, 1996), p. 138.

3. American Association for the Advancement of Science, *Science for All Americans: Summary* (Washington, DC: American Association for the Advancement of Science, 1989), p. 7. Also, if you are interested in related goals, see the following publications from the same source: *Science for All Americans* (1989) and *Benchmarks for Science Literacy* (1993).

Suggested Readings

Baab, Linda. "Middle School Computer Literacy." *The Clearing House* 72, no. 4 (March/April 1999): 197–198.

Doyle, Al. "A Practitioner's Guide to Surfing the Net." *Educational Leadership* 56, no. 5 (February 1999): 12–15.

Farenga, Stephen J., and Beverly A. Joyce. "The Truth Is Out There." *Science Scope* 22, no. 2 (October 1998): 56–57.

French, Jan L., and Peggy Hilleary. "Virtual Field Trip to Antartica." *Science and Children* 36, no. 7 (April 1999): 27–31.

Gresham, Keith. "Surfing with a Purpose." *Educom Review* 33, no. 5 (September/October 1998): 22–29.

Haymore Sandholtz, Judith, et al. *Teaching with Technology.* New York: Teachers College Press, 1997.

Holzberg, Carol. "Smart Play: Electronic Games That Make the Grade." *Media and Methods* 35, no. 3 (January/February 1999): 20–22.

———. "Surfing in Safety." *Technology and Learning* 19, no. 6 (February 1999): 10–18.

Jonassen, David H., and Kyle C. Peck. *Learning with Technology: A Constructivist Perspective.* Columbus, OH: Merrill Education, 1999.

Patti, Cheryl Ann, and Patricia Dziubek. "MCS Sets Sail on the Internet." *Science and Children* 36, no. 2 (October 1998): 32–36.

Scribner, Janet, and Kathy Lawless. "Using Real-Time Weather in the Science Classroom." *Media and Methods* 34, no. 4 (March/April 1998): 26–27.

Slattery, William, et al. "Collecting Science in a Net." *Learning and Leading with Technology* 26, no. 1 (September 1998): 25–30.

Stokes, Jackie. "Problem Solving Software, Equity, and the Allocation of Roles." *Learning and Leading with Technology* 26, no. 5 (February 1999): 6–9.

Teicher, Jim. "An Action Plan for Smart Internet Use." *Educational Leadership* 56, no. 5 (February 1999): 70–74.

Weinman, Janice, and Pamela Haag. "Gender Equity in Cyberspace." *Educational Leadership* 56, no. 5 (February 1999): 44–49.

Yoder, Maureen. "The Student WebQuest." *Learning and Leading W*ith Technology* 26, no. 7 (April 1999): 6–9, 52, 53.

9

Adapting the Science Curriculum

How can I adapt the science curriculum for children from diverse cultural backgrounds, children with special needs, and children with special gifts and talents?

A Look Ahead

Treasuring the Fleeting Moments

The time that you have with each child who steps through your classroom door into your care is fleeting—so brief that you are seldom able to respond fully to the numerous ways in which children differ from one another. This chapter will help you plan science experiences for children who have special needs. I hope that it will prepare you to say to every child who enters your classroom, "Hello, I'm glad you are going to be in my class. This is the place where *everyone* learns science."

Children from Diverse Cultural Backgrounds

Science time can be a special part of the school day for children from diverse cultural backgrounds. It can be a time when those children who happen to have difficulties reading, writing, or speaking can find success through experiences that are not wholly dependent on these skills. Each and every child, regardless of his or her abilities with language, can create a leaf collection, draw a butterfly emerging from a cocoon, get a light bulb to light after making a simple circuit, or pour muddy water through a funnel of sand, gravel, and filter paper and marvel as crystal-clear drops emerge. Best of all, the success that comes from these experiences can build the confidence necessary for children's success in other areas of the curriculum.

Acquiring Supplementary Science Materials for Non-English Speakers

"Las Cremalleras Tienen Dientes Y Otras Preguntas Sobre Inventos"

If English is your sole language, you must be puzzled by the second heading for this section. Even if you have taken high school and college courses in the language used above, my guess is that you may only partially understand it. I will give you the translation later in this section, but for now, I want you to think about what it's like for a non-English-speaking child, likely new to the United States, to see books and headings that look as foreboding as the second heading above looks to *you*. Add to this language confusion the idea that the heading probably has something to do with science, a potentially difficult subject, and you should more fully appreciate the challenge that science time must be for non-English speakers as well as their teachers.

In a perfect world, all teachers would be fluent in at least one other language. But unless you were fortunate enough to be raised in a dual-language home, the odds of your being able to communicate effectively with a newly immigrated non-English-speaking child are slim, at best. Even if you are fluent in a second language, the odds are still not in your favor (or more importantly, the child's), since that language may not be Spanish, Cantonese or Mandarin Chinese, Laotian, Cambodian, or Vietnamese—the home languages of many new arrivals to the United States.

Your success in helping non-English-speaking children learn science and expand their abilities with English will depend on whether you can bring to your classroom resources in other languages. At present, it's easiest to find age-appropriate science materials in Spanish. Whether you can acquire science-related materials in other languages will depend on your own resourcefulness.

One way to find such materials is to contact community groups that represent speakers of various languages to determine what science resources might be borrowed from scientifically literate community members. Another strategy is to contact a local university to see if undergraduate or graduate students studying a given language would be available to make translations from English. Finally, if you are a world traveler, you might consider including one or more of the countries represented by your students as additions to your itinerary. During your visit, you may be able to acquire resource materials that can be put to good use in your classroom.

If you are still curious about the secondary heading above, I will now disclose that it's the title of a book for children that, roughly translated from Spanish, reads, "I Wonder Why Zippers Have Teeth and Other Questions about Inventions." This is one of the relatively good supply of Spanish language science books you can easily find. The importance of investing energy in getting such resources is supported by Isabel Schon of the Center for the Study of Books in Spanish for Children:

> *Encouraging young Spanish speakers into the world of science is becoming easier every day. The ever-increasing number of high-quality, informative, and appealing books being published in Spanish make the observation, identification, description, experimental investigation, and/or theoretical explanation of phenomena much more rewarding.*[1]

To identify books that may be helpful in your classroom, contact the center, which maintains a database of over 3,000 titles with brief descriptions. This information is accessible at this World Wide Web location: http://www.csusm.edu/campus_centers/csb.

Reinforcing Reading and Language Arts Skills

Hands-on, discovery-based science experiences can be great confidence builders for children from diverse cultural backgrounds, even if their present reading and language arts skills in English are weak. Your challenge as a teacher is to remember that you can use a child's success in science as a starting point to build a positive attitude toward school. Lets take a unit on Weather as an example. Here are some very specific ways to extend the unit to the areas of reading and language arts, which can be applied to any science unit:

1. Use daily weather observations by students to create a language experience chart. You may have learned this technique in reading and language arts methods courses or workshops. To make such a chart, transcribe the children's oral observations onto a large sheet of paper, and have them read and discuss the material.

2. Have cooperative learning groups make model weather instruments and maintain their own language experience charts. You or a child with advanced writing abilities can transcribe the observations to the chart.

3. Expect children to make labels for the parts of their model weather instruments.

4. Expect children to keep personal logs of their daily weather observations, and occasionally read to them from their logs.

5. Have children record their individual weather reports on audiocassette tape or videotape.

6. Read or have one of the children read weather-related passages from children's books.

7. Encourage children to cut out weather-related headlines from a daily newspaper, and read them to the class.

8. Using suggestions from the class, write short poems about weather on chart-paper.

9. Have the children create dictionaries of weather terms, including pronounciation hints and drawings.

10. Have the children create a school weather report and present it on the school public address system every morning.

These techniques will be most effective if they are rooted in your belief that children from diverse cultural backgrounds who have language difficulties need every possible opportunity to practice the skills of reading, speaking, and writing. Two other techniques are especially helpful for children who are not fluent in English in the classroom: peer tutoring and parent/classroom connections.

Organizing Peer Tutoring

The key to success in peer tutoring lies in the selection of the tutors. Ideally, tutors should be good students who are fluent in both languages, who understand the content you are teaching, and who possess those special personal characteristics that permit them to function as positive, supportive tutors.

Peer tutors also need some help from teachers. If possible, you should provide them with materials that display and explain science concepts in the child's native language as well as in English. If you happen to be fluent in the native languages of the children in your classes, you may wish to prepare alternative material similar to the material shown in Figure 9.1.[2] Children who only speak English may enjoy the challenge of trying to explain what the foreign terms on such diagrams mean.

Fostering Parent/Classroom Science Connections

Science time can be a learning experience that fully and appropriately involves the parents of children from diverse cultural backgrounds. Reaching out to these parents is well worth the effort, even though time and energy are at a premium for modern

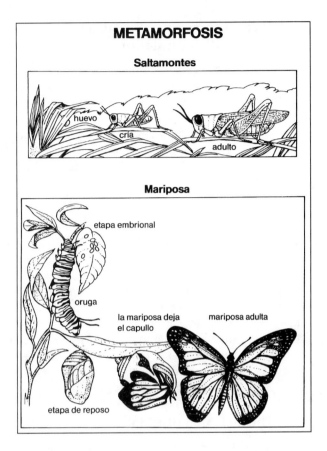

FIGURE 9.1
With a little effort, you should be able to find drawings that are labeled in children's native languages.

parents and teachers. You may need the assistance of someone who is fluent in the child's home language to use the following ideas:

1. Send a letter to parents at the beginning of the year explaining what science time for students will be like. Write the letters in English and the children's home languages, and send both copies to parents.

2. Send home a monthly science newsletter in the children's home languages that includes examples of students' work.

3. Call five parents a week to make contact for future communication.

4. Invite parents to school for a Science Open House, and invite school professionals who speak the home languages to be present.

5. Prepare home study science activity sheets in children's home languages.

6. Send a letter to parents asking for volunteers to accompany the class on field trips or to come to class when science activities are done. If you are not fluent in children's home languages, having a helper who can communicate in more than one language can be a boon.

Creating Discovery-Based Lessons with Multicultural Dimensions

Figures 9.2 and 9.3 (pages 153 and 154) are sample lesson plans that reflect instructional techniques to interconnect science and multicultural education. Notice the implementation of the discovery-learning cycle of *exploration, acquisition,* and *application* in each of the lessons.

For additional ideas on how to meet the special needs of minority and bilingual children in the classroom, contact one of the bilingual educational multifunctional support/resource centers listed in the resource materials in the final portion of this book. As you review the listing, notice that the resource centers provide services for specific geographic regions.

Children with Special Needs

 Perhaps we, as teachers, should take a vow with respect to children who have impairments—namely, that we will not give these children additional challenges while they are in our care. My language may seem a bit strong, but it is possible to put these children at even greater risk when we make content adjustments when we should be making methodology adjustments. Children with impairments need to learn the same things as other children, but they may need to learn these things in different ways or at differetn rates. Every child needs opportunities to explore, acquire knowledge and skills, and apply what he or she has learned.

The Inclusion Illusion

In many schools, children with special needs have been moved from traditional special education or resource rooms to regular classrooms in a practice known as *inclusion* or *mainstreaming*. While educating these children in classrooms with their age-mates may seem like a good idea, actually doing it can be a difficult, intense process. In too many cases, it's assumed that the physical placement alone is enough and that good things will automatically happen for everyone involved. It isn't quite that easy, however, especially in a science program designed to provide appropriate discovery-based experiences for everyone. The strategies discussed in the next few sections will help you ensure that every child who is *physically* included in your classroom will be *educationally* included, as well.

Science Experiences for Children with Visual Impairments

Children with visual impairments do not need to be placed in special classrooms. A visual impairment affects only the *manner* through which knowledge enters a child's mind; it should not in any way affect the *nature* of the knowledge you select for the curriculum. (I am, of course, using knowledge in its broadest sense to include skills, attitudes, values, and so forth.)

Food and Nutrients

Objectives

1. The children will be able to list the nutrients found in rice, corn, and wheat.
2. The children will be able to identify countries in which these cereal grains are an important part of the diet.
3. The children will develop an appreciation of the role that cereal grains play in the diet of different cultures.

Materials

Three sandwich bags for each group. Each bag should contain rice, corn, or wheat.
Newsprint and watercolor markers
Food Guide Pyramid chart for each group
Photocopies of menus from ethnic restaurants

Exploration

1. Have the children join cooperative learning groups. Distribute a sheet of newsprint and samples of rice, wheat, and corn to each group.
2. Have the groups spend 5 to 10 minutes discussing the following questions and recording their responses on the newsprint: What part of the plants did you receive? How does this part help the plants? What do you think these plants need to grow well? In what countries do people use these plants as a source of food?

Acquisition

1. Teach the term "nutrient" and write its definition on the board. Have children practice pronouncing and spelling "nutrient." Then, create a chart to show the amount of starch, water, and protein in rice, corn, and wheat.
2. Have the groups display their newsprint and give their responses to the questions.
3. Ask the children about the type of climate they think that each plant needs. Then describe the climate characteristics needed for each plant.
4. Using wall maps, show the children where the cereal grains are typically grown and identify countries that rely on rice, corn, and wheat.
5. Review their previous work on the food groups shown on the Food Guide Pyramid and ask the children to classify rice, corn, and wheat into the proper group.

Application

Distribute photocopies of menus from ethnic restaurants. Have the children identify all foods that contain cereal grains and contribute to meeting the requirements of the rice, bread, cereal, and pasta group.

Assignment

Look over the photocopied menus and write a list of the food items you would select for one day. Be sure to include foods from all six food groups but watch out for the "fats, oils, and sweets" group.

FIGURE 9.2
This science discovery lesson on nutrition has a multicultural dimension.

153

Weather and Climate

Objectives

1. The children will compare seasonal weather here with seasonal weather in their country of origin or their parents' or neighbors' countries of origin.
2. The children will make a chart comparing the climates of all the countries they have lived in or visited.

Materials

Wall map showing the continents
Index cards with weather and climate information for "mystery" countries
A "giant" mystery card
Globe

Exploration

Have the children join their cooperative learning groups. Give each group a climate information card for a mystery country. Have each group discuss the information on its card and then go the the wall map to make an educated guess about the location of their country.

Acquisition

1. At the board distinguish between "climate" and "weather." Write out a definition of each after receiving ideas from the class.
2. Discuss the seasonal differences between northern and southern hemispheres using the globe.
3. Have each group read the information from the index card and tell in what part of the world the country can be found.
4. After each group has had a turn, reveal the mystery countries and have the groups check their results.

Application

Have the students contribute ideas for a master chart that uses the climate information from their cards to show various climate types.
Display the giant mystery card and encourage each group to prepare a hypothesis about the most likely part of the world for the location of the mystery country.

Assignment

Interview relatives or neighbors about their recollections of the climate in their countries of origin and bring the information to class tomorrow.

FIGURE 9.3
This discovery lesson on weather has a multicultural dimension that extends the topic into social studies work.

If you do not modify the curriculum, then what do you do? The answer is straightforward: You modify equipment, materials, and experiences that are visually based by incorporating the use of touch, taste, and smell.

Science Reading Materials

One convenient approach to delivering printed science information to children with visual problems is to have sighted students with good oral-reading skills audiotape books, chapter sections, newspaper stories, and other printed materials. This can be an ongoing class project in which children take turns preparing instructional materials.

Another strategy is to have the school purchase large-type books, talking books, and Braille books (if your children have Braille reading skills). Major sources of such materials are the American Printing House for the Blind (Box 6085, 1839 Frankfort Avenue, Louisville, Kentucky 40206) and The Lighthouse for the Blind and Visually Impaired (1155 Mission Street, San Francisco, California 94103).

Science Activities and Equipment

Some children with visual impairments have some residual vision. That is, they may be able to distinguish light areas from dark areas and differentiate shapes. To capitalize on these abilities, you will need to speak with the child, the child's parents, and perhaps the child's physician (with parental permission, of course) to get ideas about how to modify equipment for him or her.

A small audiocassette player can be an important addition to your classroom equipment. It can take the place of a notebook by permitting the child to record the results of science experiences. The audiotaping procedure will also help the child understand that you are holding him or her as accountable as the remainder of the class for taking and maintaining notes.

Here is a challenge for you: How would you have a child with a visual impairment observe a fish in an aquarium? Since aquarium fish usually are not noisy creatures and are tucked in water, which is itself encased in glass or plastic, this problem may seem insurmountable—but it isn't. If you place within the aquarium a slightly smaller plastic aquarium that has holes drilled in it, the child will be able to lift and tip the inner aquarium until most of the water drains into the larger aquarium. The fish will become trapped in the water that remains at the bottom of the inner aquarium and can be thoroughly studied through the child's sense of touch—a pleasant educational experience for the child, if not the fish.

As the aquarium question illustrates, the real challenge to a child's learning may be the difficulty the teacher has in finding a way around or through a seemingly insurmountable problem. You are not completely on your own as you think through these problems. Through research in specialized catalogs and your personal contacts with special education personnel, you will discover that adapted equipment is available to help children and adults with visual impairments measure such variables as elapsed time, length, volume, mass, and weight. There should be an "eleventh commandment" for teachers who work with children who have visual impairments: Do not be meek in your demeanor as you go forth to make requests for special adapted materials and equipment.

Your efforts to accommodate the needs of children with visual impairments will be rewarded in many ways. The children will learn, and their peers will gain important knowledge and attitudes about people who may seem different but in fact are not.

Science Experiences for Children with Hearing Impairments

Mainstreamed children with hearing impairments range from those who do not require a hearing aid to those who have no hearing. Some of these children will be skilled lip readers, some will be adept at sign language, and some will have neither of these skills.

Children who have hearing impairments can benefit greatly from the multisensory, hands-on approach to science used in any discovery-oriented classroom. Your principal challenge will be helping these children participate fully in the experiences. Written or pictorial directions for activities and assignments, directions on task cards, and even acting out the steps of an activity will prove helpful. In the upper-elementary grades and in the middle grades, you may wish to have children take turns taking notes from your oral presentations and sharing them with students who have hearing impairments.

The child with a hearing impairment should have an unobstructed view of you and the location where you carry out demonstrations. This will allow the child to search for visual cues to supplement any information that you transmit orally. As you carry out demonstrations, explain content, and give directions, try to position your head so that the child can read your lip movements and facial expressions. You may want to remind the child's classmates to do the same.

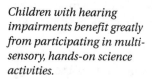

Children with hearing impairments benefit greatly from participating in multisensory, hands-on science activities.

REAL
TEACHERS
TALKING

A
Starting
Point
for
Thinking,
Talking,
and
Writing

Dale: Some teachers are really challenged when they have a child with a hearing impairment in class. I think this even happens when the child has a sign language interpreter. You've had a lot of experience with this, Karen. What are some practical things the rest of us should remember?

Karen: This sounds so obvious—but I think teachers can easily make a big mistake if there is an interpreter in the room so I am going to say it: You must direct your conversation to the child and let the interpreter facilitate the communication. Don't speak to the interpreter! A child with residual hearing or with speech-reading ability will benefit from you speaking directly to him or her. So, face the child when you talk, teach children who are in the same cooperative group with the deaf child or the child with a hearing impairment to do the same thing, and always face the child when you talk and write on the board.

Dale: I learned that lesson a long time ago. I stopped "talking to the board" because even hearing children miss instructions and information if you fall into that pattern. I've got another question that might be debatable: Should I downplay lessons and projects dealing with sound and hearing? I hate to make anyone feel uncomfortable.

Karen: Oh, no. Any activity can be made more visual or tactile with a little extra preparation. Of course, you also have the benefit of having a child who, if both the child and the parents agree, can show and explain audiograms, hearing aids, and any devices that the child uses to make sound visual or tactile. These are all items that most children will be unaware of. The rest of the class will probably be motivated to ask the child many questions about how these devices work.

Dale: So, the advice is not to stay away from sound but just take advantage of the resources that the child brings by virtue of his or her presence in the classroom. I like to think of the presence of children who may have physical impairments as an opportunity to subtly teach the rest of the class some important lessons about life. All the children need to be better prepared to live in a world where people are a little different from one another. I think *that* is the most important advantage of having a classroom that welcomes everyone.

▶ **Point to Ponder:** *What steps would you take to change the physical setting in a traditional classroom to help children who are deaf or who have hearing impairments be successful with hands-on, discovery-oriented projects?*

When working with a child who has a hearing impairment, be careful not to form an opinion about his or her intellectual abilities based only upon listening to his or her speech. The inability to articulate properly results from not having a model for the spoken words and does not indicate intellectual ability. By encouraging the child's oral responses, you will provide him or her with an opportunity to build self-confidence and practice articulation.

Science Experiences for Children with Physical Impairments

Physical impairments may range from mild to severe and differ widely in origin. Some physical challenges may result from accidents or diseases, and some may be congenital. As a science teacher, your concern should focus on the specific problems that the child may have as the class does hands-on activities. Think about whether the child has problems grasping objects, moving, stopping, or remaining steady. Also keep in mind the space needed for the child to put crutches, the room required for a wheelchair to navigate, and the access available at some field trip sites.

As you consider these matters, you may find that you have to make a few minor modifications in the classroom to accommodate a child with a physical challenge or some adaptations in the science materials or equipment that he or she will use. For example, you may need to arrange seating so that a child in a wheelchair has ready access to all parts of the room. Or you may need to be sure that a child who has a problem moving quickly has a work space that is close to the distribution point for science materials. Of course, the modifications needed will vary with each child.

A child's physical challenge can provide a growth experience for the classroom if you capitalize on the opportunities it provides for building a sense of community among all the children. By helping children interact positively with *all* their peers, you not only help the child with a physical impairment but also the entire class.

Science Experiences for Children with Emotional Problems

Some children display emotional behaviors that interfere with their ability to function well academically or with their personal and social development in the classroom. These children may have little self-confidence, be frightened easily, be depressed, be disobedient or defiant, or simply spend their time daydreaming. The child with emotional problems acts the way he or she does for a reason. Unfortunately, the reason may have eluded even the most skilled school psychologist or psychiatrist.

The causes for the behavior you observe will probably lie outside of your ability to remediate. However, the science activities you offer can serve an important therapeutic function. They can enable the child to manipulate and control variables and thus give him or her a unique opportunity to operate in responsible ways. If children can find success through such activities, they will gain self-confidence and pride in accomplishment. You may not be able to remedy children's basic emotional problems, but you can create an environment that can enhance feelings of self-worth.

As a teacher of science in a regular classroom, you should help your students welcome and encourage any child with emotional problems who joins the class for the day or a portion of the day. Remember, children with emotional problems need ever-increasing contact with children who display appropriate behavior. Some teachers may be concerned that the rest of a class will learn inappropriate behaviors from a mainstreamed child with emotional problems. If this occurs, it may be that the teacher has been unable to create a total classroom environment that values and affirms productive and appropriate social behavior.

Children with Special Gifts and Talents

 Gifted and talented children sometimes make their presence known to us; sometimes they do not. The so-called normal child may strain your patience and knowledge with such simple questions as "Why is the sky blue?" The gifted child will ask a question that reveals a far different level of thought: "Why is the sky?"

Many of the children in our schools have extraordinary intellectual abilities, and many have other abilities that are far more advanced than those of their age-mates. In fact, it is estimated that between 3% and 5% of the school-age population fits this definition. How can you tell which children have special abilities? The following definition may help:

> *Children capable of high performance, including those with demonstrated achievements or ability in any one or more of these areas—general intellectual ability, specific academic aptitude, creative or productive thinking, leadership ability, visual and performing arts, or psychomotor ability.*[3]

You may wonder what these children will do during science time that will make them stand out. Actually, some things will not be obvious at all, unless you pay very close attention to the ways children work, speak, and think. Sisk has identified the following characteristics that you should watch and listen for:

> *Early use of advanced vocabulary*
> *Keen observation and curiosity*
> *Retention of a variety of information*
> *Periods of intense concentration*
> *Ability to understand complex concepts, perceive relationships, and think abstractly*
> *Strong critical thinking skills and self-criticism*[4]

According to Sisk, children who are gifted in the visual and performing arts—talents that you certainly can use in many interdisciplinary science projects—possess some of the same characteristics as intellectually gifted children, but they also may be somewhat different:

> *Overall, children who have special creative abilities differ from intellectually gifted children in many ways. They are likely to have one or more of these characteristics: a reputation for having wild and silly ideas or ideas that are off the beaten track, a sense of playfulness and relaxation, a strong tendency to be nonconformist and to think independently, and considerable sensitivity to both emotions and problems.*[5]

Gifted and talented children may come from diverse cultural backgrounds, or they may have impairments, as discussed in previous sections of this chapter. As a teacher, try to remember that a child from a particular background or a child with a special need may also be a child with special gifts and talents. Think of your classroom as a garden in which each gifted and talented child can blossom. Science can provide these children with unique opportunities to design and carry out explorations of their environment. Because gifted and talented children may move very quickly through the planned learning experiences you provide for your class, the challenge is to keep them growing and blossoming. You will need to find ways to extend and enrich your science activities so that these children do not become bored.

Day-to-Day Enrichment Activities

Here are some activities you may wish to use even if your school has a standard science curriculum or specific set of textbooks or other resource materials:

1. Get single copies of advanced levels of the materials for each child you think will benefit from such materials or activities.
2. Each time the class begins a new unit of work, have conferences with your gifted children to identify enrichment readings and activities for them to work on in the course of the unit and establish a schedule of follow-up conferences.
3. Develop some strategy that will enable these children to share their reading and related experiences with the rest of the class.
4. In general, expect these children to participate fully in all regular activities, but try to put their special gifts and talents to use as they go beyond the basic curriculum.

Challenge Projects

Gifted and talented children are a special joy to teach because many are able to function with considerable independence in the classroom. This capacity for independent, self-directed work is well suited to long-term science projects. I call such activities *challenge projects.* Here are a few examples:

> *Can You Make:*
>   A sundial and use it as a clock?
>   A model wind-speed indicator?
>   A water filter using sand and pebbles that will clean up muddy water?
>   A compound machine from a group of simple machines?
>   A working model of a liquid-based fire extinguisher?
>   A simple battery-operated electric motor?
>   A balance that really works?
>   A clay contour map of the school grounds?

All challenge projects should begin with a teacher/student conference that focuses on the child's interest in and capacity to undertake various projects.

Responding to the special needs of gifted and talented children will provide you with many opportunities to stretch your intellectual and imaginative abilities. You will find helping these children to reach their full potential is an extremely enjoyable part of teaching.

Make the Case

The Problem Because technological innovations occur so rapidly these days, it is difficult for teachers to select the best classroom technology for children with impairments.

Assess Your Prior Knowledge and Beliefs Based on your personal experience in science classrooms, assess your present knowledge about the classroom devices that could help you achieve the fullest possible participation of children with these impairments:

1. Hearing _____

2. Visual _____

3. Orthopedic _____

The Challenge Four engineers have formed a company to design and manufacture instructional equipment for children with impairments. They have asked you to suggest ideas for new devices or for improvements in existing devices that would assist these children in a hands-on, discovery-based classroom. What will you suggest?

Internet Resources

Websites for Inclusive Classrooms

ERIC Clearinghouse on Disabilities and Gifted Education

http://www.cec.sped.org/ericec.htm

This comprehensive site will lead you to a variety of sources that will help you plan units and lessons for children with disabilities and children with special gifts and talents. It contains the results of the most recent research dealing with both groups as well as fact sheets and minibibliographies. Perhaps most important, it permits you to search the entire ERIC database to locate materials appropriate for your unique planning needs.

The National Information Center for Children and Youth with Disabilities

http://www.nichcy.org

This federally sponsored site provides information on disabilities and disability-related issues for educators, families, and others. You will find information about the nature of specific disabilities, the importance of early intervention, and most important for teachers, the preparation of IEPs (individualized education programs).

161

Top Language Groups for LEP (Limited-English-Proficiency) Students

http://www.ncbe.gwu.edu/links/langcult/toplangs.htm

This is an excellent site for anyone with a special interest in making curriculum adaptations for a child whose native language is not English. Links will take you to sites dealing with educating children representing 12 different languages, including Spanish, Vietnamese, Hmong, Tagalog, Russian, Haitian, and Arabic.

California Department of Education: Resources for English Learners

http://www.cde.ca.gov/cilbranch/bien/bien.htm

This site will be a useful resource if you teach science to children who are not fluent in English. The part of the site that offers the most help to teachers is the subsection called "Resources," which has links to very specific information on unit and lesson planning.

Bilingual Books for Kids

http://www.bilingualbooks.com/

I have included this commercial site because of the rather unique materials available from it. The books are literally bilingual in that their text is written in both English and Spanish. Look at the book selections to find detailed descriptions of "Bilingual Nonfiction" choices for science. You may want to acquire some to support teaching science- and technology-related issues.

Center for Research on Education, Diversity, and Excellence (CREDE)

http://www.cal.org/crede/

If you have a strong interest in educating children from culturally diverse backgrounds, this site will lead you to helpful resources. The center sponsors a variety of education-related projects that include attention to "Instruction in Context," which deals with teaching various subjects (including science) to these students, and "Research on Assessment," which suggests alternative ways of assessing their progress.

Summary

Appropriate reading and language-development experiences during science time are important for all children. Some children from diverse cultural backgrounds, who happen to have limited reading and language arts skills, may be encouraged to progress further as a result of hands-on science discovery activities and the stimuli such activities provide for work in reading and language arts.

Children with special needs—whether visual or physical impairments, hearing problems, or emotional problems—must participate as fully as possible in the science activities that take place in the classroom. Your response to their special needs requires both an understanding of the unique challenges they offer and the ability to develop a variety of ways to make the curriculum accessible to them.

Gifted and talented children also have special needs. The science curriculum for these children should include various enrichment activities, challenge projects, and other opportunities to use their unique talents and abilities.

Going Further

On Your Own

1. If you are part of a racial or ethnic group that was a minority in your school, comment on any special challenges you had to overcome to be a successful student in science class. If you feel that there were no such challenges, note whether this was due to special circumstances, such as a particularly responsible and encouraging teacher, parental support, and so on. If you are not a member of a minority group, interview someone who is to gather his or her responses to these questions.

2. How serious is the problem of science career awareness for children from diverse cultural backgrounds? Would broader media coverage of minority-group members in scientific fields counterbalance the underrepresentation of such individuals in curricular materials? What do you see as the teacher's role in building scientific career awareness?

3. Identify a science activity you would do with children, and then describe how you would adapt it to the needs of a child with a visual or hearing impairment.

4. Write a sample letter that you could use to establish communication among yourself, a scientist living in the community, and a gifted child with a strong interest in science. In the letter, highlight the benefits that would accrue to both the child and the scientist.

On Your Own or in a Cooperative Learning Group

5. On your own or as part of a group, interview students for whom English was not the primary language when they entered school in the United States. Try to discover what they perceive to be the special problems they faced and the techniques used by the teachers who contributed most to their success in the classroom.

6. Develop a discovery-based lesson or group of lessons that are organized around the three-step learning cycle and capitalize on the presence of children from other parts of the world in your classroom. Focus the lesson or lessons on how musical instruments from other countries produce sound. Be sure to include attention to the *exploration, acquisition,* and *application* stages of learning in each lesson or over the group of lessons you develop.

7. Role-play the following situations with your group. When you are done, discuss each situation:

   a. A parent/teacher conference regarding a gifted child whose parent is dissatisfied with your response to the child's special abilities. This parent is particularly concerned about accelerating the child's learning in both science and mathematics.

   b. Same as in "a," except the child has a hearing or visual impairment.

c. A conference in which the teacher encourages the parents of a child with a physical impairment to allow the child to participate in a field trip to a water treatment plant.

If you are doing this activity by yourself, write a brief description of what might take place in each of these three conferences.

Notes

1. Isabel Schon, "Libros de Ciencias en Espanol," *Science and Children* 35, no. 6 (March 1998): 30.

2. Many major publishers of educational materials prepare direct translations of some or all of their elementary and middle grade science books. I extend my thanks to Holt, Rinehart and Winston for their permission to reproduce the materials shown in Figures 9.2 and 9.3. These originally appeared in J. Abruscato et al., *Ciencia de Holt* (New York: Holt Rinehart and Winston, 1985), TM10, TM12.

3. Dorothy Sisk, *What If Your Child Is Gifted?* (Washington, DC: Office of the Gifted and Talented, U.S. Office of Education, n.d.).

4. Ibid.

5. Ibid.

Suggested Readings

Burtch, Joyce A. "Technology Is for Everone." *Educational Leadership* 56, no. 5 (February 1999): 33–34.

Coburn, Julia. "Making Dreams Come True." *Technology and Learning* 19, no. 7 (March 1999): 32–39.

Farmer, Jacqueline. "We Need Not Exclude Anyone." *Educational Leadership* 56, no. 6 (March 1999): 33–38.

Harris, Julia, ed. "Multicultural Approaches in Math and Science." *ENC FOCUS for Mathematics and Science Education* 5, no. 1 (1998): 1–10.

"Hispanic Heritage Month." *Science and Children* 36, no. 1 (September 1998): 43–44.

Ivy, Tamra, et al. "Battling Spring Fever? Try *Los Remedios.*" *Science Scope* 21, no. 7 (April 1998): 30–32.

Latham, Andrew S. "The Advantages of Bilingualism." *Educational Leadership* 56, no. 3 (November 1998): 79–80.

Lyman, Michael, and Mary Ann Mather. "Equal Learning Opportunity: Assistive Technology for Students with Special Needs." *Technology and Learning* 19, no. 4 (November/December 1998): 55–60.

Madrazo, Gerry, Jr. "So, How Does a Multicultural Classroom Look? Sound?" *Science and Children* 36, no. 5 (February 1999): 6–7.

McCann, Wendy Sherman. "Science Classrooms for Students with Special Needs." *ERIC Digest* (February 1998), EDO-SE-98-05.

Reiss, Sally M., et al. "Equal Does Not Mean Identical." *Educational Leadership* 56, no. 3 (November 1998): 74–77.

Renzulli, Joseph. "A Rising Tide Lifts All Ships: Developing the Gifts and Talents of All Students." *Kappan* 80, no. 2 (October 1998): 104–111.

Schon, Isabel. "Libros de Ciencias en Espanol." *Science and Children* 36, no. 6 (March 1999): 24–27.

———. "Libros de Ciencias en Espanol." *Science and Children* 35, no. 6 (March 1998): 30–32.

Verplaeste, Lorrie Stoops. "How Content Teachers Interact with English Language Learners." *TESOL Journal* 7, no. 5 (Autumn 1998): 24–28.

10

Unit, Lesson, and Enrichment Starter Ideas

The Earth/Space Sciences and Technology

A Look Ahead

Kelly's Gift

Kelly was in such a rush to get into the school that she bumped into the big, brown trash can by the front door and dropped her lunch box. She picked it up, walked through the doorway, and raced down the hallway to her classroom. The door was open and the lights were on, which meant that her teacher was somewhere in the building. She pulled a chair to the side of her teacher's desk, sat down holding her lunch box on her lap, and patiently waited.

In Kelly's lunch box was a present that Aunt Nicole had brought back from vacation. Kelly had wrapped it carefully in foil before putting it next to her sandwich. It was a very special rock, a rock filled with holes, a rock that would float!

"Good morning, Kelly. You certainly are an early bird today," her teacher said, entering the classroom.

"I've got a surprise for you," said Kelly, placing the shiny object at the front of the teacher's desk. "You can show it during science, but I wanted you to see it first."

"That's wonderful. I'll do that, but right now, I have to get the model volcano from Mr. Johnson's room." Kelly's teacher turned and hurried out the door.

Kelly went to her own desk and stared at the foil-wrapped rock. "Oh well," she thought to herself, "I guess it's OK if everybody sees it at the same time."

Science time was right after lunch. The lesson was about the earth's crust. Kelly's teacher forgot about the rock, and Kelly was too shy to mention it.

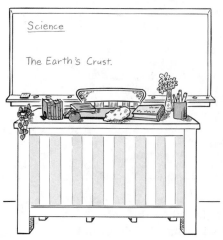

When Kelly got to school the next day, she went right to the teacher's desk, picked up the foil-wrapped object, looked at it, and without a word handed it to her teacher.

"Thanks, Kelly. I'm so sorry I forgot this yesterday. We'll unwrap it during science time today. I can't wait to see what it is."

Science time finally arrived, but just as the teacher was reaching for the foil-wrapped rock, the school fire alarm went off. There wasn't a fire, but everyone had to stay outside until someone fixed the alarm, which wouldn't stop ringing. By the time the children were able to enter the school, science time was over.

At the end of the day, Kelly quietly walked up to the teacher's desk, picked up the magic floating rock, and a minute later dropped it in the big, brown trash can just outside the school.

As you plan earth/space science and technology units and lessons, think about Kelly's magic floating rock and all children for whom rocks and oceans and outer space are sources of wonder. Once you have done this, begin to think of your plans as starting places, not ending places. You do need to plan well and to plan ahead, but you also need to be flexible enough to receive and incorporate the gifts that children bring. What are these gifts? They are the children's ideas about the natural world, their questions about things they observe that don't make sense, and of course, the occasional foil-wrapped floating rock.

Assessing Prior Knowledge and Conceptions

"But we learned all that in Mr. Greeley's class last year."

▶ Have you ever been in a classroom and observed a teacher getting ambushed? That's what happens when teachers assume that children know little or nothing about a topic, only to discover too late that they know a lot. The results are also disastrous when teachers assume that children know a lot about a topic and in fact know very little. (Plus, valuable lesson-planning time will have been wasted.) Even assumptions about children's beliefs about phenomena in the natural world can stop teachers in their tracks. Children may have very strongly held beliefs that are totally incorrect, which may not be discovered until the class is deep in a lesson or unit.

So, as a teacher in the real world of schools and classrooms, how can you quickly get a sense of what the children know, what skills they possess, and what they believe? Part of the answer is to use *probes*—basic questions and simple activities that get children thinking and talking about particular topics. The answers children give will provide very direct guidance about what you should include in science units and lessons.

The probes and sample responses that follow come from informal interviews that I or my students have done with children. I think you'll be amazed at some of the responses and motivated to develop probes that you can use *before* planning units and lessons.

Probe	*Responses That Reveal Prior Knowledge and Conceptions*
▶ After giving a young child an assortment of rocks, leaves, and twigs: *Would you please put these into groups and then tell me how you made your choices.*	"I wanted to get three in each group." "I put the big rock with these because it was lonely."
▶ After showing a fossil: *How do you think this fossil was made?*	"The animal touched the mud and it hardened. Then the bones were left behind." "When the rock was made, the object was touching it."
▶ *Why is it light outside during the day and dark outside during the night?*	"Because a different part of the country faces the sun." "Because the sun isn't around during the nighttime. The moon is there instead."
▶ *How do you think the earth began?*	"The big bang. We learned about it last year." "I don't know. I wish Adam and Eve didn't take the apple of knowledge; then we wouldn't have to go to school."

Probe	*Responses That Reveal Prior Knowledge and Conceptions*
▶ *Where do you think soil comes from?*	"It doesn't come from anything. It was always here."
	"Well, some of it comes from leaves."
	"I think it's from under the rocks and then the rocks get moved by the glaciers and the soil is left."
▶ *What are the stars?*	"They are reflections from the moon."
	"They are little balls of light."
▶ *Some people think we should send astronauts to explore Mars, and some people think doing that would be a waste of money. What do you think?*	"Well, it depends if it's safe or not. If it's safe to go, we should go to see what is there. But if it wasn't safe, we could just send more rockets with TV cameras."
	"We should send people there to see if anything there is alive. There might be some things there we could get, like metals and gold."

Internet Resources

Websites for Earth/Space Science Units, Lessons, Activities, and Demonstrations

Sharing NASA

http://quest.arc.nasa.gov/interactive/

This NASA site is dedicated to providing students and teachers with real-time experiences with ongoing NASA projects. As NASA initiates and carries out projects, students and teachers can connect to the projects and gather information about the explorations they unfold. For example, students can gather information about flying the shuttle, spacecraft explorations of distant planets, and space-based life sciences research.

NASA Space Image Libraries

http://www.okstate.edu/aesp/image.html

Finding current photographs and drawings related to the study of space is a particular problem, since ongoing developments often make the illustrations in textbooks and curriculum resource materials obsolete. This site solves that problem and more, providing graphics related to the earth, the planets, the universe, spacecraft, and almost anything else you can think of to support children's study of earth and space sciences.

CNN Interactive Weather Main Page

http://cnn.com/WEATHER/

This site will provide you and your children with a wide variety of weather resources that could serve as the basis for ongoing weather projects. Included are up-to-the-minute forecasts for every major city in the world, current weather maps, access to information about the locations and movements of major storms, and even allergy reports. This site is a gold mine of information for a creative teacher who wants to develop weather-related WebQuests for individual students or cooperative groups.

Volcano World

http://volcano.und.nodak.edu/index.html

This well-done site will provide you and your students with a wealth of information and graphics about volcanoes, including a "Volcano of the Week," video clips of volcanoes, and even " Volcanoes of Other Worlds," a presentation of volcanic activity on the moon and planets. If you enter the "Kids Door," you will find stories, games, and other activities for young people. As a teacher, you will be most interested in this site's "Lesson Plan" section.

The Science Education Gate-Way

http://cse.ssl.berkeley.edu/SEGway/

This site was created by a partnership of science museums, researchers, and educators and is sponsored by NASA and other agencies. Here, you will find information and activities that will be helpful in planning units and lessons related to the study of the earth, its weather, and a variety of topics in the space sciences. All the projects and activities are correlatated to a range of grade levels. This site will be of greatest interet if you are teaching middle-level science or above.

Earth/Space Science Lesson Plans

http://ericir.syr.edu/Virtual/Lessons/Science/

When you reach this site, select "Earth Science" or "Space Sciences" from the introductory page. Either option will take you to an extensive collection of lessons, each identified by title as well as suggested grade level. The lessons originate from a wide variety of sources and cover a broad range of topics. Some effort has been made to put them in a consistent format; however, the fact that they come from different sources has resulted in format variations. Nevertheless, this is one of the most comprehensive sources of earth and space science-related lessons you are likely to find on the Internet.

Unit Plan Starter Ideas

That great idea for a science-teaching unit may come from deep within your brain, your school curriculum guide, a state science curriculum framework, a science resource book, a course, a workshop, a discussion you have with children, or some other source. Unfortunately, a great idea (like a friend, an umbrella, and a good restaurant with cheap food) is sometimes hard to find when you really need one.

To make it easier for you to come up with great ideas for science units, I have prepared three different sources of unit starter ideas, which are presented as three lists:

1. The first is based on the National Science Education (NSE) standards for science content. I created these starter ideas for standards related to grades K–4 and 5–8.

2. The second is based on the general goals for science and scientific literacy proposed by Project 2061 in their scientific views of the world recommendations. I regrouped the goals into earth/space science, life science, and physical science and then included related goals for science and math integration.

3. The third list of starter ideas is based on my study of earth/space science topics that commonly appear in school curriculum guides. These are shown by grade level.

I am certain that this rather unique compilation of starter ideas will help you plan and create wonderful discovery-based teaching units.

Ideas Based on the NSE K–8 Content Standards

NSE

Content Standard K–4: Earth and Space Sciences [ESS]

As a result of their activities in grades K–4, all students should develop an understanding of:

> *Properties of earth materials*
>
> *Objects in the sky*
>
> *Changes in earth and sky*[1]

Starter Ideas for the Properties of Earth Materials

Unit Title/Topic: *My Rock Collection*

Unit Goal: Students gather rocks outdoors, observe them, learn that they are made of different substances, and classify them.

Unit Title/Topic: *Soils Here/Soils There*

Unit Goal: Students collect soil samples from various locations, observe them, and classify them on the basis of color, particle size, texture, and how they react with water.

Starter Ideas for Objects in the Sky

Unit Title/Topic: *The Sun and the Moon*

Unit Goal: Through class discussions and reading, students describe the general characteristics and relationships among the sun, planets, moon, and stars.

Unit Title/Topic: *The Planets and the Stars*

Unit Goal: Through class discussions and reading, students describe the general characteristics of the planets and the stars.

Starter Ideas for Changes in the Earth and Sky

Unit Title/Topic: *Our Earth Changes*

Unit Goal: Students use their memories, interviews with adults, and daily weather and climate observations to identify observable changes that occur on the earth, including the yearly changes in seasons.

Unit Title/Topic: *Our Moon*

Unit Goal: Students observe the moon, keep track of its apparent change in shape, draw its changing appearance, and search for patterns in the observations they have collected.

NSE

Content Standard 5–8: Earth and Space Sciences [ESS]

As a result of the activities in grades 5–8, all students should develop an understanding of:

> *Structure of the earth system*
>
> *Earth's history*
>
> *Earth in the solar system*

Starter Ideas for the Structure of the Earth's System

Unit Title/Topic: *The Earth Is a System*

Unit Goal: Students describe the layers of the earth, its core, and how the core and layers interact.

Unit Title/Topic: *Solid or Not?*

Unit Goal: Students give descriptions of the evidence that supports the hypothesis that the solid earth beneath their feet is constantly changing. Their descriptions will include references to the movements of plates, constructive and destructive forces, and the rock cycle (i.e., the change of old rocks to particles and their eventual reformation into rocks).

Starter Ideas for the Earth's History

Unit Title/Topic: *Yesterday and Today*

Unit Goal: Students identify modern earth processes—such as plate movement, erosion, and atmospheric changes—and make hypotheses about whether these processes have also occurred in the past.

Unit Title/Topic: *Surprising Events*

Unit Goal: Students create written research reports using information from reference books and Internet searches that describe the characteristics of possible catastrophic events in the earth's history, including asteroid or comet collisions.

Starter Ideas for the Earth in the Solar System

Unit Title/Topic: *Where Are We Really?*

Unit Goal: Students create charts, graphs, and drawings that demonstrate their knowledge of the position of the earth in the solar system and the locations of the other eight planets, moons, asteroids, and comets.

Unit Title/Topic: *The Sun Does It All*

Unit Goal: Students give evidence that supports the hypothesis that the sun is the major source of energy for phenomena such as plant growth, winds, ocean currents, and the water cycle.

NSE

Content Standards K–8 Related to:

Science and Technology {S&T]

Science in Personal and Social Perspectives [SPSP]

History and Nature of Science [HNS][2]

Unit Title/Topic: *How Do They Know?*

Unit Goal: Students identify the forms of technology used by meteorologists and build a model of at least one instrument used to gather weather observations.

Unit Title/Topic: *Protect Yourself*

Unit Goal: Students identify natural hazards that might affect them or others, their frequency of occurrence, and the protective steps individuals can take when specific hazards such as violent storms and earthquakes occur.

Unit Title/Topic: *Who Are They?*

Unit Goal: Students do library and Internet research to prepare brief biographies of Ptolemy, Tycho Brahe, Johannes Kepler, and Alfred Wegener that focus on their contributions to our understanding of the earth and its systems.

Ideas Based on Project 2061 Goals

> 2061
> GOAL
>
> *The structure and evolution of the universe with emphasis on the similarity of materials and forces found everywhere in it, the universe's response to a few general principles (such as universal gravitation and the conservation of energy), and ways in which the universe is investigated.* (p. 7)[3]

Starter Ideas for the Structure and Evolution of the Universe

Unit Title/Topic: *Does the Moon Pull, Too?*

Unit Goal: Children discover that their weight on the earth is based on the mutual attraction of their mass and the earth's mass and learn that their weight on the moon would be less than their weight on the earth.

Unit Title/Topic: *Rockets Here, Rockets There*

Unit Goal: Children learn that rocket engines can operate without an atmosphere.

> 2061
> GOAL
>
> *The general features of the planet earth, including its location, motion, origin, and resources; the dynamics by which its surface is shaped and reshaped; the effect of living organisms on its surface and atmosphere; and how its land forms, oceans and rivers, climate, and resources have influenced where and how people live and how human history has unfolded.* (p. 7)

Starter Ideas for the Features of Planet Earth

Unit Title/Topic: *Where Are We?*

Unit Goal: Children learn that the earth is one of nine planets in orbit around a star, the sun.

Unit Title/Topic: *Travels of a Drop*

Unit Goal: Children learn that human communities arise where there is a constant source of water and that various technologies are used to acquire, treat, transport, and protect the water used for life and commerce.

The mathematics of symbols and symbolic relationships, emphasizing the kinds, properties, and uses of numbers and shapes; graphic and algebraic ways of expressing relationships among things; and coordinate systems as a means of relating numbers to geometry and geography. (p. 8)

Starter Ideas for Using Numbers and Graphs

Unit Title/Topic: *What's on a Weather Map?*

Unit Goal: Children learn to express weather information using symbols found on a weather map.

Unit Title/Topic: *Where's the Quake?*

Unit Goal: Children learn to use the latitude and longitude data of recent earthquakes to determine if these earthquakes occurred along the "ring of fire."

Probability, including the kinds of uncertainty that limit knowledge, methods of estimating and expressing probabilities, and the use of such methods in predicting results when large numbers are involved. (p. 8)

Starter Ideas for Probability and Predicting

Unit Title/Topic: *Weather Forecasts: True or False?*

Unit Goal: Children keep track of official weather forecasts over an extended period of time, compare the actual weather to the forecasts, and reach conclusions about the accuracy of weather predictions.

Unit Title/Topic: *Violent Weather: Is It on the Way?*

Unit Goal: Children learn the observations that are used to predict the arrival of violent weather and the factors that can limit the ability to make such predictions.

Data analysis, with an emphasis on numerical and graphic ways of summarizing data, the nature and limitations of correlations, and the problem of sampling in data collection. (p. 9)

Starter Ideas for Studying Results and Summarizing

Unit Title/Topic: *Light-Years Away*

Unit Goal: Children apply their knowledge of the meaning of a light-year by carrying out library research and then constructing graphs to show how far various stars are from the earth.

Unit Title/Topic: *The Dew Point Changes*

Unit Goal: Children define *dew point,* find the dew points on various days, graph their data, and use their information to describe weather conditions.

2061 GOAL

Reasoning, including the nature and limitations of deductive logic, the uses and dangers of generalizing from a limited number of experiences, and reasoning by analogy. (p. 9)

Starter Ideas for Reasoning

Unit Title/Topic: *Are We Alone?*

Unit Goal: Children learn of the relationship of stars to galaxies and galaxies to the universe, do research to find the approximate numbers of stars and galaxies in the universe, and reach a conclusion about the likelihood of life existing somewhere other than on the earth.

Unit Title/Topic: *The Dinos and Us?*

Unit Goal: Children use information about the beginning and end of dinosaur life on the earth and the beginning of human life on the earth to determine whether dinosaurs and humans were contemporaries.

Ideas Based on Typical Grade Level Content

Starter Ideas for Kindergarten

Unit Topic/Title: *The Same and Different*

Unit Goal: Children compare a variety of rocks in terms of size, shape, form, color, texture, and density and create a set of rocks that each share at least two characteristics.

Unit Topic/Title: *What Is the Weather?*

Unit Goal: Children observe the daily weather, tell about it, and note any changes from the previous day's weather.

Unit Topic/Title: *What Is under Your Feet?*

Unit Goal: Children observe that rocks and soil are under their feet when they are outdoors and use a colander to sort rocks, pebbles, and soil.

Starter Ideas for First Grade

Unit Topic/Title: *The Sun, the Moon, and the Stars*

Unit Goal: Children compare the relative sizes and changing positions of the sun, moon, and stars.

Unit Topic/Title: *Water Everywhere and in the Air*

Unit Goal: Children compare various forms of precipitation and clouds and learn that water evaporates from water sources on the earth, condenses in the air, and eventually returns to the earth.

Starter Ideas for Second Grade

Unit Topic/Title: *Lakes and Oceans*

Unit Goal: Children discover that freshwater and saltwater have different characteristics, learn how beaches are made, and discover the origins of sand.

Unit Topic/Title: *The Reasons for Seasons*

Unit Goal: Children compare the four seasons and learn that they result from the position and tilt of the earth in its path around the sun.

Unit Topic/Title: *Climate Here, Climate There*

Unit Goal: Children describe the different climate zones of the world and the types of plants and animals found in them.

Starter Ideas for Third Grade

Unit Topic/Title: *A Visit to the Planets*

Unit Goal: Children learn the names of the planets, their characteristics, and their distances from the sun.

Unit Topic/Title: *Group the Rocks*

Unit Goal: Children learn that rocks can be classified into three major groups on the basis of their characteristics and origins.

Starter Ideas for Fourth Grade

Unit Topic/Title: *Earth Layers and Changes*

Unit Goal: Children learn that the earth consists of various rock layers and that changes are occurring continually in its crust.

Unit Topic/Title: *Star Search*

Unit Goal: Children learn that the sun is one of a multitude of stars in the Milky Way and learn to recognize the major constellations in the night sky.

Unit Topic/Title: *Weather Today, Weather Tomorrow*

Unit Goal: Children construct and use simple weather instruments and then use the data they have gathered to forecast the weather for the next day.

Starter Ideas for Fifth Grade

Unit Topic/Title: *The Earth Long Ago*

Unit Goal: Children learn the clues that scientists use to determine the ages of rocks, the major time periods of the earth's geologic history, and the types of living things that existed during each time period.

Unit Topic/Title: *Earth Treasures: How to Find and Use Them Carefully*
Unit Goal: Children learn how humans locate and use the earth's mineral resources and the possible environmental problems associated with the acquisition and use of these resources.

Starter Ideas for Sixth Grade

Unit Topic/Title: *Mapping the Weather*
Unit Goal: Students learn the meanings of the principal symbols used on a weather map and how to use a succession of daily weather maps to predict tomorrow's weather.

Unit Topic/Title: *Voyaging around the Earth to the Moon and Planets*
Unit Goal: Students learn how the space shuttle operates and how future space explorers will travel, work, and live in space.

Starter Ideas for Seventh Grade

Unit Topic/Title: *Making Maps*
Unit Goal: Students learn how to represent topographic features on a map.

Unit Topic/Title: *Faults and Folds*
Unit Goal: Students learn the causes and characteristics of normal faults, thrust faults, upward rock folds, and downward rock folds.

Starter Ideas for Eighth Grade

Unit Topic/Title: *Moving Plates*
Unit Goal: Students learn the basic theory of plate tectonics and the associated effects of crustal movements, including continental drift, earthquakes, and volcanoes.

Unit Topic/Title: *The Universe*
Unit Goal: Students learn the relationship between the solar system and the Milky Way and the galaxies and the universe.

Lesson Plan Starter Ideas
for Common Curriculum Topics

Sometimes you will be responsible for teaching lessons that are part of units prepared by committees of teachers in your school district or units that are commercially available. You may wonder how to break these units into lessons. To help you come up with lesson ideas for the earth/space sciences, I have analyzed a variety of teaching units and prepared a list of lesson plan starter ideas based on topics usually covered in these units. The lesson descriptions are very specific, so each description may also be viewed as the lesson's principal objective.

Characteristics of the Earth, Its Atmosphere, and the Oceans

Plan a lesson in which the children:

- Make a labeled drawing that shows that the earth consists of rock layers.
- Draw clouds they have observed and then classify each cloud into one of the following categories: cumulus, cirrus, or stratus.
- Predict tomorrow's weather based on today's weather, write a script for a weather forecast, and videotape the forecast.
- Evaluate the accuracy of a television weather forecast.
- Use a stopwatch to find the time interval between lightning and thunder.
- Calculate the distance from a thunderstorm using the time interval between lightning and thunder.
- Judge how well children could follow safety precautions if they were playing outside and thought that a thunderstorm or tornado was coming.
- Prepare a weather chart that identifies temperature, wind speed, wind direction, cloud cover, and precipitation every day for one week.

The Water Cycle

Plan a lesson in which the children:

- Describe and diagram the water cycle and then make a presentation to a class of children at an earlier grade level.
- Write a story that includes a prediction of how life in school would change if the water supply to the school was cut in half.
- Count the number of times a water fountain is used in an hour and estimate the water usage for one day.
- Observe and collect data related to the impact of people on the water cycle.
- Evaluate local streams, rivers, ponds, lakes, or ocean beaches to decide which would pose the least pollution hazard for swimmers, using newspaper articles gathered by the teacher as the basis for their evaluations.
- Make a hypothesis about how weather affects daily life and carry out a survey to test the hypothesis.
- Create labeled drawings that show the characteristics of three different climate zones.

Rocks and Minerals and the Earth's Crust

Plan a lesson in which the children:

- Compare and contrast the characteristics of the earth's crust, mantle, and core.
- Make a chart that compares the characteristics of rocks and minerals.
- Classify rocks by their characteristics and the processes by which they were formed.

- Make a cartoon in which each frame shows a stage in the process by which rock is broken down to produce soil.
- Analyze soil samples using a hand lens and separate rock and mineral particles from organic matter.
- Describe how fossils are formed and how they are used to determine the relative ages of rocks.

Space

Plan a lesson in which the children:

- Identify the major objects seen in the sky—such as the sun, moon, stars, and planets—from pictures and through direct observation.
- Infer the relative positions of the sun, earth, and moon from a list of observations made during an annular eclipse.
- Write a poem that includes the idea that the sun is the source of the earth's energy.
- Make a chart that compares the sun and the earth in terms of size, shape, color, state of matter, and temperature.
- Use an orange and a flashlight to show how the rotation of the earth determines night and day and how the earth's revolution and tilt determine the seasons.
- Create a sequence of drawings that shows how the moon appears to change shape as it revolves around the earth.
- Make a labeled diagram that shows the relative positions of the nine planets of the solar system.
- Make a chart that compares the other eight planets with the earth in terms of physical characteristics.
- Create an illustration on chart paper that shows the orbits of planets, moons, asteroids, and comets.
- Make a hypothesis to explain what motivated humans to view groupings of stars as constellations.
- Write a poem that includes the idea that a star changes size and color and goes through a life cycle.
- Describe the relative locations of the planets with respect to the sun and our solar system within the Milky Way.
- Predict what humankind will do to survive when the sun ceases to shine.

Classroom Enrichment Starter Ideas

 ### In-Class Learning Centers

Try to locate the center, which you might call *Spaceship Earth,* in a place where the students can turn out the lights when necessary. Allow space for working with clay, assembling models, and making large murals. In the center, arrange a library section containing books about the sun, earth, seasons, stars, planets, and solar system. If you have computer software or videos related to the characteristics of the earth or the solar system, place it in the center, as well.

Prepare activity cards (cards that give directions for activities you develop) based on the following ideas (***Note:*** Asterisks indicate activities that may be particularly appropriate for young children):

- *Globe Explorations*   Children mark where they live on the globe, locate large bodies of water or nearby rivers, and locate the one place they have traveled to that is farthest from where they are.

- *Seasons Mural**   Children draw or paint on shelf paper a mural illustrating the seasonal changes in their town or city.

- *Phases of the Moon*   Children take calendars home and draw the shape of the moon each night.

- *Clay Planets*   Children make models of the sun and the nine known planets from clay. (You may wish to have the children label balls with planet names and place them in order from the sun.)

- *Reflection**   Children note how visible a ball of foil or a silver tree ornament is in darkness and then note the change in visibility when light from a flash-

A well-prepared in-class learning center offers children many opportunities to make their own discoveries. This learning center—Spaceship Earth—will hold the children's interest throughout the unit.

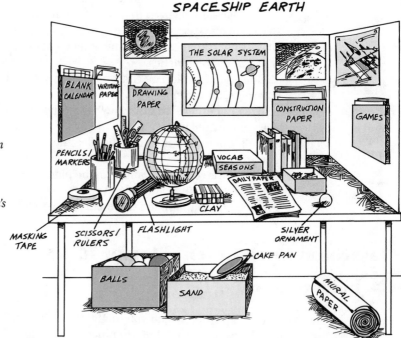

light strikes the surface of the ball or ornament. They draw parallels to the illumination of the moon by the sun.

- *Surface of the Moon** Children try to replicate the moon's surface by modeling sand in a pie plate.

Bulletin Boards

Good bulletin boards have the potential to be something that children can both look at and learn from. There are many ways to use classroom bulletin boards to enhance earth/space science units and extend your teaching to nonscience areas. The following list offers a few starter ideas for you (***Note:*** Asterisks indicate activities that may be particularly appropriate for young children):

- *The Air—Who Needs It?* Divide the bulletin board into two categories—one labeled "Needs Air to Work" and one labeled "Doesn't Need Air to Work." Show students a jar filled with air and ask, "What is inside this jar?" Pour the air out of the jar by placing it under a water-filled jar and bubbling air up into it. Then discuss the question "What can air be used for?" with the class. Provide the children with magazines and scissors, and have them cut out pictures for each category and then staple each picture on the board to form a collage.

- *Wind** How do we know the air is there? Provide and display various photographs and pictures illustrating the effects of wind (e.g., a collapsed umbrella, tree leaves blowing, and kites flying). Have the children make drawings of their observations of the presence of wind and include their drawings in the bulletin board display. Children may wish to write stories to accompany their pictures.

- *Save Water** Design a bulletin board showing a cutaway view of a typical house. Include in the diagram a bathroom, kitchen, laundry room, and outdoor hose. Prepare a set of cards listing various ideas for saving water. (Examples: "Take a short shower." "Don't leave the water running." "Don't play with the hose.") Using yarn and push pins, have children connect these ideas to the places in the house where they should be carried out.

- *Shadows on the Moon* Use cutouts representing the earth, moon, and sun to depict why the moon appears crescent shaped. Prepare other cutouts to represent the various phases of the moon, and have the children arrange them on the bulletin board in proper sequence.

- *Natural Features* Provide a set of labels for land types, including grasslands, mountains, hills, lakes, rivers, and so on. Attach pictures showing examples of each land type to the board. Challenge the children to attach the pictures under the correct headings.

Bulletin boards can draw children into the science topic you wish to introduce.

- *Land Shapes*   Place on the bulletin board a large topographical map that includes a key. Then place cards on the board representing different physical features that can be found on the map. Have the children attach the cards to the proper locations on the map.

- *Our Changing Earth*   Prepare a bulletin board so it has two distinct halves. Title one side "Changes Caused by Humans" and the other "Changes Caused by Nature." Attach an envelope containing a random assortment of pictures that depict an example for one half or the other. Have the children attach each picture to the proper half.

Field Trips for City Schools

Many of the factors that make the city an interesting and exciting place to live also make it a place that overflows with field trip possibilities. If you take the time to think about it, you will realize that streets, sidewalks, and buildings have a lot to offer children's study of earth/space science and technology. For instance, concrete has small pebbles that are readily visible; small rocks are easy to find where paths across lawns wear through the topsoil; sidewalks and school steps provide evidence of an analog to erosion as children's shoes abrade the surfaces; and water gushing from roof drain pipes recontours the soil it strikes. Many office and municipal buildings have limestone columns that contain visible fossils, and some older buildings may have marble walls and floors that can be observed and studied.

Although some celestial observations may be obscured by city lights, city astronomy is a definite field trip possibility because the moon and bright stars will still be apparent. Some world-renowned astronomers were born and raised in large, busy cities, which tells us that the evening skies can be just as much a source of wonder for city children as for children of the suburbs and country.

The field trips suggested in the next section include various explorations that can be done in the city. Pay close attention to the following topics to see if you can tailor them to the resources of the city in which you presently study or teach:

> *The Weather Station*
> *Touch the Earth*
> *Pollution Prevention Locations*
> *Water Quality Control Sites*

Here are additional starter ideas that should stimulate your thinking about field trips for children in city schools:

- *What Cracks the Sidewalks?* Children survey the sidewalks on the school grounds to find large and small cracks and make hypotheses about what causes the cracks.

- *What Happens to the Rain (Snow)?* Children search for evidence that will tell how rain or melted snow is absorbed by the soil or carried off.

- *What Clouds Are Those?* Children go outside to draw clouds, classify them, and track their movements.

- *Which Way Is North?* Children use compasses to identify north, south, east, and west on their playground.

- *Map Our Block* Children estimate distances to key buildings, count steps between landmarks, and gather related information to create a map of their block.

- *Earth Resources in the School Building* Children walk through and around the school to locate earth resources that are part of their building.

- *Trash and Treasure* Children walk around the block on recycling day (i.e., the day in which households and businesses are to use special blue or green plastic boxes to dispose of materials that may be recycled) to determine the extent to which apartment houses, homes, and businesses participate in recycling.

Field Trips for All Schools

Here are starter ideas for field trips for all schools (***Note:*** Asterisks indicate activities that may be particularly appropriate for young children):

- *The Weather Station** Even the smallest communities have locations where you can observe the operation of weather measurement and forecasting equipment. Be sure to find out ahead of time what equipment is used so you can familiarize your class with it. Contact the person who will be showing you around to let him or her know the abilities and interests of your students. Prior to the trip, discuss or review topics such as cloud types, precipitation, violent weather, and weather forecasting. During the visit, be sure that you or the guide explains the purpose of the weather station. Also discuss the instruments and procedures used in long-range forecasting. There are many follow-up activities for this trip, including the construction of simple instruments for a classroom weather station, the giving of daily weather reports, and long-range forecasting.

- *Touch the Earth*   This field trip would be helpful any time your class is studying changes in the earth's surface. The destination should be any place where the surface of the land is being disturbed (e.g., a construction site, beach, or the edge of a stream or river). Institute appropriate safety procedures depending on the location. Students should have notebooks, magnifying glasses, and something to use to carry samples. Follow-up activities could include presenting topic reports, making displays of collected items, and preparing charts showing the results of soil and water testing.

- *Visit a Potter**   A visit to a potter's or sculptor's studio can be a fascinating way for children to observe the relationship between art and earth science. At these sites, the children will be able to learn about the earth materials in use, techniques for shaping the materials, how the finished product is preserved, and how the artist thinks about the materials used as well as the origin of the design for the finished product.

- *Pollution Prevention Location!*   Many factories have added pollution controls to smokestacks and have taken other measures to reduce air pollution. Contact the public relations officer of any large company in your region to arrange for a visit. Consider a visit to a garage to see automobile air pollution devices being repaired, cleaned, or installed. Finally, many states and cities have installed pollution-monitoring stations to measure air quality. If your state has a mobile monitoring station, you might arrange for it to be brought to your school.

Additional Earth/Space Science Field Trip Ideas

Archaeological dig
Astronomy department at a local college
Building site with foundation excavation
Geology department at a local college
Gravel or sand pit
Hot-air balloon festival or exposition
Lakeshore or seashore
Museum with geological display
Road cut where rock layers can be safely observed
Stone quarry
Water reservoir
Water treatment plant

Cooperative Learning Projects

As you consider the following starter ideas for cooperative learning projects, keep in mind the importance of stressing the three key aspects of cooperative learning (discussed in detail in Chapter 5):

1. Positive interdependence
2. Individual accountability
3. Development of group process skills

- *Planet X*   Provide each cooperative learning group with access to resource books containing descriptive information about each planet in the solar system. After the students have had an opportunity to skim through the books, give each group an envelope with the words *Planet X* written on it. Inside each envelope will be an index card with the name of a planet. The groups are not to divulge the names of the planets. Provide all groups with art materials, including pâpier-maché, paint, and poster board. Give each the goal of creating a model of the planet that fits the descriptive information in the resource books and a poster that lists important information. Instruct the groups not to include the name of their planet on the poster. After the groups have completed their work, organize the mystery planets and posters in a display. Encourage members of each learning group to work as a team as they study the other planets and posters and attempt to identify them.

- *Mission Possible*   Provide each learning group with resource materials describing the characteristics of the planets of the solar system. The materials should include some information on the distances of these planets from the sun. Also provide the groups with poster board, drawing materials, and a pocket calculator. Challenge each group to select a planet, do additional library research, and prepare large drawings and charts that show the group's response to the following:
    1. How far away is the planet from the earth?
    2. Has the planet been explored with space probes?
    3. How long would it take a spaceship to get to the planet?
    4. What special features should a group of scientists exploring the planet be sure to observe?
    5. Make a drawing showing the inside of an imagined spaceship sent to explore the planet. Be sure to include places for the crew to eat, exercise, rest, and so forth.

- *Weather the Storm*   Give each group the challenge of developing a skit about the approach of a violent storm and a group of people camping outdoors. The skit must include accurate scientific information about violent storms and the safety measures that should be taken. Write the name of a violent storm (e.g., blizzard, hurricane, thunderstorm, tornado) on an index card, and give each group a different storm. Warn the groups to do their work in a way that does not reveal the storm to other groups. Encourage the groups to make simple props out of art materials. Have each group present its skit to the class as a whole.

Additional Ideas for Cooperative Groups

- Have groups create and update weather maps.
- Have each group make a weather forecast and broadcast it on the school public address system.
- Challenge groups to build model volcanoes.
- Have groups write and perform skits on earthquake safety.
- Have groups create displays of rocks found in the state or province.
- Have groups create a series of newsprint panels that illustrate the major events in a recent spaceflight.

Science and Children and Science Scope

Resource Articles for Earth/Space Science Units, Lessons, Activities, and Demonstrations

Ahlness, Mark. "The Earth Day Groceries Project." *Science and Children* 36, no. 7 (April 1999): 32–35.

Albert, Tom. "Making a Big Impact." *Science Scope* 22, no. 7 (April 1999): 26–28.

Bryan, Benjamin A., and M. Leonard Bryan "All That Snow, Where Will It Go." *Science Scope* 21, no. 5 (February 1998): 28–31.

Calkins, Andrew. "Polar Connections." *Science Scope* 21, no. 5 (February 1998): 25–27.

Edgett, Ken. "The Legend of Joe the Martian." *Science and Children* 35, no. 5 (February 1998): 14–17.

French, Jan L., and Peggy Hilleary. "Virtual Field Trip to Antartica." *Science and Children* 36, no. 7 (April 1999): 27–31, 61.

Hinshaw, Craig, and Louisa Knivilla. "Science Eruption." *Science and Children* 36, no. 2 (October 1998): 14–17, 56.

Honigsfeld, Andrea. "Global Warming: It's Not Cool." *Science and Children* 36, no. 2 (February 1999): 46–51.

Jackson, Julia A. "Discovering the Geosciences." *Science Scope* 21, no. 7 (April 1998): 28–29.

Keleher, Katherine W. P. "Star Light, Star Bright." *Science and Children* 36, no. 2 (October 1998): 18–21.

Meyer, Steve, et al. "Weather Detectives: Searching for Cool Clues." *Science and Children* 36, no. 1 (January 1999): 33–37.

The Problem Children need science experiences that range across the earth/space, life, and physical sciences. Teachers may tend to emphasize those topics they feel most comfortable with and thus inadvertently limit the scope of children's learning.

Assess Your Prior Knowledge and Beliefs

1. When you compare your knowledge of the earth/space sciences to your knowledge of the life and physical sciences, do you believe you have acquired more, less, or the same amount of basic science content in each?

	More	Less	Same
Physical sciences	_____	_____	_____
Life sciences	_____	_____	_____

2. When you were a student in grades K–8, were you exposed to more, less, or the same amount of earth/space science content as you were to life and physical sciences?

	More	Less	Same
Life sciences	_____	_____	_____
Physical sciences	_____	_____	_____

3. Dinosaurs are an ever-popular earth/space science topic for children. Identify five discrete items of knowledge that you have about dinosaurs.

   _____

   _____

   _____

   _____

4. Now identify five things about dinosaurs that you think you should know but do not.

   _____

   _____

   _____

   _____

The Challenge You are part of a team of teachers planning a unit on dinosaurs. You want the unit to include the discovery-learning stages of experiencing, acquiring, and applying. Give an example of an earth/space science activity you might include to support each of these stages.

Smith, Michael J. "Pizza Box Mining." *Science Scope* 22, no. 7 (April 1999): 24–25.

Sterling, Donna R., and Rebecca J. Graham. "And You Were There." *Science and Children* 35, no. 6 (March 1998): 41–46.

Sylvan, Patricia Kalish. "Primary Paleontologists." *Science and Children* 36, no. 1 (January 1999): 16–19, 60.

Vandas, Steve. "Coastal Hazards: Hurricanes, Tsunamis, Coastal Erosion." *Science Scope* 21, no. 8 (May 1998): 28–31.

Notes

1. This standard, as well as the others identified in later sections, are excerpted with permission from the National Research Council, *National Science Education Standards* (Washington, DC: National Academy Press, 1996), pp. 104–171. Note that the bracketed symbol to the right of each standard was prepared by this author. See also the list of all the K–8 content standards in the appendix of this book.

2. Note that I have related this sampling of NSE standards E, F, and G to the earth/space sciences.

3. This excerpt and those that follow are from *Science for All Americans, Summary/Project 2061*. Copyright © 1989 by the American Association for the Advancement of Science. Reprinted by permission of Oxford University Press. The American Association for the Advancement of Science (AAAS) grouped its Project 2061 recommendations into four categories: 1) The Scientific Endeavor, 2) The Scientific View of the World, 3) Perspective on Science, and 4) Scientific Habits of Mind. The Unit Plan Starter Ideas based on Project 2061 in Chapters 10, 13, and 16 were prepared by this author for the "Scientific View of the World" recommendations in *Science for All Americans: Summary* (Washington, DC: American Association for the Advancement of Science, 1989). I omitted three recommendations whose elementary school science implications would require a breadth of consideration beyond the scope of Chapters 10, 13, and 16. These were goals related to "consequences of cultural setting into which a person was born," "social change and conflict," and "forms of political and economic organization."

For a further specification of all the goals and the broader curriculum implications of the Project 2061 effort, see *Science for All Americans* (Washington, DC: American Association for the Advancement of Science, 1989) and *Benchmarks for Science Literacy: Project 2061, American Association for the Advancement of Science* (New York: Oxford University Press, 1993).

11A

The Earth's Surface, Atmosphere, and Weather

Content

A Look Ahead

Spaceship Earth: What Is It Made Of?

 You don't have to hitch a ride on the next space shuttle to treat yourself to a high-speed space adventure. You are having one right now! All living things—including you and me—are passengers on the most elaborate and marvelous spaceship that will ever hurl through space and time. It's the top-of-the-line luxury model, fully equipped with water, oxygen, and abundant food. And best of all, each and every seat has a fantastic view!

We can become so comfortable riding along on *Spaceship Earth* (otherwise known as the "third rock from the sun") that we take its very existence and nature for granted. If you take the time to learn more about the earth, you will discover that it's just as fascinating as the moon, planets, stars, and mysteries that lie at the far reaches of the universe.

The Earth beneath Your Feet

The earth, our personal spaceship, is full of surprises. One of the most extraordinary findings actually comes from the common misconception that we're walking around on some enormous, solid ball of rock. In fact, the earth is a giant, layered sphere made of materials that are as different as oil and water and rock and diamonds. Even more surprising is that at the center of the earth lies something completely unexpected—a liquid.

To understand the makeup of the earth, we need to figuratively peel off layers and work our way to its center. The first layer is a thin shell that ranges from 11 kilometers (about 7 miles) to 32 kilometers (about 20 miles) in thickness. This crust is thought to be divided into seven major sections called *crustal plates*. These plates are interesting for many reasons, including the fact that they are slowly moving and carrying oceans and continents along with them.

Under this first layer, we find the *mantle*, which is about 2,870 kilometers (1,780 miles) deep. Figure 11A.1 shows the crust and the mantle. Earthquake waves move faster in the upper mantle than in the crust. Knowing the rates at which earthquake waves travel through the different layers gives geologists important clues about the nature of the rock layers themselves.

Under the mantle, we find the *core*. Although no one is exactly sure of its composition, we do have an important clue: The fact that the earth has a magnetic field strong enough to turn a compass needle is evidence that a mass of molten metal exists at the center. The movement of this hot liquid metal, which is likely a mixture of iron and nickel, may create electric currents that produce the magnetic field.

Gradual Changes in the Earth's Surface

If you look outside your window, you may see mountains, prairies, a desert, a lake, or maybe just other buildings. Whatever the case, the view you see creates an illusion—an illusion of permanence. In fact, all of our surroundings are in the process of grad-

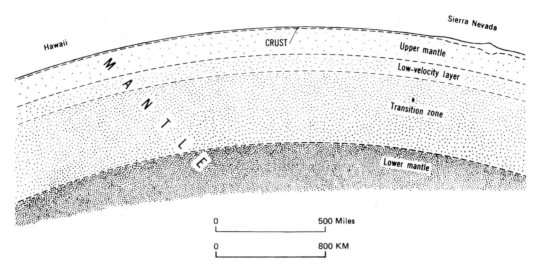

FIGURE 11A.1   The upper mantle lies between Hawaii and California.

ual change, including the walls of the buildings you may see. More startling yet is the idea that even the enormous continents are in constant motion.

Most geologists now believe that all the continents were once joined into a single, large land mass. Alfred Wegener, who proposed this theory in 1912, named this land mass *Pangaea*. He believed that it broke apart and the pieces slowly drifted to where they are now. They are still moving but only very slowly at rates of between 1 and 5 centimeters per year. Australia and Africa are moving northward, so some time in the next 50 million years, Australia may strike Asia and Africa may strike Europe. Wegener's theory seems correct because geologists have discovered similar rock structures on the west coast of Africa and the east coast of South America. This similarity, along with the discovery of similar fossils in both locations, is strong evidence that the two continents were once part of the same land mass.

Continental drift is not the only cause of change in the earth's surface. External forces, such as weathering and erosion, constantly wear down the surface, and internal forces, which come from heat and pressure, push rock layers upward and sideways to form mountains and cause plate movement.

In order to keep track of when these various changes happened during the earth's history, scientists have created a geologic time scale. The largest division in the scale is the *era*. Each era is named for the type of life that existed then. Here are the four eras of geologic time and the approximate beginning of each:

Cenozoic era	70,000,000 years ago
Mesozoic era	225,000,000 years ago
Paleozoic era	600,000,000 years ago
Precambrian era	4,500,000,000 years ago

This calendar also has other divisions. The three most recent eras have been divided into *periods,* and the period of the most recent era—the Cenozoic era—has been divided into *epochs.*

The Precambrian Era

The first part of the earth's calendar—the Precambrian era—is by far the longest, representing about 90 percent of all geologic time. It's difficult to tell a lot about how these early rocks were formed, since they have changed so much over history. Another problem for those scientists trying to study these rocks is that most of them have been covered. However, there are some large exposed areas in South America and the Middle East; smaller areas can be found in Canada, the United States, South America , Australia, Scandinavia, and Siberia. Many people and industries are quite interested in the discovery and study of Precambrian rocks, since they typically contain valuable deposits of iron, nickel, uranium, gold, and silver.

The Paleozoic Era

The Paleozoic era was a time of great changes on our planet. Sheets of ice covered much of the land in the Southern Hemisphere, and various seas and oceans formed in the Northern Hemisphere. Over time, much of the ice melted, land masses emerged from the oceans, mountain chains were pushed upward, and what was to become the North American continent began its northward path.

The Mesozoic Era

If you see some of North America when you look out your window, you are observing features that were probably formed during the Mesozoic era. For instance, the Appalachian Mountains, the Rocky Mountains, and the Sierra Nevada Mountains were all formed at this time. Great seas that were in the middle of the United States and Canada disappeared as these areas rose to form almost level plains. Many of the organisms that depended on the seas and the swampy areas along them became extinct. The levels of the great oceans dropped, and the climate became cooler. The great dinosaurs then came into existence, flourished, and disappeared all during this busy period of geologic history.

The Cenozoic Era

During the Cenozoic era, the movement of the seven crustal plates pushed up mountains and increased earthquakes and volcanic activity, and thick layers of lava covered areas in western North America. This was a time when great changes in climate began. Glaciers from both polar regions spread toward the equator, scraping the earth surface along their paths. At one point, glaciers covered North America between the Appalachian Mountains and the northern Rocky Mountains. Areas of New York, northern New Jersey, and New England east of the Appalachians were also covered with glacial ice. As the glaciers receded into south central Canada, rivers flowing northward became blocked with ice; these ice dams led to formation of a huge lake. When the ice melted, most of the gigantic lake disappeared, leaving behind hundreds of small lakes and Lake Winnipeg, which remains to this day.

Violent Changes in the Earth's Surface

If you stood between the railroad tracks in front of a freight train moving only 1 mile (less than 1 kilometer) an hour, you would gradually learn that powerful forces can have great consequences even though they are acting slowly. The same is true for the movement of crustal plates discussed earlier in this chapter. Violent changes happen where the plates meet, pushing and slowly grinding against one another.

Earthquakes

Imagine being sound asleep and being awakened by the feeling that your house was rocking back and forth. If you have actually had this experience, you know that this is what it's like to be in an earthquake.

This probably isn't news to you if you live in California, one part of North America where seismographs record a great deal of activity from the movement of plates. In western California, the Pacific plate is moving northwest and rubbing against the North American plate—the plate that North America rides on. Figure 11A.2 (page 194) shows the location of the San Andreas fault, which runs from northern to southern California. This figure also shows the dates of major earthquakes in California and areas where rock layers are very slowly being pushed out of position.

Volcanoes

On August 24, 79, the apparently extinct volcano Vesuvius suddenly exploded, destroying the cities of Pompeii and Herculaneum.[1] Vesuvius had been quiet for hundreds of years, its surface and crater were green and vine covered, and no one expected the explosion. Yet in a few hours, volcanic ash and dust buried the two cities so thoroughly that their ruins were not uncovered for more than 1,600 years!

Molten rock below the surface of the earth that rises in volcanic vents is known as *magma,* but after it erupts from a volcano, it is called *lava.* It is red hot when it pours out of the vent, but it slowly changes to dark red, gray, or black as it cools. If lava erupts in large volumes, it flows over the surface of the earth. Generally, very hot lava is fluid, like hot tar, whereas cooler lava flows more slowly, like thick honey.

All lava that comes to the surface of the earth contains dissolved gas. If the lava is a thin fluid, the gas escapes easily. But if the lava is thick and pasty, the gas escapes with explosive violence. The gas in lava may be compared with the gas in a bottle of soda pop. If you put your thumb over the top of the bottle and shake it, the gas separates from the liquid and forms bubbles. When you remove your thumb, there is a miniature explosion of gas and liquid. The gas in lava behaves in somewhat the same way; it causes the terrible explosions that throw out great masses of solid rock as well as lava, dust, and ashes.

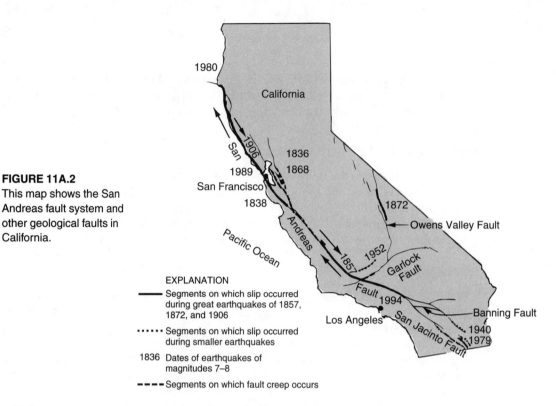

FIGURE 11A.2
This map shows the San Andreas fault system and other geological faults in California.

The violent separation of gas from lava may produce rock froth, called *pumice.* Some of this froth is so light that it floats on water. In many eruptions, the froth is broken into small fragments that are hurled high into the air in the form of volcanic ash (gray), cinders (red or black), and dust.

The Earth's Land Surface

Rocks

A rock can be much more than what it seems at first glance. Indeed, rocks provide us with many of the things that make possible an enjoyable and productive life. From rocks come the soils that nourish plants; the minerals we use for nutrients, fertilizer, adornment, and raw materials for manufacture; and, of course, the special stones that skip across the surface of a quiet pond on a hot summer day.

Igneous rocks are formed from the heating or cooling of melted materials in the earth (see Figure 11A.3). The word *igneous* comes from a Latin word meaning "coming from fire." Igneous rocks on land are exposed to the elements of the hydrosphere and atmosphere. Water, wind, and temperature changes cause the chemical and physical breakdown of igneous rocks, a process known as *weathering*. The particles and pieces removed by weathering are moved from place to place by the wind, water, and, in some cases, glaciers. This movement results in *erosion,* or the wearing away of the land. Many of the particles and pieces are washed into streams and rivers and eventually transported to the oceans. Thus, matter that was originally inland igneous

FIGURE 11A.3
Igneous rocks are the result of volcanic activity.

rock is washed up in layers at the water's edge to form beaches or, more commonly, settles in layers on the ocean floor.

Particles of rock transported to the oceans are called *sediment*. Over a long time, layers of sediment may become pressed together, eventually becoming *sedimentary rocks* (see Figure 11A.4). Sedimentary rocks are formed from particles that were originally part of any other type of rock, from chemical reactions that occur in the ocean and result in small crystals, and from organic matter.

When rocks are heated or pressed together for a long time, they can change. Rocks that have undergone this process are known as *metamorphic rocks* (see Figure 11A.5). Fashioned deep within the earth, metamorphic rocks are formed from igneous or sedimentary rocks. The term *metamorphic* comes from Greek words meaning "change" and "form."

FIGURE 11A.4
Sedimentary rocks are formed in layers.

FIGURE 11A.5
Metamorphic rocks are the result of pressure, heat, and water.

Minerals

Rocks are combinations of *minerals,* naturally occurring chemical elements or compounds. Gold, silver, and platinum, for example, are well known and highly valued minerals found in rocks. Many mineral compounds include oxygen and another element found in abundance in the earth's crust—silicon. These compounds are known as *silicates.* Quartz, feldspar, and mica are all examples of silicates. Quartz consists of one silicon atom for every two oxygen atoms. Because its atoms are tightly joined, it is a very hard mineral. Feldspar commonly contains aluminum-oxygen and silicon-oxygen combinations of atoms. In some feldspars, however, sodium, calcium, or potassium replaces the aluminum. Feldspar is a softer mineral than quartz. Mica has an atomic pattern that causes it to be easily separated into thin sheets. Biotite and muscovite are two minerals that are micas.

Ores—useful metals—and gems—crystals that have an unusual color and the ability to reflect light from their many faces, or facets—are also minerals, but they are not silicates. Other nonsilicate minerals are calcite, gypsum, halite, and fluorite. Sulfur, gold, and graphite are nonsilicate minerals that are elements. An *element* is a substance composed of just one type of atom.

Scientists are able to identify the minerals that make up rocks by performing laboratory tests. Each mineral has a variety of identifying characteristics, including color; streak—the color it leaves when it is rubbed against a piece of porcelain; luster—the property of reflecting, bending, or absorbing light; the form of its crystals; cleavage and fracture—how it splits or breaks apart; relative weight; and hardness—how easily it can be scratched. Figure 11A.6 shows the hardnesses of common minerals as determined by a measuring system known as *Mohs' hardness scale.* As you can see from this chart, if you know the Mohs' scale for some common materials, you can determine the hardness of another mineral by scratching it with the materials.

In addition to the common characteristics noted in the previous paragraph, a mineral may display some special properties, such as magnetism—being attracted to a magnet; fluorescence—glowing under ultraviolet light; phosphorescence—glowing after an ultraviolet light that has been shining on it is turned off; and radioactivity—giving off rays that can be detected by a Geiger counter.

Fossils

The earth today contains billions of living things that display amazing variety in both appearance and behavior. However, life as we know it has changed a great deal over the 5 billion years in which the earth has existed. For example, dinosaurs once lived in Utah, great mammoths lived in Canada, and swampy forests once stretched across parts of Pennsylvania and Illinois. We know this, even though none of these things exist anymore, because we have found evidence of their existence in the form of fossils.

Fossils are created in a variety of ways. Since dead plants and animals usually decay quite rapidly, only the harder parts of their bodies are preserved. These parts are fossilized as a result of the presence of water containing mineral matter that re-

FIGURE 11A.6   This chart illustrates the Mohs' hardness scale and the places of some common materials in it.

Mohs' Hardness Scale

Hardness	Mineral
1	Talc
2	Gypsum
3	Calcite
4	Fluorite
5	Apatite
6	Feldspar
7	Quartz
8	Topaz
9	Corundum
10	Diamond

Explanation: A given mineral will scratch those minerals above it in the table and will be scratched by those below it.

Some Common Materials and Their Places in the Hardness Scale

Hardness	Common Material	Comment
about 2.5	Fingernail	Will scratch gypsum with difficulty but will not scratch calcite.
about 3	Copper	Scratches calcite; will also be scratched by calcite.
about 5 to 5.5	Glass	With difficulty scratches apatite; also scratched by apatite.
about 5.5 to 6	Knife blade	Will scratch feldspar with difficulty.
about 7	File	Will scratch quartz with difficulty.
about 9	Silicon carbide	With difficulty scratches corundum; also scratched by corundum.

places the hard portions of the animal. This explains why teeth, shells, bones, and woody tissues are all commonly found fossils. If plant or animal remains are covered by a protective material soon after death, the likelihood of fossilization increases. For example, the remains of creatures that live in the water fall to the bottom of the lake or sea floor, where soft mud and sand may bury them. Fossils that form in such environments are preserved in sedimentary rocks. Some fossils are found in the form of molds or casts. For example, seashells buried in mud and sand may eventually dissolve in the water. The cavity that is left may preserve the outline of the shell and its surface. Minerals from groundwater may settle in this mold and eventually form a cast of the original shell.

Fossils are seldom found in igneous rocks, since the process by which such rocks are formed would tend to destroy any remains of living things. However, wind-blown ash from volcanic activity may settle on animal or plant material and provide a protective covering that increases the likelihood of fossilization. Yellowstone National Park in Wyoming contains fossilized remains of forests that were covered by volcanic ash and dust.

Some unfossilized remains of plants and animals that lived millions of years ago have been found. At least one mammoth has been discovered preserved in ice.

FIGURE 11A.7
This reconstruction of an American mastodon becoming entrapped in a La Brea tar pit captures the anguish of that moment in time. Fossilized remains found in the La Brea tar pits have provided a great deal of information about early life on North America.

Natural mummies have also been found. Amber, a fossilized plant resin, has served as the final resting place for a variety of small plants and animals, and tar pits have been the source of beautifully preserved animal bones. The La Brea tar pits in the Los Angeles area are probably the best-known source of information about the plants and animals that lived thousands of years ago. Apparently, the animals became stuck in these natural tar pools. The tar has acted as a preservative and has provided scientists with excellent specimens of plant and animal life (see Figure 11A.7).

Fossils of the earliest humanlike creatures have been found in Africa and are approximately 2 to 3 million years old. Modern humans—that is, creatures that would appear to us to be very much like ourselves—have probably existed for about 100,000 years. Our present physical and mental capabilities make us a species with an enormous capacity to both adapt to diverse environments and change environments to fit our needs.

Dinosaurs

Few members of the parade of life that has marched across the earth offer as much fascination to children and adults as the dinosaur. The dinosaur was an air-breathing animal that could be as small as a chicken or as large as a whale. Body forms varied considerably from species to species: Some dinosaurs walked on two feet, others on four; some had horns, others had talons, and still others had large teeth. Some dinosaurs were meat eaters, and others were vegetarians.

Tyrannosaurus was a dinosaur that reached a length of 14 meters (about 47 feet), weighed more than an elephant, had teeth that were 8 to 15 centimeters (about 3 to 6 inches) long, huge feet, powerful claws, and relatively small, grasping "animal hands." It spent most of its time on land, moved about on two legs, and was a meat eater.

Apatosaurus, a large amphibian, was probably a vegetarian. It walked on four legs and had a very large and long neck. Fossil evidence of an apatosaurus more than 21 meters (about 67 feet) long has been found in Colorado.

Stegosaurus was about 6.5 meters (21 feet) long, moved about on four limbs, and had a small head and brain and a large, curved, armor-plated back. The armor consisted of a double row of upstanding plates over the full arch of the back and two or more spikes on a powerful tail. The spikes on the tail were an effective weapon for warding off attackers. Although its brain was small, stegosaurus had a large nerve center in its pelvis that controlled the muscles of the tail and the rear legs.

Triceratops was one of a group of horned dinosaurs. Its huge head was approximately one-third its entire length. On its head were one small horn and two large ones. Its bony crest apparently protected its neck. This dinosaur was 7 meters (about 22 feet) long and was a vegetarian.

Fossil evidence reveals that the peak of the dinosaurs' development occurred near the end of the Cretaceous period in the Mesozoic era. However, no one is sure why the dinosaurs became extinct. Some scientists have suggested that a catastrophe such as an earthquake, volcano, or sunlight-blocking cloud resulting from a comet strike killed the dinosaurs. However, this theory does not explain why *only* the dinosaurs were destroyed, while other life forms survived. Scientists have also conjectured that the apatosaurus and its vegetarian relatives eventually became extinct because their huge bulk made it difficult for them to move to new environments as changes occurred in their natural habitat, but this does not explain the extinction of all the dinosaurs. Changes in climate may have changed the vegetable and animal life upon which dinosaurs fed, but there were places where such climatic changes did not occur, so some species of dinosaurs should have survived. Perhaps one of the children you teach will someday develop a theory that explains the extinction of the dinosaur satisfactorily.

The Earth's Oceans

When we look at the ocean, we see nothing but water. Imagine for a moment that the water disappeared. What would you expect the floor of the ocean to look like?

The Ocean Floor

With the water gone, you would see gently sloping areas, known as *continental shelves,* along the edges of the continents. These areas extend outward to a region of ocean floor that slopes steeply to a flatter part of the ocean floor called the *abyssal plain.* Not all continents have a gradually sloping continental shelf. In some places, the shelf extends hundreds of kilometers; in other places, the coastline drops immediately into deep water.

The continental shelf receives the sediment carried by rivers from the land surface. The material covering it is called the *continental deposit.* The edges of the continental shelf mark the beginning of a steeply sloping region known as the *continental slope.* The continental slope extends until it reaches the ocean floor, which is lined with ridges known as *midocean ridges.* Between the ridges lie the *abyssal plains.* The ridge that rises from the Atlantic Ocean floor is called the *Mid-Atlantic Ridge.* The islands known as the Azores are the peaks of the Mid-Atlantic Ridge that have risen above the water. Although there are ridges in the ocean floor beneath the Pacific Ocean, they are not as tall as the Mid-Atlantic Ridge.

The ridges on the ocean floor are made by molten rock from deep within the earth pushing upward and slowly spreading out to the east and west. Thus, the ridges indicate places where the ocean floor is actually expanding. The movement of continents away from these areas is known as *continental drift*. Since the earth is not becoming larger, there must be an explanation for what happens as new land is created at the ridges and pushed outward. The explanation can be found in *ocean trenches*. At other places on the ocean floor the earth's crust is being pushed downward, creating large trenches. Ocean trenches are the most striking feature of the Pacific Ocean floor. The trenches are thousands of kilometers long and hundreds of kilometers wide.

Ocean Currents

Throughout history, sailors have used their knowledge of the locations of ocean currents to move from place to place quickly and to avoid sailing against currents, but what causes the currents in the first place? The explanation must begin with sunlight. The equatorial regions of the earth receive more sunlight than other places on the planet's surface. Because they do, the oceans in the equatorial regions absorb an enormous amount of energy and become warm. The warmed waters have a tendency to move, and it is this moving of ocean water away from the equator that results in the major ocean currents. The earth's rotation turns these currents clockwise in the Northern Hemisphere and counterclockwise in the Southern Hemisphere. Along the eastern coast of North America, a powerful current called the *Gulf Stream* carries warm waters from the equator northward and then eastward toward England.

Although many people are familiar with the major ocean currents at the water's surface, few people realize that there are currents far beneath the surface. There is, for example, a deep current that flows out of the Mediterranean under the surface current that flows into the Mediterranean at the Straits of Gibraltar. It is said that ancient sailors familiar with this unseen current sometimes took advantage of it by putting weighted sails *into* the deep water.

Seasonal changes in the strength, direction, and temperature of currents produce a variety of effects. Fish dependent on the movement of currents to carry food to the area of the ocean in which they live may perish if the current changes. Variations in the temperature of a current can affect the hatching of fish eggs. These effects impact humans because humans depend on the ocean's resources.

Ocean Resources

The oceans of our planet are a source of food, minerals, water, and perhaps, if we discover how to convert ocean movements into a usable form, energy. The challenge we face is to harvest the ocean's resources without diminishing their richness.

The living resources of the ocean begin with *phytoplankton*—tiny, one-celled plants that carry out photosynthesis. Their capturing of sunlight is the first step in

FIGURE 11A.8
If you examine this ocean food chain closely, you will discover how energy reaching phytoplankton eventually sustains life for the shark.

creating the food chains and webs found in the oceans. Phytoplankton serve as food for microscopic animals known as *zooplankton*. Zooplankton are then eaten by larger organisms, and these organisms are eaten by still larger organisms. Thus, the energy originally received by the phytoplankton is passed along through the ocean food chains and webs (see Figure 11A.8).

The food chains and webs of the oceans can be thought of as a vast repository of protein-rich foods, and many modern technologies are used to locate and acquire fish, mollusks, and crustaceans for human consumption. Hopefully, international agreements concerning overfishing and water pollution control measures will permit future generations to benefit from these food resources.

The adage "Water, water everywhere and not a drop to drink" may have been true once with respect to salty seawater, but it is not true any longer. One important ocean resource is the water itself. Modern desalinization plants make it possible for communities that do not have access to freshwater to get it from saltwater. This is accomplished by evaporating seawater, which yields freshwater as vapor. The water vapor then condenses to form liquid water, which can be used for drinking, farming, or industrial uses. Sodium chloride and other substances are left behind as solids. The process is somewhat costly in terms of the energy required to evaporate seawater; however, as the technology improves and becomes more efficient, more of the earth's population will get its freshwater from seawater.

The ocean is a vast resource for humankind. With technological advances and a sensitivity to maintaining the quality of the water in the earth's oceans, humans will no doubt find and use other valuable ocean resources.

The Earth's Atmosphere and Weather

 The thin layer of air surrounding the earth—the *atmosphere*—changes continuously. When we use the term *weather,* we are describing the condition of the atmosphere at a given time. That condition may be hot, cold, windy, dry, wet, sunny, or cloudy. The term *climate* is used to describe the total effect of the day-to-day changes in the atmosphere.

Because the earth receives almost all its heat energy from the sun, we can say the sun is the principal cause for changes in the weather. Heat energy from the sun causes the air to warm and move upward, water to evaporate into the atmosphere, and the flow of air parallel to the earth, which we call *wind*. These changes play a part in determining the extent and type of *precipitation* (rain, snow, hail, sleet) that reaches the earth's surface.

Scientists who study the weather and predict weather changes are called *meteorologists*. Every country has meteorologists who gather weather data from a variety of sources, summarize it, record it using various symbols on a weather map, and then make predictions.

Water in the Atmosphere

The percentage a meteorologist finds when the amount of moisture in the air is compared to the amount of moisture the air could hold at a particular temperature is known as the *relative humidity*. When the relative humidity is high, the air contains a great amount of moisture and the evaporation of perspiration is slow, which makes us feel uncomfortably warm. When the temperature in the air drops to a certain point, the air can no longer hold the water vapor in it. The air at this temperature is *saturated*. The temperature at which a given body of air becomes saturated is called the *dew point*. As air rises in the atmosphere, it cools. When the rising air is cooled to its dew point, condensation may occur. Drops of water form when enough molecules of water vapor accumulate around and become attached to a particle of dust in the atmosphere. Billions of tiny droplets of water form a cloud.

Clouds

Have you ever spent part of a warm, summer afternoon watching clouds pass by, perhaps seeing in them images of animals, monsters, relatives, or friends? Scientists observe, study, and group clouds in a very different way.

Low clouds[2] include fog, stratus, stratocumulus, cumulus, and cumulonimbus. The average heights of their bases range from the surface up to 1,980 meters (about 6,500 feet). Low clouds are usually made up entirely of water droplets and are usually quite dense.

Middle clouds include both altocumulus and altostratus, and the average heights of their bases range from 1,980 to 7,000 meters (about 6,500 to 23,000 feet). They are made up of water droplets, ice crystals, or both—usually both—and they exhibit considerable variation in density. In a dense water-droplet cloud, a pilot in flight may be able to see only a few feet, whereas in an ice-crystal cloud, visibility may be as much as a mile.

High clouds are cirrus, cirrocumulus, and cirrostratus. Their bases are generally above 5,030 meters (about 16,500 feet). They are always made up of ice crystals and vary greatly in density. A distinguishing feature of cirriform clouds is the halo they produce around the sun or moon as a result of refraction of the sunlight or moonlight shining through the ice crystals. Lower clouds (altostratus) containing water droplets exhibit the solar- or lunar-corona phenomenon, rather than the halo.

Clouds exhibiting great *vertical development* constitute another major category. This category includes all the low cumulus clouds except the fair-weather cumulus and stratocumulus. The *cumulonimbus,* or "thunderhead," is in a category by itself because it may extend from the very lowest to the very highest levels of the atmosphere and during its life cycle may produce nearly all the other cloud types.

Precipitation

When you think of the word *precipitation,* you probably think of rain or snow. Actually, precipitation includes any water in the atmosphere that reaches the earth. So even *dew,* the condensation of tiny water droplets on cool objects such as grass stems or leaves, is precipitation. *Frost,* which is made when when water vapor changes directly into ice crystals, is also precipitation.

Rain, snow, hail, and sleet are other forms of precipitation. *Rain* is condensed water vapor that falls as a liquid. If the temperature of the atmosphere is low enough, water vapor may change directly into the crystals called *snowflakes.*

A snowflake is usually a six-sided, lacy-patterned product of the direct change of water to a solid. Large snowflakes result from the combination of smaller snowflakes. Surprisingly, snow that falls to the ground can insulate the soil from cold temperatures. The lack of a good snow cover can freeze soil to great depths and destroy plant roots. A good snow cover can protect the soil because there are the numerous pockets of air trapped within it. These air pockets effectively retard the loss of heat from the earth.

Hard, rounded pellets of ice or ice and compacted snow are called *hail*—a phenomenon associated with thunderstorms. If you cut a hailstone in half, you will see that it consists of concentric layers. Water droplets caught in a strong updraft of warm, moist air may be carried into cloudy regions where the temperature is quite low. At this point, the droplets acquire a coating of ice and solidify. They may then fall to a lower cloud region and gather a coating of water. Another strong updraft may carry them back up to a region of lower temperature. The ultimate size of the hailstones depends on many factors, including the number of times this up-and-down cycle is repeated. Eventually, the hailstones become so heavy that an updraft cannot carry them, and they fall to earth.

Some meteorologists think that hail is formed by a much simpler process: Water droplets fall through below-freezing layers of air and pick up extremely cold water, which is transformed into layers of ice. Although the precise way in which hail is formed is under question, its destructive effects are agreed upon. Large hailstorms can beat down crops, break tree branches, destroy roofs, shatter glass, and injure animals and humans.

Sleet, as the term is used by meteorologists, is small particles of clear ice that were originally raindrops. It results from the passing of the raindrops through a layer of cold air. Those who are not meteorologists commonly use the term to describe a mixture of rain and snow.

Violent Weather

The earth is not always a peaceful place, and the same is true of its atmosphere. Under the right conditions, violent weather—including thunderstorms, tornadoes, winter storms, and hurricanes—can have a great impact on the surface of the earth and all who live there.

Thunderstorms

Thunderstorms[3] are generated by temperature imbalances in the atmosphere. They are a violent example of *convection*—the upward and downward movement of air. The cooling of cloud tops or the warming of cloud bases puts warmer, lighter air layers below colder, denser layers. The resulting instability causes connective overturning of the layers, with heavier, denser layers sinking to the bottom and lighter, warmer layers rising rapidly.

On the ground directly beneath the storm system, strong gusts of cold wind from the downdraft and heavy precipitation (rain or hail) that typically mark the storm. Tornadoes may be associated with especially violent thunderstorms.

Lightning   Lightning is an effect of electrification within a thunderstorm. As a thunderstorm develops, interactions of charged particles produce an intense electrical field within the thundercloud. A large positive charge is usually concentrated in the frozen upper layers of the cloud, and a large negative charge along with a smaller positive area is found in the lower portions.

The earth is normally negatively charged with respect to the atmosphere. But as the thunderstorm passes over the ground, the negative charge in the base of the cloud induces a positive charge on the ground below and for several miles around the storm. The ground charge follows the storm like an electrical shadow, growing stronger as the negative cloud charge increases. But air, which is a poor conductor of electricity, insulates the cloud and ground charges, preventing a flow of current until huge electrical charges are built up.

Lightning occurs when the difference between the positive and negative charges—the *electrical potential*—becomes great enough to overcome the resistance of the insulating air and to force a conductive path that will allow current to flow between the two charges. The potential can be as much as 100 million volts. Lightning strokes proceed from cloud to cloud, cloud to ground, or, where high structures are involved, from ground to cloud.

Thunder   Thunder is the sound produced by explosive expansion of air heated by a lightning stroke. When lightning is close by, the thunder sounds like a sharp crack. More distant strokes produce rumbling noises, a result of the sound being refracted and modified by the turbulent environment of a thunderstorm. Because the speed of light is about a million times that of sound, we see a lightning bolt before the sound of the thunder reaches us. This makes it possible to estimate the distance (in miles) to a lightning stroke by counting the number of seconds between seeing lightning and hearing thunder and dividing by five.

Tornadoes

Tornadoes are short-lived local storms containing high-speed winds usually rotating in a counterclockwise direction. The winds are often observable as a funnel attached to a thundercloud. Initially, the funnel is a cloud composed of condensed water vapor. However, when it reaches the ground, it picks up dust and debris that eventually darken the entire funnel. Tornado damage can occur on the ground, even though the funnel does not seem to reach ground level.

Tornadoes occur in many parts of the world, but no area is more favorable to their formation than the Great Plains and Gulf Coast of the United States, and in these areas, no season is free of them. Normally, the number of tornadoes is lowest in December and January and at its peak in May; the months of greatest frequency are April, May, and June.

Winter Storms

In September, the sun leaves the Northern Hemisphere, its perpendicular rays drifting south of the equator. Until the sun's return in March, polar air rules the northern continental atmosphere, pushing back the tropical warmth of summer. It is autumn and then winter, a season broken by intervals of fine weather and by the seasonal parade of winter storms[4]—snow-dumping, ice-covering, blood-chilling paralyzers of cities, trappers of travelers, takers of life, destroyers of property.

Snowstorms   The word *snow* in a forecast without a qualifying word such as *occasional* or *intermittent* means that the fall of snow will probably continue for several hours without letup. Meteorologists use a variety of terms to describe winter storms: *heavy snow, snow flurries, snow squalls, blowing and drifting snow, drifting snow, blizzards, blizzard warnings, severe-blizzard warnings, travelers' warnings,* and *stockmen's warnings.*

Freezing Rain, Freezing Drizzle, and Ice Storms   Freezing rain or freezing drizzle occurs when surface temperatures are below 0°C (32°F). The rain falls in liquid form but freezes upon impact, resulting in an ice glaze on all exposed objects. The occurrence of freezing rain or drizzle is often called an *ice storm* when a substantial glaze layer accumulates. Ice forming on exposed objects generally ranges from a thin glaze to coatings of 2 or 3 centimeters (about 1 inch), but much thicker deposits have been observed.

Ice storms are sometimes referred to incorrectly as *sleet storms.* Sleet can be easily identified as frozen raindrops (ice pellets) that bounce when hitting the ground or other objects. Sleet does not stick to trees and wires, but in sufficient depth, it does cause hazardous driving conditions.

The terms *ice storm, freezing rain,* and *freezing drizzle* warn the public that a coating of ice is expected on the ground and on other exposed surfaces. The qualifying term *heavy* is used to indicate an ice coating whose weight will cause significant damage to trees, overhead wires, and the like. Damage will be greater if the freezing rain or drizzle is accompanied by high winds.

Cold Waves   Cold waves are another common form of violent weather. A *cold-wave warning* indicates an expected rapid fall in temperature within a 24-hour period that will require substantially increased protection to agricultural, industrial, commercial, and social activities. The minimum temperatures required to justify cold-wave warnings vary with the season and with geographic location. Regardless of the month or the section of the country, a cold-wave warning is a red-flag alert to the public that during a forthcoming forecast period a *change to very cold weather will require greater-than-normal protective measures.*

Hurricanes

Nothing in the atmosphere is quite like a hurricane.[5] Even seen by sensors on spacecraft thousands of miles above the earth, the uniqueness of these powerful, tightly coiled storms is clear. They are not the largest storm systems in the atmosphere or the most violent, but they combine those qualities as no other phenomenon does, as if they were designed to be engines of death and destruction.

The term *hurricanes* echoes colonial Spanish and Caribbean Indian words for "evil spirits" and "big winds." The storms are products of the tropical ocean and atmosphere, powered by heat from the sea and steered by the easterly trades, the temperate westerlies, and their own fierce energy. Around their tranquil core, winds blow with lethal velocity, the ocean develops an inundating surge, and, as they move ashore, tornadoes may descend from the advancing bands of thunderclouds.

Hurricanes have a single benefit: They are a major source of water for the land beneath their track. Perhaps there are other hidden benefits, as well, but the main consequences for people are hardship and tragedy.

Tomorrow's Weather

Because changes in the conditions of the atmosphere (the weather) tend to move in regular patterns above the earth's surface, the weather we will experience tomorrow will likely be much the same as the weather someplace else today. As a result, the most important tool that the weather forecaster has is the weather map. He or she studies the most recent weather maps and tries to predict both the strength of the disturbances observed and their path. The forecaster also studies the map to see where and how new disturbances are being formed.

Meteorologists in North America know that in the middle latitudes, the upper air moves from west to east. Storms tend to enter from the west, pass across the middle of the continent, and move toward the North Atlantic. Thus, the weather that is likely to affect a local area is predicted on the basis of the larger-scale weather movement depicted on weather maps. The map is created by first recording symbols representing the data gathered at weather stations—pressure, temperature, humidity, wind direction, wind velocity, and cloud types. Meteorologists use a variety of instruments to collect this data. The pressure of the air above us is measured with a barometer. The wind vane is used to determine the direction of the wind at the earth's surface. Wind speed is measured with an anemometer, an instrument consisting of a set of cups mounted so that they can easily be rotated by the wind. The amount of moisture in the air is determined by a hygrometer. The amount of moisture that reaches the ground as precipitation is measured by rain and snow gauges.

The characteristics of the air high above the earth are commonly determined by the use of radiosondes. These are miniature radio transmitters to which are attached a variety of weather instruments. Radiosondes are carried aloft by balloons or small rockets. Data gathered by the instruments are transmitted back to earth by the radio transmitter.

In recent years, weather satellites have greatly improved the accuracy of weather forecasts. Their photographs of the clouds over the earth's surface reveal a great deal about weather phenomena. Such satellite photography, when used with information about air temperature, atmospheric pressure, and humidity, is of great assistance to meteorologists as they develop their weather forecasts for a particular area.

Summary Outline

I. The earth consists of various layers; the outermost layer is the crust, which is divided into seven crustal plates.
   A. The crust of the earth has undergone numerous gradual and violent changes during the earth's history.
   B. The land surface of the earth is composed of a variety of rocks, minerals, and soils.
   C. Fossil evidence of life forms that have existed in various periods of the earth's history has been found.
   D. The ocean floor has many features, including the continental shelf, continental slope, and ocean ridges.
   E. Ocean currents are the result of the sun warming the water and the earth's rotation.
   F. Humankind depends on the oceans as a source of food and other natural resources.

II. The atmosphere is a thin layer of constantly moving air that surrounds the earth.
   A. Water vapor in the atmosphere sometimes condenses to form clouds.
   B. Some water vapor in the atmosphere condenses and falls to earth as precipitation.
   C. Thunderstorms, tornadoes, winter storms, and hurricanes are examples of violent weather phenomena.
   D. Barometers, anemometers, and hygrometers are some of the instruments used to measure weather phenomena.
   E. Using information from these instruments and weather maps, scientists are able to make short-term and long-term weather forecasts.

Notes

1. The discussion of volcanoes was excerpted with minor modifications from *Volcanoes*, a pamphlet prepared by the U.S. Geological Survey, U.S. Department of the Interior. This pamphlet is available for purchase from the Superintendent of Documents, Government Printing Office, Washington, DC 20402.

2. The discussion of clouds was excerpted with minor modifications from *Clouds*, a pamphlet prepared by and available from the Environmental Science Service Administration, U.S. Department of Commerce. This pamphlet may be purchased from the Superintendent of Documents, Government Printing Office, Washington, DC 20013.

3. The discussion of thunderstorms was excerpted with minor modifications from *Thunderstorms*, a pamphlet prepared by the U.S. Department of Commerce. This pamphlet (stock number NOAA/PA 77027) may be purchased from the Superintendent of Documents, Government Printing Office, Washington, DC 20402.

4. The discussion of winter storms was excerpted with minor modifications from *Winter Storms*, a pamphlet prepared by the National Oceanic and Atmospheric Administration, U.S. Department of Commerce. This pamphlet (stock number NOAA/PL 70018) may be purchased from the Superintendent of Documents, Government Printing Office, Washington, DC 20402.

5. The discussion of hurricanes was excerpted with minor modifications from a pamphlet prepared by the U.S. Department of Commerce. This pamphlet (stock number NOAA/PA 76008) may be purchased from the Superintendent of Documents, Government Printing Office, Washington, DC 20402.

11B

The Earth's Surface, Atmosphere, and Weather

Attention Getters, Discovery Activities, and Demonstrations

A Look Ahead

Attention Getters for Young Learners

How Are Rocks the Same and Different? [ESS 1]

What Is in Soil? [ESS 1]

How Does a Thermometer Change on Hot and Cold Days? [ESS 3]

Attention Getters for Middle-Level Learners

What Crushed the Can? [ESS 4]

What Pushed the Egg into the Bottle? [ESS 4]

Can We Make Fog? [S&T 4]

Discovery Activities for Young Learners

How to Make a Fossil [S&T 1]

Weather or Not [ESS 3]

Discovery Activities for Middle-Level Learners

How Do Layers of Sediment Form? [ESS 4]

Quakes and Shakes: An Earthquake Watch [ESS 4]

How to Find the Dew Point [ESS 4]

Demonstrations for Young Learners

Indoor Rainmaking [ESS 3]

Whose Fault Is It? [ESS 3]

Demonstrations for Middle-Level Learners

You've Heard of Rock Musicians, but Have You Heard of Rock Magicians? [ESS 4]

How to Find the Relative Humidity [ESS 4]

How Are Rocks the Same and Different? [ESS 1]

MATERIALS	3 locally gathered rocks 3 sheets of white paper 1 large nail

For Young Learners

MOTIVATING QUESTIONS

- Do any of the rocks look or feel like any of the other rocks?
- How can we tell if one rock is harder or softer than the others?

DIRECTIONS

1. Bring to class or take the class outside to find three rocks that look and feel different.
2. Display one rock on each sheet of paper, and have children come forward to make observations. As they do, write their observations on the board.
3. Scratch each rock with the nail, and have the children observe that some rocks are harder than others, that some rock particles scrape off, and that the scraped-off particles are of different sizes and colors.

EXPLANATION/ SCIENCE CONTENT FOR THE TEACHER

The earth's crust is made of different types of rocks. Rocks are different because of the materials within them and the ways in which they are formed. Wind, water, and ice break rocks into smaller pieces. Soil is made of small particles of rock as well as other material.

What Is in Soil? [ESS 1]

MATERIALS

1 cup of potting soil
1 cup of top soil from outdoors
1 cup of sand (aquarium sand will do)
3 sheets of white paper
3 hand lenses (magnifying glasses)

Place materials on a table so individual children can observe the soils.

MOTIVATING QUESTIONS

- Will these soils look the same or different when we examine them with a hand lens?
- What do you think we will find in the soils?

DIRECTIONS

1. Write the following terms on the board: *sand, outdoor soil, potting soil.* Read and pronounce each term with the class.
2. Sprinkle a small amount of each type of soil on a sheet of paper, and have the children use hand lenses to examine the soils.
3. As the children make observations, write them on the board under the appropriate term. ***Note:*** You may wish to sprinkle some soil particles on an overhead transparency and project the image.

EXPLANATION/ SCIENCE CONTENT FOR THE TEACHER

Over long periods of time, rocks are broken into tiny particles. These particles, mixed with other materials, make up soil. Although sand gathered from a shoreline will contain pieces of shell and other debris, soil is mostly rock particles. Top soil contains amounts of sand, water, air, and decayed organic material. Potting soil usually contains less sand and more organic material than top soil. The organic material allows it to retain water for long periods of time.

How Does a Thermometer Change on Hot and Cold Days? [ESS 3]

MATERIALS

1 outdoor thermometer containing red liquid
3 rubber bands
1 glass of cool water
1 glass of hot water

MOTIVATING QUESTIONS

Display the thermometer and ask:
- What do we call this?
- Where have you seen thermometers?

DIRECTIONS

1. Wrap a rubber band around the thermometer at the level of the liquid.
2. Put the base of the thermometer in cool water, and have volunteers observe the new level of the liquid. Put a second rubber band at this level.
3. Have the children predict how the level will change when the thermometer is placed in warm water; then place the thermometer in warm water and mark the level of the liquid with the third rubber band.
4. Discuss how looking at an outdoor thermometer might help people decide what to wear on hot and cold days.

EXPLANATION/ SCIENCE CONTENT FOR THE TEACHER

A thermometer registers the temperature of its surroundings. The level of liquid rises or falls due to increases or decreases in its volume as a result of heating or cooling. The red liquid in a typical household thermometer is tinted alcohol. Some thermometers, however, contain mercury, a silvery liquid metal.

What Crushed the Can? [ESS 4]

MATERIALS

2 empty soda cans
Tongs or heat-resistant potholder mitts
Ice cubes in a bowl of water
Access to an alcohol burner, stove top, or electric hot plate

For Middle-Level Learners

ATTENTION GETTERS

ATTENTION GETTERS

<table>
<tr><td>*MOTIVATING QUESTIONS*</td><td>• What do you think will happen if we put a little water in the can, heat the can, and plunge it into the ice water?
• What do you think causes this to happen?</td></tr>
<tr><td>*DIRECTIONS*</td><td>1. Add about one-fourth of a cup of tap water to the empty can.
2. Heat the can over the heat source until the water boils and steam is visible.
3. Using tongs or mitts, drop the can into the ice water.</td></tr>
<tr><td>*EXPLANATION/ SCIENCE CONTENT FOR THE TEACHER*</td><td>The heated water changes to steam. The steam forces some of the air out of the can. When the can is dropped into ice water, the steam in the can condenses and the pressure within the can is reduced. Atmospheric pressure (the pressure of the air outside the can) crushes the can.</td></tr>
</table>

What Pushed the Egg into the Bottle? [ESS 4]

<table>
<tr><td>*MATERIALS*</td><td>1 cooled, peeled, hard-boiled egg
1 glass gallon jug or old-fashioned milk bottle
1 sheet of paper about 8 cm square
Matches
Tongs</td></tr>
<tr><td>*MOTIVATING QUESTIONS*</td><td>• What do you think will happen if we put the egg on the empty bottle?
• What do you think will happen if we put the egg on the bottle after we have burned some paper in the bottle?</td></tr>
<tr><td>*DIRECTIONS*</td><td>1. Put the egg on the open bottle top with the narrow end down, and ask the second motivating question.
2. After listening to the predictions, remove the egg, light the paper with the match, drop it (using the tongs) into the bottle, and quickly replace the egg. The egg will be pushed into the bottle.</td></tr>
<tr><td>*EXPLANATION/ SCIENCE CONTENT FOR THE TEACHER*</td><td>The burning paper heats the air within the bottle, causing it to expand. The egg acts as a valve, allowing some but not all of the expanding air to leave the bottle around the narrow end of the egg. Thus, the air in the bottle is at a lower pressure than the air outside the bottle. The pressure of the air outside of the bottle (atmospheric pressure) slowly forces the egg into the bottle. ***Safety Note:*** Be sure to point out to the children the safety precautions you employ as you use a match and handle the burning paper. Explain that they should not try this activity at home without adult supervision.</td></tr>
</table>

Can We Make Fog? [S&T 4]

MATERIALS	2 resealable sandwich bags containing ice cubes 2 empty, clean plastic 2 liter soda bottles with labels removed 1 funnel 1 electric tea kettle or other source of very hot water 1 flashlight
MOTIVATING QUESTIONS	• What do you think will happen when we put a bag of ice cubes on top of the bottle with cool water? • What do you think will happen when we put a bag of ice cubes on top of the bottle of hot water?
DIRECTIONS	1. Add cold water to one bottle until it is about four-fifths full. Fill the second bottle with hot water to the same level. 2. Cover the top of each bottle with a sandwich bag containing ice cubes, and have the children predict the changes that will occur within the bottle. 3. Use the flashlight to illuminate the inside of each bottle. The children should be able to observe fog above the surface of the hot water. You may wish to darken the room for this part of the demonstration.
EXPLANATION/ SCIENCE CONTENT FOR THE TEACHER	Some of the hot water evaporates into the air above it. When that air is cooled by the bag of ice cubes, the water vapor condenses into tiny droplets. These droplets are in fact a cloud. When a cloud is formed at the earth's surface above land or water, it is called *fog*. Depending on the room's temperature and other factors, the children may be able to see some fog above the hot water even without the use of the sandwich bag with ice cubes.

How to Make a Fossil [S&T 1]

OBJECTIVES	• The children will create fossils from samples of plant material. • The children will explain the process by which fossils are produced in nature.
SCIENCE PROCESSES EMPHASIZED	Hypothesizing Experimenting Communicating

MATERIALS FOR EACH CHILD OR GROUP	Aluminum foil pie plate Water
	Plastic spoon Vaseline
	Assortment of plant materials, Plaster of paris
	   including portions of a carrot,
	   a leaf, and a twig

For Young Learners

DISCOVERY ACTIVITIES

D I S C O V E R Y   A C T I V I T I E S

MOTIVATION   Be sure to have two or three real fossils on hand, if possible, or reference books with pictures of various fossils. Display the fossils or pictures of the fossils, and have children make observations about their characteristics. Encourage the children to discuss how the fossils may have been formed. Tell the children that they will create their own fossils during this activity.

DIRECTIONS

1. Have the children coat each portion of the plants they are using with a thin layer of vaseline.
2. Have the children mix the plaster of paris with water in the bottom of the pie plate until they obtain a thick, smooth mixture.
3. Have the children gently press the plant material into the upper surface of the plaster of paris and set the plaster aside to harden.
4. Bring the children together for a group discussion. Emphasize that what they have done represents *one* way in which fossils are formed; that is, plant or animal material falls into sediment, making an imprint. If the sediment then hardens into rock, the imprint will remain even though the organic matter decays.
5. When the plaster is dry and they have removed the plant material, the children will be able to observe a permanent imprint.
6. Establish a display of reference books showing pictures of fossils. Have the children look at pictures of fossils and hypothesize about how they were formed.

KEY DISCUSSION QUESTIONS

1. Have you ever found any fossils or seen any fossils on display? If so, what were they like and where did you see them? *Answers will vary.*
2. The fossils you made are known as *molds.* How could a scientist use a mold fossil to make something that looked like the object that formed the mold? *He or she could use something like clay to press against the mold fossil. The surface of the clay would take the shape of the original material.*

SCIENCE CONTENT FOR THE TEACHER   A fossil is any preserved part or trace of something that lived in the past. Leaves, stems, bones, and even footprints have been preserved as fossils. Some fossils are formed when water passing over and through portions of animal or plant remains deposits minerals that replace the original materials. In other cases, animal and plant remains are buried in sediment. An imprint of the shape is left in mud even when the material decays, and if the mud hardens and turns to rock, the imprint is preserved. This type of impression, which the children have replicated in this activity, is known as a *mold.*

EXTENSION   *Science:* You may wish to encourage some children to do an activity that will extend their knowledge of fossil molds to fossil casts. They can replicate the formation of a cast fossil by mixing plaster of paris outdoors and filling in animal tracks with it.

Weather or Not [ESS 3]

OBJECTIVES	• The children will observe and record daily weather conditions.
	• The children will compare their observations with information on weather maps.

*SCIENCE
PROCESSES
EMPHASIZED*

Observing
Measuring
Comparing

*MATERIALS FOR
EACH CHILD
OR GROUP*

Outdoor thermometer marked in Celsius
Newspaper weather map for the days of the activity
Legend from weather map showing symbols and meanings

MOTIVATION

Create a weather chart on the chalkboard that has columns for temperature, cloud, wind, and precipitation data. While the children watch, fill the columns of the chart with your personal observations of the present weather, using the appropriate symbols from a weather map. Challenge the children to guess what is meant by each symbol. After some discussion, explain what each symbol represents and indicate that the children will use these symbols on the charts they make.

DIRECTIONS

1. After giving the children some time to practice drawing each weather symbol that you have explained, have them make blank charts.
2. For the next two to three days, have the groups take their charts to some location on the school grounds where they can make weather observations. They should use weather symbols to record their observations. **Safety Note:** Be sure that each group is visible to you in a safe location.
3. You can generate additional excitement if you have the children compare the observations from their weather charts with weather maps for the same days.

*KEY
DISCUSSION
QUESTIONS*

1. What kinds of measurements can we make of weather conditions outside? *Temperature, whether it's raining, how hard the wind is blowing, and whether there are clouds in the sky.*
2. How are clouds different from one another? *Some are white and puffy, some are flat and gray, some are high in the sky, and some you can see through.*

*SCIENCE
CONTENT FOR
THE TEACHER*

There are three major types of clouds: *cirrus, cumulus,* and *stratus.* Clouds that are high in the sky and wispy are cirrus clouds. Cumulous clouds are often billowing with white tops. Stratus clouds are sheets of gray clouds that are close to the ground. Depending on your climate, precipitation may take the form of rain or snow. Temperature varies from place to place on a given day as well as from day to day.

DISCOVERY ACTIVITIES

EXTENSION   *Science/Art:* Encourage some children to create a cloud display. After consulting reference books for pictures of various types of clouds, they can use cotton balls, cotton batting, and Styrofoam to create their displays.

How Do Layers of Sediment Form? [ESS 4]

For Middle-Level Learners

OBJECTIVES
- The children make a model and use it to discover the order in which particles of different sizes settle to the bottom.
- The children make drawings to document the results of their experimentation and discuss their results.

SCIENCE
PROCESSES
EMPHASIZED
Observing
Experimenting
Communicating

MATERIALS FOR
EACH CHILD
OR GROUP

Large glass jar with lid	Pebbles
Source of water	Gravel
Soil	Sand

MOTIVATION   This is a good activity to do before the children begin studying how various types of rocks are formed. Display at the front of the room or at a learning station all of the materials in the materials list. Ask the children to guess what this activity will be about. After some initial discussion, focus their attention on the soil, pebbles, gravel, and sand. Ask them to think about what would happen if a stream carrying these materials slowed down. Once the children have begun to think about the materials settling into layers on the bottom of a stream or river, begin the activity.

DIRECTIONS
1. Have each group fill one-third of a large glass jar with equal amounts of soil, pebbles, gravel, and sand.
2. Have the groups fill the jars the rest of the way with water and screw on the lids.
3. Have the groups shake the jars so that all the materials are thoroughly stirred in the water.
4. Ask the groups to let the materials settle.
5. Have the groups observe the settling and then make drawings of the layers they observe.
6. Engage the class in a discussion of the results of the activity.

KEY
DISCUSSION
QUESTIONS
1. Which of the materials settled to the bottom of the jar first? *The gravel.*
2. How can you explain the results in this activity? *The large pieces of gravel settled first because they were heavier than the other materials. The heaviest materials are at the bottom, and the lightest materials are at the top.*

3. What type of rock is formed from layers of earth materials that settle out of water? *Sedimentary*.

SCIENCE CONTENT FOR THE TEACHER   When water moves across the surface of the earth, it picks up tiny rocks, pebbles, grains of sand, and soil. This flow of water and materials eventually reaches streams, rivers, and the ocean, and the particles within the water become known as *sediment*. Whenever a flow of water is slowed, some of the sediment is deposited on the bottom of the flow. Layers of sediment pile up under the water. After hundreds of years have passed, the weight of these layers may have become so great that the bottom layers are turned into rock.

EXTENSION   *Science/Social Studies:* Some children may be encouraged to do research on the effect of moving water on farmland. The loss of topsoil due to water erosion is a significant threat to agriculture. Through research, these children will find that there are many government agencies that assist farmers who are trying to protect their soil from erosion.

Quakes and Shakes: An Earthquake Watch [ESS 4]

OBJECTIVES
- The children will be able to locate those regions of the earth that have more earthquake activity than others.
- The children will study earthquake occurrence data and make hypotheses to explain any patterns they observe.

SCIENCE PROCESSES EMPHASIZED   Interpreting data
Making hypotheses

MATERIALS FOR EACH CHILD OR GROUP   *Note:* This is a long-term activity in which children plot data from current government information on earthquakes. Thus, you will need to order the the *Preliminary Determination of Epicenters: Monthly Listing* from the Superintendent of Documents, Government Printing Office, Washington, DC 20402.

Copies of the epicenter charts
World map with latitude and longitude marked
Access to an atlas
Paper
Pencil

MOTIVATION   Ask the children if they have ever been to a part of the country that has a lot of earthquake activity, such as San Francisco. If any of them have, encourage them to discuss anything they may have heard about earthquakes from persons who live there. If no one has, engage the children in a discussion about earthquakes. Stress their cause and possible hazards. Explain that scientists are able to study information about previous earthquakes to predict the general locations of future earthquakes. Tell the children that they will be working with some of the same information that scientists use. Then display the collection of epicenter charts and the world maps.

DIRECTIONS

1. Give a map and copies of the epicenter charts to each child or group. Explain that the information on the charts shows where scientists believe the source of an earthquake was; then explain the information. Although there is a lot of information on each chart, the children should work with only the date, time of eruption, latitude, longitude, region, depth, and *magnitude.* Explain that magnitude indicates the strength of the earthquake.

2. Have the children refer to an atlas to find the specific location of each earthquake and then mark their copy of the world map with a symbol for the earthquake. They should plot all earthquakes with a source from 0 to 69 kilometers deep with one symbol, 70 to 299 kilometers with another symbol, and more than 299 kilometers with a third symbol.

3. When they have recorded data from the epicenter chart, you may wish to have a discussion of the patterns they observe.

4. Have the children maintain their maps for a few months and repeat the activity each time you receive a monthly epicenter chart.

KEY DISCUSSION QUESTIONS

1. Do you see any pattern on your map that tells you what parts of the earth seem to have the most earthquakes? Where are those places? *Yes, along the western portion of the Pacific Ocean, from the Mediterranean Sea across Asia, and along the west coast of North and South America.*

2. What problems do you think are caused by earthquakes? *Answers will vary. Some may include comments such as the following: buildings may fall; earthquakes in the ocean may cause great waves.*

SCIENCE CONTENT FOR THE TEACHER

An earthquake is the shaking of the ground caused by the shifting of the plates that make up the earth's surface and the release of pressure through faults in the earth's crust, which results in the movement of blocks of rocks past each other. The vibrations at ground level are sometimes strong enough to do structural damage to buildings and threaten life. The shaking of the ocean floor can produce gigantic waves that roll across the ocean. Scientists record the presence of an earthquake with an instrument known as a seismograph. To pinpoint the source of an earthquake's vibrations, scientists gather data from seismographs all over the world. The epicenter is thought to be directly above the place where the initial rock fractures occurred. When the locations of epicenters are plotted on a map, they roughly mark the places on the earth where crustal plates grind against each other.

EXTENSION   *Science/Social Studies:* Some children may wish to research the effects of the San Francisco earthquake of 1906. They will be able to find pictures in encyclopedias showing how the city looked after the earthquake. Ask the children what effects the earthquake likely had on community life immediately after it occurred and its effect after a few years had passed.

How to Find the Dew Point [ESS 4]

OBJECTIVES
- The children will find the temperature at which water vapor in the air condenses.
- The children will analyze their data and offer an explanation of how changes in treatment of moisture in the air will affect dew point readings.

SCIENCE
PROCESSES
EMPHASIZED

Observing
Gathering data
Interpreting

MATERIALS FOR
EACH CHILD
OR GROUP

Empty soup can with one end cut out
Outdoor thermometer that will fit into the soup can
Supply of ice cubes
Rag

MOTIVATION   Begin a discussion with the children about the invisible water vapor present in the air. Ask them if they have ever observed any evidence of the presence of water vapor in the air. They will probably share such observations as the steaming up of mirrors in bathrooms and the steam that seems to come out of their mouths when they breathe on a cold day. Tell the children that water vapor in the air is usually not observed because the air temperature is sufficiently high to keep the water vapor a gas. As a gas, water vapor is invisible. Display the equipment that will be used for this activity and tell the children that they will be using it to find the temperature at which the water vapor presently in the air will condense. Explain that this temperature is known as the *dew point*. The dew point is the point at which water vapor changes from a gas to a liquid.

DIRECTIONS   1. Distribute the soup cans to the children and have them remove the labels, scrub the outside of the cans with soap and water, and polish the surfaces.

Checking the dew point

2. Demonstrate the following procedure for the children: Fill the shiny can about two-thirds full of water at room temperature, and place a thermometer in it. Then add small amounts of ice, and stir the mixture until the ice melts. Have the children observe the outside of the can as you add small amounts of ice and stir. Eventually, the outside will begin to lose its shine, and a layer of moisture will be observable.

3. Have the children do this activity on their own. Ask them to keep track of the temperature on the thermometer and to pay close attention to the outside of the can as the temperature drops. Stress the importance of observing the precise temperature at which the film forms.

4. After the children have found the dew point inside the classroom, you may wish to have them find it outside. When the children have completed the activity, begin a class discussion of their results. Be sure the children understand that the drier the air, the lower the temperature must be in order for moisture to condense.

SCIENCE FOR THE TEACHER

The air's capacity to hold moisture is determined by its temperature. The The temperature at which air can no longer hold water vapor is known as the *dew point*. Condensation, the change from water as a gas to water as a liquid, is usually observable in the atmosphere as dew, fog, or clouds. Condensation occurs when the air is saturated with water vapor. Saturation occurs when the temperature of the air reaches its dew point. In this activity, the air near the outside surface of the can is cooled to its dew point. The moisture in that layer of air condenses on the available surface—the outside of the can.

KEY DISCUSSION QUESTIONS

1. Why do you think we use a shiny can for this activity? *It makes it easy to tell when the moisture condenses. The moisture makes the shiny can look dull.*

2. Why do you think knowing the dew point might be important to weather forecasters? *If they know the dew point, they will know the temperature at which the moisture in the air will condense. Then they can more easily predict when fog, clouds, or rain will happen.*

3. Why do you think dew forms only at night? *During the night, the temperature of the air falls because the earth is not receiving sunlight. Sometimes the temperature falls so low that the dew point is reached. When this happens, the moisture condenses on grass and on the leaves and branches of plants.*

EXTENSION

Science/Math: You may wish to have some children find the dew point with both Celsius and Fahrenheit thermometers. After they have done this, they can use conversion charts to be sure the dew point expressed in the number of degrees Celsius is equivalent to that expressed in the number of degrees Fahrenheit.

Indoor Rainmaking[1] [ESS 3]

OBJECTIVES	• The children will observe the production of rain. • The children will explain how the rainmaking model can be used to illustrate the water cycle.

For Young Learners

SCIENCE PROCESSES EMPHASIZED	Observing Inferring Explaining

MATERIALS	Hot plate or stove Teakettle	Large pot Water	Ice cubes

MOTIVATION Show the materials to the children, and ask how the materials could be used to make a model that shows how rain forms. After some discussion, they will be ready to observe the demonstration and follow the path of the water. You may wish to have a volunteer assist you.

DIRECTIONS
1. Place water in the teakettle and begin to heat it. As the water is heating, put the ice cubes in the pot.
2. When the water in the teakettle is boiling, hold the pot with the ice cubes above the steam emerging from the teakettle. Have children observe the formation of water droplets on the bottom of the pot.
3. Have the children note when the water droplets become large enough to fall.
4. Using the questions below, discuss the rainmaking process as a model illustrating the water cycle.

KEY DISCUSSION QUESTIONS
1. What do you think the teakettle of boiling water stands for in the model? *Oceans and lakes.*
2. How does water from the oceans and lakes get into the atmosphere? *The sun heats the water and it evaporates.*
3. Where are the clouds in our model? *The steam stands for the clouds.*
4. Rainmaking is part of the water cycle. What do you think scientists mean when they talk about the water cycle? *Water is always moving. Water that leaves the lakes and oceans moves into the air. Water that is in the air forms clouds and sometimes falls to the earth. Rain, snow, sleet, and hail fall onto the land and oceans. Water that reaches the land flows back into the oceans and lakes.*

SCIENCE CONTENT FOR THE TEACHER Water on the earth is continually recycled. The path that water takes in nature is known as the *water cycle*. Water that evaporates from oceans, lakes, and rivers enters the atmosphere. Precipitation forms when this water vapor accumulates around dust particles at low temperatures and high altitudes. The water then returns to earth.

EXTENSION   *Science/Language Arts:* Some children may wish to use this demonstration as a starting point for writing poetry about the principal form of precipitation in their area. They could write their poetry on large sheets of paper suitable for display.

Whose Fault Is It? [ESS 3]

OBJECTIVES
- The children will observe the occurrence of folds and faults in simulated rock layers.
- The children will infer the causes of changes in rock layers.

SCIENCE PROCESSES EMPHASIZED
Observing
Inferring

MATERIALS
2 blocks of wood
4 sticks of modeling clay, each a different color

MOTIVATION
Ask the children how you could use clay to make rock layers. Flatten each stick of clay into a strip that is about 1 centimeter (less than 1/2 inch) thick and 8 to 10 centimeters (about 3 to 4 inches) wide.

DIRECTIONS
1. Place the clay strips on top of one another. Ask the children to guess whether the strips represent sedimentary, igneous, or metamorphic rocks.
2. Gently press the wood blocks against the ends of the clay layers, and have the children observe changes.
3. Eventually, small cracks will appear on the layers, and the layers will be forced into a hump. *Note:* If the clay is too soft or too warm, the fractures will not occur. You may wish to allow the layers to dry or cool for a day before performing this part of the demonstration.

KEY DISCUSSION QUESTIONS
1. If the clay layers were layers of rock, which layer would probably be the youngest? Why? *The top one. The material in it was deposited last.*
2. What causes the bends and breaks in real rock layers? *Answers will vary. Some children may be aware that the pushing together of the plates of the earth's crust produces great forces that change and fracture rock layers.*
3. Do you think that breaks in the rock layers might allow molten rock to move toward the earth's surface? Why? *Yes. The molten rock can flow up through the cracks because there is nothing to hold it back.*

SCIENCE CONTENT FOR THE TEACHER
Layers of sedimentary rock provide important clues about the relative ages of rocks. Top layers are *usually* younger than lower layers. Sometimes, however, layers of rocks are turned upside down as a result of the collusion of the crustal plates and the movement of molten rock beneath the surface.

EXTENSION *Science/Art:* You may wish to have children construct detailed models of various types of faults described in reference books.

You've Heard of Rock Musicians, but Have You Heard of Rock Magicians? [ESS 4]

OBJECTIVES
- The children will observe one unusual characteristic in each of five rocks.
- The children will describe each characteristic observed.
- The children will name each of the rocks used in the demonstration.

For Middle-Level Learners

SCIENCE PROCESSES EMPHASIZED
Observing
Communicating

MATERIALS
Samples of the following rocks: pumice, anthracite, asbestos, calcite, willemite (or any other rock that will fluoresce)
Bowl of water
Sheet of paper
Matches
White vinegar or any dilute acid
Any ultraviolet-light source (you may be able to borrow one from a high school earth science teacher)

Optional: bow tie, magic wand

Very optional: top hat and/or cape

MOTIVATION
Because of the nature of this demonstration, it will take little to get the children's attention. You may wish to be the rock magician yourself, or you may happen to have a child who would be perfect for the part! Be sure that all the children have a good view of what is to transpire.

DIRECTIONS
1. The rock magician should use the materials in the list to demonstrate the following:
   a. The floating rock: Pumice will float in water.
   b. The writing rock: Anthracite will write on paper.
   c. The rock that can resist flame: Asbestos fibers will not burn.

A rock magician

d. The fizzing rock: A few drops of vinegar will cause calcite to fizz.

e. The fluorescent rock: With the room darkened, the willemite will fluoresce when placed under ultraviolet light.

2. Before each demonstration, the magician should name the rock, spell it, and write its name on the chalkboard. The children will thereby learn the name of each rock displayed.

3. Have the children write down their observations.

KEY DISCUSSION QUESTIONS

1. Why do you think geologists are interested in the special characteristics of these rocks? *They can tell a lot about what the rock is made of if it does certain things.*

2. Why do you think the pumice floated? *It has a lot of air trapped in it.*

3. Do you think the material in your pencils might be something like the anthracite? Why? *Yes, both can make marks on paper.* **Note:** The material in pencils these days is not lead but graphite. Graphite is essentially carbon. Anthracite is also carbon.

SCIENCE CONTENT FOR THE TEACHER

Pumice is magma (molten rock) that trapped bubbles of steam or gas when it was thrown out of a volcano in liquid form. When magma solidifies, it is honeycombed with gas-bubble holes. This gives it the buoyancy to float on water. *Anthracite* is a type of coal that results from the partial decomposition of plants. The carbon in the plants is the primary constituent of anthracite and other forms of coal. *Asbestos* is the popular name of the mineral chrysotile. The silky fibers of asbestos can be woven into a yarn that is used in brake linings and in heat- and fire-retardant fabrics. *Calcite* is a mineral found in such rocks as limestone and marble. Geologists test for its presence by placing a few drops of a warm acid on the rock under study. If calcite is present, carbon dioxide gas will be released with a fizz by the chemical reaction. *Willemite* is a mineral that fluoresces; that is, it gives off light when exposed to ultraviolet light. Some other minerals, generally available from science supply companies, that can be used to demonstrate fluorescence are calcite, tremolite, fluorite, and scapolite.

EXTENSION

Science/Social Studies: You may wish to follow this demonstration with a map or study exercise in which the children find out where the various rocks come from. They will need some earth science reference books and an atlas.

How to Find the Relative Humidity [ESS 4]

OBJECTIVES

• The children will observe how to construct a wet/dry bulb hygrometer.

• The children will measure the relative humidity.

SCIENCE PROCESSES EMPHASIZED

Observing

Using numbers

MATERIALS 2 identical Celsius thermometers
Small piece of gauze
Small rubber band
Baby food jar full of water at room temperature
Small board or piece of heavy cardboard
Relative humidity table

MOTIVATION Ask the children if they have ever heard the term *relative humidity*. After some discussion, indicate that the term represents a comparison of the amount of water in the air to the amount of water the air could hold at the present temperature. Tell the children that they are about to observe how to construct an instrument that will permit them to find the relative humidity.

DIRECTIONS 1. With the help of a student volunteer, tape both thermometers about 6 centimeters (about 2 inches) apart on a piece of cardboard. The bulb end of one thermometer should extend 6 centimeters beyond the edge of the cardboard.

Relative humidity expressed as a percentage

Dry Bulb Reading (°C)	Difference between Wet Bulb Reading and Dry Bulb Reading (°C)									
	1	2	3	4	5	6	7	8	9	10
0	81	64	46	29	13					
2	84	68	52	37	22	7				
4	85	71	57	43	29	16				
6	86	73	60	48	35	24	11			
8	87	75	63	51	40	29	19	8		
10	88	77	66	55	44	34	24	15	6	
12	89	78	68	58	48	39	29	21	12	
14	90	79	70	60	51	42	34	26	18	10
16	90	81	71	63	54	46	38	30	23	15
18	91	82	73	65	57	49	41	34	27	20
20	91	83	74	66	59	51	44	38	31	24
22	92	83	76	68	61	54	47	41	34	28
24	92	84	77	69	62	56	49	44	37	31
26	92	85	78	71	64	58	51	47	40	34
28	93	85	78	72	65	59	53	48	42	37
30	93	86	79	73	67	61	55	50	44	39

2. Wrap the extending end in gauze. Fasten the gauze with a rubber band, but leave a tail of gauze that can be inserted into the baby food jar.

3. Place the tail in the baby food jar filled with water, and moisten the gauze around the bulb. The tail will serve as a wick to keep the bulb moist.

4. Fan both thermometers vigorously. In a few minutes, the volunteer will observe that the thermometers display different temperatures. Use the wet/dry bulb table to find the relative humidity.

KEY DISCUSSION QUESTIONS

1. Why do you think the wet bulb showed a lower reading than the dry bulb? *Water evaporated from the gauze and cooled the thermometer.*

2. Would more or less water evaporate on a drier day? *More, because water enters the air faster if there is little water in the air to begin with.*

SCIENCE CONTENT FOR THE TEACHER

Hygrometers are used to measure relative humidity. The evaporation of water lowers the wet bulb temperature. The amount of lowering depends on a variety of factors, including the amount of water vapor already in the air.

EXTENSION

Science/Social Studies: Have the children interview adults to find out if they have lived in places where the relative humidity is high or low. The interviewers can find out how this affected the way of life in each place. Children can practice geography skills by locating various high and low humidity regions on a world map.

Note

1. The activity on indoor rainmaking is based on an activity of the same name in J. Abruscato and J. Hassard, *The Whole Cosmos Catalog* (Glenview, IL: Scott, Foresman, 1991), 60.

12A

The Cosmos

Content

A Look Ahead

Are We Alone?

Are we all alone in the vastness of space?

Are other planets in orbit around distant stars?

 Although we still don't have an answer to the first question, we do have an answer to the second. Humankind has made an extraordinary discovery—there *are* planets around other stars!

Powerful telescopes, the careful study of light spectra from stars, advanced computer software, new techniques for studying the wobbles in the movements of stars (an important clue for the presence of a planet), and diligent work by astronomers have revealed that there are stars in the evening sky that do have planets. The names of three of them are 51 Pegasi in the Pegasus constellation, 70 Virginis in the Virgo constellation, and 47 Ursae Majoris in the Big Dipper. Even more amazing, a family of planets has been discovered orbitting Upsilon Andromedae, a star similar to our sun and 44 light-years away.

So, now we know that planets may be far more common in the universe than we would have ever believed. But where does that leave us? Will we *ever* get the answer to that first question—*Are we alone?* Perhaps, but as we use powerful radiotelescopes to search the sky for signals sent by intelligent life, we can also pursue other questions that are just as interesting. For instance: How did the universe come into existence? When did the universe come into existence? What is the real meaning of *time?* and Did time exist before the universe came into being? There are even more mind-wrenching questions, such as whether universes parallel to ours exist or whether matter that enters a black hole can pop out somewhere else in our universe or another universe—if there are other universes.

All of these questions bring us very close to the edge of what people call *science fiction,* yet each day, real-live and very respectable scientists search for the answers. These esoteric questions, as well as those focused more closely on our planet and solar system, will eventually produce answers. We are moving closer and closer to the time when we'll finally be able to answer the question *Are we alone?*

What Is the Universe and How Was It Formed?

The universe is all of the matter, energy, and space that exists. But how did this matter, energy, and space begin? Scientific debate over how the universe began seems to be endless. One important theory, known as the *Big Bang theory,* suggests that the universe had a definite beginning. According to the theory, approximately 8 to 20 billion years ago, the universe was created as a result of a fiery explosion. Astronomical observations that reveal all galaxies have been moving apart from one another at enormous speeds and other evidence suppports this theory. By reasoning backward from the present outward movement of galaxies, we can assume that all the matter of the universe was once packed together.

The theory of a cosmic explosion is also supported by a discovery made in 1965 by Arno Penzias and Robert Wilson of the Bell Laboratories. Penzias and Wilson discovered and measured the strength of faint radiation that came from every direction in the sky. The entire universe seems to be immersed in this radiation. Measurements of the strengths and forms of radiation coincide with the strengths and forms that would have resulted from an enormous explosion occurring billions of years ago.

Maps of the sky made from data gathered by the Cosmic Background Explorer (COBE) satellite show slight differences in the background radiation discovered by Penzias and Wilson. Advocates of the Big Bang theory claim the data are exactly what a scientist would predict if the universe began with a Big Bang.

Although the Big Bang theory offers many explanations for astronomical phenomena, some recent discoveries have strongly challenged it. Observational studies of galaxies by Dr. Margaret J. Geller and Dr. H. P. Huchra of the Harvard–Smithsonian Center for Astrophysics and others have found some organized patterns of galaxies. However, according to the Big Bang theory, these patterns or structures, including an enormous chain of galaxies about 500 billion light-years across and known as the *Great Wall*, should not exist because galaxies should be homogeneously distributed.

Perhaps future studies will be able to explain the organized pattern of galaxies within the confines of the Big Bang theory. On the other hand, future studies may provide data that suggest alternate theories that better explain the nature of the universe we observe today.

Magnetars

A new type of star has been discovered, and we know of its existence because for one brief moment, it affected our environment. Called a *magnetar*, it is believed to be a neutron star that has a magnetic field billions of times more powerful than the earth's magnetic field. A neutron star is a remnant of a collapsed star and is extremely dense. The forces that form a neutron star are so powerful that the original star's protons and electrons were compressed together to form neutrons.

Some scientists have thought for awhile that this strange type of star existed, but there was no proof until recently, when an intense pulse of x-rays and gamma rays entered our solar system and set off detectors on spacecraft orbiting our earth and surveying other planets. The intensity of the radiation was powerful enough to cause some spacecraft to automatically shut down their instruments to prevent them from being damaged. Fortunately, the radiation didn't penetrate our atmosphere any further than a distance of 48 kilometers (about 30 miles) from our planet's surface. The burst of radiation probably occurred when something caused the magnetic field around the magnetar to become rearranged. No real harm was done, except to disappoint those scientists who were confident that magnetars didn't exist in the first place.

Quasars, Pulsars, and Black Holes

Magnetars aren't the only fascinating objects in the universe.[1] There are faint blue celestial objects that are thought to be the most distant and luminous objects in the universe. There are rotating neutron stars thought to be remnants of *supernovas,* exploding stars that at peak intensity can outshine their galaxies. Astronomers have even found evidence that some stars have collapsed, forming such a powerful gravitational field that no light or any other radiation can escape. These objects, known as *black holes,* along with quasars and pulsars, raise many interesting questions about the universe in which we exist.

Quasars

Quasars may be the same size as large stars, yet they emit energy at all wavelengths equivalent to that of a thousand galaxies and produce more energy in a given volume than any other object in the sky. They were first called *quasi-stellar objects* when discovered in 1963 by radio astronomers because they were point sources of radio energy—starlike—instead of diffused over large areas of the sky, like all previously discovered radio sources. Understanding their energy processes could be a key link to new theories on the structure of matter itself.

Quasars are controversial objects because observations don't yet permit conclusive interpretation. They are believed to be receding at enormous velocities—up to 92% of the speed of light—because of the huge red-shifts of their spectral lines. Objects moving at this speed must be billions of light-years distant, near the limits of the observable universe. One newly discovered quasar, OQ 172, is believed to be the most remote recorded object in the universe. Calculated to be 10 billion light-years from Earth, it started sending out energy before the sun, the earth, or the moon existed—even as stellar dust. If quasars are that remote from us, they may be among the oldest observed objects and may prove important to cosmological research by revealing what the early universe was like.

Pulsars

Formed from the collapsed remnants of supernovae explosions, *pulsars* are extremely dense, rotating neutron stars with intense magnetic fields. They are believed to generate beams of directional energy that sweep across space like lighthouse beacons. According to this model, when such a beam wipes across Earth, it appears as a pulse.

When first formed, pulsars may spin up to 1,000 revolutions per second. Their diameter is typically 19.3 kilometers (about 12 miles). When the first pulsar was discovered in 1967, the remarkable regularity of its pulse rate was initially interpreted as a meaningful signal from another intelligent civilization.

A very rich pulsating source for future investigations is Hercules X-1, a binary x-ray star that exhibits a wide variety of pulse periods and interactions with its visible companion. At least one of the pulse periods is produced by eclipses of the x-ray star by this larger companion.

Another important pulsar in the Crab Nebula has been observed in the radio, optical, x-ray, gamma-ray, and infrared regions of the spectrum. This spinning star, like the rotor in an electrical power generator, produces most of the Crab Nebula's energy. Collapse to a neutron star converts the gravitational potential energy of the particles in the original star into kinetic energy of explosion and rotation. Squeezed by its collapse, the star explodes, blowing off the matter in its outer shell, or mantle. Next, continued collapse spins up the remnant star as it grows smaller. The detailed mechanism of this gravitational collapse is one of the major problems being studied by astrophysicists.

Black Holes

Black holes are former stars that, having collapsed to an extremely dense state, have an extraordinarily powerful gravitational field. This field is so strong that no object, light, radio waves, or other radiation can escape to reveal the presence of the black hole.

Black holes may account for 90 percent of the content of our universe. Potentially, there are 1 billion black holes in our galaxy. Astrophysicists speculate that black holes may be bridges connecting one part of our universe to another. Similarly, the other violent sources that we have observed may be white holes through which this energy is surging toward us.

Cygnus X-1, believed to be the first identifiable black hole, was discovered by the *Uhru* satellite in 1972. This black hole is the invisible but dominant component of a binary pair of stars and is shown sucking the material of its visible companion into a rotating disk. The black hole is at the center of the disk. The violence of the transfer and shredding action heats the atoms of gas into emitting x-rays at the edge of the black hole. These x-rays indirectly reveal its presence.

The total energy of the particles and radiation near a black hole is enormous. This energy is produced by the conversion of gravitational energy into radiation energy as the matter falls inward, accelerating into the hole. This mechanism is many times more efficient than nuclear fusion, which produces stellar and solar energy. A black hole converts mass to energy more efficiently than any other mechanism known in physics—except for matter–antimatter annihilation. Accordingly, black holes have been called an ultimate source of cosmic energy.

You might think that the black holes described above are the strangest objects in our universe, but recently, more mysterious objects have been discovered. Astronomers have acquired evidence to suggest that even more complex black holes exist. They are called *supermassive black holes* and may exist at the center of some galaxies. Supermassive black holes are thought to contain the mass of millions or perhaps even billions of stars. How they actually are formed is not known, but one theory is that they may begin as black holes and over long periods of time take in the masses of large numbers of surrounding stars. Another theory suggests that supermassive black holes were formed during the Big Bang.

FIGURE 12A.1
The Andromeda Spiral Galaxy, which is visible as a faint patch in the constellation Andromeda, is about 2 million light-years from Earth.

Galaxies

Within the universe are billions of clusters of stars, known as *galaxies*. Each galaxy contains hundreds of millions of stars, clouds of dust, and gas. Galaxies themselves are thought to be parts of clusters of other galaxies and nebulae, which are huge bodies of dust and gas (see Figure 12A.1).

The galaxy of stars that contains our sun is known as the *Milky Way*. The stars in the Milky Way are so far from one another that measurement in kilometers (or miles) would be impossible to imagine. As a result, astronomers use a measuring unit called the *light-year*. A light-year represents the distance that light travels in one year. Light travels 299,792 kilometers (about 186,000 miles) in just one second, so one light-year represents a distance of 9,450,000,000,000 kilometers (about 6,000,000,000,000 miles). Astronomers have estimated that the Milky Way is tens of thousands of light-years in length and one-eighth that distance in width. Their evidence seems to indicate that our galaxy has a spiral shape. The closest star to our sun, Alpha Centauri, is more than four light-years away. The distance from the Milky Way to the nearest galaxy is 1,500,000 light-years.

Constellations

Constellations are groups of stars that seem to form specific patterns when viewed from Earth. Ages ago, people on Earth looked up at the night sky and saw that the stars that make up the Milky Way seemed to be organized into patterns. Each area of the sky containing such a pattern was identified as a constellation, and all the stars within the pattern were considered part of it. Many constellations were given names from mythology. Others were named for their apparent resemblance to familiar animals and objects. At present, there are 88 named constellations.

The easiest constellations to recognize are the polar constellations, those groups of stars located around the North Star (Polaris). To locate the North Star, find the constellation known as the Big Dipper. By sighting along an imaginary line between the two stars at the rim of the Big Dipper, you should be able to locate the North Star.

Our Solar System

 Our sun, the planets revolving around it, and associated clouds and bodies of matter make up what we call the *solar system,* which scientists believe was formed about 4.6 billions years ago. The sun's gravitational pull is the dominant force in the solar system, and the sun itself is the most massive part of the solar system.

Our Sun, a Star

With all of the new solar data pouring in from spacecraft, the sun is proving to be a more complex star[2] than we ever realized. Of course, the answers to many of our questions may be hidden in the data now on hand. Most scientists seem to agree on how the sun was born and how it will die. They have even calculated how much longer it has to live: 5 billion years as a normal, or main-sequence, star.

Astronomers believe that the sun and planets were formed from an enormous contracting cloud of dust and gas. All parts of this cloud did not move uniformly. Some parts formed local condensations that eventually became our planets, moons, comets, and asteroids. Gradually, the main cloud became spherical. Gravitational contraction increased its temperature. Eventually, the core temperature rose to a point at which the cloud's hydrogen nuclei began to fuse. Nuclear energy then produced enough outward pressure of heated gas to balance the inward force of gravity and maintain the sun as a glowing star. This process is believed to have begun about 5 billion years ago.

About 5 billion years from now, the sun will have depleted the hydrogen fuel in its core. Its thermonuclear reactions will then move outward where unused hydrogen exists. At the same time, the tremendous nuclear heat at the sun's core will also move outward, expanding the sun by as much as 60 times. As the sun cools by expansion, its surface color will become a deep red. It will then be a *red giant*—not a main-sequence star. Looming across much of our sky, it will boil off our water and air and incinerate any remnants of life.

When the sun exhausts its hydrogen fuel, it will no longer be able to withstand gravitational contraction. Eventually, it will shrink to a *white dwarf,* no bigger than the earth but so dense that a piece the size of a sugar cube would weigh thousands of kilograms. Eventually, after billions of years, our sun will cool and dim to a *black cinder.* Only then will eternal night fall upon the solar system.

The Moon

Earth has a single natural satellite—the moon. The first human footsteps on the moon were made by American astronauts, who explored its dusty surface in 1969. Six two-man crews brought back a collection of rocks and soil weighing 382 kilograms (842 pounds) and consisting of more than 2,000 separate samples.

Rocks collected from the lunar highlands date from 4.0 to 4.3 billion years ago. The first few million years of the moon's existence were so violent that little trace of

FIGURE 12A.2
This lunar landscape photo was transmitted to Earth by a *Surveyor* spacecraft.

this period remains. As a molten outer layer gradually cooled and solidified into different kinds of rock, the moon was bombarded by huge asteroids and smaller objects. Some of the asteroids were the size of Rhode Island or Delaware, and their collisions with the moon created huge basins hundreds of kilometers across.

The catastrophic bombardment died away about 4 billion years ago, leaving the lunar highlands covered with huge overlapping craters and a deep layer of shattered and broken rock (see Figure 12A.2). Heat produced by the decay of radioactive elements began to melt the inside of the moon at depths of about 200 kilometers (124 miles) below its surface. Then, from 3.1 to 3.8 billion years ago, great floods of lava rose from inside the moon and poured over its surface, filling the large impact basins to form the dark parts of the moon, called *maria,* or seas. Surprisingly, recent analysis of data from the moon has revealed the presence of water trapped as ice at its polar regions.

Planets

Nine planets,[3] including Earth, revolve around the sun. Four of these planets—Mercury, Venus, Mars, and Pluto—resemble Earth in size, density, and chemical composition. The other four—Jupiter, Saturn, Uranus, and Neptune—are larger and have thick, gaseous atmospheres (see Figure 12A.3).

Mercury

The *Mariner 10* space probe passed within 805 kilometers (500 miles) of the solar system's innermost planet. Photographs from *Mariner 10* revealed an ancient, heavily cratered surface with huge cliffs crisscrossing it. The planet clearly resembles our moon. The cliffs apparently were created when Mercury's interior cooled and shrank, compressing the planet's crust. The cliffs are as high as 2 kilometers (1 mile) and as long as 1,500 kilometers (932 miles). Mercury, like Earth, appears to have a crust of light silicate rock.

FIGURE 12A.3
The relative sizes
of the planets

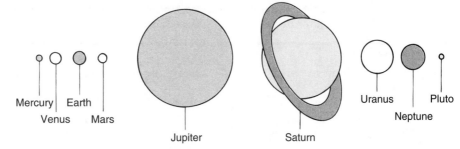

Mercury | Earth
Venus | Mars
Jupiter
Saturn
Uranus | Pluto
Neptune

The spacecraft reported temperatures ranging from 510°C (950°F) on Mercury's sunlit side to –210°C (–346°F) on the dark side. Mercury literally bakes in daylight and freezes at night. The days and nights are long on Mercury. It takes 59 Earth days for Mercury to make a single rotation. It spins at a rate of about 10 kilometers (6 miles) per hour (see Figure 12A.4 on page 236).

Venus

The *Mariner 2* space probe passed within 34,762 kilometers (21,600 miles) of Venus and was the first spacecraft to scan another planet. *Mariner 5* flew much closer to the planet, passing within 4,023 kilometers (2,500 miles).

Venus more nearly resembles Earth in size, physical composition, and density than any other known planet. Its surface temperature reaches 482°C (900°F), hot enough to melt lead.

Among the features discovered by the space probes are two continentlike highland areas. One, about half the size of Africa, is located in the equatorial region. The other, about the size of Australia, is to the north. There is also evidence of two major active volcanic areas, one larger than Earth's Hawaii–Midway volcanic chain (Earth's largest), with a mountain higher than Everest (Earth's highest mountain).

Venus's predominant weather pattern is a high-speed circulation of clouds, which are made up of sulfuric acid. These speeds reach as high as 362 kilometers (225 miles) per hour. The circulation is in the same direction—east to west—as Venus's slow retrograde rotation.

Earth

As viewed from space, Earth's distinguishing characteristics are its blue waters and white clouds. Enveloped by an ocean of air consisting of 78% nitrogen and 21% oxygen, the planet is the only one in our solar system known to harbor life. We now know that our wispy upper atmosphere, once believed calm and quiescent, seethes with activity, swelling by day and contracting by night. It is affected by changes in solar activity and contributes to weather and climate on Earth.

Circling the sun at an average distance of 149 million kilometers (93 million miles), Earth is the third planet from the sun and the fifth largest in the solar system. The American satellite *Explorer I* discovered an intense radiation zone, now called the *Van Allen Radiation Belt*, surrounding Earth.

FIGURE 12A.4   As this chart indicates, Mercury is the planet closest to the sun. A study of the chart will reveal the special characteristics of each planet.

Categories	Mercury	Venus	Earth	Mars	Jupiter	Saturn	Uranus	Neptune	Pluto
1. *Mean distance from Sun (millions of kilometers)*	57.9	108.2	149.6	227.9	778.3	1,427	2,871	4,497	5,914
2. *Period of revolution*	88 days	224.7 days	365.3 days	687 days	11.86 years	29.46 years	84 years	165 years	248 years
3. *Equatorial diameter (kilometers)*	4,880	12,100	12,756	6,794	143,200	120,000	51,800	49,528	~2,330
4. *Atmosphere (main components)*	Virtually none	Carbon Dioxide	Nitrogen Oxygen	Carbon Dioxide	Hydrogen Helium	Hydrogen Helium	Helium Hydrogen Methane	Hydrogen Helium Methane	Methane + ?
5. *Moons*	0	0	1	2	16	18	15	8	1
6. *Rings*	0	0	0	0	3	1,000 (?)	11	4	0
7. *Inclination of orbit to ecliptic*	7°	3.4°	0°	1.9°	1.3°	2.5°	0.8°	1.8°	17.1°
8. *Eccentricity of orbit*	.206	.007	.017	.093	.048	.056	.046	.009	.248
9. *Rotation period*	59 days	243 days retrograde	23 hours 56 min.	24 hours 37 min.	9 hours 55 min.	10 hours 40 min.	17.2 hours retrograde	16 hours 7 min.	6 days 9 hours 18 min. retrograde
10. *Inclination of axis**	Near 0°	177.2°	23° 27'	25° 12'	3° 5'	26° 44'	97° 55'	28° 48'	120°

*Inclinations greater than 90° imply retrograde rotation.

The planet's rapid spin and molten nickel–iron core produce an extensive magnetic field, which, coupled with the atmosphere, shields us from nearly all of the harmful radiation coming from the sun and other stars. Most meteors burn up in Earth's atmosphere before they can strike the surface. The planet's active geological processes have left no evidence of the pelting it almost certainly received soon after it formed.

Mars

In 1997, the world's attention was riveted to the televised sight of a tiny, 10 kilogram (about 22 pound), Tinker Toy–like vehicle, traveling from a small base station to investigate rocks with names like *Barnacle Bill* and *Yogi*. The vehicle was called *Sojourner*, and the brilliant pictures it was sending to Earth were coming from the surface of Mars. The red planet was grudgingly giving up some more of its secrets, and humans could watch it all happen on television or on the World Wide Web.

Of all the planets, Mars has long been considered the solar system's primary candidate for harboring extraterrestrial life. Apparent seasonal color changes on the planet's surface led scientists to speculate that atmospheric conditions might support a bloom of vegetation during the warmer months that would go dormant during colder periods. It was thought that the *Sojourner* rover vehicle (see Figure 12A.5), as well as two *Viking* spacecraft that had reached Mars years before, might answer the question Is there life on Mars? Unfortunately, even with all the information already received, that question remains a mystery.

The Martian atmosphere, like that of Venus, is primarily carbon dioxide. Present in small percentages are nitrogen, oxygen, and argon with trace amounts of krypton and xenon. Martian air contains only about 1/1,000 as much water as Earth's, but even this small amount can condense and form clouds that ride high in the atmosphere or swirl around the slopes of towering Martian volcanoes. Local patches of early morning fog can form in valleys.

There is evidence that in the past, a denser Martian atmosphere may have allowed water to flow on the planet. Physical features closely resembling shorelines, gorges, riverbeds, and islands suggest that great rivers once existed on the planet.

Mars has two small, irregularly shaped moons, Phobos and Deimos, each with ancient cratered surfaces.

FIGURE 12A.5
Sojourner on the surface of Mars

Jupiter

Exploring spacecraft found Jupiter to be a whirling ball of liquid hydrogen topped with a uniquely colorful atmosphere that is mostly hydrogen and helium. It also contains small amounts of methane, ammonia, ethane, acetylene, phosphene, germanium tetrahydride, and possibly hydrogen cyanide. The Great Red Spot is a tremendous atmospheric storm, similar to a hurricane, that rotates counterclockwise.

Largest of the solar system's planets, Jupiter rotates at a dizzying pace—once every 9 hours and 55 minutes. It takes the massive planet almost 12 Earth years to complete a journey around the sun.

Saturn

Saturn is composed mostly of hydrogen and has a subtle butterscotch hue. Its markings are often muted by high-altitude haze. The *Pioneer* spacecraft discovered that there are actually thousands of ringlets encircling Saturn, each composed of countless low-density particles orbiting individually around the equator at progressive distances from the planet's cloud tops. Unable either to form into a moon or to drift away from each other, individual ring particles appear to be held in place by the gravitational pulls of Saturn and its satellites (see Figure 12A.6). Analysis of radio waves passing through the rings showed that the particles vary widely in size, ranging from dust to boulders. Most of the material is ice and frosted rock.

Uranus and Neptune

These two planets are roughly the same in mass and diameter. They are colder and significantly denser than Saturn. The atmospheres of both Uranus and Neptune are known to contain methane, which gives the planets their unusual greenish color. Both planets are believed to possess deep atmospheres that are principally composed of hydrogen and helium. Scientists theorize the planets have cores of rock and metal surrounded by layers of ice, liquid hydrogen, and gaseous hydrogen. Uranus has a system of faint rings, discovered in 1977, and 15 known moons.

FIGURE 12A.6
This photomontage of Saturn and its rings and moons was created by an artist who juxtaposed a series of photographs transmitted by the *Voyager* spacecraft.

Pluto

Pluto is the oddity of the solar system. It has nothing in common with the gas giants. It travels farther from the sun than any of the rest, yet the eccentricity of its orbit periodically carries it inside Neptune's orbit. Pluto's orbit is also highly inclined; that is, it is well above and below the plane of the other planets' orbits.

Observations calculate its diameter to be between 3,000 and 3,500 kilometers (1,864 and 2,175 miles), which is about the same size or somewhat smaller than our moon. Earth-based observations indicate Pluto's surface is covered with methane ice. Small as it is, Pluto has a satellite. The moon, discovered in 1978, was named *Charon*.

Meteors

Meteors are masses of stone and iron from space that sometimes strike Earth. Some meteors have a mass of less than one gram; others have masses of thousands of kilograms. Although many meteors enter Earth's atmosphere, few reach the planet's surface. Most are simply burned up by the friction they produce as they move through the atmosphere. Some meteors are so large that parts of them remain after their journey through the atmosphere. If they reach Earth's surface, they are known as *meteorites*. Scientists have various theories about the origin of meteorites. Most think they originated in our solar system, perhaps from the band of planetlike objects between the orbits of Mars and Jupiter.

Comets

Comets are heavenly bodies surrounding the solar system. They move in large orbits; occasionally, a comet may be pulled from its normal orbit and move toward the sun. Comets are thought to be composed of solidified ammonia, carbon dioxide, and ice. The solid portion of a comet is known as its *head*. The comet's *tail* is formed by the evaporation of solidified matter by energy from the sun. The tail of a comet always points away from the sun. Although comets do not produce light themselves, energy from the sun causes the material in their heads and tails to give off light.

Asteroids

Between the orbits of Mars and Jupiter lies a belt of objects that are smaller than any of the planets. These objects are called *asteroids*. Scientists are not sure how the asteroids were formed. Some believe they are the remnants of a planet that once existed between Mars and Jupiter. Others think they are leftovers from the materials that combined to form Mars and Jupiter.

Some asteroids leave their orbits and cross the paths of planets or moons. Craters observed on the moon and on Mars are probably the result of collisions with asteroids. Some craters on Earth can be explained most easily as the results of collisions with asteroids millions of years ago.

Exploring Space: The First Steps

The development of powerful rockets has made possible the exploration of outer space. (An explanation of the scientific principles involved in rocket propulsion may be found in Chapter 17A.) The first step toward space exploration began in earnest in 1957 with the Soviet Union's launch of the first artificial space satellite—*Sputnik I.*

On August 17, 1958, the United States attempted its first launch of a rocket to the moon. Intended to place an artificial satellite in orbit around the moon, this mission was a failure. On July 2, 1959, the Soviet Union fired a rocket that went into orbit around the sun. A later rocket in the launch series was sent past the moon and transmitted pictures from its far side, but humans did not visit the moon until July 20, 1969, when Neil Armstrong stepped upon its surface. This was one of the many outcomes of the *Apollo* space exploration program, which witnessed visits on the moon's surface by 12 astronauts in all from 1969 to 1972. To date, however, the moon is the only place in space that humans have visited.

Four years earlier, in 1965, both American and Soviet unmanned spacecraft had flown by Mars and taken pictures of its surface. In 1971, *Mariner 9* was placed in orbit about that planet. The pictures it transmitted to Earth showed a surface that looked as if it had been sculptured by intensive flooding millions of years ago. Curiosity about another planet—Mercury—led to the launch of *Mariner 10,* which flew within 720 kilometers (about 450 miles) of the planet in 1974. Television cameras and scientific instruments sent back information concerning temperature, solar wind, and the planet's surface.

Since that time, various spacecraft have been used to explore Venus and other planets. American *Mariner* and Soviet *Venera* rockets both have reached the Venusian atmosphere and transmitted information. *Venera IX* and *X* landed on the surface of Venus in 1975. A year later, in 1976, more detailed information about the surface of Mars was gathered by the spacecraft *Viking 1* and *2,* which dropped small instrument packages to the surface.

The first American spacecraft to orbit Venus was *Pioneer Venus I,* which reached the Venusian atmosphere on December 5, 1978. A few days later, *Pioneer Venus 2* discharged five probes toward the planet's surface. Each transmitted important information about the Venusian atmosphere before being destroyed by the planet's heat. Soviet *Venera* spacecraft parachuted instrument packages to the surface of Venus in 1978. These landers sent information to orbiting spacecraft, which reflected it to Earth.

Space Probes

Voyager 1 and *2* are rocket probes launched in 1977 to observe phenomena on Jupiter, Saturn, Uranus, and Neptune. It is hoped that one or both of these probes will be able to reach the edges of our solar system and beyond. At present, the probes are sending back an enormous amount of data about the outer planets. Data gathered by *Voyager 2*'s flyby of Uranus in 1986 provided extremely sharp pictures of its major satellite.

FIGURE 12A.7
This *Magellan* radar image of Venus shows a set of valleys nicknamed "Gumby."

If they are not destroyed, the *Voyager* spacecraft will escape the solar system at a speed of 62,000 kilometers (about 38,700 miles) per hour. On board each spacecraft are a phonograph record, sound-reproduction equipment, and playing instructions. The records include music, spoken languages, and common sounds from nature. Also included is a plaque that shows pictures of humans and describes, in scientific symbols, Earth, its location, and its people. The *Voyager* spacecraft will reach the first star in their interstellar voyage in about 40,000 years. Perhaps someone or something will interrupt them before then and learn about our planet and its people from the information, equipment, and pictures on board.

The *Magellan* spacecraft was deployed by the space shuttle *Atlantis*. Its interplanetary journey includes a careful study of Venus. *Magellan's* onboard instruments, which include radar imaging systems, have transmitted rather spectacular images of the Venusian surface. Early radar images include that shown in Figure 12A.7, which shows 75 kilometer (46 mile) long valleys that have been nicknamed "Gumby" by photoanalysts.

The National Aeronautics and Space Administration (NASA) has an aggressive schedule for sending spacecraft to explore Mars. Additional orbiter/landers using more advanced technology than the *Pathfinder* mission that placed *Sojourner* on the surface will be launched. In the first decade of the twenty-first century, we should expect some landers to reach Mars, retrieve soil and rock samples, and carry them back to Earth. The success of these missions will lay the foundation for astronauts to visit Mars some time in the not too distant future.

The Hubble Space Telescope

The Hubble Space Telescope (HST) was deployed from a space shuttle launched on April 24, 1990, and just one month later, on May 20, humans saw the first pictures transmitted from the telescope. The HST was designed to gather the sharpest pictures ever of astronomical objects (see Figure 12A.8, page 242). Unfortunately, defects in one of the Hubble's mirrors limited its effectiveness. To correct this problem as well as upgrade related equipment, astronauts from the space shuttle *Endeavor* carried out the most complicated space repairs ever attempted. They secured the HST in the shuttle cargo bay, replaced its solar panels, installed a device to correct the mirror defects, replaced gyroscopes (instruments that sense the telescope's ori-

FIGURE 12A.8   Compare these photographs of the nearest star burst spiral galaxy, NGC-35. The image on the left was taken with a land-based telescope. The detailed area shown on the right is an image by the Hubble Space Telescope (HST). The HST's high resolution allows astronomers to quantify complex structures in the starburst core of the galaxy for the first time.

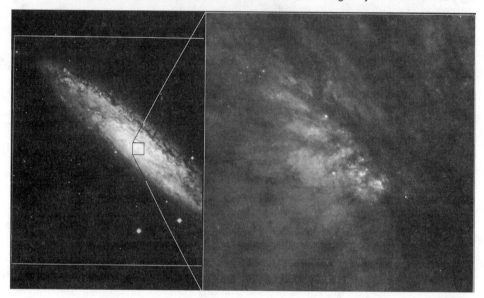

entation in space), replaced one of its cameras, and released the upgraded HST into orbit on December 10, 1993. The repaired Hubble Space Telescope is able to detect stars that are 10 billion or more light-years away.

The Space Shuttle

The American space shuttle[4] continues to offer great potential in the exploration of outer space because of its ability to carry scientists and its great maneuverability. It can orbit Earth like a spacecraft and land like an airplane. The shuttle is designed to carry heavy loads into orbit around Earth. Other launch vehicles have done this, but unlike these vehicles, which can be used only once, each space shuttle orbiter can be reused more than 100 times (see Figure 12A.9).

The shuttle permits the checkout and repair of satellites in orbit and the return of satellites to Earth for repairs that cannot be done in space. Thus, the shuttle makes possible considerable savings in spacecraft costs. The types of satellites that the shuttle can orbit and maintain include those involved in environmental protection, energy, weather forecasting, navigation, fishing, farming, mapping, and oceanography.

Principal Components

The space shuttle has three main units: the *orbiter,* the *external tank,* and two solid rocket *boosters.* The orbiter is the crew- and payload-carrying unit of the shuttle sys-

FIGURE 12A.9
A successful shuttle launch

tem. It is 37 meters (122 feet) long, has a wingspan of 24 meters (78 feet), and without fuel weighs about 68,000 kilograms (150,000 pounds). It is about the size and weight of a DC-9 commercial airplane.

The orbiter can transport a payload of 29,500 kilograms (65,000 pounds). It carries its cargo in a cavernous payload bay 18.3 meters (60 feet) long and 4.6 meters (15 feet) in diameter. The bay is flexible enough to provide accommodations for unmanned spacecraft in a variety of shapes and for fully equipped scientific laboratories.

The orbiter's three main liquid rocket engines are fed propellants from the external tank, which is 47 meters (154 feet) long and 8.7 meters (28.6 feet) in diameter. At liftoff, the tank holds 703,000 kilograms (1,550,000 pounds) of propellants, consisting of liquid hydrogen (fuel) and liquid oxygen (oxidizer). The hydrogen and oxygen are in separate pressurized compartments of the tank. The external tank is the only part of the shuttle system that is not reusable.

A Typical Shuttle Mission

In a typical shuttle mission, lasting from 7 to 30 days, the orbiter's main engines and the booster ignite simultaneously to rocket the shuttle from the launch pad. Launches are made from the John F. Kennedy Space Center in Florida for east–west orbits and from Vandenberg Air Force Base in California for north–south orbits.

At a predetermined point, the two solid rocket boosters separate from the orbiter and parachute to the sea, where they are recovered for reuse. The orbiter continues into space, jettisoning its external propellant tank just before orbiting. The external tank enters the atmosphere and breaks up over a remote ocean area.

The orbiter then proceeds on its mission in space. When its work is completed, the crew directs the orbiter on a flight path that will take it back to the Earth's atmosphere. Various rocket systems are used to slow its speed and adjust its direction. Previous spacecraft followed a direct path from space to the predetermined landing area. The orbiter is quite different. It can maneuver from the right to the left of its entry path a distance of about 2,035 kilometers (about 1,270 miles). The orbiter has the capability of landing like an airplane at Kennedy Space Center or Vandenberg Air Force Base. Its landing speed is about 335 kilometers (about 210 miles) per hour.

Exploring Space: The Next Steps

 ### *VentureStar:* The X-33

> *"May we have your attention please? VentureStar Flight 271 is now ready for boarding at gate number 6. Please have your boarding pass available for the flight attendant at the gate."*

At some time in your life, you may be sitting at a "rocketport," listening to an announcement that will be remarkably close to the one reported above. As we begin this new century, the possibility of relatively inexpensive spaceflight is very real. Someday, it will happen. What's needed is the invention of new technologies to replace those that have taken us this far.

NASA has now launched an effort to design and test a replacement for the space shuttle. The early version of this replacement craft is the X-33 Reusable Launch Vehicle, which has been given the name *VentureStar* by its prime contractor, the Lockheed Martin Skunk Works in Palmdale, California. The demonstration version of *VentureStar* is a 273,000 pound (123,831 kilogram), web-shaped vehicle that will lower the cost of putting 1 pound (about 2.2 kilograms) of payload into space from $10,000 dollars to $1,000 (see Figure 12A.10).

Although *VentureStar* won't take humans to other planets, it will make it possible to use limited resources to explore our own planet's surroundings and test new technologies more fully. To go further, we need an orbiting space station that uses expertise and resources from around the world as well as knowledge gained from the operation of the Russian space station *Mir.* That space station will be the *International Space Station Alpha.*

International Space Station Alpha: A Rest Stop on the Road to Mars?

When completed, the *International Space Station Alpha* will house astronauts and scientists in a laboratory that's permanently orbiting Earth at a distance of 200 miles (323 kilometers). It will be a place for the intensive study of how the human body and other biological systems respond to prolonged time in space. Even the construction of the space station will produce knowledge every bit as important as what will be

FIGURE 12A.10
VentureStar is the prototype for a new generation of spacecraft that will likely replace the shuttle.

learned from the basic science research that will happen in its onboard laboratory. Engineers will discover the best possible procedures for coordinating the design and construction of very complex structures designed on Earth but assembled in space.

International Space Station Alpha will consist of various modules and components built by the United States and other countries; these parts will be rocketed into space and then joined together. Constructing all these parts on Earth and then assembling them in space will be the largest cooperative scientific and engineering effort in human history. When it is complete, the new space station will contain facilities for biotechnology, fluids and combustion, a space station furnace, gravitational biology, centrifuge, and human research.

Although the very construction of the space station will be an amazing feat, it will be only the beginning. If all goes well and humans successfully create and operate the structure, its mission will likely change. *International Space Station Alpha* may become the launching pad that will take humankind deep into space.

Summary Outline

   I. The universe is all the matter, energy, and space that exist.
     A. Recent discoveries of patterns of galaxies pose a challenge to the Big Bang theory.
     B. In recent years, scientists have discovered and begun studies of extraordinary astronomical phenomena, such as magnetars, quasars, pulsars, and black holes.

II. The solar system consists of the sun, its nine planets, and associated clouds of matter, including meteors, comets, and asteroids.

    A. The sun is a star that will use up its supply of hydrogen and come to the end of its existence in about 5 billion years.

    B. The moon, which is a satellite of Earth, is airless and lifeless.

    C. The nine planets that circle the sun are Mercury, Venus, Earth, Mars, Jupiter, Saturn, Uranus, Neptune, and Pluto.

III. Powerful rockets have enabled humans to explore outer space in a variety of ways.

    A. Manned and unmanned space probes have explored space since 1957.

    B. The space shuttle is a space vehicle that can return to Earth and be reused in subsequent space journeys.

    C. *VentureStar* will serve as the prototype for a spacecraft that will eventually replace the space shuttle.

    D. *International Space Station Alpha* will be a permanently orbiting scientifically laboratory. It may also serve as a launching pad for the human exploration of Mars.

Notes

1. The discussion of quasars, pulsars, and black holes was excerpted with minor modifications from *Quasars, Pulsars, Black Holes . . . and HEAO's*, a pamphlet prepared by the National Aeronautics and Space Administration. This pamphlet (stock number 003-000-00542-3) is available for purchase from the Superintendent of Documents, Government Printing Office, Washington, DC 20402.

2. The discussion of the sun was excerpted with modifications from *Our Prodigal Sun*, a pamphlet prepared by the National Aeronautics and Space Administration. This pamphlet (stock number 3300-00569) can be purchased from the Superintendent of Documents, Government Printing Office, Washington, DC 20402.

3. Portions of this discussion of the planets are excerpted with modification from the NASA publication *A Look at the Planets*. This pamphlet is available for purchase from the Superintendent of Documents, Government Printing Office, Washington, DC 20402.

4. The discussion of the space shuttle was excerpted with minor modifications from *NASA Facts: The Space Shuttle*, prepared by the National Aeronautics and Space Administration. This publication (stock number 003-000-00679-9) is available for purchase from the Superintendent of Documents, Government Printing Office, Washington, DC 20402.

12B

The Cosmos

Attention Getters, Discovery Activities, and Demonstrations

A Look Ahead

Can You Move Like the Planets? [ESS 2]

MATERIALS   9 sheets of 8½ × 11 in. pastel paper for each group
1 larger sheet of orange paper
Crayons or water-based markers for each group

MOTIVATING QUESTIONS
- What are some of the things you see in the sky on a bright day?
- Display a globe and ask: Do you think our earth moves or stays still?

For Young Learners

DIRECTIONS
1. Write the planet names on the chalkboard, distribute the paper, and assign a planet name to each group.
2. Write the word *sun* on the orange sheet, and have each group write the name of its planet on the paper it received.
3. Have volunteers from each group join you at a central place in the room. Arrange the volunteers in proper sequence from the sun (the orange sheet that you are holding), and have the children circle around you.
4. Finally, indicate that the planets spin (rotate) as they move (revolve), and have the children do the same, slowly.

SCIENCE CONTENT FOR THE TEACHER   Nine major planets travel around the sun in orbits. These planets do not emit light. They reflect the sun's light. The sun is a star whose apparent motion is due to the earth's rotation. Seasonal changes are due to the change in the relative position of the earth as it orbits around the sun.

Can You Move Like the Moon? [ESS 3]

MATERIALS   1 orange sheet of paper
1 white sheet of paper
1 blue sheet of paper
Crayons or water-based markers

MOTIVATING QUESTIONS
- Do you think the earth moves around the sun, or do you think the sun moves around the earth?
- Do you think the moon moves around the earth, or do you think the earth moves around the moon?

DIRECTIONS
1. Write the word *sun* on the orange sheet of paper, the word *earth* on the blue sheet, and the word *moon* on the white sheet. (You may wish to have children copy the words from the board.)
2. Select one student to stand and hold the orange sheet to represent the sun.
3. Select another student to hold the blue sheet and move in orbit around the sun.

4. Finally, select a student to hold the white sheet and orbit the earth as it travels around the sun.

SCIENCE CONTENT FOR THE TEACHER

The moon is a satellite of the earth. This means that the moon revolves around the earth as the earth rotates and revolves around the sun. The moon also rotates as it orbits the earth.

Why Is Earth Called the "Blue Planet"? [ESS 1]

MATERIALS

1 model car, plane, and doll
1 globe

MOTIVATING QUESTIONS

- Is this a real car, plane, or person?
- How are these the same or different from real cars, planes, and people?

DIRECTIONS

1. Write the words *sun* and *earth* on the chalkboard.
2. Pronounce each word, and then display the toys. Discuss how models are different from real things.
3. Display the globe, and ask what it is a model of. Have children point out the locations of lands and oceans on the globe, and discuss the relative amounts of each.
4. Move the globe as far from the children as possible, and ask how astronauts in space might describe the earth.

SCIENCE CONTENT FOR THE TEACHER

Scientists often use models. Just as toys stand for real things, a globe stands for, or is a model of, the earth. A globe is roughly the same shape as our planet and shows the predominant colors as seen from space.

Is Day Always as Long as Night? [ESS 6]

MATERIALS

1 tennis ball
1 steel knitting needle
1 small lamp without lampshade

Chalk
1 m of string
1 marking pen

MOTIVATING QUESTIONS

- If you didn't have to go to school, would you have more time to play outside in the summer months or in the winter months?
- Are the lengths of the days and nights the same all through the year?

For Middle-Level Learners

ATTENTION GETTERS

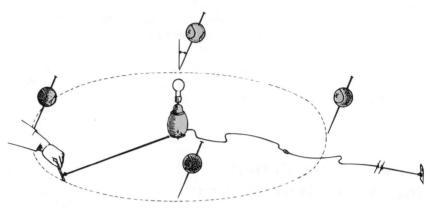

Earth in orbit in the classroom

DIRECTIONS

1. Before class, carefully push the knitting needle through the tennis ball from top to bottom. Use a marking pen to make a dot that stands for your city or town on the tennis ball.
2. Use the string to make a circle on the classroom floor. Put the lamp at the center of the circle. Use the chalk to label the furthest-left part of the circle *June 21*. Label the furthest-right part of the circle *December 21*, the topmost point *March 21*, and the lowest point *September 21*.
3. At the start of class, have the children gather around the model. Explain that the circle *almost* represents the path of the earth.
4. Tell the children that the path is really a flattened-out circle called an *ellipse*. Convert the circle to an ellipse by using the original circle as a guideline and drawing an ellipse with chalk.
5. Incline the tennis ball approximately 23° from the vertical, and have a child hold it at the spot marked March 21 and slowly rotate it. The children will note that their town gets light for half the rotation (12 hours). When this procedure is repeated at June 21, the children will note that the town is lit for approximately two-thirds of a rotation (16 hours). At the December 21 spot, the children will note their town gets few hours of sunlight (8–10 hours). To make this more obvious, have a child sit at sun's location and tell whether she or he sees the town for a long or short period of time on June 21 and December 21.

*SCIENCE
CONTENT FOR
THE TEACHER*

Spring and fall are times when the earth's axis is not tilted toward or away from the sun. At these times, day and night are of equal length. During summer in the Northern Hemisphere, the earth's axis is tilted in the direction of the sun, so any location in the Northern Hemisphere has longer days.

Can You Draw an Orbit? [ESS 6]

MATERIALS   1 m of string   1 large sheet of paper
                 1 pencil   2 pushpins or thumbtacks
                 1 sheet of cardboard about the same size as the paper

MOTIVATING   • What shape is the earth's path around the sun?
QUESTIONS   • Do you think the shape is a circle?

DIRECTIONS   1. Place the paper on the cardboard. Stick the pushpins through the paper
                    and cardboard toward the center of the paper but about 20 centimeters
                    apart.
                 2. Tie a knot in the string to make a closed loop, and put the loop around
                    the pushpins.
                 3. Holding the pencil vertically inside the loop
                    and pushed against the string, move it
                    in a complete path
                    around the pins. Be
                    sure to keep the
                    tension of the pencil
                    against the loop
                    constant.

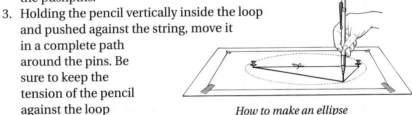

How to make an ellipse

                 4. Explain to the children that the figure you have drawn is an *ellipse* and
                    that the planets travel in ellipses around the sun. If you wish, remove
                    one of the pushpins after you have drawn the ellipse and explain that
                    the remaining pushpin represents the sun.

SCIENCE   Although people often describe the orbits of the planets as circles, they are
CONTENT FOR   in fact ellipses. An ellipse has two foci. The sun is at the location of one of
THE TEACHER   the foci for the earth's orbit.

Where Does the Sun Rise and Set? [ESS 6]

MATERIALS   2 sheets of drawing paper for each child
                 Pencils, crayons, or markers

MOTIVATING   • Can you remember where the sun sets?
QUESTIONS   • Can you remember where the sun rises?

DIRECTIONS   1. Have each child place the drawing paper so the long side runs from left
                    to right in front of him or her.

2. On one sheet of paper, have each child draw some of the objects he or she would see while looking toward the east of where he or she lives: buildings, trees, fields, forests, parks, or whatever is toward the east of his or her home. On the other sheet, have each child do the same for the west.

3. Next, have each child draw a rising sun on the sheet at the place that represents where the sun rises and a setting sun at the place that they think represents where the sun sets.

4. Have the children take both papers home for a few days to correct, if they need to, the locations of their suns. *Safety Note:* Remind the children never to look directly at the sun.

SCIENCE CONTENT FOR THE TEACHER   It seems to us that the sun is moving across our sky every day, rising in the east and setting in the west. However, the sunrise and sunset that we see are due to the earth's rotation. In this activity, the children simply compare their memories of where the sun rises and sets to the actualities.

Planets on Parade [ESS 2]

OBJECTIVE   • The children will place the planets in sequential order from the sun.

SCIENCE PROCESSES EMPHASIZED   Using numbers
Using space/time relationships

MATERIALS FOR EACH CHILD OR GROUP   1 deck of 9 index cards, each labeled with a different
    planet name

MOTIVATION   Tell the children that they are going to play a game that will help them learn about the planets. Display the nine index cards you will be distributing.

DIRECTIONS   1. Before beginning this activity, create a set of clues for each planet, such as "I am Venus; I am closer to the sun than the Earth"; "I am Neptune; I am further from the Sun than Mars."

2. Distribute a randomly sequenced deck of index cards to each group. Explain that each card represents a planet that is traveling around the sun but that the cards are not in the proper order. Challenge the groups to rearrange the cards based on the clues you give.

3. Read each clue, and encourage the children to rearrange the cards on the basis of the clues.

DISCOVERY ACTIVITIES

For Young Learners

KEY *DISCUSSION* *QUESTIONS*	1. Which planet is closest to the sun? *Mercury* 2. Which planet is furthest from the sun? *Pluto* 3. Which planet is just before Earth, and which planet is right after Earth? *Venus, Mars*
SCIENCE *CONTENT FOR* *THE TEACHER*	The nine known planets of our solar system in order from the sun are Mercury, Venus, Earth, Mars, Jupiter, Saturn, Uranus, Neptune, and Pluto.
EXTENSION	*Science/Math:* After the children have put their decks in order, have them turn the decks over and number each card sequentially from 1 to 9. Have pairs of children play a game in which one child removes one of the numbered cards and the other child has to guess the planet name that is on the reverse side.

Making a Simple Sundial [ESS 3]

OBJECTIVES	• The children will use numbers to write time measurements. • The children will predict the actual time from the position of the shadow on a sundial.
SCIENCE *PROCESSES* *EMPHASIZED*	Using numbers Predicting
MATERIALS FOR *EACH CHILD* *OR GROUP*	Sheet of light cardboard 25 cm (10 in.) square Straw Masking tape
MOTIVATION	Display the materials and tell the children that they are going to be making their own clocks. Indicate that they will be strange clocks because they will only work when the sun is shining.
DIRECTIONS	1. Prior to class, make a 20 centimeter (about 9 inch) circle on each sheet of cardboard and punch a small hole at the center of each circle. Be sure to have a compass available for step 3. 2. Distribute a straw and a few strips of masking tape to each group. Have the groups insert one end of the straw into the hole and tape the straw so that it can stand upright. Tell them to write the letter *N* at any point along the edge of the circle.

3. On a sunny day, take the groups and their sundials outside. Using the compass, point north and have the children orient their sundials so that the *N's* are pointed north. Have them mark the location of the straw's shadow, and then tell the children the actual time. Have them write the time on the cardboard at the end of the shadow.

4. After repeating this procedure at various times on consecutive days, have the children predict where the straw's shadow will be at a given time and take them outside at that time to check. As a final step, take the children outside and have them use their sundials to tell you the time.

KEY
DISCUSSION
QUESTIONS

1. There is one time in the day when the shadow is shortest or does not exist at all. What time is that? *When the sun is directly overhead.*

2. What are some of the problems with using sundials to tell time? *You can't tell the time on a cloudy day or at night.*

SCIENCE
CONTENT FOR
THE TEACHER

Since Earth is constantly changing its position in relation to the sun, the sundials made in this activity will be fairly accurate for only a few days. Sundials in gardens or parks are constructed to compensate for Earth's changing position. They usually do not use a vertical object for the shadow but rather a rod that is inclined at the angle of the location's latitude and pointed toward the North Star.

EXTENSION

Science/Social Studies: Do library research to locate pictures or drawings of various time-keeping devices used through the ages. Show the pictures to the children and ask them to suggest any problems, such as the size of the devices, that people might have had using these devices.

Sunlight in Winter and Summer [ESS 3]

OBJECTIVE

• The children will observe that light striking an inclined surface does not appear as bright as light striking a surface directly.

SCIENCE
PROCESSES
EMPHASIZED

Measuring

MATERIALS FOR
EACH CHILD
OR GROUP

Black construction paper	Book
Chalk	Tape
Flashlight	

MOTIVATION

Ask the children if they have ever wondered why it is colder in winter than in summer. Tell them that they will discover one of the reasons in this activity.

DIRECTIONS

1. Be sure to have a globe available before beginning this activity. Darken the classroom and distribute a book, tape, chalk, paper, and flashlight to each child or group.
2. Have each child or group tape the paper to the book and hold the book vertically on a flat surface. Ask them to shine the flashlight on the paper and use the chalk to draw a circle outlining the lit area.
3. Next, tell the children to keep the flashlight at the same distance from the book but to move it so the light strikes a different part of the paper. Have them tilt the book away from the flashlight and outline the lit area.
4. Turn the lights on and display the globe. Use a flashlight to represent the sun, and tilt the globe to show that the earth's tilt causes the Northern Hemisphere to be angled away from the sun during the winter months. Relate this to the light striking the paper that was tilted away from the light source.

KEY DISCUSSION QUESTIONS

1. How are the drawings you made different from one another? *The first was smaller.*
2. Was the patch of light brighter the first or second time you had the light strike the paper? *The first.*

SCIENCE CONTENT FOR THE TEACHER

Although many people believe that winter occurs because the earth is farther from the sun at that time of the year than it is in summer, the principal cause for winter is the earth's tilt, not its orbit. This tilt serves to spread out the sun's energy more in the Northern Hemisphere during the winter months. Sunlight strikes the Northern Hemisphere more directly in June than in December.

EXTENSION

Science/Social Studies: Have the children look at the globe and consider how their lives would be different if they lived in an equatorial region, which receives a great deal of direct sunlight all through the year, or in a polar region, which receives much less sunlight.

Make a Solar System Mobile [ESS 2]

OBJECTIVE

- The children will construct mobiles showing the nine planets of the solar system.

SCIENCE PROCESSES EMPHASIZED

Measuring
Using space/time relationships

MATERIALS

1 wire coat hanger
String
Crayons
9 circles of oak tag 8 cm
   (about 3 in.) across

3 or 4 straws
Scissors
Tape

MOTIVATION

Tell the children they are going to create an art project that illustrates some science knowledge they have. You may wish to display a sample planet mobile at this point.

DIRECTIONS

1. Prior to class, create a mobile using a coat hanger as a base and an arrangement of strings and horizontal straws. Attach the nine oak tag circles to the strings that dangle from the straw ends.
2. Display the mobile, and explain that each circle represents one of the planets in the solar system. Write the names of the planets on the chalkboard, and distribute the materials. Tell the children to write the name of a planet on each circle.
3. Once the circles are labeled, have the children construct the mobiles. Be ready to assist those children who need help tying knots to attach string to straws or to oak tag circles. Some children may find it easier to tape the parts of their mobile together. You may wish to suggest that the children construct some of the subparts of the mobile first—for example, a straw with two or three planets hanging from it. If you are fortunate enough to have parent volunteers or assistants in the classroom, urge them to help those children who have limited psychomotor abilities.
4. When the children are done, have them hang their mobiles in the classroom.

KEY DISCUSSION QUESTIONS

Since this activity is focused on the construction of a mobile, the questions you raise should facilitate the children's use of psychomotor skills.

1. If you wanted to hang two planets from a straw, where would you tie them? *One at each end.*
2. If you hung one planet from each end of a straw, where would you tie the string that attaches the straw to the hanger? *At the center.*

SCIENCE CONTENT FOR THE TEACHER

Be sure to remind the children that although their planets are all the same size, the real planets are of different sizes.

EXTENSION

Science: Children with advanced reading and writing skills may be asked to use resource books to locate key descriptive words and write them on the planet circles. Challenge these children to find words that tell about the colors or temperatures of the planets.

How to Build an Altitude Finder (Astrolabe) [S&T 4]

OBJECTIVES
- The children will construct a simple device for measuring the heights of planets and stars above the horizon.
- The children will measure how many degrees an object is above the horizon.

*SCIENCE
PROCESSES
EMPHASIZED*
Observing
Using numbers
Measuring

*MATERIALS FOR
EACH CHILD
OR GROUP*
Piece of cardboard 25 × 25 cm (about 10 × 10 in.)
25 cm (10 in.) length of string
Small weight, such as a washer or nut
Protractor
Tape

**For Middle-
Level
Learners**

MOTIVATION
Tell the children that they will be building an instrument that the Greeks invented long ago to discover how far above the horizon the planets and stars are. Explain to the children that scientists call this instrument an *astrolabe* but that they can call it an *altitude finder* because it finds altitudes.

DIRECTIONS
1. Distribute a protractor to each child or group. Show the children that the protractor scale can be used to measure angles from 0° to 180°.
2. Distribute a cardboard square to each group, and have the children place a 0° mark at the lower-left-hand corner of the cardboard. Have them place a 90° mark at the upper-right-hand corner.

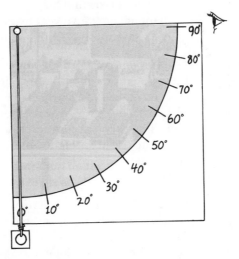

An altitude finder

3. Have the children attach one end of the string to the upper-left-hand corner of the cardboard with the tape and tie a pencil to the free end of the string. Now they can use the string and pencil as a compass to draw an arc from the lower-left-hand corner to the upper-right-hand corner.

4. Have the children divide the arc they have drawn into 10° intervals from 0° to 90°—that is, 0°, 10°, 20°, . . . , 90°. The protractor can be used to help mark these divisions.

5. The children should now untie the pencil and tie the nut or washer to the string. The string should cross the 0° mark when the upper edge of the cardboard is held horizontally. Tell the children that they will be sighting objects along the top of the cardboard with the string on the edge of the cardboard that is farthest away from them.

6. When the children have constructed their altitude finders, you may wish to take them outside to find how many degrees such things as chimneys, treetops, or lampposts are above the horizon. Be sure they do not try to sight the sun with their altitude finders.

7. Encourage the children to take their altitude finders home and measure the number of degrees the visible heavenly bodies are above the horizon.

KEY DISCUSSION QUESTIONS

1. Why do you think we attached a weight to the string? *To pull the string straight down.*

2. Sometimes people use the term *angle of elevation* when they use an astrolabe. What do you think the term means? *How many degrees the object is above the horizon.*

3. Does the altitude finder tell you anything about the direction the object is from you? *No.*

4. How could you find the direction? *Use a compass.* **Note:** The next activity in this chapter involves creating an instrument that measures the angle of a heavenly body from true north.

SCIENCE CONTENT FOR THE TEACHER

The astrolabe was invented by the Greeks for observing heavenly bodies. It consisted of a movable rod that was pointed at a star or planet. The position of the rod against a circle indicated the altitude of the sun, moon, and stars. The astrolabe was eventually refined for use as a navigational tool. The sextant, a more accurate device that fulfills the same purpose, came into use in the eighteenth century. It uses a small telescope and a system of mirrors to compare the position of a heavenly body with the horizon.

EXTENSION

Science/Social Studies: You may wish to have a group of children do some library research to find out more about the extent to which the ancient Greeks were involved in astronomy. This group can also research the importance of the astrolabe and sextant in the exploration of the world by seafaring countries.

How to Build an Azimuth Finder [S&T 4]

OBJECTIVE	• The children will construct a simple device that will tell them how many degrees from north, measured in a clockwise direction, a heavenly body is.

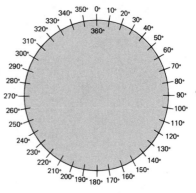

An azimuth finder

SCIENCE PROCESSES EMPHASIZED	Observing Using numbers Measuring
MATERIALS FOR EACH CHILD OR GROUP	Magnetic compass 50 cm (20 in.) square of cardboard 25 cm (10 in.) length of string Pencil Protractor

DISCOVERY ACTIVITIES

MOTIVATION Tell the children that astronomers usually keep track of both the positions of heavenly bodies above the horizon and their direction in relation to north. Write the word *azimuth* on the chalkboard, and explain that this term refers to how far an object is from north. Distribute the materials, and begin a discussion of how they can be used to make an azimuth finder.

DIRECTIONS
1. Have the children use the protractor and pencil to draw a circle on the cardboard square.
2. Show the children that they can divide the circle into 10° units by placing the protractor so that its center measuring point is at the center of the circle. Have the children label any point on the circle 0° (north). Then have them mark off 10° positions from 0° to 360°, going in a clockwise direction. Once they have marked off the 10° units, they can use the bottom of the protractor as a straightedge. *Note:* Since the protractor goes from 0° to 180°, the children should simply turn it upside down in order to continue around the circle in 10° intervals from 180° to 360° (0°).
3. When the azimuth finders are complete, take the children outside to use them to find the azimuths of chimneys, treetops, and other tall objects. In order to do this, they must first rotate the case of the compass so the needle is pointing north. (You may wish to introduce the difference between true north and magnetic north at this point. Refer to Science Content for the Teacher for information on this subject.) Have each child align the azimuth finder so that the 0° mark is oriented to the north.
4. The children can find various azimuths by noting the number of degrees clockwise the object is from the 0° reading.

5. Encourage the children to take their azimuth finders home to make evening measurements of the positions of heavenly bodies. They will need flashlights to read the finders.

KEY
DISCUSSION
QUESTIONS

1. What would be the azimuth of a planet that was due east of you? *90°*.
2. What would be the azimuth of a planet that was due south of you? *180°*.
3. What would be the azimuth of a planet that was due west of you? *270°*.

SCIENCE
CONTENT FOR
THE TEACHER

You can readily find the azimuth of a heavenly body by using true north as a reference point. Navigators generally label true north as 0° and describe the azimuth of an object in terms of the number of degrees, measured in a clockwise direction, by which its direction differs from true north. (Astronomers tend to use true south as 0°. However, for school use, the 0° north reading used by navigators is a perfectly acceptable method of measurement.)

One problem in the use of an azimuth finder is that the magnetic north measured by a compass is displaced from geographic north, except for a small portion of North America. The amounts of deviation for some representative cities are as follows:

Portland, Oregon	21°E
San Francisco	17°E
Denver	13°E
St. Paul	5°E
Atlanta	0°
Cleveland	5°W
Philadelphia	9°W
Portland, Maine	17°W

EXTENSION

Science/Social Studies: You may wish to have some children do library research on the history of astronomy. The children can find information on Egyptian, Babylonian, Chinese, and Mayan astronomy in most reference books. They may also be interested in gathering pictures of Stonehenge to share with the rest of the class.

Using Altitude and Azimuth Finders to Follow the Motion of a Planet [S&T 4]

OBJECTIVE

• The children will use simple altitude- and azimuth-measuring instruments to observe the motion of a planet.

SCIENCE
PROCESSES
EMPHASIZED

Observing
Measuring
Communicating

MATERIALS FOR EACH CHILD OR GROUP	Altitude-measuring instrument (see first discovery activity for middle-level learners, pp. 257–258) Azimuth-measuring instrument (see previous activity) Chart with the following headings: *Observation, Date, Time, Altitude, Azimuth* Paper and pencil

MOTIVATION Ask the children if they have ever seen planets in the evening sky. They may have observed that planets do not twinkle and that some appear other than white in color. Discuss with the children the importance of making observations of planets over an extended time in order to see patterns of motion. Indicate that this activity is going to extend over a period of months and will require them to do their observations at home.

DIRECTIONS

1. Review the use of the altitude and azimuth measurers described in the two previous activities. If the children have not constructed these instruments, they will need to do so before beginning this extended activity.
2. Have each child prepare an observation chart.
3. Explain to the children that they should attempt to locate one planet in the evening sky and record observations at the same time each day. To help them locate a planet, find one for yourself and determine its altitude and azimuth. (You can get help from any almanac that describes the locations of visible planets for your area at various times of the year.) Share the location of this planet with the class. The children can then try to find it on their own with their measuring devices.
4. Every few months, hold a class discussion of the observations that have been made as of that time.

KEY DISCUSSION QUESTIONS

1. What planet did you observe? How did you know what planet it was? *Answers will vary.*
2. What problems did you have during the activity? *Answers will vary but may include such problems as cloud cover obscuring the planets, precipitation making outdoor work difficult, misplacing instruments, and forgetting to make observations at the same time every day.*

SCIENCE CONTENT FOR THE TEACHER See the content presented in the previous two activities.

EXTENSIONS *Science:* You may wish to encourage a group of children to carry out some long-term library research to coincide with this extended activity. Children can focus on such topics as the astronomers Tycho Brahe and Copernicus, the invention of the telescope, and the use of modern astronomical instruments, such as the radio telescope.

Science/Social Studies: You may wish to have some children explore the resistance of society to Copernicus's and Galileo's conclusion that the sun is the physical center of the solar system.

Moon Watcher [ESS 2]

OBJECTIVES	• Using a model, the children will observe the phases of the moon. • The children will explain why the moon seems to change in shape.
SCIENCE PROCESSES EMPHASIZED	Observing Communicating
MATERIALS	Small lamp with ordinary light bulb and removable shade Orange Paper and pencil Signs with the labels *Earth, Moon,* and *Sun*
MOTIVATION	Ask the children to describe and draw the various shapes that the moon seems to take. Have them show their drawings to the class. Ask if they think the moon really changes shape. After some discussion, display the materials for the demonstration, and tell the children that they will be observing a model of the moon in orbit around Earth that will help them understand the changes in its shape.

DEMONSTRATIONS

For Young Learners

What phase of the moon is this?

DIRECTIONS

1. Remove the lampshade, and place the sun label on the lamp. Place the sun at the center of the front of the room. Select one child, and affix the *Earth* label to him or her.
2. Darken the room by drawing the shades and shutting off the classroom lights.
3. Now have the child hold the orange (the moon) so that his or her hand is fully outstretched. Have the child first stand so that he or she is facing the sun and holding the moon directly in line with it. The child should be about 1 meter (a little more than 3 feet) from the sun.
4. The lamp should be turned on at this point. Have the child holding the orange describe how much of the orange's lit surface is seen. None of the lit surface should be seen; the moon is not visible in the sky.
5. Have the child turn sideways, and ask him or her how much of the lit surface of the orange he or she can see. Half the lit surface should be visible; the child sees a half-moon.
6. Have the child stand so that his or her back is to the lamp and the orange is about 30 centimeters (1 foot) away from his or her eyes and slightly to the left of the head. Ask how much of the lit surface of the moon can be seen. All of it should be visible; the child sees a full moon.
7. Repeat the demonstration so that the crescent moon and three-quarter moon can be seen.

KEY DISCUSSION QUESTIONS

1. Does the moon produce light? *No, it just reflects light from the sun.*
2. What name do we give to the shapes that the moon seems to take? *Phases.*
3. Does the moon really change in shape? Why? *No. The only thing that changes is the pattern of the light we can see bouncing off the moon.*

SCIENCE CONTENT FOR THE TEACHER

The sun shines on only half the surface of the moon. This entire lit surface is not always visible from the earth. The apparent shape of the moon at any given time is really the portion of the lit surface that is visible. The different portions of the surface that are lit at different times are the phases of the moon. The *full moon* is that phase in which we see the entire lit surface. When full, the moon appears as a round disk in the sky. We refer to the phase in which we see half the lit surface as the *half-moon*. The *crescent moon* is a phase in which we see only a sliver of the lit surface. The *new moon* is the phase in which none of the lit surface can be seen.

EXTENSIONS

Science: You may wish to encourage a group of children to use the lamp, orange, and other round objects to demonstrate other astronomical phenomena, such as lunar and solar eclipses.

Science/Arts: A group of children may wish to draw a sequence of pictures to represent an imaginary incident that occurs as astronauts explore a mysterious crater on the moon.

The Shoe Box Planetarium [ESS 3]

OBJECTIVE

- The children will observe the Big Dipper constellation projected in the classroom and will be able to locate it in the night sky.

SCIENCE PROCESS EMPHASIZED

Observing

MATERIALS

Shoe box with lid	Electrical tape
Index card	Scissors
Flashlight	

MOTIVATION

Tell the children that they will observe something they can then ask a parent or other adult to help them find in the night sky.

DIRECTIONS

1. Tape the lid to the shoe box. At one end, cut out a hole sufficiently large for you to insert the lamp end of a flashlight. Cut a rectangular window the size of a small index card in the other end.
2. Using the electrical tape, seal one end of the box around the flashlight so that the switch is not in the box.
3. Poke small holes in an index card in the shape of the Big Dipper. Attach the index card to the window in the shoe box. *Note:* For somewhat older children, you may wish to prepare additional index cards to use to project images of other constellations.
4. Darken the room, turn on the flashlight, and project the Big Dipper on a screen or wall. Have the children note the shape of the handle and the cup. Encourage the children to ask an adult to help them find it in the night sky.

KEY DISCUSSION QUESTIONS

1. Look at the sides of the Big Dipper. What do you notice about them? *Answers will vary. If no one mentions that sides of the dipper slope inward, do so.*
2. Look at the handle of the Big Dipper. What do you notice about it? *Answers will vary. If no one mentions that the handle is curved, do so.*

SCIENCE CONTENT FOR THE TEACHER

We are able to observe thousands of stars with the naked eye. Groupings of stars that seem to move together in an apparent path around the North Star are known as *constellations*. The following is a sample of the many constellations visible from the northern latitudes at various times in the year: *spring*, Leo, the Lion; *summer*, Cygnus, the Swan; *fall*, Andromeda, the Maiden; *winter*, the Hunter. This demonstration focuses on the constellation known as the Big Dipper, which is visible throughout the year. The Big Dipper is part of another constellation known as Ursa Major, the Bear, with the tail of the bear made from the handle of the Big Dipper.

EXTENSION

Science/Math: Have the children create their own connect-the-dots puzzles that include numbers representing the seven stars of the Big Dipper. Have the children exchange papers so each can complete a puzzle made by someone else.

Space Journey [ESS 6]

For Middle-Level Learners

Note: Due to the unique nature of this demonstration, motivation, direction, key discussion questions, and extensions have been integrated under one heading.

OBJECTIVES

- Each child will take the role of a member of a space exploration team and describe his or her imaginary adventure.
- The children will explain the similarities and differences between their imaginary journeys and a possible real journey into outer space.

MATERIALS

A classroom that can be darkened by shutting off the light and adjusting the blinds

MOTIVATION, DIRECTIONS, KEY DISCUSSION QUESTIONS, AND EXTENSIONS

Through this simulation of a journey into outer space, children have an opportunity to use their knowledge of the solar system to form mental images of the planet their spaceship lands on. The experience encourages children to use their imagination, to communicate orally with the remainder of the class, and at a later time, to use their creative writing and artistic abilities.

Prior to the simulated space journey, divide the class into teams of space explorers. Each team will have four members—a pilot, a navigator, a scientist, and a medical officer. Allow group members to select their roles, and change the classroom seating arrangement so that team members can sit side by side. Have various team members explain what their jobs will be at the time of launch and during planetary exploration. You may, with the assistance of the class, redecorate the classroom so it looks like the interior of a spacecraft. To add realism to the experience, use a sound effects record of a rocket launch, if you can obtain one. The record can be played during blastoff.

Have each team prepare for the launch by sitting quietly in their seats for a few seconds. Indicate that you will soon begin the countdown for blastoff. Tell them that they should shut their eyes and listen to your words.

Begin the countdown. Tell the children that the rocket engines are beginning to work. When you reach 0, tell them that the rocket is lifting off the launchpad.

Space journey

Use phrases such as the following to guide their thinking during the flight:

You are being pressed backward. . . . You are in the most dangerous part of the flight, a time when a group of astronauts once lost their lives. . . . Your journey will be a safe one. Imagine that you are looking back at the earth. . . . You are flying higher and higher. . . . The earth is getting smaller and smaller. . . . It is a tiny blue dot. Ahead of you is the blackness of space. . . . The stars are bright. Brighter than you have ever seen them before. . . . Way ahead you see a tiny reddish-colored dot. . . . The pilot puts the spacecraft on automatic pilot and all the members of the crew go to special sleeping compartments, where they will sleep for months as the spacecraft approaches its target. . . . You are sleeping.

Many weeks later, a buzzer rings to awaken you. You return to your seats and see that the planet is now a large reddish ball directly ahead.

As the spacecraft gets closer, the pilot prepares for a landing. The spacecraft gently lands. You look out the windows and see the surface of the planet. . . . Think about the way it looks. Is it flat or bumpy? Does it have mountains? Don't answer. Just think about how it seems to you.

The science officer checks some instruments that tell about the planet's surface and atmosphere. The science officer says that it is safe to explore the planet if you wear spacesuits.

Imagine that you put the bulky spacesuits on. You check each other's suits to be sure they are working properly. Imagine that the pilot opens the door and you go down a ladder to the surface of the planet.

You look around and then look back at one another. You check to be sure that your radios are working. Now each of you starts out in a different direction. After you've walked for a few minutes, you stop and look around to see if you can still see the other crew members. You can see each of them. Keep walking and making observations. . . . You notice something very interesting at your feet. You bend down, pick it up, and gently place it in your collection bag. You reach a large boulder and walk behind it. There on the ground, you see something in the shadows. You are amazed at what you see. You try to move it but you can't. You pull and pull and finally get it free. Just as you are getting ready to call the other crew members to tell them what you have found, you hear the pilot's voice: "Emergency, get back to the ship immediately." You take what you discovered and race back to the ship. You and the other crew members are safely on board. Relax . . . the pilot makes a safe liftoff. You begin the long journey back to Earth. . . . A few months later, you see a tiny blue speck straight ahead. It gets larger and larger. . . . It is Earth, your home. The pilot makes a safe landing. . . . You may open your eyes. Welcome home!

When all the spacecraft have made safe landings, engage the participants in discussions of what they observed and how their observations compare with what they have learned about the solar system and planets. You may wish to have the children prepare illustrated written reports about their adventures.

SCIENCE CONTENT FOR THE TEACHER   Prior to this demonstration, study the physical characteristics of the various planets in our solar system as well as the stars. This knowledge will enable you to assist the children when they discuss their experiences.

What Is a Light-Year? [ESS 6]

OBJECTIVES
- The children will interpret data given to them and calculate the distance light travels in one year.
- The children will interpret data given them and develop a strategy for finding the time it takes for light to reach the earth from the sun.

SCIENCE PROCESSES EMPHASIZED
Interpreting data
Using space/time relationships

MATERIALS
Transparency and transparency pen
Flashlight
Clock with second hand
Globe

MOTIVATION   Clap your hands, and ask the children how long they thought it took the sound waves to reach them. Write down their estimates. Then position yourself so that they can watch you clap and also see the clock. Tell them that you want them to try to time the travel of sound waves. Clap once again. The children will note that it was either impossible to time the sound waves or that it took less than a second. Explain that they have been trying to time the rate at which sound travels and that the speed of sound, although high (340 meters/second, 1090 feet/second at 0° Celsius), is much less than the speed of light. Tell the children that they are going to discuss the speed of light.

**D
E
M
O
N
S
T
R
A
T
I
O
N
S**

DIRECTIONS

1. Write *300,000 km/sec* on the transparency. Aim the flashlight toward the children, and turn it on briefly. Explain that light from the flashlight traveled to their eyes at the rate shown on the transparency. Tell them that at this speed, if light could travel around the earth, it would circle the earth seven times in 1 second. Hold up the globe and illustrate the seven trips by moving your finger around the equator as the children snap their fingers to represent 1 second. As you obviously cannot get your finger around a tiny globe seven times in 1 second, the children should appreciate the magnitude of the speed of light.
2. Challenge the children to calculate the actual number of kilometers a beam of light can travel in a year. Begin by having them determine the number of seconds in a year (60 seconds/minute /60 minutes/hour/24 hours/day/365 days/year = 31,536,000 seconds/year).
3. Again direct the flashlight toward the students, and flick it on and off. Tell them to imagine that the flashlight is the sun. Ask them how long it takes light to travel from the sun to the earth. Write *149,600,000 km* on the transparency. Indicate that this is the average distance that the earth is from the sun as it travels in orbit. Have the children invent a strategy for finding out how many seconds it takes for light to get to the earth. *Hint:* Round off the kilometer distance to 150,000,000 and divide it by 300,000 kilometers per second, which will equal 500 seconds. Remind the children that they did some rounding, so the actual number of seconds is somewhat less.

*KEY
DISCUSSION
QUESTIONS*

1. How far away from the flashlight would you have to be in order for the light to reach you in exactly 1 second? *300,000 kilometers.*
2. If the sun were to stop shining right now, how long would it be before we would notice it? *Between 7 and 8 minutes.*

*SCIENCE
CONTENT FOR
THE TEACHER*

Light waves travel at a speed of 300,000 kilometers per second (about 186,000 miles per second). Light does not require a medium and can travel through empty space. The speed of light is constant in the universe. Scientists use the distance that light can travel in one year, a *light-year,* as a standard measurement of distance.

EXTENSION

Science/Math: Ask the children to determine how long it takes light to travel from the sun to Pluto (about 5 hours) and from the sun to Proxima Centauri, the closest star to the sun (about 4 years). This extension requires library research, the ability to round numbers, and the use of a calculator.

13

Unit, Lesson, and Enrichment Starter Ideas

The Life Sciences and Technology

A Look Ahead

The Tapper

Assessing Prior Knowledge and Conceptions

Internet Resources: Websites for Life Science Units, Lessons, Activities, and Demonstrations

Unit Plan Starter Ideas

Ideas Based on the NSE K–8 Content Standards

Ideas Based on Project 2061 Goals

Ideas Based on Typical Grade Level Content

Lesson Plan Starter Ideas for Common Curriculum Topics

Classroom Enrichment Starter Ideas

In-Class Learning Centers

Bulletin Boards

Field Trips for City Schools

Field Trips for All Schools

Cooperative Learning Projects

Science and Children and *Science Scope*: **Resource Articles for Life Science Units, Lessons, Activities, and Demonstrations**

Make the Case: An Individual or Group Challenge

The Tapper

The sound of John Williams's footsteps bounced off the walls lining the dimly lit hallway and echoed after him as he counted down the classroom numbers. Room 12, 11, 10, 9, 8. And there it was—Room 7. With excitement and more than a little apprehension, he opened the door. His first quick look around the room brought a sinking feeling. Drab, drab, drab—25 desks with firmly attached chairs, an old wooden teacher's desk, green chalkboards, bookshelf after bookshelf filled with school books, and some bulletin boards swiss-cheesed with tack holes. No real tables or even counter space for science work or hands-on projects of any kind.

John walked to the front of the room and sat down behind the old wooden desk. The eerie silence and warmth of the last days of summer soothed him only slightly.

What would it be like teaching in this school? Would the other teachers accept him? Where was he going to get the materials he was going to need? What would the children be like? That was his primary question. What would the children be like?

He didn't notice the tapping sound for a while. Finally, a particularly loud tap broke him from his reverie. He turned to his right and saw the concerned face of a child outside, tapping on the window pane with one hand to get his attention. He left his chair, walked to the window, and opened it wide.

"Hi, I'm Mr. Williams. I'm going to be the teacher in this room."
"I found this nest in the bushes. It was on the ground."
John asked, "What grade are you going to be in?"
"It's got some pieces of eggshell in it," the Tapper answered.
John tried again, "What's your name? Do you live near here?"
"The birds. What happened to the little birds?"

Children are concerned about life. They want to know what happens to baby birds, and they want to know the names for the colorful, creepy-crawly caterpillars they find on the way to school. In this chapter, you will find ideas and resources to assist you as you plan discovery-oriented life science experiences for children that will develop and extend their curiosity, knowledge, and concern for life in its multitude of forms.

Assessing Prior Knowledge and Conceptions

"But we learned all that in Mr. Greeley's class last year."

Have you ever been in a classroom and observed a teacher getting ambushed? That's what happens when teachers assume that children know little or nothing about a topic, only to discover too late that they know a lot. The results are also disastrous when teachers assume that children know a lot about a topic and in fact know very little. (Plus, valuable lesson-planning time will have been wasted.) Even assumptions about children's beliefs about phenomena in the natural world can stop teachers in their tracks. Children may have very strongly held beliefs that are totally incorrect, which may not be discovered until the class is deep in a lesson or unit.

So, as a teacher in the real world of schools and classrooms, how can you quickly get a sense of what the children know, what skills they possess, and what they believe? Part of the answer is to use *probes*—basic questions and simple activities that get children thinking and talking about particular topics. The answers children give will provide very direct guidance about what you should include in science units and lessons.

The probes and sample responses that follow come from informal interviews that I or my students have done with children. I think you'll be amazed at some of the responses and motivated to develop probes that you can use *before* planning units and lessons.

Probe	*Responses That Reveal Prior Knowledge and Conceptions*
▶ *Is the wind a living thing?*	"Yes. It moves things."
	"No. It just blows stuff around."
	"No. It's just cold."
	"No. You can't see it."
▶ *Is fire a living thing?*	"No. It burns things."
	"Yes. It makes smoke."
	"Yes. It's hot and red and moves."
	"No. I don't know why."
▶ *Is the sun a living thing?*	"Yes. If it wasn't, it couldn't make things hot."
	"No. It's like a star."

Probe	*Responses That Reveal Prior Knowledge and Conceptions*
▶ After pointing out some clouds overhead: *Are those clouds living things?*	"Yes. They work by bringing the rain down."
	"No. They are just a bunch of rain."
	"No. They are just puffy and float."
	"No. They don't breathe or have babies."
▶ *What is a seed?*	"Something you stick in the ground."
	"A thing that makes flowers grow."
	"A plant grows out of them."
	"Little thing you put in the ground."
	"They get bigger to make a plant."
▶ After having the child observe a variety of seeds: *Where do seeds come from?*	"Plants. Some have things that make the air put it somewhere else. They have fuzz on them."
	"Other plants."
	"Flowers."
	"Pumpkins. Sometimes if you eat one, it will stay there and grow."
	"When someone plants two seeds and if one of them doesn't grow, then someone digs the other seed up."
	"Sometimes ants make them and lay them like eggs."
	"They come from big, big bags."
▶ *Do you eat any plants or parts of plants?*	"Yes. Raspberries."
	"Yes. I eat carrots."
	"We can eat berries and beans."
	"Corn. I eat the whole thing."
	"No. Brian eats clovers. He's bad."
	"No way. They are bad for you."
▶ After showing a collection of forest pictures: *What animals and plants live in a forest?*	"All of them except dogs and cats."
	"Spiders. Lots of spiders."
	"Trees and wolves."
	"Lions and bears."
	"People could, but they don't. I don't think anybody lives there now."

Probe	*Responses That Reveal Prior Knowledge and Conceptions*
▶ After showing a child pictures of the desert: *What animals and plants do you think live in a desert like this one?*	"No dogs and cats." "Snakes." "Tigers." "Dinosaurs used to live there." "Some cows do." "Wolves . . . no, maybe no wolves."
▶ *What is pollution?*	"Dirty air." "Cars give pollution." "Big cities have pollution." "Garbage on the ground." "It comes from cars on the street." "Where the air gets dirty and mixes up with the bad stuff then we can't breathe." "When people litter with cars." "Air . . . disgusting air." "Stuff that flies around the world."

Internet Resources

Websites for Life Science Units, Lessons, Activities, and Demonstrations

The Electronic Zoo

http://netvet.wustl.edu/pix.htm

If your students are engaged in discovery units, lessons, or Internet research about animals, this page will prove to be extremely valuable. In addition to subsections on all major areas of the animal kingdom, you will find excellent photographs, graphics, and even animal sounds! Be advised that some of the links on the pages will take young people to rather advanced science content. You may wish to spend some time at this site yourself so you can tailor your students' web research to content that is at an appropriate difficulty level for them. Older students will also find career-awareness information, if they have an interest in veterinary medicine.

ERIC Life Science Lesson Plans

http://ericir.syr.edu/Virtual/Lessons/Science/

This is one of the best-organized compilations of science lesson plans on the Internet. When you reach the site, select "Biological and Life Sciences," which will take you to an alphabetized list of lessons at all grade levels. Be advised that although the lessons have been placed in a consistent format, they come from a variety of sources. (Or to put it more directly, they vary in quality.)

The Natural History Museum (London) "Quest"

http://www.nhm.ac.uk/education/quest/index.html

This is the "Quest" portion of a rather amazing site. The Natural History Museum provides virtual tools that your students can use to explore at least 12 different objects related to the natural sciences. Each Quest excursion can easily be adapted to a discovery-based lesson for your classroom. Imagine the possibilities as your students explore science materials in London using the Internet.

The Natural History Museum (London) "The Life Galleries"

http://www.nhm.ac.uk/museum/lifegal/interface/p1.html

At this site, students can view a variety of the life science exhibits available at the Natural History Museum. Each location—whether on birds, mammals, ecology, or any of the other important topics presented—contains extremely well done visual presentations and an abundance of information about the topic. Creative teachers will find this a useful site to direct students to.

The Wild Ones

http://www.thewildones.org/Curric/curricLib.html

This site, sponsored by the Wildlife Preservation Trust International, seeks to provide "students ages 7 to 14 with an international perspective, opportunities for cooperative science activities, and a positive outlook on their capacity as individuals to improve the prospects for endangered species." At this Interent location of The Wild Ones, you will find a variety of resources, including classroom, school yard, and field trip activities related to the organization's mission. An interesting feature of this site is that a portion of the resources are presented in Spanish.

Sea World: Science Information

http://www.seaworld.org/infobook.html

This beautifully presented and quite helpful site represents Sea World's presence on the Internet. This specific portion of the site includes science content and illustrations on a variety of topics related to ocean and shore life and other environmental topics: beluga whales, coral reefs, endangered species, and many other topics commonly taught in the schools. The information about particular species of animals is quite extensive, and the photographs and related graphics are of the highest quality.

Sea World: Science Information

http://www.seaworld.org/teacherguides/teacherguides.html

This portion of the Sea World site focuses directly on teaching resources (in contrast to the previous site, which presents science content). This is one of the very few places on the Internet that provides complete science units referred to as "Teacher's Guides," including "All About Seals, Sea Lions, and Walruses," "Ocean Olympians," and "Animals Abound." Again, some of the units are in Spanish.

The Tree of Life

http://phylogeny.arizona.edu/tree/

Don't be misled by the use of the word *tree* in the name for this site. It's about *all* life on our planet. Be advised that this site presents science content in a somewhat sophisticated manner, which should be understandable to you and perhaps a few of your most advanced students. Even so, this is one of the most carefully organized and well-presented compilations of science content on the Internet and must be visited by any teacher who wants to be sure that he or she presents accurate scientific content to children when life on Earth is being studied. Use the "Search" choice on the opening page, and key in the name of a living thing your class is studying. You will be amazed at the information and associated graphics available.

Unit Plan Starter Ideas

That great idea for a science-teaching unit may come from deep within your brain, your school curriculum guide, a state science curriculum framework, a science resource book, a course, a workshop, a discussion you have with children, or some other source. Unfortunately, a great idea (like a friend, an umbrella, and a good restaurant with cheap food) is sometimes hard to find when you really need one.

To make it easier for you to come up with great ideas for science units, I have prepared three different sources of unit starter ideas, which are presented as three lists:

1. The first is based on the National Science Education (NSE) standards for science content. I created these starter ideas for standards related to grades K–4 and 5–8.

2. The second is based on the general goals for science and scientific literacy proposed by Project 2061 in their scientific views of the world recommendations. I regrouped the goals into earth/space science, life science, and physical science and then included related goals for science and math integration.

3. The third list of starter ideas is based on my study of life science topics that commonly appear in school curriculum guides. These are shown by grade level.

I am certain that this rather unique compilation of starter ideas will help you plan and create wonderful discovery-based teaching units.

Ideas Based on the NSE K–8 Content Standards

NSE

Content Standard K–4: Life Sciences [LS]

As a result of activities in grades K–4, all students should develop an understanding of:

The characteristics of organisms

Life cycles of organisms

Organisms and environments[1]

Starter Ideas for the Characteristics of Organisms

Unit Title/Topic: *Taking Care of Plants*

Unit Goal: Children care for classroom plants for a two-week period and then prepare charts and drawings to show how they helped the plants meet their requirements for life (e.g., air, water, nutrients, and light).

Unit Title/Topic: *Taking Care of Animals*

Unit Goal: Children care for classroom chameleons, gerbils, and guinea pigs and identify through diagrams and written explanations how they have helped the animals meet their requirements for life (e.g., air, water, and food).

Starter Ideas for Life Cycles of Organisms

Unit Title/Topic: *Cycles in a Garden*

Unit Goal: Children maintain an outdoor garden, observe plants growing into adulthood from seeds, and maintain logs that show the changes that occur as the plants go through their life cycles.

Unit Title/Topic: *Seed Cycles/Frog Cycles*

Unit Goal: After raising plants from seeds and frogs from eggs, children compare plant and animal life cycles, including attention to birth, adulthood, reproduction, and death.

Starter Ideas for Organisms and Environments

Unit Title/Topic: *Find the Chains*

Unit Goal: Through library research, Internet research, and direct observations at a local nature area, children prepare diagrams to show five sample food chains that could be found in each of the following environments: forest, desert, tundra, meadow, and ocean.

Unit Title/Topic: *The Grasshopper's Lawn*

Unit Goal: Children make careful observations of the school lawn and identify the living things, food, and water present in the grasshopper's environment.

> **NSE**
>
> ### Content Standard 5–8: Life Sciences [LS]
>
> *As a result of the activities in grades 5–8, all students should develop an understanding of:*
>
> *Structure and function in living systems*
>
> *Reproduction and heredity*
>
> *Regulation and behavior*
>
> *Populations and ecosystems*
>
> *Diversity and adaptation of organisms*

Starter Ideas for Structure and Function in Living Systems

Unit Title/Topic: *Cells—What Are They? What Do They Do?*

Unit Goal: Children prepare written reports on cell structure and function based on their study of cells using a microscope and library research.

Unit Title/Topic: *Body Systems*

Unit Goal: Children describe the characteristics of body systems that provide for digestion, respiration, reproduction, circulation, excretion, movement, control and coordination, and protection from disease.

Starter Ideas for Reproduction and Heredity

Unit Title/Topic: *You and Heredity*

Unit Goal: Children describe how each new human being receives a "set of instructions" that specifies his or her inherited traits.

Unit Title/Topic: *My Traits and My Environment*

Unit Goal: Children identify five of their inherited traits and five traits that may have been acquired from their environment.

Starter Ideas for Regulation and Behavior

Unit Title/Topic: *Changes on My Inside*

Unit Goal: Children describe and prepare labeled diagrams to show how the human nervous system senses internal environmental changes and the body adapts to changes in internal stimuli.

Unit Title/Topic: *Changes on My Outside*

Unit Goal: Children describe and prepare labeled diagrams to show how the human nervous system senses external environmental changes and the body adapts to changes in internal stimuli.

Starter Ideas for Populations and Ecosystems

Unit Title/Topic: *Producers*

Unit Goal: Children identify those organisms that capture the sun's energy in a desert, a woodland, a meadow, and an ocean ecosystem.

Unit Title/Topic: *Consumers*

Unit Goal: Children identify those organisms that use energy captured by others in a desert, a woodland, a meadow, and an ocean ecosystem.

Starter Ideas for Diversity and Adaptation of Organisms

Unit Title/Topic: *Special Species*

Unit Goal: Children identify the external adaptations and the related advantages possessed by five birds of prey, five land predators, and five ocean predators.

Unit Title/Topic: *Dinosaurs' Disappearance*

Unit Goal: As a result of library research and classroom discussion, children identify and prepare support for three hypotheses that explain why dinosaurs became extinct.

NSE

Content Standards Related to:

Science and Technology [S&T]

Science in Personal and Social Perspectives [SPSP]

History and Nature of Science [HNS][2]

Unit Title/Topic: *Acid Rain*

Unit Goal: Children write and perform a classroom skit that identifies the natural and human causes of acid rain and its environmental impact.

Unit Title/Topic: *They Study Life*

Unit Goal: Children conduct library and Internet research to gather information about the lives and work of three scientists in the field of ecology and present their information through oral reports.

Ideas Based on Project 2061 Goals

> **2061 GOAL**
>
> *The living environment, emphasizing the rich diversity of the earth's organisms and the surprising similarity in the structure and functions of their cells; the dependence of species on each other and on the physical environment; and the flow of matter and energy through the cycles of life.* (p. 7)

Starter Ideas for the Living Environment

Unit Title/Topic: *Animals Need Plants*

Unit Goal: Children learn how all animal life (even meat eaters) depends on the growth of green plants.

Unit Title/Topic: *It's All about Energy*

Unit Goal: Children learn that the food chain and food web are used to explain the flow of energy through an ecosystem.

> **2061 GOAL**
>
> *Biological evolution as a concept based on extensive geological and molecular evidence, as an explanation for the diversity and similarity of life forms, and as a central organizing principle for all of biology.* (p. 7)

Starter Ideas for the Diversity and Similarity of Life Forms

Unit Title/Topic: *What Happened to the Dinosaurs?*

Unit Goal: Children learn that there may be some environmental changes to which a species is unable to adapt.

Unit Title/Topic: *What Happens Next?*

Unit Goal: Children make hypotheses about what may occur as a result of environmental changes, including changes in the availability of clean air and water.

> **2061 GOAL**
>
> *The human organism as a biological, social, and technological species—including its similarities to other organisms, its unique capacity for learning, and the strong biological similarity among all humans in contrast to the large cultural differences among groups of them.* (p. 7)

Starter Ideas for the Human Organism as a Biological, Social, and Technological Species

Unit Title/Topic: *You and the Bee*

Unit Goal: Children learn the organizational structure of a beehive and try to discern the similarities and differences between a hive and human society.

Unit Title/Topic: *Human Body Systems*

Unit Goal: Children learn that humans, like all living things, have systems that carry out essential life processes, such as growth and reproduction.

> **2061 GOAL**
>
> *The human life cycle through all stages of development and maturation, emphasizing the factors that contribute to the birth of a healthy child, to the fullest development of human potential, and to improved life expectancy.* (p. 7)

Starter Ideas for the Human Life Cycle

Unit Title/Topic: *Healthy Baby, Healthy You*

Unit Goal: Children identify the factors that contribute to the birth of a healthy child and the factors that affect healthy human growth and development to adulthood.

Unit Title/Topic: *You Are Growing and Changing*

Unit Goal: Children learn that their growth and change will proceed along a predictable sequence from childhood to adulthood.

> **2061 GOAL**
>
> *The basic structure and functioning of the human body, seen as a complex system of cells and organs that serve the fundamental functions of deriving energy from food, protection against injury, internal coordination, and reproduction.* (p. 8)

Starter Ideas for the Structure and Functions of the Human Body

Unit Title/Topic: *From Food to Energy*

Unit Goal: Children learn how the human body transforms food into the energy required for life processes.

Unit Title/Topic: *From Life Comes Life*

Unit Goal: Children learn how the human reproductive system functions and what child-care responsibilities parents have.

> **2061 GOAL**
>
> *Physical and mental health as they involve the interaction of biological, physiological, psychological, social, economic, cultural, and environmental factors, including the effects of food, exercise, drugs, and air and water quality.* (p. 8)

Starter Ideas for Physical and Mental Health

Unit Title/Topic: *Drugs That Help, Drugs That Hurt*

Unit Goal: Children learn that street drugs have deleterious effects and that drugs prescribed by a physician may assist the body's natural response to ailments but may have side effects.

Unit Title/Topic: *Food Choosing*

Unit Goal: Children learn about the food guide pyramid and how to use it to analyze the food they eat at home, at school, and at their favorite fast-food restaurant.

> **2061 GOAL**
>
> *Medical technologies, including mechanical, chemical, electronic, biological, and genetic materials and techniques; their use in enhancing the functioning of the human body; their role in the detection, diagnosis, monitoring, and treatment of disease; and the ethical and economic issues raised by their use.* (p. 8)

Starter Ideas for Medical Technologies

Unit Title/Topic: *Healthy Babies on the Way*

Unit Goal: Children learn about nutrition, exercise, and the dangers of drug, alcohol, and tobacco use during pregnancy.

Unit Title/Topic: *Robo-You?*

Unit Goal: Children learn of advances in technology related to organ transplants and mechanical devices used to compensate for problems caused by disease or injury.

> **2061 GOAL**
>
> *The human population, including its size, density, and distribution, the technological factors that have led to its rapid increase and dominance, its impact on other species and the environment, and its future in relation to resources and their use.* (p. 8)

Starter Ideas for the Human Population

Unit Title/Topic: *Many Mouths to Feed*

Unit Goal: Children learn of the technological advances used to increase the food supply for the human population and the possible adverse affects of using these technologies.

Unit Title/Topic: *A Perfect Space Colony*

Unit Goal: Children learn what the requirements would be for the creation of a self-sustaining space colony on a planet.

> **2061 GOAL**
>
> *The nature of technologies, including agriculture, with emphasis on both the agricultural revolution in ancient times and the effects on twentieth-century agricultural productivity of the use of biological and chemical technologies; the acquisition, processing, and use of materials and energy, with particular attention to both the Industrial Revolution and the current revolution in manufacturing based on the use of computers; and information processing and communications, with emphasis on the impact of computers and electronic communications on contemporary society. (p. 8)*

Starter Ideas for the Nature of Technologies

Unit Title/Topic: *Perfect Food: What Is the Price?*

Unit Goal: Children learn that our desire for perfect, unblemished fruits and vegetables may have hidden costs in terms of challenges to farmers and adverse environmental effects.

Unit Title/Topic: *Computers Here, Computers There*

Unit Goal: Children learn that the computers they use in school and at home are only a few of those that are part of their daily lives and discover that computer technology is found in automobile and school bus engines, television sets, home appliances, and other things.

> **2061 GOAL**
>
> *The mathematics of symbols and symbolic relationships, emphasizing the kinds, properties, and uses of numbers and shapes; graphic and algebraic ways of expressing relationships among things; and coordinate systems as a means of relating numbers to geometry and geography. (p. 8)*

Starter Ideas for Using Numbers and Graphs

Unit Title/Topic: *Slow Plants, Fast Plants*

Unit Goal: Children learn how light affects plant growth and use simple bar graphs to illustrate growth.

Unit Title/Topic: *Graph It*

Unit Goal: Children use graphs and charts to report the results of their analyses of the number and kinds of living things discovered in 1 square meter of lawn.

2061 GOAL

Probability, including the kinds of uncertainty that limit knowledge, methods of estimating and expressing probabilities, and the use of such methods in predicting results when large numbers are involved. (p. 8)

Starter Ideas for Probability and Predicting

Unit Title/Topic: *How Many Pea Plants?*

Unit Goal: Children learn to estimate the likely germination rate of a seed packet of peas from previous experience with similar seed packets.

Unit Title/Topic: *The Same or Different?*

Unit Goal: Children gather data from a sample of children in their class regarding resting pulse rate, eye color, and hair color; what their results would be if they carried out the same procedures for another classroom; and then compare their results with their predictions.

2061 GOAL

Data analysis, with an emphasis on numerical and graphic ways of summarizing data, the nature and limitations of correlations and the problem of sampling in data collection. (p. 9)

Starter Ideas for Studying Results and Summarizing

Unit Title/Topic: *Waste Watch*

Unit Goal: Children study the amount of food left on a sample of dishes disposed of after hot lunch time, prepare charts and graphs to show the results of their study, and then estimate the total amounts of various types of food wasted.

Unit Title/Topic: *How Many Seeds?*

Unit Goal: Children create rules to accurately estimate the number of seeds in a variety of fruits and vegetables. After counting and graphing the seeds in a sample, they use the rules with a different sample and compare the results.

> **2061 GOAL**
>
> *Reasoning, including the nature and limitations of deductive logic, the uses and dangers of generalizing from a limited number of experiences, and reasoning by analogy.* (p. 9)

Starter Ideas for Reasoning

Unit Title/Topic: *Model Frog/Real Frog*

Unit Goal: Children compare what they learn from a plastic model of a frog to what they learn from a real frog and discuss the differences between a model and the reality it represents.

Unit Title/Topic: *Can't Fool Me!*

Unit Goal: Children analyze the advertising copy from magazines or video-taped commercials for such products as exercise machines, diet plans, and beauty aids to determine whether the benefits advertised are likely or unlikely to occur.

Ideas Based on Typical Grade Level Content

Starter Ideas for Kindergarten

Unit Topic/Title: *The Senses*

Unit Goal: Children learn that the senses of touch, sight, hearing, taste, and smell are their tools for exploring the world around them.

Unit Topic/Title: *Plant or Animal?*

Unit Goal: Children learn the characteristics they can use to classify things as plants or animals.

Starter Ideas for First Grade

Unit Topic/Title: *What Do Green Plants Need?*

Unit Goal: Children learn that green plants need sunlight, air, and water to live.

Unit Topic/Title: *What Do Animals Need?*

Unit Goal: Children learn that animals need food, air, water, and shelter to live.

Starter Ideas for Second Grade

Unit Topic/Title: *Plants Have Parts*

Unit Goal: Children learn the basic structures and functions of such plant parts as roots, stems, leaves, flowers, and seeds.

Unit Topic/Title: *Animals Have Parts*

Unit Goal: Children learn the basic structures and functions of the principal organs outside and inside animals.

Starter Ideas for Third Grade

Unit Topic/Title: *Looking for Plants*

Unit Goal: Children learn that plants display characteristics that reflect adaptations to the environments in which they live.

Unit Topic/Title: *Looking for Animals*

Unit Goal: Children learn that animals display characteristics that reflect adaptations to the environments in which they live.

Starter Ideas for Fourth Grade

Unit Topic/Title: *Life Is a Cycle*

Unit Goal: Children learn the life cycles of various plants and animals.

Unit Topic/Title: *What Is a Population?*

Unit Goal: Children learn that a *population* is all the individuals of a particular species in an environment and that populations are affected by changes in the environment.

Starter Ideas for Fifth Grade

Unit Topic/Title: *Cells Tell*

Unit Goal: Children learn to use a microscope and reference material to identify basic structures in animal and plant cells.

Unit Topic/Title: *Cells, Tissues, Organs, Systems*

Unit Goal: Children learn that their bodies and other living things are composed of a variety of systems and subsystems.

Starter Ideas for Sixth Grade

Unit Topic/Title: *Taking Care of Your Business*

Unit Goal: Children learn about the basics of personal health care, the existence of sexually transmitted diseases (STDs), and the general modalities for the prevention of STDs, including abstinence.

Unit Topic/Title: *The Dinosaurs*

Unit Goal: Children learn the characteristics of various species of dinosaurs and their places in the food chains that existed when they did and make hypotheses about whether particular species could survive in the climatic conditions that now exist in the students' region.

Starter Ideas for Seventh Grade

Unit Topic/Title: *Animals without Backbones*

Unit Goal: Students learn the basic characteristics and biological adaptations of sponges, coelenterates, worms, mollusks, echinoderms, and arthropods.

Unit Topic/Title: *Animals with Backbones*

Unit Goal: Students learn the basic characteristics and biological adaptations of fish, amphibians, reptiles, and birds.

Starter Ideas for Eighth Grade

Unit Topic/Title: *Plants with Flowers, Plants Without*

Unit Goal: Students learn how flowering (angiosperms) and nonflowering (gymnosperms) plants reproduce.

Unit Topic/Title: *Our Earth, Our Ecosystem*

Unit Goal: Students learn that the earth can be studied as one large ecosystem, which is affected by our technologies.

Lesson Plan Starter Ideas for Common Curriculum Topics

 Sometimes you will be responsible for teaching lessons that are part of units prepared by committees of teachers in your school district or units that are commercially available. You may wonder how to break these units into lessons. To help you come up with lesson ideas for the life sciences, I have analyzed a variety of teaching units and prepared a list of lesson plan starter ideas based on topics usually covered in these units. The lesson descriptions are very specific, so each description may also be viewed as the lesson's principal objective.

Characteristics of Living Things

Plan a lesson in which the children:

- Observe and measure the growth and movement of living things that are kept in the classroom.
- Count the number of living things in the classroom, and prepare a bar graph that shows the number of each type of living thing.
- Orally describe the similarities and differences between plant and animal parts.
- Analyze the conditions under which animals at a local zoo are kept and list the observed conditions on a chart.

Plant and Animal Life Processes

Plan a lesson in which the children:

- Analyze food samples provided by the teacher to determine whether they are sweet, sour, bitter, or salty.
- Identify from a list of foods those that are the best sources of protein, fiber, carbohydrates, and fat, and locate each food in the nutrition food pyramid.
- Explain orally how humans can prevent the spread of diseases, including sexually transmitted diseases.
- Explain orally the effects of tobacco, alcohol, and drug use on the human body.
- Evaluate the effectiveness of posters created by classmates to encourage people not to smoke, use alcohol, or take drugs.
- Recognize and identify different patterns of animal growth (continuous, molting, metamorphosis).
- Identify the functions of the principal organs of the human reproductive system for both males and females.

Populations

Plan a lesson in which the children:

- Identify factors that might cause a population of animals or plants to become extinct.
- Explain the factors that trigger the migration of a population from one place to another.
- After doing library and Internet research to evaluate explanations for successful migration to distant locations, select the two most likely explanations.
- Explain the similarities and differences in the survival needs of the following populations: bees, ants, deer, humans.
- Make a labeled diagram that shows the role decomposers play in returning water, minerals, and other nutrients to a population.

The Environment

Plan a lesson in which the children:

- Describe the adaptations that an organism has that help it fit into its environment.
- Predict the impact of humankind on plants and animals.
- Infer the requirements for keeping an ecosystem self-sustaining.
- Create a timeline for the last 100 years that shows the changes described by senior citizens in the local environment.
- Identify the human use of natural resources found in the environment.

Life Adapts and Changes

Plan a lesson in which the children:

- Evaluate how an animal's characteristics increase its chances for survival in its environment.
- Given illustrations of the ancient and modern forms of horses and dogs, infer any advantages the modern form would have over the ancient form in today's world.
- Create a timeline that shows when life began on Earth, the origin and extinction of dinosaurs, and the origin of humans.
- Identify the major changes that have occurred in the bodies and behaviors of humans over the past 3 million years.
- Predict changes that will occur in human bodies as the species adapts to increased water and air pollution.

Ecosystems

Plan a lesson in which the children:

- Explain how all animals depend on the food-making ability of green plants.
- Classify the members of a community as producers, consumers, and decomposers.
- Count the number of organisms found in a sample of water from a pond ecosystem.
- Explain that an ecosystem consists of the physical environment and a group of interacting living things that also interact with the environment.
- Infer how changes in the characteristics of an ecosystem can affect the balance among producers, consumers, and decomposers.
- Given specific information about the components of an ecosystem, infer how the introduction of a population of new producers changes the rest of the ecosystem.
- Describe an experiment that could test the effects of drastic changes in each of the following on an ecosystem: water, food, temperature, and availability of light.

Classroom Enrichment Starter Ideas

 ## In-Class Learning Centers

You may wish to use a corner of your room for this learning center, which you might call the *Wonder Machine.* Allow enough floor space for the children to make outlines of themselves by rolling out shelfpaper and tracing around their bodies. You may want to cover part of the floor with newspapers, on which the children can work with clay and paste. If you have computer software or videos related to the human body, make them available in this center, too.

Prepare activity cards (cards that give directions for activities you develop) based on the following ideas (***Note:*** Asterisks indicate activities that may be particularly appropriate for young children):

- *Find Your Pulse* Children use a stopwatch or the second hand of a clock to count heartbeats, do mild exercise, and count heartbeats again. Have the children graph their results.

- *Take a Breather** Children breathe on a mirror and record what they observe.

- *Bright Eyes* Children observe changes in their partners' eyes when they briefly shine a flashlight at them.

- *Different Bodies** Children trace each other while lying on shelfpaper, and then refer to materials on the principal organs of the body and their locations and draw the organs on the shelfpaper. Some children may use a tape measure to gather data for a chart on foot sizes.

- *What's Inside?* Children use clay, construction paper, and other art materials to construct models of organ systems.

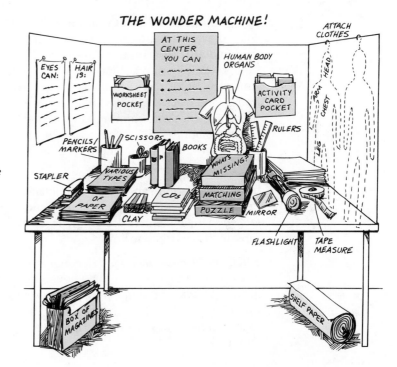

This in-class learning center—the Wonder Machine—holds a host of activities to interest children.

Bulletin Boards

Good bulletin boards have the potential to be something that children can both look at and learn from. There are many ways to use classroom bulletin boards to enhance life science units and extend your teaching to nonscience areas. The following list offers a few starter ideas for you (**Note:** Asterisks indicate activities that may be particularly appropriate for young children):

- *Flower Power** Create vocabulary word cards for the words *stem, leaf, roots, petals, soil, air, sun,* and *water.* Make construction paper cutouts of a plant stem, leaves, petals, roots, the sun, clouds, soil, and raindrops, and display them on the bulletin board with the word cards. After the children have become familiar with the vocabulary on the word cards, have them attach the cards to the appropriate parts with pushpins. Provide a self-correcting key.

- *I'm Lost** Divide a bulletin board into six areas, all of which can be reached by a young child. Each area should have one of the following labels and magazine pictures illustrating the label: *Insects, Fish, Amphibians, Reptiles, Birds, Mammals.* Place at the bottom of the bulletin board a folder or envelope containing a random assortment of pictures or drawings for each of the six categories. Provide some age-appropriate method for attaching the pictures to the areas and encourage the children to spend free time at the bulletin board, placing each picture from the folder in the appropriate category.

- *Desert Animal Homes** Cover the bulletin board with easel paper, and use colored paper, crayons, pastels, paint, and other art supplies to create, with the children's assistance, a desert scene without animals. Include cactus, sand, rocks, blue sky, a shining sun, and so forth. Draw or cut out 10 magazine pictures of desert animals (e.g., a hawk, rattlesnake, scorpion, and lizard), and place these in a folder or envelope at the bottom of the bulletin board. Provide an age-appropriate method for children to attach the pictures to the bulletin board. Encourage children to use their free time to work on putting the animals in their proper places.

- *Plant Munchers** Create a large, generic plant that includes a flower, seed, fruits, leaves, stems, and roots. Add unlabeled arrows that point to each part. Put pictures of commonly eaten fruits and vegetables in a large envelope attached to the bulletin board. In their free time, have children attach the pictures to the appropriate arrows.

- *Producers, Consumers, and Decomposers* Cover the bulletin board with easel paper. Divide it into three equal-sized parts, and label each with the heading *Producer, Consumer,* or *Decomposer.* As the children have free time, ask them individually or in groups to draw and label an example of each organism following this rule: "The three organisms must interact with one another."

- *Body Systems*   Place a large drawing of the human body at one side of the bulletin board. Each week, place a large index card with the name of a body system (e.g., digestion, circulation, respiration) at the top of the other side of the bulletin board. Challenge children to attach smaller cards with labels to show the sequence of steps that occur in the identified system. For example, if the system was digestion, the children might attach cards under it that said "Food eaten," "Food enters stomach," and so on.

Field Trips for City Schools

Many of the factors that make the city an interesting and exciting place to live also make it a place that overflows with field trip possibilities. When you teach children life science concepts and technology, don't forget that life is in full bloom right outside the school door. There, at the borders of sidewalks, in moist areas along the foundations of buildings, in little-used parts of the school playground, and many other places, life carries out its silent struggle for survival. Even so-called vacant lots are filled with life. Moss, weeds, insects, birds, and squirrels grow and thrive in old building foundations, chunks of pavement from long-forgotten parking lots, and discarded shopping carts. City parks are nature reserves where life flourishes and awaits discovery by those children fortunate enough to have a clever teacher who sees science discovery possibilities that others miss.

The field trips suggested in the next section include explorations that can be done in the city. Pay close attention to the following topics to see if you can tailor them to the resources of the city in which you presently teach or study:

Animal Study	*Plants on Parade*
Is It Alive?	*Eggs and Seeds*
Seasonal Changes	*Supermarket Survey*

Here are additional starter ideas that should stimulate your thinking about field trips for children in city schools:

- *Mud Puddle Life*   Children observe living things in and at the margins of a mud puddle after a rainstorm.

- *Dandelion Detectives*   Children count dandelions, note where they are found, and observe their structures.

- *Squirrel Detectives*   Children count the squirrels they see on a nature walk and note their behavior.

- *Bushes Change*   Children study hedges and other plants growing on the school grounds to observe seasonal changes.

- *City Birds*   Children study pigeons, sparrows, starlings, and other birds that live in the city.

- *Bug Business*   Children go on a nature walk to locate (without touching) as many insects as they can and note what the insects are doing.

- *Is There Life in That Lot?*   Under close supervision and at a vacant lot that is safe in every respect, children note the presence of such living things as ragweed and milkweed plants, fungi, moths, butterflies, and so forth.

- *Pyramid Power*   Children visit restaurants and neighborhood grocery stores to learn what foods people from various cultures enjoy and then use the nutrition food pyramid to classify the foods.

Field Trips for All Schools

Here are starter ideas for field trips for all schools (***Note:*** Asterisks indicate activities that may be particularly appropriate for young children):

- *Animal Study**   Visiting a zoological park, aquarium, or farm gives children the opportunity to observe some of the animals they have seen only in pictures, movies, and television shows. Consider having individual children or cooperative learning groups become "experts" on one animal they will see during the trip, and have them compare their research with what they actually observe during the trip. Any nearby stream, field, or park also can offer the children a chance to obtain firsthand knowledge about animal life. Because such trips can also provide opportunities for students to draw and write about interesting animals, art materials and notebooks should be available. If the location is easily accessible, visit it at different times in the year so variations in animal life can be observed.

- *Is It Alive?**   A field trip on school grounds or to a nearby park or nature area will provide many opportunities for young children to differentiate between living and nonliving things. Prior to the trip, have children discuss the characteristics of living and nonliving things. You may wish to create a checklist that children can take along on the trip. They may discover that some objects do not easily fit into the two categories. Such an observation could prompt a good discussion of the problems that arise when objects are classified.

- *Searching for Changes*   A walk through the school neighborhood can provide opportunities to observe how the environment has been modified to meet the needs of people. If farmland has been converted to a residential area, you may see some signs of previous farm use. Have the children look for evidence of resources being brought into the environment, such as electric poles, water pipes, and so forth. Also look for evidence of materials being taken out of the area, such as sewage pipes and trash bins. Emphasize that an environment may look stable, but if we observe it for any length of time, we can see many changes occurring.

- *Plants on Parade*   A nature walk focused on plants may reveal a great deal to children about the types and quantities of plants that live on or near the school grounds. Prior to the trip, have children predict the number of different plants they will see. During the trip, have them keep track of the kinds of plants they observe.

Additional Life Science Field Trip Destinations

Aquarium

Botany or zoology department
  at local college

Bird/wildlife sanctuary

Commercial greenhouse

Fish hatchery

Flower or garden show

Food-processing facility

Forest preserve

Natural history museum

Orchard

Petstore

Ranch, dairy, chicken, or vegetable farm

Cooperative Learning Projects

As you consider the following starter ideas for cooperative learning projects, keep in mind the importance of stressing the three key aspects of cooperative learning (discussed in detail in Chapter 5):

1. Positive interdependence

2. Individual accountability

3. Development of group process skills

- *"Life's My Game, Amy's the Name"* Have each group research career options available to people interested in the life sciences. After the groups have finished their research, have each group select one career and train one person in the group to present the career to the remainder of the class. Emphasize that the group is responsible for getting the information needed, rehearsing the person, and providing constructive feedback. On the presentation day, the person trained should come to class dressed as a person in the career is dressed and prepared to describe what he or she does, the working conditions, the rewards, and the educational background required.

- *We Are the . . .* Give each group a choice of an animal or plant phylum (you may wish to include protists), and have the groups prepare presentations that creatively teach the characteristics of the phyla. Groups should be encouraged to use music, dance, art, puppets, poetry, and other media for their presentations. Each group should build into the presentation a way of assessing whether the audience has learned the characteristics.

- *Big as a Whale* Have each group prepare life-sized outlines of three animals on the school lawn using lengths of clothesline pulled around popsicle sticks that have been placed at points marking the ends of the animal's tail, head, feet, and other body parts. In preparation for this project, each group should choose the animals they will create and carry out library research to acquire the needed information. All the groups should create their animals on the lawn at the same time. This will permit the children to compare their own size to the sizes of various animals.

Additional Ideas for Cooperative Groups

- Have each group select a human body system, research the system, and then present the system to the remainder of the class in a creative way.
- Challenge groups to raise popcorn plants to see which group can produce the healthiest and largest plants in the shortest period of time.
- Have groups prepare arguments for or against the operation of zoos. This can serve as the basis for a debate or discussion among groups.
- Have groups research and design a truly healthy breakfast that reflects knowledge of the nutrition food pyramid. Groups can be challenged to prepare portions of their proposed breakfasts that can be sampled by the rest of the class.

Science and Children and *Science Scope*

Resource Articles for Life Science Units, Lessons, Activities, and Demonstrations

Berglund, Kay. "Thought for Food." *Science and Children* 36, no. 1 (January 1999): 38–42.

Chudler, Eric, et al. "Brain Awareness Week Open House." *Science Scope* 22, no. 4 (March 1999): 54–55.

Dyche, Steven E. "Meaworms, Real Worms?" *Science Scope* 22, no. 2 (October 1998): 19–23.

El-Harim, Jean Love. "Treemendous Learning Experience." *Science and Children* 35, no. 8 (May 1998): 26–29.

Fischer, Daniel. "Science Is a Day at the Beach." *Science Scope* 21, no. 8 (May 1998): 14–17.

Gaylen, Nancy. "Encouraging Curiosity at Home." *Science and Children* 35, no. 4 (January 1998): 24–25.

Glanville, Linda. "Bug Buddies." *Science and Children* 35, no. 7 (April 1998): 22–25.

Guerrierie, Frank W. "Beak Adaptations." *Science Scope* 22, no. 4 (January 1999): 19–25.

Hibbitt, Catherine. "A Growth Opportunity." *Science Scope* 22, no. 4 (March 1999): 34–35.

Holden, Janet C. "Corn Dehydration Lab." *Science and Children* 35, no. 1 (September 1998): 26–29.

Johnson, Kerry Ann. "El Niño and the Teacher at Sea." *Science and Children* 35, no. 4 (April 1998): 23–27.

Make the Case

The Problem Children need science experiences that range across the earth/space,
life, and physical sciences. Teachers may tend to emphasize those topics
they feel most comfortable with and thus inadvertently limit the scope of
children's learning.

***Assess
Your Prior
Knowledge
and Beliefs***

1. When you compare your knowledge of the life sciences to your knowledge of
    the earth/space and physical sciences, do you believe you have acquired more,
    less, or the same amount of basic science content in each?

	More	Less	Same
Earth/space sciences	_____	_____	_____
Physical sciences	_____	_____	_____

2. When you were a student in grades K–8, were you exposed to more, less, or the
    same amount of life science content as you were to earth/space and physical
    science content?

	More	Less	Same
Earth/space sciences	_____	_____	_____
Physical sciences	_____	_____	_____

3. Whether life as we know it exists on other planets is an ever-popular life science
    topic for children. Identify five discrete items of knowledge that you have about
    the topic.

    _____

    _____

    _____

    _____

4. Now identify five things about the requirements for life that you think you
    should know but do not.

    _____

    _____

    _____

    _____

The Challenge You are part of a team of teachers planning a unit on the requirements for life. You
want the unit to include the discovery-learning stages of experiencing, acquiring,
and applying. Give an example of a life science activity you might include to support each of these stages.

295

Laubenthal, Gail. "Web of Life Connections." *Science and Children* 36, no. 1 (January 1999): 20–23.

May, Janet L. "Celling the Drama." *Science Scope* 22, no. 1 (September 1998): 28–32.

McCann-Keach, Anne. "Bats—Masters of the Night." *Science and Children* 35, no. 1 (September 1998): 30–34.

McClaughlin, Charles W., et al. "Shining Light on Photosynthesis." *Science and Children* 36, no. 5 (February 1999): 26–31.

Palopoli, Maria L. "The Mantis Project." *Science and Children* 35, no. 5 (February 1998): 34–39, 54.

Pottle, Jean L. "Something to Crow About." *Science Scope* 22, no. 4 (January 1999): 14–18.

Roychoudhury, Anita, and Daniel K. Gladish. "How Plants Work." *Science Scope* 22, no. 2 (October 1998): 14–18.

Scribner-MacLean, and Anita Greenwood. "Invertebrate Inquiry. *Science and Children* 35, no. 5 (May 1998): 18–21.

Shimkanin, A. John, et al. "Hopping Good Time: Wood Frogs in the Classroom." *Science and Children* 35, no. 4 (April 1998): 34–39.

Tippins, Deborah, et al. "A Fishy Adventure." *Science and Children* 36, no. 5 (February 1999): 16–20.

Notes

1. This standard, as well as the others identified in later sections, are excerpted with permission from the National Research Council, *National Science Education Standards* (Washington, DC: National Academy Press, 1996), pp. 104–171. Note that the bracketed symbol to the right of each standard was prepared by this author. See also the list of all the K–8 content standards in the appendix of this book.

2. Note that I have related this sampling of NSE standards E, F, and G to the life sciences.

3. This excerpt and those that follow are from *Science for All Americans, Summary/Project 2061*. Copyright © 1989 by the American Association for the Advancement of Science. Reprinted by permission of Oxford University Press. The American Association for the Advancement of Science (AAAS) grouped its Project 2061 recommendations into four categories: 1) The Scientific Endeavor, 2) The Scientific View of the World, 3) Perspective on Science, and 4) Scientific Habits of Mind. The Unit Plan Starter Ideas based on Project 2061 in Chapters 10, 13, and 16 were prepared by this author for the "Scientific View of the World" recommendations in *Science for All Americans: Summary* (Washington, DC: American Association for the Advancement of Science, 1989). I omitted three recommendations whose elementary school science implications would require a breadth of consideration beyond the scope of Chapters 10, 13, and 16. These were goals related to "consequences of cultural setting into which a person was born," "social change and conflict," and "forms of political and economic organization."

For a further specification of all the goals and the broader curriculum implications of the Project 2061 effort, see *Science for All Americans* (Washington, DC: American Association for the Advancement of Science, 1989) and *Benchmarks for Science Literacy: Project 2061, American Association for the Advancement of Science* (New York: Oxford University Press, 1993).

14A

Living Things

Content

A Look Ahead

Living or Nonliving? That's the Question

 Dust from the surface of an African plain, dotted with grass and small plants, is kicked into clouds by the plodding feet of a rhinoceros. As the huge, lumbering beast moves along munching plants, it frightens insects into confused flight. Some of these insects land on the rhino's body and are carried to greener pastures as the rhino moves across the plain. Some of these insects become food for the tick birds that also ride on the rhino's back (see Figure 14A.1). As the rhino feeds on grasses and weeds, the tick birds flutter about, feasting upon the newly arrived insects. The rhino, the insects, the tick birds, and the grass are all living things, but the dust, of course, is not.

What makes the dust fundamentally different from the rhino, insects, tick birds, and grass? When scientists make observations to determine whether something is living or nonliving, they search for the eight characteristics, or functions, of life:

1. The ability to respire, or to release the chemical energy locked in nutrients (respiration)
2. The ability to produce or acquire and use food
3. The ability to get rid of waste products (secretion and excretion)
4. The ability to move a variety of materials within it (transport)
5. The ability to move
6. The ability to respond to changes (irritability)
7. The ability to grow
8. The ability to produce more of its own kind (reproduction)

Scientists who study the characteristics of living things are known as *biologists.* Life on Earth is so complex that biologists can specialize in one or more parts of biology:

Zoology, the study of animals
Botany, the study of plants
Anatomy, the study of the structure of living things
Ecology, the study of the relationships among living things
and their surroundings

Similarities in Living Things

Believe it or not, you have a lot in common with a cactus plant. This hopefully doesn't apply to your outward appearance, but it most definitely applies to your inside appearance. You, the cactus plant, and every other living thing is made up of one or more cells. Within every cell is a gelatinlike, colorless, semitransparent substance called *protoplasm,* which is made up of a variety of elements: carbon, hydrogen, oxygen, potassium, phosphorous, iodine, sulfur, nitrogen, calcium, iron, magnesium, sodium, chlorine, and traces of other elements.

In living things that contain more than one cell, any group of cells that performs a similar function is called a *tissue.* A group of tissues that function together is

FIGURE 14A.1
The tick birds and the rhinoceros both benefit from their relationship.

called an *organ*. And a group of organs that work together to perform a major function is known as a *system*. For instance, in plants, the various cells and tissues that enable the food made in the leaves to be transported to the stems and roots make up the vascular system. Plants contains many different systems that all perform different functions. So does the human body. Those systems include the skeletal system, muscular system, respiratory system, nervous system, excretory system, and reproductive system.

Differences in Living Things

You and that cactus plant are also different in many ways. The protoplasm in the cells of a particular type of living thing is unique to that thing. The ptotoplasm of a cactus enables cactus cells to carry on the unique functions that permit the cactus to function as a cactus. So it is with the protoplasm of the human body and every other living thing.

The cells that make up living things also differ. Most have clearly defined nuclei, but some one-celled organisms do not. And while plants and animals have clearly defined nuclei in their cells, the cell walls of plants contain cellulose while the cells of animals are bound by membranes that do not contain cellulose. Plants and animals, of course, possess other characteristics that allow us to distinguish between them:

Plants	Animals
Organs are external to the plant's body—for example, leaves and flowers.	Most organs are internal to the animal's body—for instance, the heart and the stomach.
They produce their own food.	They cannot produce food internally.
They show little movement.	Most can move freely.
No organs have a specific excretory function.	They possess excretory organs.
They respond slowly to changes in the environment.	They can respond quickly to changes in the environment.

299

Even within any given multicellular living thing, the cells are not all similar to one another. For example, your skin cells, although they contain protoplasm and a nucleus, differ in many ways from the cells that make up the muscles of your heart. Similarly, every plant and every animal contains a variety of very specialized cells that make up its tissues and organs.

Classifying Living Things

 Long ago, biologists classified all living things into just the two categories we've already discussed—plants and animals. With further study and more sophisticated equipment, biologists were surprised to discover living things that really didn't fit into either group.

The Five Kingdoms

Modern biologists use a classification system that includes five distinct kingdoms (see Figure 14A.2):

1. *Monera*—This kingdom includes one-celled living things that don't have a membrane around the cell's genetic material. In other words, none of these things has a nucleus. Monerans include bacteria, which don't produce their own food, and blue-green algae, which can produce food through photosynthesis. Most of the earth's oxygen is produced by blue-green algae. A few species of bacteria live deep underwater near thermal vents and are able to manufacture food using chemical energy.

2. *Protista*—This group includes single-celled organisms that do have a membrane surrounding the cell's genetic material—for example, diatoms, protozoa, and euglena. Common amebas and paramecia are also protozoans. All protists are found in moist or aquatic habitats and get their nutrition in a variety of ways. Protists are believed to be early examples of the types of life forms that eventually became the fungi, plants, and animals that live on the earth today.

3. *Fungi*—This group of living things may be one celled or multicelled. They gain their nutrition by absorbing nutrients from their surroundings, and they store energy in the chemical compound glycogen, which makes them different from plants that store food as starch. Fungi can reproduce sexually or asexually. Asexual reproduction is carried out through the production and release of tiny spores that can be carried long distances through the air. Sexual reproduction occurs from the fusion of cell material from two types of fungi competing on the same food source.

4. *Plantae*—This kingdom includes living things that are multicellular and have true cell nuclei and cell walls. Most use photosynthesis to produce food. The green plants in this kingdom—mosses, ferns, grasses, trees, and so on—reproduce sexually or asexually.

5. *Animalia*—This group is made up of multicelled living things that are able to ingest food directly from their environments. Animal cells contain nuclei. Members of this kingdom reproduce sexually, with a few exceptions. Sponges, for example, reproduce asexually by forming buds that can break free of the parent sponge and be carried to a place they can develop into a complete sponge. Although some animals, such as sponges, are sessile (i.e., they remain in one specific place during their life cycle), most are able to move freely from place to place.

FIGURE 14A.2 A five-kingdom classification system

Kingdom	Characteristics	Examples			
Monera	One celled, lack nuclear membranes and other cell structures with membranes, sometimes form groups or filaments, nutrition usually by absorption, reproduction usually by fission or budding	Bacteria Blue-green algae			
Protista	Includes one-celled and multicelled living things, have an organized nucleus and organelles with membranes, reproduction usually by fission	Ameba Paramecium			
Fungi	Some one celled, some multicelled, nutrition by absorption, cell walls made of chitin, sexual or asexual reproduction	Bread molds Mildews Yeasts Mushrooms			
Plantae	Multicellular, produce own food through photosynthesis, cells surrounded by cell wall, sexual and asexual reproduction	Mosses Ferns Trees Grasses Palms Roses			
Animalia	Multicellular, nutrition by ingestion, cells surrounded by cell membrane, have complex organ systems, mainly sexual reproduction	Sponges Flatworms Starfish Insects Amphibians Reptiles Mammals			

How to Classify a Particular Living Thing

When biologists classify an organism, they must first decide which of the five kingdoms provides the best fit. Then, because kingdoms are divided into various categories and subcategories, biologists must identify the appropriate subcategory. They do so by looking at how other living things with the identical characteristics as the mystery organism have already been classified.

Every living thing is classified according to the following system, in order from the largest (most general) to the smallest (most specific) group:

Kingdom
Phylum
Class
Order
Family
Genus
Species

This means, of course, that every living thing actually has seven names that ultimately specify its exact place among all living things. Let's see how this would work for a relatively easy-to-find organism—the common grasshopper:

Kingdom	Animalia
Phylum	Arthropoda
Class	Insecta
Order	Orthoptera
Family	Acridiidae
Genus	*Schistocerca*
Species	*americana*

The grasshopper is an animal, so its kingdom is Animalia. And since the animal kingdom has so many members, it is further classified as a member of the Arthropoda phylum. There are thousands of other arthropods, so the grasshopper is placed in the class Insecta. The process continues until the grasshopper is identified by the series of seven names. Notice how the classification of a grasshopper and a human differ:

	Grasshopper	**Human**
Kingdom	Animalia	Animalia
Phylum	Arthropoda	Chordata
Class	Insecta	Mammalia
Order	Orthoptera	Primates
Family	Acridiidae	Hominidae
Genus	*Schistocerca*	*Homo*
Species	*americana*	*sapiens*

The use of a classification system helps biologists avoid confusion when they talk and write about living things.

The Plant Kingdom: A Closer Look

 Recent classification systems have grouped the organisms of the plant kingdom into two major phyla: the Bryophytes (Bryophyta) and the Tracheophytes (Tracheophyta). *Bryophytes* are small plants that lack conducting vessels for transporting water and nutrients. This phylum includes mosses, liverworts, and hornworts. The phylum *Tracheophyta* includes all vascular plants—that is, plants that have vessels for transporting water and nutrients.

Ferns, conifers, and flowering plants are all tracheophytes. Ferns do not produce true seeds. Both conifers and flowering plants are seed-producing tracheophytes. These seed-producing plants are grouped into two classes: the Gymnosperms and the Angiosperms. Most Gymnosperms do not produce flowers—they produce cones. Evergreen trees such as pines, redwoods, and spruces are all Gymnosperms. Angiosperms produce flowers. Fruit trees, rose plants, and daisies are all examples of Angiosperms.

The Structure of Flowering Plants

With more than 250,000 species, flowering plants—the Angiosperms—are the most advanced form of plant life on the earth. They are able to survive and thrive in a wide variety of soils and climatic conditions. To understand how they can, we need to take a closer look at their structure.

The Root

Roots have two major functions: to anchor the plant in the soil and to absorb water and dissolved minerals. The tip of the root is made of a group of loose cells called the *root cap*. As the root makes its way through the ground, the cells of the root cap are worn away. New cells behind the root cap continue to grow and take the place of the cells worn away. Fuzzy hairs, called *root hairs,* grow behind the root cap. Each of these root hairs is quite thin and able to take in large amounts of water and dissolved minerals. Water that enters the root hair is transported upward through tubes in the center of the root. These tubes ultimately carry water and also dissolved minerals to the stem and leaves of the plant. Surrounding these tubes are other tubes that carry food from the leaf and stem to the root. Many roots also contain large storage cells. Food that is produced in the leaves and stem and then transported to the root is stored in such cells.

The Stem

The stem of a plant can be thought of as an elaborate pipeline through which a two-way flow of materials occurs. At the outside of the stem is a group of tubes that carry food produced in the leaves downward through the stem into the root. Closer to the center of the stem is a group of tubes that carries water and dissolved minerals upward to the leaves. In the center of the stem are groups of cells that store food. This region is known as the *pith.*

There are two types of stems. Soft, green stems, called *herbacious stems,* are usually found in plants that live one or two years. Woody stems, which are made of thick, tough tissue, are found in plants that live for more than two years. Trees and shrubs such as forsythia and lilac have woody stems.

The Leaf

Food for the plant is made in its leaves. Leaves use water and dissolved minerals, which are absorbed by the roots and carried upward by the stem, carbon dioxide in the air, and the energy of the sun to produce food. While there is a wide variety of leaf shapes, all green leaves—regardless of their shape—contain *chlorophyll,* the vital substance that enables them to produce food. Leaves contain an elaborate network of tubes that carry liquid through the stalk of the leaf to all areas of the leaf. These tubes, or *veins,* carry the water and dissolved minerals brought by the stem from the root to the leaf and then transport the food produced there to the stems, roots, and fruit. Some of the food produced in the leaf is stored in the leaf, but most of it is carried to other parts of the plant.

The Reproductive Organs of Flowering Plants

A flowering plant's reproductive organs are found in the center of its flowers (see Figure 14A.3). A flower in the bud stage is protected by an outer covering of sepals. Seen at the base of most flowers, *sepals* are usually green and look like small leaves. The parts of the flower that are most familiar to us are the petals. *Petals* are usually brightly colored and possess an odor that attracts insects. The petals of a flower produce a sugary material called *nectar,* which insects and some birds use as a source of food.

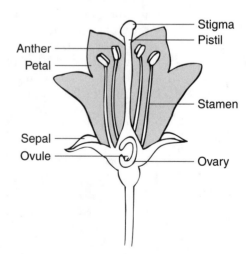

FIGURE 14A.3
The flower is a reproductive organ, and each structure has a function. What is the function of each of these structures?

In the center of the flower is the *pistil*, the female reproductive organ. Some flowers have many pistils, whereas others have only one. At the base of the pistil is a swollen area called the *ovary*. In it are tiny *ovules* that can eventually develop into seeds. The ovule contains an egg nucleus that, if fertilized, can produce a new plant.

The pistil is surrounded by a group of male organs called *stamens*. A stamen consists of a slender stalk with a yellow or orange pollen box on top. This pollen box, which is called an *anther*, contains many pollen grains. Within each grain is a sperm nucleus that can eventually unite with an egg nucleus to form a seed that can become a new plant.

Most flowers contain both male and female organs. However, some contain just one or the other. Reproduction in flowering plants is similar to that in animals in that an egg nucleus and sperm nucleus must unite before an offspring can be formed.

Sexual Reproduction in Flowering Plants

Pollination is the process through which the sperm cell in a pollen grain unites with the egg nucleus of the ovule. Pollen grains are carried to the stigma at the top of the pistil by wind, water, or insects. The bee, for example, is a principal agent of pollination. As the bee visits the flower, pollen grains may stick to its many bristles when it brushes against the stamen. If the bee then brushes against the tip of the pistil, some pollen grains may rub off its body and become attached to the stigma.

Soon after the pollen grain becomes attached to the stigma, it begins to produce a slender pollen tube that grows down through the pistil toward the ovary. If the pollen tube reaches the ovary, the sperm cells inside the pollen grain may move from the pollen grain down the tube to the ovary and eventually unite with the nuclei of egg cells. Fertilized egg cells from the ovary will divide, multiply, and eventually form seeds. Within each seed is an embryo that is surrounded by stored food—a tiny plant. If the seed reaches moist soil, a new plant will grow.

Asexual Reproduction in Flowering Plants

Some plants reproduce without the union of sperm and egg cells. Reproduction that does not require seeds produced by the fusion of male and female cells is known as *asexual reproduction.* Florists and fruit and vegetable growers utilize a number of different ways to produce plants without using seeds.

Some plants, such as the begonia, can be reproduced simply from a piece of stem with leaves on it. Such a stem is called a *cutting* or *slip*. Cuttings are usually placed in water or moist sand and then kept warm. Eventually, a new plant begins to form. Other plants, such as lilies and tulips, reproduce from bulbs—large portions of stems that store food. All that is usually required in this case is warmth and moisture.

The white potato is an underground stem that contains stored food. Farmers who wish to grow new potato plants simply cut a potato into pieces. Each piece must contain a bud, or *eye*. When planted, the buds sprout to form a new plant.

The Animal Kingdom: A Closer Look

 Animals are multicellular organisms that obtain food from their environments. Most have systems that allow them to move, and most reproduce sexually. Almost 1 million different kinds of animals inhabit the earth. In order to keep track of them, biologists have found it useful to classify them into two major groups: animals without backbones and animals with backbones. Animals without backbones are called *invertebrates*. They include sponges, jellyfishes, starfishes, worms, mollusks, lobsters, spiders, and insects. The second major group, those with backbones, are called *vertebrates*. This group includes fishes, frogs, snakes, birds, and mammals. Vertebrates and invertebrates are divided into various phyla.

Vertebrates: Mammals

Mammals are vertebrates who nourish their young with milk produced by mammary glands. Their bodies are usually covered with hair or fur, although in some mammals, the hair takes the form of a few whiskers around the mouth. While many mammals have four legs, some mammals—for example, whales, dolphins, and manatees—do not. In other mammals, the forelegs and rear legs are modified to perform particular functions. For instance, the forelimbs of kangaroos enable them to grasp food, whereas their strong, enlarged back legs enable them to hop.

The eggs of mammals are usually fertilized internally, and most mammals produce young by giving birth to them (although the duck-billed platypus, which is a monotreme mammal, does lay eggs). Female mammals suckle their young and care for them as they mature. The amount of time for a young mammal to mature into an adult varies greatly. Mammals seem able to teach their young to perform functions that will ensure their survival. Some mammals care for their young until they are fully grown and able to survive on their own.

Female opossums and kangaroos are marsupial mammals. They have pouches in which they place their young as soon as they are born. Although bats appear to be birds, they have hair rather than feathers. Bats can fly through the use of a leathery membrane stretching between their forelimbs and hind legs.

Although whales look like fish, they are really sea-living mammals. The hair on their bodies takes the form of whiskers around the mouth. The blue whale can reach almost 30 meters (about 100 feet) in length and weigh more than 140,000 kilograms (about 150 tons).

The primates, which include monkeys and apes, are the most intelligent of the mammals. They have the best-developed brains of all animals, fingers that are able to grasp objects, opposable thumbs, and nails instead of claws. (An opposable thumb can be positioned opposite of the other fingers, making it possible to manipulate objects with one hand.) The largest of all apes is the gorilla, which can weigh as much as 180 kilograms (about 400 pounds). The gorilla is able to walk upright and to support itself by placing its hands on the ground. The most intelligent of all animals is probably the chimpanzee, though some people feel that a sea mammal, the dolphin, may be more intelligent than the chimpanzee and perhaps as intelligent as humans.

Biologists usually group the human species with the primates. The characteristics that have traditionally differentiated humans from other primates include the ability to reason, the use of complex communication systems, and the use of tools. In recent years, the observation of chimpanzees and gorillas in the wild, as well as laboratory research, has revealed that primates may have capabilities that challenge traditional views.

Sexual Reproduction in Vertebrates

Reproduction in the vertebrates may take a number of forms. Some vertebrates lay eggs; others give birth to living young. Fertilization may occur externally or internally. The young may be born fully developed, or the young may be born in a very immature condition. Because reproduction can take a number of forms, this section will examine reproduction in general in frogs, birds, and some mammals. Human reproduction is discussed in Chapter 15A.

Frogs

Although frogs are able to live on both land and water, they reproduce in the water. The male frog releases sperm cells over egg cells expelled into the water by the female. The egg cells are surrounded by a jellylike material and are attached to one another in long strands. The sperm cells fertilize the eggs.

After fertilization, a many-celled embryo begins to develop (see Figure 14A.4). Eventually, the embryo takes the form of a tadpole. When the tadpole is sufficiently mature, it breaks free of its jellylike envelope and swims away. The tadpole absorbs oxygen from water through a pair of gills in its neck.

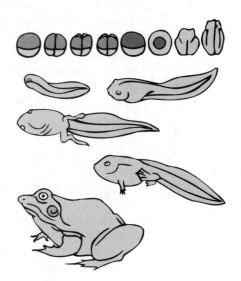

FIGURE 14A.4
Frog development begins when the fertilized egg divides into many cells. In time, the tadpole's gills will disappear and legs will develop.

The tadpole changes in form as time passes. Its tail shrinks, hind and front legs appear, and its gills get smaller. As the gills shrink, lungs begin to form, and the tadpole must rely on air for oxygen. At this stage, it has become a young frog.

Birds

Birds reproduce as a result of internal fertilization. Because the basic process is the same for most types of birds, the chicken will serve as a good example. Within the body of the female chicken, or hen, is an ovary. The ovary produces the hen's egg cells. As a tiny egg cell within the ovary matures, it fills with yolk. After this has occurred, the egg leaves the ovary and enters the upper part of the oviduct, the channel through which sperm deposited by a male chicken, or rooster, can swim. If a sperm cell that swims up the oviduct meets an unfertilized egg cell, a fertilized egg will be produced. The fertilized egg passes down the oviduct and develops an external membrane. The material that we call egg white is also added in the oviduct. As the fertilized egg—now containing both egg white and yolk—moves toward the outside world, glands at the bottom of the oviduct produce a hard substance that surrounds the egg. This shell prevents the fertilized egg from drying out and keeps it from crushing when it reaches the outside world.

Mammals

In mammals, sperm cells enter the female reproductive system and internally fertilize an egg cell. The fertilized egg journeys to the uterus, an organ in which it will grow and develop until it is sufficiently mature to survive in the outside world. The amount of time the developing egg, or embryo, spends in the uterus is known as the *gestation period*. A few mammals, such as the spiny anteater and the duck-billed platypus, resemble lower forms of vertebrate life in that they lay eggs in a manner similar to birds and reptiles. As we have seen, opossum and kangaroo females have an external pocket, or pouch. Newborn animals of these species are extremely undeveloped at birth and complete development in the pouch, where they are fed from mammary glands.

The gestation period for a human being is about 9 months. A human baby is virtually helpless at birth and takes a very long time to become fully grown. (See Chapter 15A for greater detail.)

Two Very Small but Very Interesting Living Things

 When you think of the really exotic living things on the earth, you may think of a field of flowering plants, a school of multicolored fish, or even a large magnificent creature such as a Bengal tiger. In fact, there are far more exotic creatures—creatures that are there but too small for you to see. We will consider just two of them. One can be found in most freshwater ponds, and the other can be found in a place you might not typically search for an exotic creature—in the intestines of a fish!

Euglena

One of the strangest protists is a tiny one-celled organism called the *euglena*. There are over 150 species of this freshwater organism, which has both plant *and* animal characteristics. You have seen evidence of euglena, whether or not you recognized it, if you have ever noticed green scum on the surface of a pond.

Euglena contain green chloroplasts that enable them to make food in the presence of sunlight. Obviously, this is a characteristic of green plants, so euglena are clearly food producers. Unlike other green plants, however, euglena can move to environments rich in food. Locomotion is accomplished through the use of a whiplike organ called a *flagellum*. In environments rich in food, euglena can absorb food through cell membranes. Thus, euglena are both producers and consumers.

Like other common protists, such as amoeba and paramecium, the euglena has a clearly defined nucleus in its interior. The interior contains a structure known as a *vacuole* that permits the euglena to excrete excess water that is absorbed during the direct acquisition of food. The euglena also has an eyespot located near the base of the flagellum that permits it to sense changes in light levels. If the euglena senses a stronger light in one portion of its environment, it may use its flagellum to move there. Presumably, the presence of strong light permits the euglena to engage in increased food production through photosynthesis. Euglena reproduce through asexual reproduction. One parent euglena divides to produce two daughter cells.

The World's Largest Bacterium

Dr. Ester R. Angert's research has proven that an enormous one-celled creature found in the intestines of an Australian fish is in fact a bacterium. Prior to Dr. Angert's research, bacteria were thought to be the world's smallest living cells. They have three possible shapes—round, rod, or spiral. Many bacteria have flagella, which permit them to move from place to place, but they do not have clearly defined nuclei. Although many bacteria cause disease, most are beneficial.

Dr. Angert's bacterium, named *Epulopiscium fisheloni,* is 50 times as large as a common paramecium (see Figure 14A.5). By studying the genetic material that

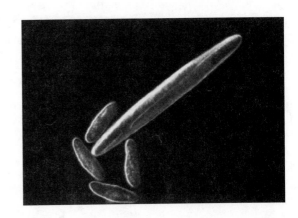

FIGURE 14A.5

To understand how large the *Epulopiscium fisheloni* is when compared to most protists, study this photomicrograph of one near four paramecium. Then imagine a bacterium that's 100 times bigger!

makes up the organism's nucleus, Dr. Angert demonstrated that the organism is part of a family of protists that includes the bacterium that causes botulism, a deadly disease. So far, *Epulopiscium fisheloni* has only been found in fish intestines and seemingly causes no damage to the fish. The organism's scientific name, *Epulopiscium fisheloni*, can be roughly translated as "guest at a fish's banquet," which makes it very appropriate.

A bacterium that's even larger than *Epulopiscium fisheloni* has recently been discovered! *Thiomargarita namibiensis*, a strange sulfur-eating bacterium discovered off the coast of Africa, is 100 times larger. Its common name is the *sulfur pearl*.

Summary Outline

I. Living things can be distinguished from nonliving things on the basis of characteristics known as functions of life.
   A. The life functions are respiration; food production, acquisition, and use; secretion and excretion; transport; ability to move; irritability; growth; and reproduction.
   B. *Biology* is the study of living things.
   C. All living things are made up of one or more cells. Plants have cellulose in their cell walls; animals do not.

II. Living things can be classified into groups based on their common characteristics.
   A. The major groupings are the five kingdoms: Monera, Protista, Fungi, Plantae, and Animalia.
   B. Living things can be further classified into the following categories: phylum, class, order, family, genus, and species.

III. The plant kingdom can be divided into several phyla and subdivided into several classes.
   A. Flowering plants, or Angiosperms, are the most advanced form of plant life on the earth.
   B. Plants can reproduce through sexual or asexual reproduction

IV. The animal kingdom includes the invertebrates and vertebrates.
   A. Invertebrates are animals with backbones, including hydra, jellyfishes, corals, worms, mollusks, and jointed-leg animals.
   B. Vertebrates are animals with backbones, including fish, frogs, birds, and mammals.

V. Two small but very interesting living things are Euglena and the world's largest bacterium

14B

Living Things

Attention Getters, Discovery Activities, and Demonstrations

A Look Ahead

Attention Getters for Young Learners

Is It a Plant or an Animal? [LS 1]

How Does Color Help Animals? [LS 3]

Are You a Good Animal Detective? [SPSP 2]

Attention Getters for Middle-Level Learners

How Are Seeds the Same and Different? [LS 5]

Can You Grow a Sweet Potato Plant Indoors? [LS 5]

Do Insects Have the Same Kinds of Body Parts? [LS 4]

Discovery Activities for Young Learners

How Is a Kitten Different from a Stone? [S&T 3]

What Is a Seed? [LS 2]

Who Goes There? [LS 3]

Discovery Activities for Middle-Level Learners

Male and Female Guppies: What's the Difference? [LS 5]

Do Mealworms Like or Dislike Light? [LS 6]

How Does Light Affect the Growth of Plants? [LS 7]

Demonstrations for Young Learners

The Curious Gerbils [LS 3]

Is It Alive? [S&T 3]

Demonstrations for Middle-Level Learners

The Birth of Guppies [LS 5]

The Insect Aquarium [LS 7]

Is It a Plant or an Animal? [LS 1]

For Young Learners

MATERIALS FOR EACH CHILD OR GROUP	10 colorful magazine pages that show plants and animals Scissors 3 mailing envelopes
MOTIVATING QUESTIONS	• Do you see any living things in the pictures? • What is the same (different) about all the plants (animals)?
DIRECTIONS	1. Distribute the materials, and ask the children to cut out all of the pictures they find of living things. 2. Write the words *animals* and *plants* on the board, pronounce them, and have the children write each word on one of the envelopes. Tell the children that there is another type of living thing called a *protist*. Make a protist envelope, and then explain that most protists are too small to see. 3. Have the children sort their pictures into the plant and animal envelopes.
SCIENCE CONTENT FOR THE TEACHER	There are many different ways to group living things. A common classification system uses three categories: plants, animals, and protists. Plants have cell walls that have cellulose and make food through photosynthesis. Animal cells do not have cell walls. Their cells are bounded by cell membranes. Animals take food into their bodies. Bacteria, viruses, protozoa, and slime molds are classified as protists.

How Does Color Help Animals? [LS 3]

MATERIALS FOR EACH CHILD OR GROUP	Sheet of green construction paper Scissors Sheet of brown construction paper Paper leaf pattern
MOTIVATING QUESTIONS	• What kinds of animals eat insects? • What are some ways that insects can escape from other animals?
DIRECTIONS	1. Distribute the materials, and have the children use the leaf pattern to draw and then cut out one brown leaf and one green leaf. Have them cut out a few small green and brown squares that are about 2.5 centimeters (1 inch) on edge. 2. Tell the children that they should pretend the squares are insects. Have them place the green insects on the brown leaf and the brown insects on the green leaf. 3. Ask them how hard they think it would be to find the insects if they were birds. 4. Have the children put the green insects on the green leaf, and ask the question again.

SCIENCE CONTENT FOR THE TEACHER Many animals have protective coloration that increases their chances of escaping predators. Insects that have the same color as their background stay still when predators are near and blend into their background, which increases their chances of survival.

Are You a Good Animal Detective? [SPSP 2]

MATERIALS Sheet of easel paper
Marking pen

MOTIVATING QUESTIONS
- What animals do you think we will see outside?
- How many animals do you think we will see?

DIRECTIONS
1. Take the children on a 10-minute nature walk around the school grounds to identify the animals that live around the school.
2. On your return to the classroom, prepare a three-column chart and list the children's recollections of the types and quantities of animals seen. Also note where the animals were seen—for example, under a rock.

SCIENCE CONTENT FOR THE TEACHER Life is both diverse and widespread. Any lawn, playground, or natural area on or near the school will have an abundance of animals. Depending on your locale and the season, expect to see squirrels, birds, cats, and dogs. Search for insects and other small creatures under rocks and near moist areas such as the ground near a water fountain or a mud puddle as well as on the bark of trees.

How Are Seeds the Same and Different? [LS 5]

MATERIALS FOR EACH CHILD OR GROUP One common fruit per group. (*Note:* Try to have a variety of fruits available, including oranges, apples, pears, grapefruit, peaches, and plums.)
Lightweight plastic serrated knives (if you are working with older children)
Paper towels
Drawing paper
Hand lens

For Middle-Level Learners

MOTIVATING QUESTIONS
- Do you think your fruit has a seed?
- Do you think your fruit has more than one seed?
- What do you think the seed or seeds in your fruit will look like?
- Do you think different fruits will have seeds that are the same or different?

A T T E N T I O N G E T T E R S

DIRECTIONS

1. Distribute the materials, and give each group one or more fruits. Before they cut open their fruits, have the groups predict the number, shape, size, and color of the seed or seeds and then draw what they think their seed or seeds will look like.
2. Have the groups cut open the fruits and examine the seeds. *Safety Note:* Cut open the fruit for younger children after the groups have completed their drawings.
3. Have the groups compare the seeds, and then discuss the variety in the number and types of seeds in fruits.

SCIENCE CONTENT FOR THE TEACHER

Although there is great variety in the seeds of common fruits, fruits of the same type have the same type of seeds. An interesting addition to your discussion would be a consideration of the great size and variation in seeds, with the coconut as one of the largest seeds in the natural world. You may wish to point out to the children that many types of seeds are important to humans. Examples would include corn, oats, and wheat.

Can You Grow a Sweet Potato Plant Indoors? [LS 5]

MATERIALS

1 small sweet potato
6 toothpicks
1 glass that is wider than the potato's diameter
Water

MOTIVATING QUESTIONS

- Do you think the sweet potato is a root or a stem?
- Where does a new potato plant get food?

DIRECTIONS

1. Distribute the materials and have the children wash the sweet potatoes to remove any excess dirt.
2. Have each group of children stick the toothpicks into the potato so it can be suspended in the glass with the narrow end submerged in the water. (About one-fourth should be in the water.)
3. After each group has prepared its potato, put the potatoes in a warm, well-lit area of the room. Children will need to add water periodically to replace that used by the growing potato plant and lost through evaporation.

SCIENCE CONTENT FOR THE TEACHER

Unlike the white potato, which is a tuber, or underground stem, the sweet potato is a root. The rapid root and leaf growth that will occur is partially due to the availability of starch in the fleshy material within the potato root.

Do Insects Have the Same Kinds of Body Parts? [LS 4]

MATERIALS	1 collection of common insects with different insects in different jars with net tops (grasshoppers, crickets, butterflies, flies, ants) Hand lens Drawing paper

MOTIVATING QUESTIONS
- Are all these animals insects?
- How are these animals alike? How are they different?

DIRECTIONS
1. Have the groups observe the insect or insects in each jar. Provide a hand lens for those who want to make closer observations. Encourage the children to make a drawing of each insect.
2. After each group has made observations and drawings, begin a discussion of how the insects are the same and different.

SCIENCE CONTENT FOR THE TEACHER

Although insects vary greatly in size, color, and the detailed shapes of their body parts, all insects have three main body parts: head, thorax, and abdomen. Unlike spiders and other arachnids that have eight legs, insects are six-legged creatures. Insects have two antennae and wings. They are invertebrates with exoskeletons, relatively hard exterior body coverings that protect the softer interior parts.

How Is a Kitten Different from a Stone? [S&T 3]

OBJECTIVE
- Children will describe three ways in which a kitten (or other small animal) is different from a stone.

SCIENCE PROCESSES EMPHASIZED

Observing
Classifying
Communicating
Inferring

MATERIALS FOR EACH CHILD OR GROUP

Small animal (or a picture of a small animal)
Stone
One picture of a living thing and one picture of a nonliving thing

MOTIVATION

Keep both the kitten and the stone out of sight at the beginning of the activity. Secretly pick up the stone and tell the class that you would like them to guess what is in your hand. After a few guesses, show the stone and tell them that today's activity will teach them how a stone is different from a living thing. Show them the kitten (or picture of a kitten), and begin the lesson.

For
Young
Learners

DISCOVERY ACTIVITIES

DIRECTIONS

1. Ask the children to make observations of both the kitten and the stone.
2. Make a list of their observations on the chalkboard.
3. Begin a discussion of their observations of the stone and the kitten, focusing on the differences between living and nonliving things.
4. Distribute one picture of a living thing and one picture of a nonliving thing to each child or group. Have them study the pictures and think about the differences between the living and nonliving things depicted in them.
5. Have the children summarize what they have learned about the differences between living and nonliving things.

KEY
DISCUSSION
QUESTIONS

1. What are some nonliving things you have noticed on your way to school? *Water. Sun. Wind.*
2. What are some living things you have noticed on your way to school? *Children. Plants. Animals.*
3. What are some of the living things in this classroom? *Children. Teachers. Plants.*
4. What are some of the nonliving things in this classroom? *Books. Desks. Pencils.*

SCIENCE
CONTENT FOR
THE TEACHER

Living things differ in many ways from nonliving things. The characteristics of living things—the functions of life—include reproduction; food production, acquisition, and/or use; growth from within; internal transport of materials; responsiveness to stimuli; secretion and excretion of waste products; and respiration.

*Discovering similarities
and differences*

EXTENSIONS   *Science:* A field trip in conjunction with this activity will enable children to observe living and nonliving things in the environment and begin to differentiate one type of living thing—plants—from another type of living thing—animals. This would be an excellent time for children to begin thinking about the fact that a specific living thing (such as the kitten) more closely resembles its parents in appearance than it resembles other living things.

Social Studies: Some children may begin to think about the relationships of living things to nonliving things. Shelter and implements are among the uses of nonliving things that you can highlight. You may wish to have children begin to think about and discuss how nonliving things, such as volcanoes, violent weather, and landslides, affect the lives of humans.

What Is a Seed? [LS 2]

OBJECTIVE   • The children will be able to describe a seed as something capable of growth.

SCIENCE   Predicting   Interpreting data
PROCESSES   Observing   Contrasting variables
EMPHASIZED   Recording

MATERIALS FOR   Large cardboard box cut 2 to 4 inches tall and lined with plastic
EACH CHILD   Soil or starting mixture (vermiculite plus soil)
OR GROUP   Collections of seeds and other small things ("red-hot" candy,
                      marbles, pebbles)
                   Chart paper
                   1 index card per student

MOTIVATION   Ask the children to bring in seeds and other small items for some science experiments. When the candy comes in, tell them they will begin their study of seeds and discover whether the candy will grow.

DIRECTIONS   1. Begin by setting out samples of the small things that have been brought in. Ask the students to describe the items while you list their observations on the chart paper.
                   2. Have each group record in pictures and in words the appearance of each item at the start of the experiment. In addition, each group can glue an item to an index card and then use the index card to record observations from the activity.
                   3. Have each group decide how many of each item should be planted and the depth of planting. Explain that the amount of water, light, warmth, and so on should be the same for each item. These things will be easy to control if the samples are planted in the same box.

4. Have each group label each row with the name of the item planted. Then, set aside a short period of time each day for maintenance and data gathering. Encourage the children to keep a daily log of what they see.

5. Some children may want to peek at the seeds during the experiment. If they do this, they need to think about the number of each item that was planted and how they can make their inspection without disturbing the others. One way to observe germination without disturbing the seeds is to place moist paper toweling in a glass jar and "plant" the item between the toweling and the glass. Such a jar will allow students to see what is going on in the soil in the boxes, but perhaps it can be kept a secret until the students have had the pleasure of digging up a few of their own seeds.

6. When the seeds have been growing for awhile, have the children dig up samples of each type of seed. They can make observations, record them, and compare their new observations with the observations they made at the start of the experiment.

7. After some items have sprouted, it would be useful to divide the original set of items into growers and nongrowers. With this set to examine, students should begin to investigate where the items come from and develop a general definition of a *true seed*.

KEY DISCUSSION QUESTIONS

1. In what ways are all these items alike? *They are all small.*
2. How many items of each type should be planted? *More than one or two, since some might die before they come up and can be seen.*
3. How deeply should they be planted? *Answers will vary based upon gardening experience, but common sense usually prevails.*
4. What should be done about the amount of water, sunlight, temperature, and so on that the items receive? *They should be kept the same so that all seeds have the same chance of living.*
5. What is the biggest difference among the items at the end of the experiment? *Some grow and some don't.*
6. What did some seeds become? *They grew into new plants.*

SCIENCE CONTENT FOR THE TEACHER

Seeds come in all sizes, from those as small as the period at the end of a sentence to others as big as a walnut. Shape can also vary dramatically, from round and smooth to pyramidlike. Seeds have protective shells (seed coats) that keep the embryonic plant alive. Stored food will provide the energy for the seedling to reach the soil surface and begin producing food of its own.

In order to survive, some plants produce *great* numbers of seeds, and others produce seeds with structures (such as the hooks on burrs and the "wings" on maple seeds) that enable them to be dispersed. Some seeds even look like insects, which discourages seed-eating birds from consuming them.

Even with this great diversity, seeds differ significantly from all the nonseed items in this activity by being able to *grow* and reproduce their own kind (much to the despair of some candy lovers!).

EXTENSIONS *Science:* You may wish to cut open some fruits and vegetables and have the children find and describe the seeds. Some students may then wish to produce a poster or bulletin board with as many kinds of seeds as can be collected. The seeds can be grouped by size, shape, or color.

Math: Some students may be interested in collecting seeds to be used as "counters." These students can sort the seeds into sets and arrange them in order from smallest to largest.

Who Goes There? [LS 3]

OBJECTIVE
- The children will be able to match pictures of common animals with the animals' footprints.

SCIENCE PROCESSES EMPHASIZED
Observing
Inferring

MATERIALS FOR EACH CHILD OR GROUP
Set of pictures of the animals for which you have footprints
Set of pictures showing the various environments in which the
   animals live
Set of animal name cards
Construction paper headband
Paper feathers of various colors

MOTIVATION
Hand out the animal pictures and headbands to each group. Suggest that they pretend they are teams of animal trackers, and explain that each team will be awarded one feather for each animal they successfully track.

DIRECTIONS
1. Before beginning this activity, you will need a set of unlabeled animal footprints and a set of pictures illustrating environments in which the animals are likely to be found. *Note:* A good source of information on tracks is the ESS unit *Animal Tracks* originally published by McGraw-Hill but now available from Educational Resources Information Center: Clearinghouse for Science, Mathematics, and Environmental Education; Ohio State University, Columbus, Ohio.
2. Hold up pictures of the animal track and its environment. After some discussion, have the children try to think of the animal being described. The group members can discuss the possibilities among themselves before the group suggests an animal.
3. When all the teams are ready, have each chief hold up the picture of the animal they have selected. Encourage each group to tell why they think their choice is the correct one.
4. Staple a paper feather to the headband of each team that is correct. The job of being chief is then rotated to the next person in each group, and the game continues.

KEY DISCUSSION QUESTIONS

1. Which of the tracks comes from the biggest animal? *Answers will depend on the tracks and the pictures you are using.*
2. Which of the tracks comes from the smallest animal? *Answers will vary.*
3. Which of the tracks comes from an animal with claws that stick out? *Answers will vary.*
4. Which of the tracks belongs to an animal that can climb trees? *Answers will vary.*
5. Hold up the pictures of various environments (e.g., a treetop for squirrels and an open plain with trees in Africa for elephants), and ask which of the animals might be found in them. Ask the students to try to guess which footprint might be found in most environments. (Be sure to have the teams explain why they decided on particular footprints.)

SCIENCE CONTENT FOR THE TEACHER

Footprints hold clues about the lives and environments of the animals that made them. Very large footprints often belong to large animals or to animals that travel over soft terrain. For example, the relatively large feet of the snowshoe rabbit support its weight on snow, thus allowing it to travel well on terrain that hinders most other animals. Most animals that live on the open range have evolved smaller feet with hooves that allow them to run fast on fairly smooth, hard land. Some footprints show evidence of claws used for defense as well as climbing. Retractable claws are an obvious benefit to animals that must be able to run quickly and silently before catching their prey.

EXTENSIONS

Science: Obtain or reproduce pictures of various tracks showing something happening (e.g., animals walking and then running). Have the teams determine what happened.

Some students may wish to research the topic of fossils, especially fossilized tracks, and what scientists have learned about the animals that made them. Other students may enjoy making answer boards on which others try to match pictures of animals with pictures of their footprints.

Art: Students may want to make pictures from a set of linoleum printing blocks of footprints.

Male and Female Guppies: What's the Difference? [LS 5]

OBJECTIVE

• The children will observe the physical characteristics of male and female guppies.

SCIENCE PROCESSES EMPHASIZED

Observing
Classifying

MATERIALS FOR	Male and female guppies
EACH CHILD	2 clean liter- or quart-size jars filled with aquarium water
OR GROUP	Dry fish food
	Hand lens

MOTIVATION   Ask the children if they know what a guppy is. If possible, have them describe guppies without the benefit of guppies to observe. Now display the guppies you will be using for the activity, and tell the children that they will have a chance to make careful observations of male and female guppies.

DIRECTIONS
1. Distribute a jar containing aquarium water, a female guppy, and a hand lens to each child or group.
2. Ask each child or group to observe the external characteristics of the guppy and make a drawing of it, labeling the body parts. Encourage them to shade in parts of their drawing to show the guppy's markings.
3. Once the drawings are completed, distribute a jar containing aquarium water and a male guppy. Have the children observe the male guppy and then make a labeled drawing of it.
4. Allow the children to visit with one another to see if their male guppy resembles other male guppies and if their female guppy resembles other female guppies.
5. Circulate around the room and sprinkle a small amount of dry fish food on the surface of each container. Ask the children to observe the feeding behavior of the guppy.

KEY
DISCUSSION
QUESTIONS
1. How can you tell the difference between male and female guppies? *The female is usually larger, with a gray color and a fan-shaped fin; the male is smaller, with patches of color and a tubelike part at the base of its tail.*
2. How does the location of the guppy's mouth make it easier and safer for the guppy to feed? *It's at the top of its head, which lets it feed on surface food without having to lift its head out of the water; this makes it easier for it to sneak up on food.*

SCIENCE   Guppies are tropical fish. The male is smaller than the female but has a
CONTENT FOR   larger tail. It is also more lightly colored. The female is usually a uniform
THE TEACHER   gray. The female has a fan-shaped anal fin. The male's anal fin is pointed and tubelike.

EXTENSIONS   *Science:* The demonstration on the birth of guppies, described later in this chapter (pages 327–329), is an effective follow-up to this activity.

Art: Some children may wish to create larger drawings of the guppies they have observed. Drawing paper and a supply of pastels will assist them in such a project. Encourage the children to reproduce nature's coloration faithfully by using the appropriate colors and shades of pastels. You may wish to spray fixative on the children's finished drawings to preserve them.

Do Mealworms Like or Dislike Light? [LS 6]

OBJECTIVES	• The children will set up and carry out an experiment to determine how a mealworm responds to light.
	• The children will collect, summarize, and interpret the data they gather.

SCIENCE PROCESSES EMPHASIZED

Observing
Recording data
Interpreting data

MATERIALS FOR EACH CHILD OR GROUP

Live mealworm (available in a petstore)
Small flashlight
20 cm (about 8 in.) circle of paper divided into 8 pie-shaped
   sections

MOTIVATION

Ask the class how they can find out what people like. The children will suggest that they can ask people or try something and see if people smile, frown, or become angry. Some children may suggest that the number of times a person does something could be used to determine what the person likes. Tell the children that they will be finding out how well mealworms like being in the dark and that since mealworms do not talk, the children will have to do an experiment to find the answer.

DIRECTIONS

1. Display the mealworms, and discuss some strategies that the children could use to find out what a mealworm likes. Show the circle that has been divided into eight parts, and explain that it is the tool they will use to find out whether a mealworm likes light.
2. Have the children prepare their own circles and divide them into eight parts. They should number the sections from 1 to 8.
3. Place the flashlight about 30 centimeters from section 1 on the circle. Direct the light toward the center of the circle, darken the room, and have the children observe your setup.
4. Have the children place a light source near their section 8 and the mealworm in the center of the circle where all the lines intersect. The children should record the number of the section toward which the mealworm moves. This should be repeated 10 times.
5. Have the children develop charts or graphs to summarize their findings. Finally, have the class suggest a strategy for combining the results from all the groups so that conclusions can be drawn.

SCIENCE CONTENT FOR THE TEACHER

Mealworms usually avoid lighted areas. They are frequently found in bins of old grain or meal, which provide dark, dry environments. A mealworm that enters a lit area would lose touch with its food supply and possibly fall prey to birds or other predators.

KEY
DISCUSSION
QUESTIONS

1. Why should you do this experiment many times before concluding that a mealworm likes or dislikes light? *Mealworms don't always move in the right direction. It takes the mealworm a few tries before it figures things out.*
2. What other things might make a mealworm respond by moving? *They might be afraid of us. They might not like the heat that comes from the light. They see light from other parts of the room.*
3. Why might a mealworm avoid light? *It likes dark. The light may mean danger to the mealworm.*

EXTENSIONS

Science: Some children may wish to design and conduct experiments to see how mealworms respond to heat, cold, moisture, dryness, loud sounds, and different kinds of food.

Language Arts: Have the children pretend that they are mealworms and write stories describing their adventures in a land of giants.

How Does Light Affect the Growth of Plants? [LS 7]

OBJECTIVES

- The children will design and conduct an experiment to test the effect of light on the growth of grass.
- The children will observe and record the color and length of grass grown under two conditions (light and darkness).

SCIENCE
PROCESSES
EMPHASIZED

Formulating hypotheses
Interpreting data
Experimenting

MATERIALS
NEEDED

2 paper cups
1/4 tsp. of grass seed
Potting soil or synthetic plant-growing material
Light source that can be placed about 25 cm (about 10 in.) above
    the cup (a fluorescent grow-light fixture would be best)
Ruler
Graph paper
Easel paper for class data

Finding out how light affects plant growth

D
I
S
C
O
V
E
R
Y

A
C
T
I
V
I
T
I
E
S

MOTIVATION   Tell the class that they are going to observe and measure the effect something has on plants. Display the grass seeds and related materials. Ask the children to guess what they will be investigating.

DIRECTIONS   1. Distribute the materials, and have the children label one cup *light* and one cup *dark*. They should also record the date on each cup. Tell them to fill each cup two-thirds full of soil, scatter a pinch of seeds across the surface, and then lightly cover the seeds with more soil. Tell the children to punch a few holes into the bottom of the cup to allow excess water to drain.

2. Ask each group to predict what will happen if one cup is placed in a dark location and one cup is placed in a light location for three days. Have the groups record their predictions. This would be a good time to have a class discussion about the range of predictions that are made.

3. Have the children add the same amount of water to each cup and then put their cups in the appropriate environments. *They should plan to observe the cups every three days.*

4. When the groups make their observations, they should record the appearance, color, and average length of plants. The determination of length will be challenging because the groups will need to invent a strategy that does not require the measurement of every plant. One strategy might be to measure five plants from different parts of the cup and average the measurements. Another would be to simply record the total height of the sample. The length measurements as well as other observations should be recorded on a data sheet, which should be maintained for about two weeks.

KEY DISCUSSION QUESTIONS   1. If we want to see if the seeds need light to grow, what must we do to the water and temperature of the plants? *We have to keep the water and temperature the same for both cups.*

2. Why did all the seeds start to grow equally well? *Seeds don't need light to sprout.*

3. Why did the plants in the dark stop growing and turn yellow after awhile? *They ran out of food. They needed light to grow.*

SCIENCE CONTENT FOR THE TEACHER   Grass seeds contain a small amount of stored food in their cotyledons, which allows them to begin growing. When the food is used up, the plant must rely on sunlight for the energy required for further growth.

EXTENSION   *Science/Nutrition:* Some students may wish to obtain seeds at a health food store that are appropriate for sprouting (mung beans, alfalfa, lettuce). Once the seeds have sprouted, the class can have a feast while discussing the nutrients found in the sprouts.

The Curious Gerbils [LS 3]

Note: This demonstration is a long-term classroom project that involves proper care for living organisms. There are many questions you must face if you embark upon it, not the least of which is what you will do with the gerbils that are born in the classroom. You will quickly run out of appropriate living space for these creatures, as they are capable of reproducing at an alarming rate. The children will undoubtedly volunteer to take excess gerbils. However, do not assume that every child who wants a gerbil will be able to provide appropriate care or that his or her family will want to have a new addition to the household. Also be aware that some of the children who may want gerbils may be allergic to them. You should spend time thinking about both the benefits and problems associated with the raising of animals in the classroom before beginning this project.

OBJECTIVES
- The children will observe the characteristics of gerbils.
- The children will provide appropriate care for gerbils in the classroom.
- The children will observe the birth of gerbils in the classroom.

SCIENCE PROCESSES EMPHASIZED

Observing
Inferring

For Young Learners

MATERIALS

Male gerbil	Gerbil food
Female gerbil	Supply of lettuce

Gerbil cage with exercise wheel, water bottle, nesting material (cedar shavings, newspaper, cloth, and so on)

MOTIVATION

Keep the presence of the gerbils and the cage supplies secret. Tell the children that they are going to have an opportunity to meet some classroom pets. Do not divulge what kind of animals the pets are. Ask the children if they think they can be responsible for the care of some pets in the classroom. Assuming the answer is yes, proceed with the demonstration.

DIRECTIONS

1. Display all the materials and the male and female gerbils.
2. Place the nesting material, food, and exercise wheel in the cage and fill the water bottle. Have the children discuss the purpose of each object in the cage.
3. Before placing the male and female gerbils in the cage, allow the children to observe them.
4. Discuss the importance of proper care of the gerbils. Talk about the children's responsibilities and appropriate rules for the gerbils' care.

DEMONSTRATIONS

5. If you are fortunate, within a month or two you may have a litter of ger-bils. In this event, have the children observe the changes that occur as the tiny creatures begin to appear more and more like their parents.

KEY DISCUSSION QUESTIONS

1. Are gerbils mammals? *Yes. They are alive, they drink their mother's milk, and their bodies are covered with hair/fur.*
2. What do you think gerbils need in order to survive and stay healthy in the classroom? *Answers will vary but may include food, water, nesting material, air, exercise, and some peace and quiet.*
3. Various other questions concerning the children's responsibilities for the continuing care and feeding of the gerbils should be asked. Such questions should focus upon what the responsibilities will be, how they should be carried out, and who will carry them out.

SCIENCE CONTENT FOR THE TEACHER

Gerbils are small animals that are easy to care for in the classroom. They are covered with hair, give birth, and suckle their young; they are true mammals. Young female gerbils may bear young every six to eight weeks.

EXTENSIONS

Science: Students may be interested in learning about the care of puppies, cats, guinea pigs, hamsters, and other animals.

Art: The class may want to make drawings of both the male and female gerbil and any babies. The children can use commercially available crayon-like pastels to reproduce the coloring of the animals.

Is It Alive? [S&T 3]

OBJECTIVE

• The children will observe and describe the differences between living and nonliving things.

SCIENCE PROCESSES EMPHASIZED

Observing
Communicating
Inferring

MATERIALS

Living animal (fish, insect, mouse)
Living plant
Nonliving thing (shoe, pencil, book)
Wind-up toy that makes sounds (or nonelectric ticking clock with second hand)
Cardboard box with fitted top

MOTIVATION

Prior to class, place the mechanical toy or ticking clock in a box with a fitted top. Do not tell the children what is in the box. Have volunteers come forward to listen to the toy or clock in the box. Tell the children that they are going to discover some things about the object in the box and how to tell the difference between things that are alive and things that are not.

DIRECTIONS

1. Hold up for observation the animal, the plant, and the shoe, book, or pencil. Display each object one at a time so that the children can focus their observations.
2. On the chalkboard, create a chart on which to record the children's observations. Provide a space at the bottom of the chart to write their guesses about the object in the box and whether or not it is alive.
3. Once all the observations have been recorded, play a game of 20 questions with the children to help them refine their thinking. Suggest that they use their observation when asking questions. *Hint:* Actually peek into the box after each question. A little acting on your part will help maintain interest in the game.
4. Finally, display the object in the box and engage the children in a discussion of the differences between living and nonliving things.

KEY DISCUSSION QUESTIONS

1. In what ways are living and nonliving things the same? *Answers will vary and may include such observations as living and nonliving things can be the same color or size. They can both be soft or hard.*
2. In what ways are living things and nonliving things different? *Answers will vary and may include the idea that nonliving things stay the same, last a long time, don't change very much; living things like plants have seeds; animals have baby animals.*

SCIENCE CONTENT FOR THE TEACHER

Living things and nonliving things may share some common characteristics. They both may move; they both may make noise; they may be the same color or weight. However, things that are alive grow, change, or develop from infant to adult and are able to reproduce their own kind.

EXTENSION

Health: Discuss the special responsibilities involved in caring for living things that are different from the responsibilities involved in caring for nonliving things. Some children may want to make drawings or posters that show how to care for pets or other living things.

The Birth of Guppies [LS 5]

For Middle-Level Learners

Note: This demonstration can be used as a follow-up to the discovery activity on male and female guppies described earlier in this chapter (pages 320–321).

OBJECTIVES

- The children will observe the construction of an aquarium.
- The children will describe the roles of male and female guppies in the reproductive process.

SCIENCE PROCESSES EMPHASIZED	Observing Inferring

MATERIALS

Fish aquarium
Aged tapwater at room temperature
Aquarium sand and gravel
Assorted freshwater plants, including *Anarchis,* duckweed,
   and eelgrass
1 dip net
2 or 3 nursery traps
Small container with 2 male guppies
Small container with 4 female guppies
Thermometer
Light source (a reading lamp can be used)
Dry fish food

MOTIVATION

Ask the children if they have ever seen the birth of guppies. After a discussion of any observations they have made of guppies reproducing, tell them that within the next few weeks they may be able to see guppies being born. Display the aquarium and other materials.

DIRECTIONS

1. Have the children observe all the materials that you have placed on display.
2. Begin assembling the aquarium by placing a 5-centimeter (2-inch) layer of sand on its floor. Plant eelgrass in the sand. Now add the aged tap water; do it gently so as to avoid stirring up the sand. Float the duckweed and *Anarchis* in the water.
3. Put the thermometer in the water and place the light source nearby. The light source will need to be moved back and forth during the demonstration so as to maintain the water temperature at 25°C (75°F).
4. Place the male and female guppies in the aquarium.
5. Float the nursery traps in the aquarium, and sprinkle some fish food on the water's surface.
6. Maintain the aquarium over a two- or three-week period, and encourage the children to make observations of any changes that occur in the shape of the female guppies. A pregnant female will develop a bulging abdomen. Use the dip net to place each pregnant female in its own nursery trap. This increases the chances that the soon-to-be-born babies will survive, for the traps will protect the new guppies from hungry adult fish.

KEY DISCUSSION QUESTIONS

1. Why did we plant eelgrass and other aquarium plants in the aquarium? *Answers will vary. They may include: So that some living things in the aquarium would have plants to eat.*

2. What does the male guppy do in the reproductive process? *Places sperm in the female guppy.*
3. What does the female guppy do in the reproductive process? *Produces the eggs that get fertilized; has a place inside her body where the new guppies begin to develop.*

SCIENCE CONTENT FOR THE TEACHER

For this demonstration, you must know how to assemble and maintain a simple freshwater aquarium. The preceding directions provide some of the basic information. If you wish to increase the likelihood of maintaining a healthy aquarium for more than one or two weeks, it would be worthwhile to talk with a knowledgeable salesperson in a petstore to learn the details of raising and caring for tropical fish in general and guppies in particular. Additional materials—such as water heaters, pumps, and filters—are necessary if you wish to keep the aquarium functioning all through the year. This equipment is commonly available at petshops.

The Insect Aquarium [LS 7]

Note: This demonstration should be done in the spring.

OBJECTIVES
- The children will observe the construction of a freshwater aquarium.
- Children will infer the reasons for the placement of various materials in the aquarium.

SCIENCE PROCESSES EMPHASIZED

Observing
Inferring

MATERIALS

4 liter wide-mouth jar (about a gallon) or a small plastic or
    glass aquarium
Source of fresh pond or stream water
Collection of live water plants and insects from a pond or stream
Small twigs from the pond or stream
Pebbles and rocks found at the water's edge
Clean aquarium sand (available from a petshop)
Fine mesh screening to cover the top of the aquarium

MOTIVATION

Tell the children that you have gathered a variety of materials to use to construct a freshwater aquarium. Discuss the difference between freshwater and saltwater. Tell the children that the aquarium you are going to build will not contain fish but may contain other interesting creatures. Their job will be to give you ideas as you construct it.

D
E
M
O
N
S
T
R
A
T
I
O
N
S

DIRECTIONS

1. In the spring prior to the demonstration, gather freshwater and a variety of plants and aquatic insects from a local pond or stream. Keep the specimens fresh and take them to class.
2. In the classroom, fill the bottom of the container with about 5 centimeters (about 2 inches) of sand, and root the water plants in the sand. Place a few large twigs at the side of the jar in a way that roots their ends in the sand, and put some rocks and pebbles on the surface of the sand.
3. Gently add freshwater until the water level is about 12 centimeters (about 5 inches) from the top. Float some twigs on the surface so that any insects emerging from the water have a place to stay. Cover the top with the mesh, and put the aquarium where it can receive sunlight and benefit from air circulation.
4. Encourage the children to make daily observations of the aquarium and to infer the reasons for some of the changes they observe.

KEY DISCUSSION QUESTIONS

1. Why do you think we are doing this demonstration in the spring? *Answers will vary and may include the idea that insects hatch in the spring.*
2. Why do you think we put the aquarium in the sunlight? *Answers will vary and may include the idea that the plants need sunlight to make food.*

SCIENCE CONTENT FOR THE TEACHER

Insects you may be able to find in a pond are the nymphs of dragonflies, water boatmen, mosquito larvae, mayflies, and water beetles. Insects are easily found in the shallow water at the edge of a pond or stream.

EXTENSION

Science/Language Arts: After about a week of observation, ask the children to write a poem entitled "Changes" that will include at least three observations they have made of the aquarium.

15A

The Human Body

Content

A Look Ahead

The Body's Systems

Silently in the cold gray light of dawn, a runner moves briskly along the pavement. The row houses look quietly on as her footsteps echo off their walls. Her stride is steady and firm. Her breathing barely reflects the strain of four miles of running. Her gaze is clear and her ears are sensitive to the sounds of the neighborhood awakening. The blood courses through her arteries, bringing oxygen and nourishment to her body's cells and carrying away by-products produced by the cells. The runner's body systems are functioning well when she arrives home. Within minutes, her body has recovered from this morning's ritual run. She feels refreshed and alive.

The well-functioning systems of the runner's body enable her to concentrate on the things that matter in her life. The discipline of her body is matched by the discipline of her mind, which wills her to rise early each day to run. To understand fully how the human body is able to perform, we need to consider its basic systems. *Body systems* are groups of organs that work together to carry out a particular function. For example, the heart, arteries, and veins each perform specific tasks that together enable the bloodstream to transport oxygen, nutrients, and waste products. This system of heart, arteries, and veins is called the *circulatory system*. The other basic body systems are the digestive, skeletal-muscular, respiratory, nervous, excretory, and reproductive systems. To understand them, you need to know both their structures and their functions.

The Digestive System

Thinking a thought, blinking an eye, and taking a step are not possible without energy. The basic source of this energy is the food we eat. The process of digestion changes food from its original form to a fuel that can release energy when it reacts with oxygen. Digestion also releases and transforms proteins—the materials necessary for building new cells and repairing old ones. The hamburger, french fries, and ear of corn on your plate at a late-summer picnic are the raw materials for the conduct of life itself.

Structure and Function

Digestion is the process through which the body breaks down the molecules that make up the food that has been eaten and prepares them to react with oxygen to produce energy. Digestion begins in your mouth. As you chew food, glands in your mouth secrete *saliva,* a digestive juice that mixes with the food particles. Saliva contains water, mucus, and an enzyme that begins the process of breaking down the food.

As food moves through the digestive system, enzymes continue to act on it. Each enzyme breaks down a particular material found in food. The seeds of certain fruits, the cellulose in vegetables, and some meat tissues are indigestible. Such material passes into the large intestine and is eventually excreted.

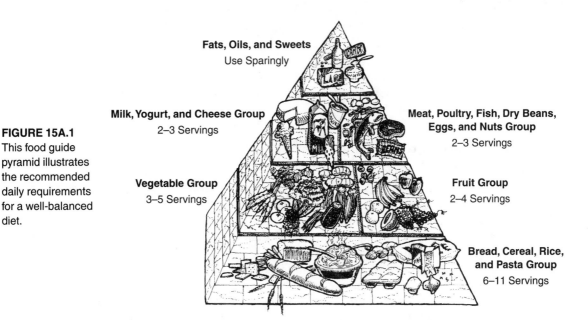

FIGURE 15A.1
This food guide pyramid illustrates the recommended daily requirements for a well-balanced diet.

Fats, Oils, and Sweets
Use Sparingly

Milk, Yogurt, and Cheese Group
2–3 Servings

Meat, Poultry, Fish, Dry Beans, Eggs, and Nuts Group
2–3 Servings

Vegetable Group
3–5 Servings

Fruit Group
2–4 Servings

Bread, Cereal, Rice, and Pasta Group
6–11 Servings

Food and Nutrition

All food contains *nutrients,* specific substances that provide the energy and materials the body requires to function properly. The nutrients in the food we eat are used in one of two basic ways by the body. Some are converted into energy and used immediately. Others are used to build new cells. Six specific nutrients are necessary for health and growth: carbohydrates (starches and sugars), fats, proteins, minerals, vitamins, and water. The foods we eat contain different amounts of these nutrients.

The United States Department of Agriculture recommends that we all eat more grains, fruits, and vegetables and less meat, fat, and sweets. To convey this view of appropriate nutrition, the Department of Agriculture has created a food guide pyramid that can help you make wise decisions about what you eat (see Figure 15A.1).

The Skeletal-Muscular System

Bones: Structure and Function

Your bones and muscles work together to give your body its form and structure. The bones provide support, protection for vital organs, a place in which red blood cells and some white blood cells are produced, a storage area for minerals, and surfaces to which muscles are attached. Although many people think that bones are hard, dry objects within the body, they are really alive.

Bone tissue is composed of living bone cells, which require food and oxygen, just as other body cells do, the products of bone-cell respiration, and deposits of minerals. Most bones in the human body originate from softer bonelike structures, or *cartilage.* As you age, the cartilage present in your body when you were very young becomes strong bone. This process continues until you are 20 to 25 years old.

A *joint* is a place where two bones meet. There are five types of joints in the human body: immovable, hinge, ball-and-socket, pivot, and gliding. Each provides flexibility of movement. In some joints—such as the one that connects the upper arm to the shoulder—bands of strong connective tissue, called *ligaments*, hold the bones of the joint together.

Muscles: Structure and Function

The muscles in your body provide you with the ability to move. This results from the ability of muscle cells to contract. There are three types of muscles in your body: smooth muscle, skeletal muscle, and cardiac muscle. Smooth muscles are those that act involuntarily. For example, the muscles that line the stomach and intestinal walls and the arteries are all involuntary muscles. This means they are able to operate quickly and without the direct control of the brain.

The involuntary muscle found in your heart is called *cardiac muscle*. When the fibers in this muscle contract, the chambers of the heart are squeezed and blood is forced out through blood vessels. If the cardiac muscle was not involuntary, your brain would have to tell your heart to beat each time blood needed to be pumped through your circulatory system.

Skeletal muscles are voluntary muscles. They work because the brain tells them to bend or flex or stretch. Skeletal muscles attach directly either to bones or to other muscles. *Tendons* are bands of connective tissue that attach the ends of some skeletal muscles to bones. When a skeletal muscle such as one in your upper arm contracts as a result of a message your brain gives it, it pulls on the muscles of your lower arm. The movement of the lower arm results from the contraction of the voluntary skeletal muscle.

The Respiratory System

 The food you eat supplies your body with energy through a series of chemical reactions that take place in the body's cells and require oxygen. Without oxygen, the food molecules could not be broken down and energy would not be released. While some of this energy is released as heat, much of it is stored in chemical form. Carbon dioxide and water are given off during this energy-producing process. The stored energy is used by body cells, tissues, organs, nerves, and other body organs. This simple equation shows the process by which energy is produced in your body cells:

$$\text{food} + \text{oxygen} \rightarrow \text{carbon dioxide} + \text{water} + \text{energy}$$

The Diaphragm, Windpipe, and Lungs: Structure and Function

The oxygen your body needs to produce energy from food is contained in the air you breathe. Air is about 21% oxygen and about 78% nitrogen. When you inhale, both oxygen and nitrogen enter your lungs. The nitrogen, however, is not used by the body. The in-and-out action of your lungs is controlled by the *diaphragm*, a large curved muscle that lies underneath them. As the diaphragm contracts, it moves downward. At the same time, the rib muscles separate the ribs and move them forward. These actions increase the amount of space in your chest and allow the lungs to expand.

After the air space in your chest has been enlarged, outside air pressure forces air through your nose and throat, down your windpipe, and into your lungs. After you have inhaled air, the action of your diaphragm and rib muscles increases the pressure within your chest and pushes air out through your windpipe, throat, and nose. This occurs each time you exhale.

The *windpipe* is a tube that stretches from your throat to your lungs. At your lungs it divides into two branches. Each of these branches subdivides into smaller and smaller branches within the lungs. These small branches end in tiny air sacs, each of which is surrounded by tiny blood vessels called *capillaries*. The air sacs have very thin walls, which permit the oxygen to pass through them and into the capillaries.

Oxygen Transport

Once oxygen has entered the air sacs of the lungs and diffused into the capillaries, it is picked up by red blood cells and carried to all parts of the body, where it reacts chemically with food to produce energy, carbon dioxide, and water. Carbon dioxide produced in the cells enters the bloodstream and is carried back to the air sacs in the lungs. There it leaves the bloodstream, enters the lungs, and is exhaled. The paper-thin walls of the air sacs are continually allowing oxygen to pass from the lungs to the bloodstream and carbon dioxide to pass from the bloodstream to the lungs.

The Nervous System

 A chirping bird catches your attention during a quiet morning walk along a wooded path. You stop and turn your head in an attempt to locate the source of this early morning joy. Your ears help focus your attention on the uppermost branch of a nearby tree. The song seems to come from somewhere behind a clump of leaves and twigs attached to the branch. Suddenly, your eyes pick out a slight movement and come to rest on a brownish head that pokes its way over the nest top and looks directly at you.

Your sight and hearing are precious gifts that, along with your other senses, gather information about the surrounding world. These sense organs are the farthest outposts of your nervous system. It is your nervous system that permits you to see, hear, touch, smell, taste, and—of course—become aware of and enjoy the existence of chirping birds on quiet morning walks through the woods.

Nerves: Structure and Function

The nervous system consists of the brain, the spinal cord, and many nerve cells. A *nerve cell* has three parts: a cell body, short, branchlike fibers that receive impulses from the brain, and long thin fibers that carry impulses away from the cell body. Bundles of either short or long fibers are known as *nerves.* Nerves carry messages from the brain to other parts of the body and from other parts of the body to the brain. Messages are carried by nerve impulses, chemical changes that cause electrical charges to be transmitted through the nervous system.

Twelve pairs of nerves directly connect the brain to the eyes, ears, nose, and tongue. These nerves are called *cranial nerves.* Branches of some of these nerves leave the head and connect with the variety of muscles and other internal organs in other parts of your body.

The principal way in which messages are sent from the brain to the body is through the *spinal cord,* a column of nerves that extends from the base of the brain down through the backbone. Thirty-one pairs of nerves directly connect the spinal cord with such organs as the lungs, intestines, stomach, and kidneys. These organs usually function without voluntary control. Thus, the nerves that control these functions make up what is known as the *autonomic nervous system.* Actions over which the individual has some control or awareness of are controlled by the *somatic nervous system.*

A *reflex* is another type of automatic action controlled by the nervous system. A reflex, the simplest way in which your nervous system operates, occurs when some part of the body is stimulated. The knee-jerk reaction is a good example of a reflex. If a person taps your kneecap with an object, your lower leg swings upward. The tapping of the kneecap stimulates a nerve cell in your lower leg. The nerve impulse travels along nerves to the spinal cord. When the impulse reaches the spinal cord, a message is immediately sent to the leg muscle, which causes the jerking movement. In this and many other reflex reactions, the response is not controlled by the brain. Reflex reactions are completed well before the brain is aware of their occurrence. Other reflexes are coughing, blinking, and laughing when you're tickled.

The Senses

The sense organs, the farthest outposts of the human nervous system, contain specialized nerve cells that receive stimulation from the outside world and carry messages to the brain. Nerve cells that are capable of receiving information from the external environment are called *receptors.* Each of your sense organs has special receptors.

The Skin Sensors

Your skin is able to sense a variety of stimuli, including touch, pressure, pain, heat, and cold. Whenever a receptor is stimulated, an impulse, or nerve message, begins traveling along the nerve to which the receptor is connected and eventually arrives at the central nervous system. Receptors for the various skin senses are distributed at different locations and different depths in the skin. The touch receptors are close to the surface of the skin. Your fingertips contain many touch receptors. Pressure receptors are deeper in the skin.

Taste

Your ability to taste results from specialized nerve receptors on your tongue. The areas containing these receptors are called *taste buds*. There are specialized taste buds for each of the following flavors: sour, sweet, salt, and bitter. What you interpret as taste is actually a combination of taste and smell, for when you chew food, vapors from it reach your nose. Thus, you simultaneously taste and smell the food you're eating. You may have noticed that when you have a cold, food does not taste as good as usual. This is due to the fact that you cannot smell it as you eat it.

Smell

The principal nerve that carries information about smell to the brain is the *olfactory nerve*. Branches of this nerve are contained in a cavity in your nasal passage. Vapor from the food you eat enters your nasal cavity, is dissolved in a liquid, and stimulates the endings of the olfactory nerve.

Hearing

The ear is the principal organ through which sound waves enter the body. Sound waves enter the opening in your external ear and travel through a tube called the *auditory canal*. This canal ends at a membrane called the *eardrum*. The sound waves stimulate the eardrum, causing it to vibrate. On the other side of the eardrum a group of tiny bones—the hammer, the anvil, and the stirrup—transmit vibrations from the eardrum to the cochlea and the semicircular canals, located in the inner ear. These organs relay the vibrations to the sensitive receptors at the end of the auditory nerve, which carries them to the brain.

Sight

Your eyes receive information in the form of light from the external world (see Figure 15A.2). Light passes through a transparent covering called the *cornea* and enters the

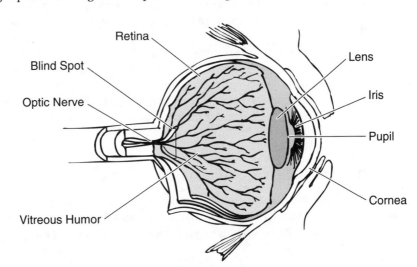

FIGURE 15A.2
The human eye receives information from the external environment.

pupil, a small opening at the front of the eyeball. The size of the pupil is controlled by the opening and closing of the *iris,* the colored portion of the eyeball. Directly behind the pupil is the *lens,* which focuses your sight. Focusing is achieved by a muscular contraction that changes the shape of the lens. Between the lens and the cornea is a watery liquid known as the *aqueous humor.* Within the eyeball is a thicker, transparent substance called the *vitreous humor.* The structures at the front of the eyeball all serve to focus light on the *retina,* the rear portion of the eyeball containing light receptors. These receptors are of two types: cones and rods. The cones are responsible for color vision; the rods produce a material that helps you see in dim light. Focused light rays, or images, that reach the retina stimulate the receptors, which in turn transmit information about them to the brain via the optic nerve. In interpreting these messages, the brain gives us the sense we call sight.

The Excretory System

 The process by which your body rids itself of wastes is called *excretion.* Virtually all forms of energy production create waste by-products. The human body produces both energy and an abundance of gaseous, liquid, and solid wastes. These wastes result from the production of energy and the process through which complex food materials are changed to simpler, more usable ones. If, for some reason, wastes cannot leave the body, sickness and death are certain to follow. The human body is able to rid itself of wastes by means of a very efficient group of organs.

The Kidneys: Structure and Function

Wastes from your body's cells enter the bloodstream and are carried to specific excretory organs. The major excretory organs are the kidneys and the skin. The kidneys lie on each side of the spine in the lower back. Each kidney is protected by a layer of fat. Waste-containing blood enters the kidneys and is divided into smaller and smaller amounts as the arteries transporting it branch into capillaries. From the capillaries, the blood flows through filters that separate the wastes from the blood and combine them into urine. *Urine* is a liquid that contains, in addition to the body's waste by-products, water and excess mineral salts that have also been filtered from the blood by the kidneys. Tubes called *urethras* carry the urine from the kidneys to the *urinary bladder.* This muscular organ then expels the urine from the body through the *urethra.* Meanwhile, the cleansed blood exits the kidneys through the renal veins.

The Skin and Lungs: Function

You may be surprised to learn that your skin is an important excretory organ. Its principal role is the removal of excess heat. When the body becomes too warm, blood vessels in the skin open wide, increasing the flow of blood to the capillaries, which allows heat to be given off to the air. Through pores in the skin exit water, salts, and small amounts of *urea*, a waste found principally in the urine. The liquid that contains these body wastes is *perspiration*. As perspiration evaporates, it helps cool the body. The lungs are considered part of the excretory system because they rid the body of carbon dioxide and excess water in the form of water vapor.

The Liver and Intestines: Function

Although the liver is principally a digestive organ, it is also able to form urea and secrete it into the bloodstream. Bacteria, some drugs, and hormones are removed from the blood in the liver and converted into less harmful substances. These substances are returned to the blood and eventually excreted from the body by the kidneys.

The large intestine performs an important excretory function by removing from the body food that has not been digested by the small intestine. Solid waste that moves through the large intestine is composed largely of undigested food and bacteria. It is eliminated from the body through the *anus*—the end of the digestive tract. The *rectum* is that portion of the large intestine that lies directly above the anus.

The Circulatory System

 A complex system consisting of a pump and conducting vessels keeps you alive. This system, known as the circulatory system, operates efficiently whether you are sitting, standing, walking, running, or sleeping. The circulatory system is an extraordinarily complex system but so efficient and automatic that you are able to carry out the activities of living without even an awareness of its existence.

The Heart and Blood Vessels: Structure and Function

The heart is the powerful pump that moves blood through your body's blood vessels. It has four chambers: a right atrium, a left atrium, a right ventricle, and a left ventricle. Blood enters this marvelous pump through the *atria* (the upper chambers) and is pumped out of the heart by the *ventricles* (the lower chambers). Between the atria and the ventricles are *valves* that prevent the blood from flowing backward. Once blood passes from the atria to the ventricles, it is impossible for it to return through these controlling valves. The opening and closing of the heart valves produce the sound that a physician hears when he or she uses a stethoscope to listen to your heart. The "lub-dub, lub-dub" is simply the opening and shutting of the valves. If the heart valves are damaged and blood is able to leak backward from the ventricles to the atria, a health problem results. Physicians can usually detect this problem by listening through their stethoscope for the sound produced by blood moving in the wrong direction. This sound is called a *heart murmur.*

The vessels that carry blood from the ventricles to various parts of the body are called *arteries.* The vessels that return blood to the heart are called *veins.* Within the body tissues the major arteries branch into smaller and smaller arteries and small veins merge to form large veins. A series of microscopic *capillaries* connect small arteries and veins and permit the exchange of dissolved nutrients, oxygen, wastes, and other substances.

The right side of the heart receives blood from the body cells and pumps it to the lungs. This blood contains the carbon dioxide produced by the cells as they converted nutrients to energy. In the lungs, the carbon dioxide is removed from the blood, and oxygen from inhaled air is added. The oxygen-rich blood is then carried to the left side of the heart, which pumps it to the remaining organs of your body (see Figure 15A.3). To understand the circulatory system, you must remember that the heart seems to act like two pumps. On the right side, blood that contains carbon dioxide is pumped to the lungs. On the left side, blood that is rich in oxygen, as a result of having passed through the lungs, is pumped to all parts of the body.

Blood

Human blood is made of a variety of materials. One such material is *plasma,* which is 90% water and 10% various dissolved substances. Among the most important of these substances are *antibodies,* which help your body fight diseases.

Red blood cells are another component of blood. They contain *hemoglobin,* the iron-rich substance that receives oxygen from the lungs and carries it to the tissue cells.

Another type of cell found in the bloodstream is the *white blood cell.* White blood cells do not contain hemoglobin. Rather, they are your body's first line of defense against infection. If you have an infection, the number of white cells in your blood increases very rapidly. White blood cells are able to surround disease-causing bacteria and kill them.

Fibrinogen, which makes possible the process of clotting, is found in plasma. If you cut yourself, substances called *platelets* release a chemical that causes fibrinogen to turn into needlelike fibers that trap blood cells and form a clot. It is this clotting process that allows the bloodstream to repair itself in the event of a cut. It simply restricts the flow of blood to an open cut or puncture.

As blood passes through the body, it picks up many things. In the capillaries of the small intestine, it absorbs dissolved food, which it then carries to the liver, an organ that is able to store sugar. Other nutrients in the blood are carried to the various body cells, where, in combination with oxygen, they are converted to energy. This energy production results in carbon dioxide, water, and other waste by-products. These wastes leave the cells and are carried by the bloodstream to organs that are able to rid the body of them.

FIGURE 15A.3

The human heart consists of two pumps lying side by side to form a single organ. The right side of the heart sends oxygen-poor blood to the lungs; the left side of the heart sends oxygen-rich blood to the rest of the body.

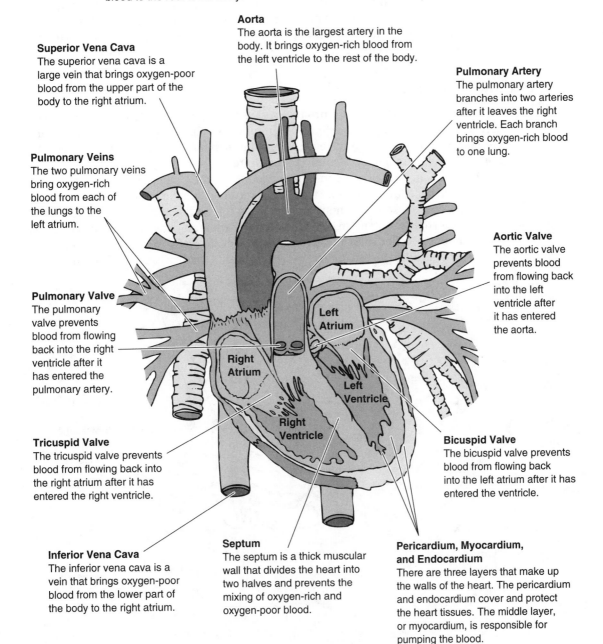

Aorta
The aorta is the largest artery in the body. It brings oxygen-rich blood from the left ventricle to the rest of the body.

Superior Vena Cava
The superior vena cava is a large vein that brings oxygen-poor blood from the upper part of the body to the right atrium.

Pulmonary Artery
The pulmonary artery branches into two arteries after it leaves the right ventricle. Each branch brings oxygen-rich blood to one lung.

Pulmonary Veins
The two pulmonary veins bring oxygen-rich blood from each of the lungs to the left atrium.

Aortic Valve
The aortic valve prevents blood from flowing back into the left ventricle after it has entered the aorta.

Pulmonary Valve
The pulmonary valve prevents blood from flowing back into the right ventricle after it has entered the pulmonary artery.

Left Atrium

Right Atrium

Left Ventricle

Right Ventricle

Tricuspid Valve
The tricuspid valve prevents blood from flowing back into the right atrium after it has entered the right ventricle.

Bicuspid Valve
The bicuspid valve prevents blood from flowing back into the left atrium after it has entered the ventricle.

Inferior Vena Cava
The inferior vena cava is a vein that brings oxygen-poor blood from the lower part of the body to the right atrium.

Septum
The septum is a thick muscular wall that divides the heart into two halves and prevents the mixing of oxygen-rich and oxygen-poor blood.

Pericardium, Myocardium, and Endocardium
There are three layers that make up the walls of the heart. The pericardium and endocardium cover and protect the heart tissues. The middle layer, or myocardium, is responsible for pumping the blood.

The Reproductive System

The egg or sperm cells within your body are so tiny that they can be seen only with a microscope, yet within each reposes half of a blueprint for a new human being, who may one day contribute one of its own reproductive cells to the process of creating a new person. We are bound backward in time to our parents, grandparents, and all those who have preceded us.

Structure and Function

The male reproductive organs produce *sperm*, or male reproductive cells. The female reproductive organs produce female reproductive cells, or *eggs*. Through sexual intercourse, a sperm cell and an egg cell may unite to form a human embryo. The embryo has the potential for becoming a new human being.

Sperm are produced in an organ called the *testis*. A pair of testes are contained in a pouch called the *scrotum*. Since this scrotum is outside the body wall, the temperature of the testes is somewhat lower than the body temperature. However, the production of healthy sperm cells requires this lower temperature. Within each testis are numerous coiled tubes. The cells that line the walls of these tubes produce sperm. These tubes merge to form a larger tube, the *sperm duct*. The sperm duct car-

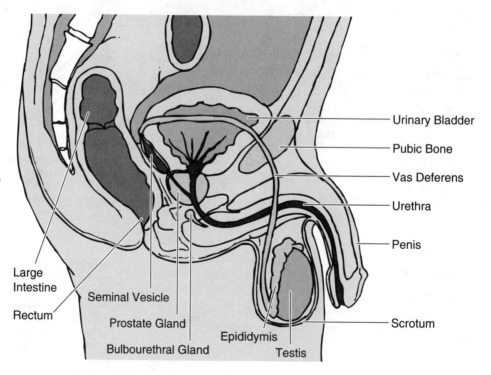

FIGURE 15A.4
The human male reproductive system

Large Intestine

Rectum

Seminal Vesicle

Prostate Gland

Bulbourethral Gland

Epididymis

Testis

Urinary Bladder

Pubic Bone

Vas Deferens

Urethra

Penis

Scrotum

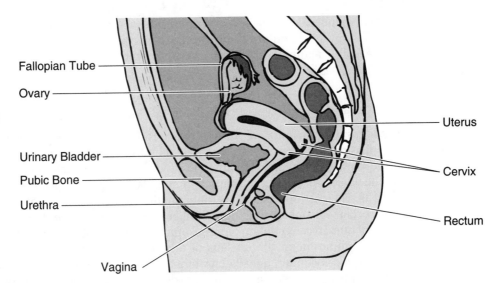

FIGURE 15A.5
The human female reproductive system

Fallopian Tube

Ovary

Uterus

Urinary Bladder

Cervix

Pubic Bone

Urethra

Rectum

Vagina

ries sperm and fluids produced by other glands (Cowper's gland, the prostate gland, and the seminal vesicles) into the body and then through the external sexual organ, the *penis.* The penis is used to fertilize egg cells in a female (see Figure 15A.4).

Human egg cells are produced in a pair of *ovaries* in the female body. During a human female's lifetime, about 500 eggs, or *ova,* will mature and be released by the ovaries. Usually one ovum matures and is released at one time. A mature ovum leaves the ovary and passes into a tubelike organ known as an *oviduct,* where it is pushed along by hairlike projections to a large muscle-lined tube called the *uterus.* If the egg is fertilized by a sperm, it will become attached to the uterus wall and develop into an embryo (see Figure 15A.5).

The *vagina* is a tube that connects the uterus with the outside of the body. During intercourse, sperm cells placed here may swim through the uterus and reach the oviducts. If a healthy sperm cell reaches a healthy, mature egg cell, fertilization occurs. The nucleus of the female egg cell and the nucleus of the male sperm unite to form the beginning of a new human being.

Within one week of fertilization, the cell produced by the union of the sperm and egg will divide into about 100 cells. Nine months later, the embryo will consist of more than 200 billion cells, each designed to carry out a particular life function.

The developing embryo gets its food through a membrane called the *placenta.* Nutrients and oxygen in the mother's bloodstream pass from the uterus into the blood vessels of the placenta and from there into the embryo, by way of blood vessels in an umbilical cord. The belly button, or *navel,* marks the place where the umbilical cord entered the developing embryo's body. Wastes produced by the cells of the developing embryo enter the embryo's bloodstream and are eventually carried by the placenta to the mother's bloodstream. However, the blood of the mother and the embryo do not mix.

When the embryo reaches maturity, birth occurs. At birth, the embryo is forced through the vagina and out of the mother's body as a result of contractions of the uterine wall. The umbilical cord that had connected the embryo with its mother is cut. The baby is born.

Reproduction and Heredity

Heredity is the transmission of the physical traits of the parents to their offspring. Your physical traits result from the transmittal of hereditary information that occurred when a sperm and egg united to produce you. The nucleus of the sperm cell and the nucleus of the egg cell contain material that determines the embryo's physical traits. The part of the nucleus that contains hereditary information is the *gene*. Genes occupy distinct places on ribbonlike structures called *chromosomes*. The nuclei of all human cells contain chromosomes. Although the nuclei of most cells contain 46 chromosomes, the nucleus of a human sperm cell and the nucleus of a human egg cell contain only 23 chromosomes. When a sperm cell and an egg cell unite, the resulting cell has 46 chromosomes. Twenty-three carry genes from the male parent, and 23 carry genes from the female parent. The genes on the chromosomes of the first complete cell and the particular order in which they are located on the chromosome give the offspring its inherited traits.

Identical twins result when an embryo splits in two. The two halves develop into individuals who have the same physical traits. *Fraternal twins* are the result of two ova being fertilized by two sperm. They are simply siblings who happened to be conceived and born at the same time.

Summary Outline

I. The digestive system converts food into energy or cell-building material.

II. The skeletal-muscular system provides the body with its shape and structure and gives it the ability to move.

III. The respiratory system secures the oxygen necessary for the conversion of food to energy and eliminates carbon dioxide.

IV. The nervous system receives stimuli and carries them to the brain; it then transmits the brain's messages to various parts of the body by means of nerve impulses.

V. The excretory system rids the body of gaseous, liquid, and solid wastes.

VI. The circulatory system moves a variety of substances from place to place in the body.

VII. The reproductive system of a male produces sperm cells capable of fertilizing an ovum, the reproductive cell of a female.

15B

The Human Body

Attention Getters, Discovery Activities, and Demonstrations

A Look Ahead

How Can We Help People See Us at Night? [S&T 1]

MATERIALS

1 sheet of dark construction paper
1 small mirror
Silver glitter
Glue

Transparent tape
1 flashlight
Bicycle reflector (optional)

MOTIVATING QUESTIONS

- Is it hard or easy to see people who are walking or riding bikes at night?
- What should people who are out at night do to keep themselves from being hit by a car?

DIRECTIONS

1. Darken the room, and ask the children if it would be hard or easy to see a person on a bicycle at night wearing a shirt that is the color of the construction paper. *Note:* This would be an excellent time to have a brief discussion of bicycle safety.
2. Shine the flashlight near the paper, and have the children pretend that the light is an automobile headlight. Ask how visible the person would be if the children were in a car. Tape the mirror to one side of the paper, and repeat the demonstration. Be sure the children notice that mirrors do not help if the light beam does not shine directly on them.
3. Draw a circle on the paper, fill the circle with glue, and sprinkle it with silver glitter. Try to produce some layers of glitter so that not all the glitter is flat on the paper. Your intent is to replicate a bicycle reflector. Have the children compare the extent to which the paper is lit without anything on it, with the mirror on it, and with the glued-on glitter. If you are able to obtain a bicycle reflector, attach that to the paper, as well.

SCIENCE CONTENT FOR THE TEACHER

How well we see something depends on how well light is reflected from the object. A bicycle reflector contains many tiny mirrorlike objects that reflect light from many directions so it is easy to see at night.

When Do We Do Things That Keep Us Healthy and Strong? [SPSP 1]

MATERIALS

1 large clock with hour and minute hands
Easel paper and marker

MOTIVATING QUESTIONS

- What things do you do before, during, and after school that help keep you healthy and strong?
- What things could you do that you are not doing now?

DIRECTIONS

1. Begin by explaining to the children that they are going to discuss what an imaginary child named Pat might do to stay healthy and strong. Tell them that you are going to make a chart on which you will record their ideas.
2. Set the hands of the clock to 7:00 A.M., review or teach time telling, and have the children give their ideas about what Pat might be doing. For example, 7:00 A.M. might be the time for washing, 7:15 A.M. might be the time that Pat eats a healthy breakfast, 7:30 A.M. might be the time that Pat brushes her/his teeth, and 7:45 A.M. might be the time that Pat puts on a seat belt for the bus ride to school. Carry this through the school day.

SCIENCE CONTENT FOR THE TEACHER

Children do many things in the course of a day that contribute to their health and well-being. The sequence of activities is relatively constant. By thinking about what more they could do and by trying to fit new ideas into their sequence, they can improve their health.

How Do Your Ears Help You Learn Things? [LS 3]

MATERIALS

1 small rubber ball
1 sheet of newspaper
1 empty soda bottle
1 empty glass
1 glass of water
Movable room divider or other object to use as a visual screen

MOTIVATING QUESTIONS

• Which sounds are easy (hard) to guess?
• Why are some sounds easy to guess and some sounds hard to guess?

DIRECTIONS

1. Keep all materials behind a screen for the duration of the demonstration. Ask for volunteers to sit in front of the screen facing the class.
2. Use the newspaper, ball, soda bottle, and glass of water to produce various sounds—such as the crumpling of paper, the bounce of a ball, the noise of water poured from glass to glass, or the sound made blowing across the soda bottle—and have the volunteers try to identify them. Discuss what factors make it easy or difficulty to recognize the sources of sounds.

SCIENCE CONTENT FOR THE TEACHER

The human senses are important because they allow us to take in information about our surroundings. The sense we make of the sounds we hear depends on a variety of factors, including our previous experience, whether the sound is clear or muffled, how loud the sound is, and the sensitivity of our ears.

How Does Light Affect Your Eyes? [LS 4]

Note: This Attention Getter can be done as a cooperative group activity if you have a flashlight and drawing paper for each group.

MATERIALS
1 flashlight
Drawing paper

MOTIVATING QUESTIONS
- Why do people sometimes wear dark glasses?
- Does your vision change when you go from a well-lit room to a dark room?

DIRECTIONS

For Middle-Level Learners

1. Distribute the drawing paper to the children. Have the children carefully observe one another's eyes and make drawings that show the iris (the pigmented part of the eye) and the pupil (the entryway of light into the eye).
2. Darken the room somewhat so that the children can observe changes in the pupil, and have them note additional changes when the lights are turned on.
3. Ask for a volunteer to come to the front of the room, and then select two observers. Have the observers look into the volunteer's eyes and tell the rest of the class how large the pupils are.
4. While the observers are studying the volunteer's eyes, briefly shine the flashlight perpendicular to the volunteer's eyes. Have the observers describe any changes they see. *Safety Note:* Do not shine the light into the volunteer's eyes. Light coming from the side will be sufficient to cause the pupils to dilate.

SCIENCE CONTENT FOR THE TEACHER
Our capacity to see depends on how much light enters the pupil and reaches the retina. It is difficult to see when too little light enters. Too much light can cause severe damage to the eyes. Muscles in the iris of the eye cause the pupil to become larger or smaller, depending on the availability of light. It is interesting to note that both eyes will react to changes in light intensity even if the changing light conditions occur for one eye.

What Is in That Cereal? [SPSP 6]

MATERIALS
2 or 3 large cereal boxes, including at least one heavily
   sweetened cereal
1 small cereal box for each group
1 transparency made from a cereal nutrition label

MOTIVATING QUESTIONS	• Which of these boxes of cereal do you think has the most calories per serving? • Which of these boxes of cereal do you think has the most vitamins and minerals?
DIRECTIONS	1. Project the cereal nutrition label, and review the categories of information on the label. 2. Distribute one cereal box to each group, and ask the groups to interpret the information on the nutrition labels. Be sure they note the number of calories per serving, the suggested serving size, and the percentage of sugars and fats in the cereal as well as the types and amounts of vitamins and minerals.
SCIENCE CONTENT FOR THE TEACHER	While cereal can provide some of the carbohydrates the body needs, many cereals have added sugar, which is not good for you. The nutrition information provided on a food label can be very helpful to consumers. As children study the labels, they should note the differences between various cereals and the contributions made by milk to the nutrient values of the cereals.

What Is in Cream? [SPSP 6]

MATERIALS	1 pt. of pasteurized heavy whipping cream Electric hand mixer or eggbeater 1 mixing bowl
MOTIVATING QUESTIONS	• How is cream the same or different from milk? • What do you predict will happen if we beat cream with a hand mixer?
DIRECTIONS	1. Ask the children how cream differs from milk. Pour the cream into the bowl, and have children make observations about its consistency and color. 2. Ask for volunteers to take turns using the mixer or eggbeater to churn the cream. Have some children act as observers who describe to the class the changes they observe as the cream is beaten. 3. In time, butter will begin to form and the bowl will contain butter and buttermilk. Ask for volunteers to taste the buttermilk and butter.
SCIENCE CONTENT FOR THE TEACHER	Cream has a very high fat content. When it is shaken vigorously, the fat begins to form granules. These granules gradually clump together, making butter. Although the color of butter we buy in the store is yellow, in some cases this color is due to the addition of food coloring. The actual color of butter varies greatly and depends on the type of cows that produced the milk and the type of food the cows consumed.

DISCOVERY ACTIVITIES

For Young Learners

The Mystery Bag [S&T 3]

OBJECTIVES
- Using their sense of touch, the children will name assorted objects.
- The students will match objects that they see with ones that they feel.

SCIENCE PROCESSES EMPHASIZED

Observing
Inferring

MATERIALS FOR EACH CHILD OR GROUP

Assorted objects, including pencils, erasers, paper clips, rubber bands, wooden blocks, marshmallows, and coins of various sizes
Boxes for the objects
Large paper bags with two holes (large enough for a hand to fit through) cut near the bottom of each bag
2 paper clips to close the tops of the bags

MOTIVATION

Before class begins, place one of the objects in a bag. Explain to the children that they are going to discover how their sense of touch can help them identify things. Begin the activity by placing your hand in one of the holes in the bag to feel the object inside. Describe the object to the children. Have various children come to the front of the room to feel the object in the bag. On the chalkboard or easel pad, record what they think the object is.

DIRECTIONS

1. Form two-person cooperative learning teams, and give each team a box containing the objects listed for this activity. Have the teams decide who will go first in each team, and have that person close his or her eyes. At the front of the room, hold up the type of object for the other team member to place in the bag.
2. Have the children who have had their eyes closed put one hand through each hole and feel the mystery object.
3. Ask the children to identify the object. If they are unable to name the object, hold up an assortment of objects and have the children vote for the one they think is correct.

KEY DISCUSSION QUESTIONS

1. What part of the body do we use most to feel things? *The hands.*
2. What are some of the things that the hands can feel? *How hot or cold things are. Whether objects are sharp, smooth, rough, soft, hard, and so on.*

Involving students in the creation of the activity

The mystery bag

3. What are some things that hands can't tell? *What color an object is, how shiny or bright it is, and so on.*

SCIENCE CONTENT FOR THE TEACHER   The skin has sense receptors that are sensitive to touch, warmth, cold, pain, and pressure. These sense receptors are not evenly distributed. Pressure is felt most accurately by the tip of the nose, the tongue, and the fingers. Sense receptors in our hands give us our awareness of heat, cold, pain, and pressure.

EXTENSIONS   *Math:* You may want to place a set of rods of different lengths in the bags and ask the children to select the biggest rod, the smallest, the second biggest, and so on.

Art: Some children may want to build a "feely board" collage out of materials of various textures, shapes, and sizes.

Sniff, Snuff, and Sneeze [LS 1]

OBJECTIVES
- The students will use their sense of smell to determine the contents of closed paper bags.
- The students will be able to identify various common odors (those of an onion, vinegar, an apple, and an orange).

SCIENCE PROCESSES EMPHASIZED
Observing
Inferring

MATERIALS FOR EACH CHILD OR GROUP

Paper bags (lunch size)	Plastic sandwich bags
25 cm (10 in.) of string for each bag	Paper towels
Peppermint oil	Vinegar
Wintergreen oil	Onion
Lemon extract	Apple
Camphor oil	Orange

MOTIVATION   Place a small amount of one of the odor-producing substances in one of the bags. Tie the bag loosely with string so that odors are able to escape but the students cannot see into it. Invite the students to identify the scent in the bag without looking in it and without using their hands.

DIRECTIONS

1. Distribute the paper bags and string, and have the children write their names on the bags. Have them select one of the odor-producing foods (apple, orange, or onion), place a small piece of it on a small piece of paper toweling in the bag, and loosely tie the bag.
2. Divide the children into cooperative learning groups, and have the members of the groups try to identify what is in each bag without looking.
3. Have each group select one bag to share with another group. Each group should discuss their observations and reach some agreement about what is in the other group's bag.
4. Place one or two drops of each oil and the vinegar on a small piece of paper towel, and seal it in a plastic bag.
5. Give each group a set of bags. Tell them to smell all of the bags and then identify and classify the scents any way they can.

KEY
DISCUSSION
QUESTIONS

1. How can we tell what is in the bag without opening it or touching it? *By smell.*
2. What are some words that can be used to describe odors? *Good, bad, strong, sour, sweet, medicine-smelling, food-smelling.*
3. How does smelling help animals survive? *By helping them track prey. By helping them sense enemies.*

SCIENCE
CONTENT FOR
THE TEACHER

When we smell something, we sample the air by inhaling it and having it move over receptors deep in our nasal cavity. These receptors analyze the chemicals in the air sample with great precision and transmit the findings to our brain for analysis and storage. Minute odors can trigger vivid memories.

EXTENSION   *Art:* Some children may want to produce a collage of pictures of good- and bad-smelling things. The children may be able to scent portions of the collage, such as pictures of flowers.

Using Your Senses to Classify Things [LS 1]

OBJECTIVE   • The children will use their senses of sight and touch to classify seeds.

SCIENCE
PROCESSES
EMPHASIZED

Classifying

MATERIALS FOR   Paper plate
EACH CHILD   Small plastic bag containing a variety of dried seeds, including
OR GROUP   sunflower seeds, kidney beans, lima beans, lentils, and so forth
               Hand lens

MOTIVATION   Display a bag of seeds, and tell the children that they are going to see how well they can sort through such a bag. Explain to them that they are to sort the seeds into different groups on their paper plates.

DIRECTIONS   1. Distribute a bag, paper plate, and hand lens to each group, and have the groups classify the seeds by placing them in like piles on a paper plate. ***Safety Note:*** If you are doing this activity with very young children, caution them not to eat any of the seeds or to put them in their nose, ears, or mouth.

               2. After the groups have begun their work, display the hand lenses and ask how they could be used to help classify the seeds.

KEY   1. How did your sense of sight help you group the seeds? *Answers will vary*
DISCUSSION   *but might include references to color or shape.*
QUESTIONS   2. If I asked you to group the seeds by how smooth or rough they were, what sense would you use? *Touch.* (After you ask this question, have the groups reclassify their seeds on the basis of smoothness and roughness.)

SCIENCE   Our senses provide us with detailed information about our surroundings.
CONTENT FOR Even something as simple as calling a person by name requires us to first
THE TEACHER use our senses to identify the person and then to decide whether we know the person or not. We can identify the person by sight or by the sound of her or his voice.

EXTENSION   *Science/Health:* You may want to bring in a variety of healthy foods and have the children group them according to taste—sweet, salty, sour, or bitter.

How Does Smell Affect Taste? [LS 4]

OBJECTIVES
- The children will predict the effect of the smell of a substance on its taste.
- The children will observe how the ability to smell affects taste.
- The children will infer the relationship between the senses of smell and taste.

SCIENCE   Observing
PROCESSES   Predicting
EMPHASIZED   Inferring

For Middle-Level Learners

DISCOVERY ACTIVITIES

MATERIALS FOR   Onion slice in a closed container
EACH CHILD   Apple slice in a closed container
OR GROUP   White potato slice in a closed container
                    5 packs of small hard candies, such as Lifesavers or Charms,
                        each of a different flavor
                    2 glasses of water
                    2 blindfolds

MOTIVATION   Keep the materials out of sight, and ask the children if they have ever no-
                    ticed that they sometimes lose some of their ability to taste foods. Some
                    children may note that food lost some of its taste when they had colds. Tell
                    the children that in this activity, they will discover how the smell of a sub-
                    stance affects its taste.

DIRECTIONS   ***Note:*** This activity has two parts. Begin by doing steps 1–5 as a demonstra-
                    tion. Then have the children work in groups to try the experiment using a
                    volunteer from their group.
                    1. Tell the children that you need a volunteer for a taste test of hard can-
                       dies. Blindfold the volunteer, and have the class predict how well the
                       volunteer will do.
                    2. Give the volunteer one of the candies, and have him or her taste it and
                       tell its flavor. Have the class record the accuracy of the result.
                    3. Have the volunteer take a drink of water to rinse the taste from his or
                       her mouth, and repeat the taste test with a different flavor of candy.
                       Continue repeating the taste test until all the flavors have been tested.
                       Be sure the volunteer rinses his or her mouth after each test and that
                       the class records the results of each test.
                    4. Blindfold the volunteer, hold an apple slice under his or her nose, and
                       have him or her take a small bit of the potato slice. Ask the volunteer
                       what kind of food was eaten.
                    5. Have the volunteer take a sip of water before beginning the second test.
                       Place an onion slice in front of the child's nose, provide an apple slice
                       for him or her to chew on, and ask him or her to identify the food.
                    6. Now have the class form cooperative learning groups to carry out steps
                       1–5 with a volunteer from each group.

KEY   1. Were you surprised at any of the things you observed during this activ-
DISCUSSION   ity? Why? *Answers will vary.*
QUESTIONS   2. How do you think the way something smells affects its taste? *When we
                       taste something our brain also discovers how it smells. The taste of food
                       depends in part on how it smells.*

SCIENCE   Substances must be dissolved in liquid before sensory nerves are able to
CONTENT FOR   detect their presence. The nerve endings in the taste buds are stimulated
THE TEACHER   by the dissolved substances and send information about them to the brain.

The nerve that carries information about smells to the brain branches into receptors that line the nasal cavities. Particles of food that enter the air as gases are dissolved in the liquids on the surface of the nasal cavities and stimulate the smell receptors. A cold or allergic reaction that produces large quantities of mucus in the lining of the nasal cavities limits the ability of the olfactory nerve to receive information.

EXTENSION   *Art:* Have the children discover the relationship between what we see when we look at food and how we think the food is going to taste. Using food colorings, they can prepare cookies, bread, and fried eggs in different colors and investigate why some people may not wish to sample them.

How Does Rest Affect Tired Muscles? [SPSP 6]

OBJECTIVES
- The children will gather data about the number of exercises they can do within a given period of time.
- The children will determine the effect of rest on the amount of exercise they can do.

SCIENCE   Observing and gathering data
PROCESSES   Inferring
EMPHASIZED

MATERIALS FOR   Pencil   Chart with 10 columns
EACH CHILD   Paper   Watch or clock with a second hand
OR GROUP

MOTIVATION   Ask the children if they remember that in the lower grades, their parents or teachers tried to make them rest or take naps. Have the children discuss why the adults wanted them to rest. You may wish to point out that young children are very active and tire quickly. Explain that rest gives muscles a chance to regain some strength. Tell the children that in this activity, they will find out how rest affects their muscles.

DIRECTIONS   1. Divide the class into two-member teams. One member will perform the exercise while the other member records data. Have the member who is going to perform the exercise make a clenched fist with one hand and then extend his or her fingers. Have the other member count how many times this exercise can be completed within 15 seconds. He or she should then enter the number in the first column of the chart.
                   2. Have all teams repeat this procedure four times, with no rest between trials. After the first member has completed five trials, have him or her rest for 10 or 15 minutes. During this rest period, have the other member of the team do the exercise.

D
I
S
C
O
V
E
R
Y

A
C
T
I
V
I
T
I
E
S

3. After the other member has completed five trials, have the teams repeat the activity but this time with a minute of rest between trials. Have the partners record the data as they did before.

KEY DISCUSSION QUESTIONS

1. How did resting for a minute between trials affect the results? *When I rested between trials, I was able to do more exercises during the trials.*
2. How can you use what you learned in this activity? *If I want to improve how well my muscles work when I play a sport or a game, I should rest as much as possible during time-outs or between innings.*

SCIENCE CONTENT FOR THE TEACHER

Skeletal muscles are voluntary muscles. They contract because we tell them to do so. When they contract, they cause various body parts to move. The energy that produces this movement comes from food that is digested in our body. As the cells produce energy, wastes accumulate. When too much waste has accumulated in the muscle cells and tissues, the cells are no longer able to contract normally. If this occurs, we experience muscle fatigue. One way of dealing with muscle fatigue is to allow muscles to rest. This permits the bloodstream to remove excess wastes that have built up in the muscle tissue.

EXTENSION

Math: You may wish to have some students synthesize all the data from this activity and prepare a classroom graph showing the average number of exercises performed during each trial for both the first part of the activity (exercises without rest periods) and the second part of the activity (exercises with intervening rest periods).

Are You Part of Any Food Chains? [LS 7]

OBJECTIVES

- The children will trace the locations of foods they have eaten in the food chain and discover their own location in the food chain.
- The children will communicate orally or in writing information about the factors that may affect the quantity and quality of the food that reaches them.

SCIENCE PROCESSES EMPHASIZED

Inferring
Communicating

MATERIALS

Potato   Magazine picture of a hamburger

MOTIVATION

After a brief discussion of what the children's favorite meals are, ask whether they have ever thought about how the food was produced. Hold up a potato and a picture of a hamburger, and tell the children that they are going to discover how they receive energy from the sun through each of these foods.

DISCOVERY ACTIVITIES

DIRECTIONS

1. Distribute a small potato and a magazine picture to each group. Ask the groups to make food chain charts that relate the foods to them. The chart for the potato, for example, would simply show the potato and a human. The chart for the hamburger would identify grass or grain, beef cattle, and humans.

2. Challenge some of the students to create a food chain that includes a human and a great white shark. When they are done, ask them to look at their food chain to see if they have shown the complete sequence of events that leads from the sun's energy to the energy the shark needs to survive to their own needs for energy.

KEY DISCUSSION QUESTIONS

1. How would changes in soil, water, air, or amount of sunlight affect the food you eat? *Answers will vary but should note that poor soil, limited water or sunlight, and air pollution can affect plant growth and thus affect animals that eat the plants and people who eat the plants and animals.*

2. If you are a vegetarian, is your food chain longer or shorter than the food chain of a person who is a meat eater? Why? *Shorter because the energy from the sun that is captured through photosynthesis goes directly from the vegetables to the person.*

SCIENCE CONTENT FOR THE TEACHER

Photosynthesis, the process by which the sun's energy is captured by plants, depends on the quantity and quality of the soil, water, sunlight, and air. Meat eaters as well as vegetarians require access to this captured energy in order to carry out life processes.

EXTENSION

Science/Social Studies: Encourage the children to identify the specific geographic locales where some of their favorite foods are produced. Have them describe and illustrate the various modes of transportation used to move the food products to them.

What Can Change Bones? [SPSP 1]

OBJECTIVES

- The children will observe two changes in bones.
- The children will infer the presence of minerals and water in bones.

SCIENCE PROCESSES EMPHASIZED

Observing
Inferring

For Young Learners

MATERIALS

4 small chicken bones
Jar of white vinegar
Alcohol or propane burner (if one is not available in your school, you may be able to borrow one from a high school science teacher)
Paper label

DEMONSTRATIONS

MOTIVATION   Tell the children that this demonstration will help them understand what bones are made of. Display the bones, vinegar, and burner. Ask the children to guess how these materials could be used to discover some things about bones.

DIRECTIONS

1. Place two of the bones in the jar of vinegar. Put a label on the jar, and write the date on the label. Tell the children that you are putting the jar aside and will remove the bones from the jar in about a week. Encourage the children to make observations of the contents of the jar each day during the week.
2. Compare the flexibility of the two remaining bones by bending each slightly.
3. Heat one of the bones over the burner. After the bone has been dried by this process, allow it to cool and then try to bend it. If it has been thoroughly dried, it will break in two easily. *Note:* Be sure the room is well ventilated, since heating the bone will produce some strong odors.
4. After a week has passed, retrieve the bones that were placed in the vinegar. Show the children that these bones bend easily.

KEY
DISCUSSION
QUESTIONS

1. How did heating affect the bone? *It made the bone break easily.*
2. How were the bones that were placed in vinegar changed? *They could be bent very easily.*

SCIENCE
CONTENT FOR
THE TEACHER

Vinegar is a weak acid that is able to react with the calcium in bones. Calcium gives bones the strength to support weight. Bones contain living cells as well as calcium and other minerals. Heating a bone dries out the water contained in the cells. Without water, the bone becomes brittle.

EXTENSION   *Art:* You may wish to have some of the children research how artists use their knowledge of bone structure in animals and humans in creating paintings and sculptures.

Your Nose Knows [LS 1]

OBJECTIVES
- The children will observe how long it takes for them to notice a substance introduced into the air in the classroom.
- The children will infer how the scent of a substance travels to their noses.

SCIENCE
PROCESSES
EMPHASIZED

Observing
Inferring

MATERIALS

Perfume	Oil of citronella	Oil of peppermint
Ammonia cleaner	4 saucers	

MOTIVATION	Pinch your nostrils closed, and ask the children if they have ever done this. Tell them that they are going to discover how much their sense of smell tells them about their world.

DIRECTIONS

1. Have the children sit around the room at various distances from the table you will use for the demonstration. Open one of the containers, and pour a few drops of one of the substances on a saucer. Tilt the saucer to spread the liquid over its surface.
2. Ask the children to raise their hands when they smell the substance.
3. After you have repeated the process for each substance, ask the children to try to explain how the smell got from the substance on the saucer to their noses. This is an opportunity for you to discuss the idea of particles entering the air from the substance and gradually spreading out, or diffusing.

KEY DISCUSSION QUESTIONS

1. Would opening a window or turning on a fan help us notice the smell more quickly or less quickly? *Answers will vary. If the movement of air directs molecules of the substance toward the children, they will smell the substances more quickly than they will if the window is closed or there is no fan.*
2. Do you think dogs have a better sense of smell than humans? *Answers will vary. Some children may have seen television programs or movies showing dogs used to track crime suspects.*

SCIENCE CONTENT FOR THE TEACHER

Sense organs gather information about our surroundings and send the information to the brain. Our sense of smell, or olfactory sense, results from the stimulation of olfactory cells in the nose by odors in the air. Nerve impulses carry information from the olfactory cells to the brain. What we know as smell is in fact the brain's response to the information it receives.

EXTENSION

Science/Health: Engage the children in a discussion of the possible safety advantages provided by the ability to smell odors. Ask: Does your nose help keep you safe? As the children respond, be sure to comment on how the smell of food going bad gives our brains important information.

What Is Your Lung Capacity? [LS 4]

OBJECTIVES

- The children will estimate the capacity of the teacher's lungs.
- The children will measure the capacity of the teacher's lungs.

SCIENCE PROCESSES EMPHASIZED

Observing
Predicting
Measuring
Using numbers

DEMONSTRATIONS

For Middle-Level Learners

MATERIALS   4 liter (1 gallon) glass or translucent plastic jug
1 liter container of water
1 m (about 3 feet) of clear plastic tubing (available for purchase in any hobby store)
Bucket large enough for the jug to be totally immersed
Source of water
Reference book that has a diagram of the human lungs and upper torso

MOTIVATION   Tell the children that this demonstration will give them an idea of the amount of air that can be contained by the lungs. Display the drawing of the lungs. Ask the children to estimate how many liters of air the lungs can hold. Have the children write down their predictions.

DIRECTIONS   1. Involving the children as assistants, fill the bucket to a depth of 10 centimeters (about 4 inches) with water. Fill the jug completely with water.
2. Cover the mouth of the jug with your hand, invert the jug, and place it in the bucket. When the mouth of the jug is under water in the bucket, carefully remove your hand. The water in the jug will remain in place. Have a child hold the inverted jug in position.
3. Place one end of the tube inside the jug, at least 10 centimeters (about 4 inches) up from its mouth. Leave the other end of the tube free.
4. Take a deep breath and exhale as much of the air in your lungs as possible through the free end of the tube. This air will displace some of the water in the jug.
5. Cover the free end of the tube with your thumb, and have a child cover the inverted end of the jug with his or her hand. Now extract the tube and have the child completely seal the mouth of the jug.
6. Turn the jug upright. The jug will be partly empty. This empty region represents the amount of water displaced by your exhaled air and, therefore, represents your lung capacity.
7. Have the children determine the number of liters of air that were exhaled. To do this, have them pour water into the jug from the liter container.
8. The children can compare the resulting figure with their predictions.

Apparatus for testing lung capacity

KEY DISCUSSION QUESTIONS

1. How could we make a jug that would tell us the amount of air that was exhaled? *Fill the jug with liters of water, and make a mark on the outside of the jug to show where the water level is for each liter of water. When the jug is turned upside down and used, measure the amount of air in it by seeing how many liters of water were pushed out.*
2. How did your prediction of lung capacity compare with the lung capacity we measured? *Answers will vary.*
3. What are some things that might shrink a person's lung capacity? *Answers will vary but may include any injury or disease that affects one or both lungs.*

SCIENCE CONTENT FOR THE TEACHER

Each time you breathe, the diaphragm muscle (located under your lungs) contracts, enabling the rib cage to expand. This expansion allows the lungs to expand to full capacity. As this occurs, air is taken into the lungs. As the diaphragm returns to its normal state, the contents of the lungs are expelled. The capacity of the lungs depends on a variety of factors, including general body size, the condition of the diaphragm and lung tissues, and the health of the respiratory system in general.

EXTENSION

Art: You may wish to encourage some children to make a series of large labeled drawings that show the location and size of the lungs in a variety of animals. These children will need access to reference books in order to carry out this activity.

How Fast Is Your Reaction Time? [LS 6]

OBJECTIVES

- The children will gather, graph, and interpret reaction time data.
- The children will suggest strategies for decreasing their reaction time.

SCIENCE PROCESSES EMPHASIZED

Interpreting data
Controlling variables

Testing reaction time with a dropped penny

MATERIALS

Penny
Meterstick

MOTIVATION

Display the materials, and ask the children to guess how you will use them. Explain that the demonstration will deal with reaction time, and ask them to suggest techniques that you could use to assess reaction time with a penny and with a meterstick.

DIRECTIONS

1. Ask for several volunteers. Have one volunteer extend his or her hand with the thumb and forefinger separated. Hold a meterstick by one end, and have the other end dangle between the volunteer's thumb and forefinger. Tell the volunteer that you are going to let go of your end of the meterstick, and ask him or her to catch it with his or her thumb and forefinger. The distance that the meterstick drops before it is caught is an indicator of reaction time. Repeat this exercise a number of times, and have the children create and interpret a graph of the data gathered.

2. Hold a penny above the outstretched hand of one of the volunteers. Tell the volunteer to try to move his or her hand away from the penny as it falls. Hold the penny at various distances above the child's hand. When the penny is close to the child's hand, it will be difficult for the child to move his or her hand away before the penny hits.

3. Ask the children what variables might affect reaction time. For example, a penny dropper might inadvertently signal a forthcoming drop with a facial gesture. Encourage them to invent ways to control some of the variables.

*KEY
DISCUSSION
QUESTIONS*

1. Can you think of an invention for a bicycle that might decrease the time between seeing a danger and braking? *Answers will vary. One example would be a radarlike device that would automatically engage the brakes when it sensed an object directly in the rider's path.*

2. What can an automobile driver do or avoid doing to improve his or her reaction time? *Answers will vary. Responses might include never driving while impaired by alcohol or drugs, keeping windshields clean, or playing the automobile radio at moderate volume levels so horns or sirens can be heard.*

*SCIENCE
CONTENT FOR
THE TEACHER*

Reaction time is the time between the receipt of sense information by our brain and the movement of muscles in response to the information. In everyday life, this movement can have important safety consequences. Alcohol is one example of a substance that can increase reaction time.

EXTENSION

Science/Language Arts: Have the children create a story about a superhero or -heroine whose principal advantage is the speed of his or her reaction time. Have the children focus on developing a central incident in which this advantage leads to the capture of a villain.

16

Unit, Lesson, and Enrichment Starter Ideas

The Physical Sciences and Technology

A Look Ahead

The Letter

Her throat was hoarse, her eyes itched, and her feet ached. It had been one of those long, long school days. On her way out of the building, she stopped in the main office to check her mailbox. A pink envelope, which signified interoffice mail, was tucked in the back of the box. Fishing it out, she opened it and began to read:

Dear Elizabeth:

You will recall that last year our elementary science curriculum committee recommended that we revise our entire elementary science curriculum this year. In order to accomplish this, each teacher will be a member of a subcommittee responsible for making recommendations about various parts of the curriculum. I would like to ask you to serve on the subcommittee that will review the physical science units that are presently in the curriculum. Part of that review should include assessing the extent to which the units are correlated to the NSE standards.

Each subcommittee should be prepared to make recommendations concerning the appropriateness of various units, activities, and materials to the full elementary science curriculum review committee within three months. I would like to thank you in advance for your contribution to this very important effort.

Cordially,

Margaret Stephanson

Margaret Stephanson
Elementary School Curriculum Coordinator

At the bottom of the page, there was a handwritten note: "P.S. Beth, would you mind being the chairperson for the subcommittee? Your principal and I both feel that you would be terrific for the job. Thanks. Margaret." A wry smile crossed Beth's face as she thought about her consistent avoidance of, and lack of interest in, physical science in high school and college and the irony of being appointed chairperson of a subcommittee that was going to focus on physical science units. She shook her head, tucked the letter in the pile of papers under her arm, and walked out the door.

Regardless of whether you enjoy learning about atoms, molecules, and energy, physical science topics make up a substantial portion of any curriculum or textbook series that you are likely to work with. If you enjoyed working with magnets, pushing on levers, playing with tuning forks, and making light bulbs light, you are going to have a lot of fun observing children's involvement in these activities. If you didn't enjoy physical science, you will discover how interesting it can be when approached with a child's sense of wonder.

Assessing Prior Knowledge and Conceptions

"But we learned all that in Mr. Greeley's class last year."

Have you ever been in a classroom and observed a teacher getting ambushed? That's what happens when teachers assume that children know little or nothing about a topic, only to discover too late that they know a lot. The results are also disastrous when teachers assume that children know a lot about a topic and in fact know very little. (Plus, valuable lesson-planning time will have been wasted.) Even assumptions about children's beliefs about phenomena in the natural world can stop teachers in their tracks. Children may have very strongly held beliefs that are totally incorrect, which may not be discovered until the class is deep in a lesson or unit.

So, as a teacher in the real world of schools and classrooms, how can you quickly get a sense of what the children know, what skills they possess, and what they believe? Part of the answer is to use *probes*—basic questions and simple activities that get children thinking and talking about particular topics. The answers children give will provide very direct guidance about what you should include in science units and lessons.

The probes and sample responses that follow come from informal interviews that I or my students have done with children. I think you'll be amazed at some of the responses and motivated to develop probes that you can use *before* planning units and lessons.

Probe	*Responses That Reveal Prior Knowledge and Conceptions*
▶ After showing a child an ice cube and a glass of water: *What is the difference between these two things?*	"Ice is frozen and water is plain." "One's colder, it's been frozen. Oh and how fast the molecules are moving."
▶ After putting a magnet on a metal file cabinet: *Why do you think the magnet sticks?*	"Because the drawer is metal and the magnet is a different kind of metal that sticks." "Because it's a magnet." "Because one has got negative charges and one has got positive or something like that."
▶ After showing some eyeglasses: *How do eyeglasses work?*	"I'm not sure. I think it has something to do with the shape and the way that they carved it."
▶ *Why is it easier to bike down a hill than up a hill?*	"The gravity pulls on the bicycle when you are going down the hill."

Probe	*Responses That Reveal Prior Knowledge and Conceptions*
▶ *What are some ways that people could save energy?*	"Turn off the lights, radio, and TV. "Wear a sweater instead of turning up the heat." "Be careful of what you throw away."
▶ After turning a desk lamp on for a minute: *Slowly move your hand toward the bulb, but don't touch it. How is it possible for you to feel the warmth from a fire, the sun, or a light bulb when you are not touching it?*	"Because they are so hot that it comes on so strong. It comes all the way down to the earth from the sun or comes to your hand from the light bulb."
▶ *How is an airplane able to stay in the air?*	"The pressure from the air keeps it up some-how—it can dip up or down—I really don't know."

Internet Resources

Websites for Physical Science Units, Lessons, Activities, and Demonstrations

Bill Nye Demo of the Day

http://nyelabs.kcts.org

This site showcases ideas from popular educational television personality Bill Nye, "The Science Guy." When you reach this site, select "Demo of the Day," which provides a daily demonstration that can be done with inexpensive, readily available materials. Most of these demonstrations are related to some aspect of the physical sciences. To receive each demonstration automatically, change your Internet browser's default startup page to this one.

The Atoms Family

http://www.miamisci.org/af/sln/

This site, sponsored by the Miami Museum of Science, presents information about energy concepts, the power of the sun, energy conservation, energy transformation, electricity, and fossil fuels. You and your students will find physical science activities in places with rather interesting names, such as "Dracula's Library," "Frankenstein's Lightning Laboratory," and the "Phantom's Portrait Parlor."

Early and Later Elementary Chemistry Lessons

http://www.eecs.umich.edu/~coalitn/sciedoutreach

Selecting the "Lessons and Activities" choice on this website will take you to a page where you can then select "Physical Science," "Technology," or "Chemistry." At these locations, you will discover an excellent collection of activities/demonstrations to do with children. Each is preceded by a "Guiding Question" you can use to focus their efforts. Safety concerns for each activity are noted, as well.

Science Try Its

http://www.ktca.org/newtons/tryits

This site, sponsored by the *Newton's Apple* television program, is a collection of physical science activities that students can try at home. When you reach this page, select any of the "Science Try Its." Each activity has an accompanying illustration to help you and your students assemble the materials and equipment needed. A brief presentation of the science concepts that explain each activity is also included.

The Science Explorer

http://www.exploratorium.com/science_explorer

Teachers and students who visit this site, sponsored by the world-famous Exploratorium in San Francisco, California, will find many adventures. This URL will take you to the part of the site that provides science activities students can do at home or school. Each is well illustrated and in a consistent format that includes "What do I need?" "What do I do?" and "What's going on?" The latter subsection explains the science concepts that are part of each activity.

Kids Web: Science

http://www.npac.syr.edu/textbook/kidsweb

Selecting the "Sciences" option at this site will bring up more options for such physical science–related topics as "Chemistry," "Physics," and "Computers." This is a very comprehensive site, so you should be able to find resource ideas appropriate for any grade level. Those resources will include projects and activities as well as science subject matter presentations.

Unit Plan Starter Ideas

That great idea for a science-teaching unit may come from deep within your brain, your school curriculum guide, a state science curriculum framework, a science resource book, a course, a workshop, a discussion you have with children, or some other source. Unfortunately, a great idea (like a friend, an umbrella, and a good restaurant with cheap food) is sometimes hard to find when you really need one.

To make it easier for you to come up with great ideas for science units, I have prepared three different sources of unit starter ideas, which are presented as three lists:

1. The first is based on the National Science Education (NSE) standards for science content. I created these starter ideas for standards related to grades K–4 and 5–8.

2. The second is based on the general goals for science and scientific literacy proposed by Project 2061 in their scientific views of the world recommendations. I regrouped the goals into earth/space science, life science, and physical science and then included related goals for science and math integration.

3. The third list of starter ideas is based on my study of physical science topics that commonly appear in school curriculum guides. These are shown by grade level.

I am certain that this rather unique compilation of starter ideas will help you plan and create wonderful discovery-based teaching units.

Ideas Based on the NSE K–8 Content Standards

NSE

Content Standard K–4: Physical Sciences [PS]

As a result of activities in grades K–4, all students should develop an understanding of:

> *Properties of objects and materials*
>
> *Position and motion of objects*
>
> *Light, heat, electricity and magnetism*[1]

Starter Ideas for Objects and Materials

Unit Title/Topic: *Observe, Think, Sort*
Unit Goal: Children classify the objects in collections of marbles, blocks, small tiles, and pebbles into categories based on weight, shape, color, and size.

Unit Title/Topic: *Tell Me about It*
Unit Goal: Children use tools such as rulers, balances, and thermometers to take, write down, and tell about measurements they make about the items in a collection of solid objects and containers of liquids.

Unit Title/Topic: *Water Changes*
Unit Goal: Children observe and explain why water and other substances can be changed from a solid to a liquid to a gas and from a gas to a liquid to a solid.

Starter Ideas for Position and Motion of Objects

Unit Title/Topic: *Where Is It?*
Unit Goal: Using three objects labeled "a," "b," and "c," children describe their relative positions using the terms *in back of, in front of, above, below,* and *beside.*

Unit Title/Topic: *Forces Cause Changes*
Unit Goal: Children demonstrate to their peers how an object's change in position is related to the strength and direction of the applied force.

Unit Title/Topic: *Vibrations Cause Changes*
Unit Goal: Using a variety of objects, children demonstrate that sound is produced by vibrating objects and that pitch can be changed by changing the object's rate of vibration.

Starter Ideas for Light, Heat, Electricity, and Magnetism

Unit Title/Topic: *Paths of Light*
Unit Goal: Using mirrors, lenses, focused-beam flashlights, and pins to mark path positions, children compare the actual paths of beams of light to predicted paths.

Unit Title/Topic: *Electrical Energy*
Unit Goal: Children identify the characteristics of a simple series circuit, build a circuit, and use it to produce light, heat, sound, or magnetic effects.

Unit Title/Topic: *Magnets*
Unit Goal: Children use permanent magnets to demonstrate attraction, repulsion, the presence of poles, and the existence of magnetic fields.

NSE

Content Standard 5–8: Physical Sciences [PS]

As a result of the activities in grades 5–8, all students should develop an understanding of:

>   *Properties and changes of properties in matter*
>
>   *Motion and forces*
>
>   *Transfer of energy*

Starter Ideas for Properties and Changes of Properties in Matter

Unit Title/Topic: *It's Dense*
Unit Goal: Students calculate the densities of regular and irregular objects using tools such as a ruler, graduated cylinder, overflow container, and balance.

Unit Title/Topic: *Matter Changes*

Unit Goal: Students gather, organize, and chart data about the changes in characteristics of sugar, cornstarch, baking soda, and flour as a result of testing each by heating, adding water, and adding vinegar.

Unit Title/Topic: *Physical or Chemical?*

Unit Goal: Students observe teacher demonstrations of physical and chemical changes, make observations, and correctly group the demonstrations into those that show physical changes and those that show chemical changes.

Starter Ideas for Motion and Forces

Unit Title/Topic: *Observe the Motion*

Unit Goal: Children gather and record data about the positions, directions of motion, and speeds of battery-powered toy cars moving across the classroom floor.

Unit Title/Topic: *Graph the Motion*

Unit Goal: Children graph the positions, directions of motion, and speeds of battery-powered toy cars moving across the classroom floor.

Unit Title/Topic: *Predicting Motion*

Unit Goal: Children predict the motions of objects acted upon by unbalanced forces that cause changes in speed or direction.

Starter Ideas for Transfer of Energy

Unit Title/Topic: *Generators Small and Large*

Unit Goal: After classroom science activities and field work at a power station, children make labeled diagrams that compare the initial energy sources and the energy transfers that occur in a classroom hand-operated generator and at the power station.

Unit Title/Topic: *Energy Changes*

Unit Goal: Children construct hands-on displays for a school science fair that demonstrate the transfer of electrical energy into heat, light, and sound.

Unit Title/Topic: *Energy—The Space Traveler*

Unit Goal: After library research work and class discussions, children explain how energy is produced by the sun, transmitted through space, and captured by green plants.

NSE

Content Standards Related to:

Science and Technology [S&T]

Science in Personal and Social Perspectives [SPSP]

History and Nature of Science [HNS][2]

Unit Title/Topic: *Egg Saver*
Unit Goal: Using everyday materials, children design containers that can protect an uncooked egg dropped from the height of a stepladder to a school sidewalk.

Unit Title/Topic: *Safest, Cleanest, Cheapest*
Unit Goal: After library research work, Internet research, field work, and classroom discussions, children compare three alternate forms of energy with respect to safety, pollution, and economy.

Unit Title/Topic: *Who Are They?*
Unit Goal: After library research work, Internet research, and classroom discussions, children identify and write brief biographies of five women scientists who have had made significant contributions to the physical sciences.

Ideas Based on Project 2061 Goals

2061
GOAL

The structure and evolution of the universe with emphasis on the similarity of materials and forces found everywhere in it, the universe's response to a few general principles (such as universal gravitation and the conservation of energy), and ways in which the universe is investigated. (p. 7)[3]

Starter Ideas for Structure and Evolution of the Universe

Unit Title/Topic: *Measure Here, Measure There*
Unit Goal: Children learn how to use such basic measuring tools of science as a meterstick, pan balance, and thermometer.

Unit Title/Topic: *Close Up and Far Away*
Unit Goal: Children learn how scientists use powerful tools to make visible and observe objects that are too small or too far away to see.

The basic concepts related to matter, energy, force and motion, with emphasis on their use in models to explain a vast and diverse array of natural phenomena from the birth of stars to the behavior of cells. (p. 7)

Starter Ideas for Energy, Force, and Motion

Unit Title/Topic: *What's the Matter?*

Unit Goal: Children learn the basic properties of matter and the alternative forms that matter can take.

Unit Title/Topic: *Space Toys*

Unit Goal: Using toys with moving parts, children assess whether the toys would work on board a spacecraft in a weightless environment and design new toys that could be used in such an environment.

The mathematics of symbols and symbolic relationships, emphasizing the kinds, properties, and uses of numbers and shapes; graphic and algebraic ways of expressing relationships among things; and coordinate systems as a means of relating numbers to geometry and geography. (p. 8)

Starter Ideas for Using Numbers and Graphs

Unit Title/Topic: *Wild and Wacky Units*

Unit Goal: Children learn that units of measure are arbitrary and invent a new system of units and unit symbols to describe the path that must be taken to find an object hidden somewhere on school property.

Unit Title/Topic: *How Much Stretch?*

Unit Goal: Children make a simple scale using a rubber band and paper clips, plot on graph paper how far the rubber band stretches when various objects are added, make a graph to predict how far the rubber band will stretch when other objects are added, and calibrate their scale using known weights.

Probability, including the kinds of uncertainty that limit knowledge, methods of estimating and expressing probabilities, and the use of such methods in predicting results when large numbers are involved. (p. 8)

Starter Ideas for Probability and Predicting

Unit Title/Topic: *What's a Bias?*

Unit Goal: Children learn that there are some circumstances that occur while making measurements that can reduce the accuracy of results (e.g., counting the loudest sounds heard during a study of sounds in the environment will reduce the accuracy of a count of sounds in the environment).

Unit Title/Topic: *Quality Control*

Unit Goal: Children learn of common methods for assuring the quality of products without testing each individual item.

> **2061 GOAL**
>
> *Data analysis, with an emphasis on numerical and graphic ways of summarizing data, the nature and limitations of correlations and the problem of sampling in data collection.* (p. 9)

Starter Ideas for Studying Results and Summarizing

Unit Title/Topic: *Energy Costs*

Unit Goal: Children survey a group of automobile owners to determine how much gasoline is required to move a car from one city to another, prepare a chart to summarize their data, and list variables that might affect their results.

Unit Title/Topic: *Measurement Errors*

Unit Goal: Children study the results produced when each child independently measures the length and width of the classroom. The class then prepares a graph showing all of the measurements and develops an explanation for the highest and lowest measurements.

> **2061 GOAL**
>
> *Reasoning, including the nature and limitations of deductive logic, the uses and dangers of generalizing from a limited number of experiences, and reasoning by analogy.* (p. 9)

Starter Ideas for Reasoning

Unit Title/Topic: *Mystery Boxes*

Unit Goal: After examining a variety of closed boxes that contain objects of different sizes and shapes, children predict the sizes and shapes of the objects within the boxes and create their own mystery boxes that can be used with children in other classrooms.

Unit Title/Topic: *Seesaw (Teeter-Totter) Study*

Unit Goal: Children learn about the operation of levers and then design an imaginary seesaw that can be used by children of widely varying weights.

Ideas Based on Typical Grade Level Content

Starter Ideas for Kindergarten

Unit Topic/Title: *Push It, Pull It*

Unit Goal: Children learn that forces cause things to move or change shape.

Unit Topic/Title: *Hot and Cold*

Unit Goal: Children learn that heating and cooling things can change them.

Unit Topic/Title: *What Is It?*

Unit Goal: Children learn how to describe and compare objects on the basis of their properties.

Starter Ideas for First Grade

Unit Topic/Title: *Water Changes*

Unit Goal: Children learn that liquid water can be changed to a solid or a gas and that heating and cooling produce changes in form.

Unit Topic/Title: *Like and Unlike*

Unit Goal: Children learn to compare material objects by using the terms *bigger, smaller, longer, shorter, heavier,* and *lighter* appropriately.

Starter Ideas for Second Grade

Unit Topic/Title: *I Can Measure*

Unit Goal: Children learn how to use such measuring devices as clocks, metersticks, and scales to measure time, length, and weight.

Unit Topic/Title: *Sounds Are All Around*

Unit Goal: Children learn the requirements for the production, transmission, and reception of sound waves.

Starter Ideas for Third Grade

Unit Topic/Title: *Matter Can Change Its Form*

Unit Goal: Children learn that matter can exist as a solid, liquid, or gas.

Unit Topic/Title: *Electricity: Where Does It Come From?*

Unit Goal: Children learn the alternate ways in which electrical energy is produced, the environmental effects of the alternatives, and the importance of conserving electrical energy.

Starter Ideas for Fourth Grade

Unit Topic/Title: *Bending Light and Making Colors*
Unit Goal: Children learn how to use various lenses and prisms to affect the movement of light rays.

Unit Topic/Title: *Simple Machines*
Unit Goal: Children learn how simple machines operate and are able to identify the effort force, resistance, effort distance, and resistance distance for a variety of simple machines.

Starter Ideas for Fifth Grade

Unit Topic/Title: *Two Kinds of Electricity*
Unit Goal: Children learn the effects produced by static and current electricity.

Unit Topic/Title: *Changes*
Unit Goal: Children learn to distinguish between physical and chemical changes.

Starter Ideas for Sixth Grade

Unit Topic/Title: *Matter in Motion*
Unit Goal: Children observe and classify the everyday interactions of objects and forces in terms of Newton's laws of motion.

Unit Topic/Title: *Chemical Reactions*
Unit Goal: Children learn the variables that can affect the rate of chemical reactions.

Starter Ideas for Seventh Grade

Unit Topic/Title: *Energy of Position and Energy of Motion*
Unit Goal: Students learn the difference between potential and kinetic energy.

Unit Topic/Title: *Atoms and Molecules*
Unit Goal: Students learn the fundamental structures of atoms and molecules.

Starter Ideas for Eighth Grade

Unit Topic/Title: *Matter Is Conserved*
Unit Goal: Students learn that matter is neither created nor destroyed in ordinary chemical reactions.

Unit Topic/Title: *Energy Is Conserved*
Unit Goal: Students learn that energy can be changed in form and that the total amount of energy in a system remains constant.

Lesson Plan Starter Ideas
for Common Curriculum Topics

 Sometimes you will be responsible for teaching lessons that are part of units pre-pared by committees of teachers in your school district or units that are commer-cially available. You may wonder how to break these units into lessons. To help you come up with lesson ideas for the physical sciences, I have analyzed a variety of teaching units and prepared a list of lesson plan starter ideas based on topics usually covered in these units. The lesson descriptions are very specific, so each description may also be viewed as the lesson's principal objective.

Characteristics of Matter

Plan a lesson in which the children:

- Identify, compare, and classify objects on the basis of touch, taste, smell, and emitted sounds.
- Describe objects using the characteristics of size, shape, and color.
- Infer the characteristics of a small object in a closed box without looking in the box.
- Name three forms of matter (gas, liquid, and solid), and give an example of each.
- Illustrate how the movement of molecules in solids, liquids, and gases differs using body movements.
- Create a diagram illustrating an imaginary experiment that shows that air ex-pands when it is heated and contracts when it is cooled.

Energy and Its Changes

Plan a lesson in which the children:

- Observe that sound waves are produced by objects vibrating in a medium.
- Use a stopwatch correctly during an outdoor activity to calculate the speed of sound.
- Identify light, heat, electricity, and magnetism as forms of energy, and pre-pare a two-column chart that shows a human use for each form.
- Evaluate three different light bulbs to determine which will provide the most light, which will last the longest, and which is the best value for the money.
- Given appropriate safe materials, construct a simple electromagnet.
- Make a graph that compares the speed of sound with the speed of light.
- Make a hypothesis about the ability of light waves to travel without the pres-ence of a medium, and invent an experiment to test the hypothesis.
- Make a hypothesis to explain the formation of rainbows using the knowledge that water droplets can act as prisms.
- Make a labeled diagram that shows how convex and concave lenses differ in shape.

Forces and Motion

Plan a lesson in which the children:

- Observe the operation of various machines, and then identify the effort, force, and resistance.
- Create an illustrated chart identifying the characteristics of six simple machines.
- Draw an imaginary "wake-me-up-and-get-me-out-of-bed" machine that uses at least six different simple machines.
- Make a labeled drawing of one frequently used object that is made up of at least two simple machines.
- Using simple instruments, measure direction, distance, mass, and force of gravity (weight).
- Describe the position of an object relative to another object using the terms *north, south, east,* and *west.*
- Construct a simple machine, and use it to do work.
- Make a hypothesis to explain how a pulley system is able to multiply force, and invent an experiment to test the hypothesis.

Airplane, Jet, and Rocket Motion

Plan a lesson in which the children:

- Make a diagram of an airplane in flight, and label the forces of gravity, lift, thrust, and drag.
- Explain how a jet engine takes advantage of the law of action and reaction.
- Explain how gravity affects large objects and that the strength of attraction between objects depends on their masses and distance apart.
- Write a story about a boy or girl who lives on an imaginary planet that doesn't have gravity.
- Make a diagram of a rocket in flight, and label the action and reaction forces.
- After doing library research on the exploration of Mars, evaluate the likelihood of humans reaching the planet by the year 2020.

Classroom Enrichment Starter Ideas

 ### In-Class Learning Centers

Try to locate the center, which you might call *Energy Savers,* in an area that has enough space for writing, game-playing, dramatizing, and constructing activities. Be sure to provide construction paper, cardboard boxes of various sizes, foam packing peanuts, ice cream buckets, and a scrapbook. Have the children sign up to work for a half-hour on one activity per day in the center. If you have computer software or videos related to energy, make them available in this center, too.

An in-class learning center like this one, called Energy Savers, can encourage students to discover more about the physical sciences.

Prepare activity cards (cards that give directions for activities you develop) based on the following ideas (***Note:*** Asterisks indicate activities that may be particularly appropriate for young children):

- *Felt Board** Have the children make figures out of paper or cardboard. Glue strips of felt to the backs of the figures, and give them names such as "Walter Waste Energy," "Conni the Conserver," and so forth. Have the children invent and dramatize the adventures of these characters and their friends.

- *Ice Cube Race* Challenge the children to build ice cube keepers. Provide foam packing peanuts, ice cream buckets, cardboard, tape, and small cardboard boxes. Have the children use baby food jars to hold ice cubes that are allowed to melt at room temperature to get data for a control.

- *Energy Scrapbook** Have the children cut out pictures and articles from newspapers and magazines on such energy issues as nuclear power and solar energy. Then have them prepare scrapbook pages for an energy scrapbook that will be kept in the center.

- *Power Play* Have the children invent and construct a board game that employs a die, tokens, and a set of "chance" cards that say such things as "You left the TV on; go back two spaces" or "You took a 30-minute shower; go back four spaces" or "You put on a sweater instead of turning up the heat; go ahead ten spaces." The children can use file folders or construction paper to make the board.

Bulletin Boards

Good bulletin boards have the potential to be something that children can both look at and learn from. There are many ways to use classroom bulletin boards to enhance physical science units and extend your teaching to nonscience areas. The following list offers a few starter ideas for you (***Note:*** Asterisks indicate activities that may be particularly appropriate for young children):

- *Matter and Its Composition*   Divide the bulletin board into four columns going down and four columns going across. Leave the top of the first column blank but label the next three columns *Solid, Liquid,* and *Gas.* Label the four rows going down *Object, Molecules, Characteristics,* and *Containers.* Set aside three cards and draw a rock on one, a vial filled with colored water on another, and an inflated balloon on the third. Create three cards illustrating the organization of molecules in solids, liquids, and gases; three cards illustrating a solid, a liquid, and a gas in flasks; and six cards listing the characteristics of solids, liquids, and gases. Place the cards in manila envelopes labeled *Objects, Molecules, Characteristics,* and *Containers.* After discussing the characteristics of solids, liquids, and gases and demonstrating how matter can change from one state to another by melting ice and boiling water, have the children take the cards from the envelopes and arrange them in the appropriate rows and columns, using pushpins to hold the cards in place. Children should do this in their free time; they can check their work using an answer key provided by you.

This bulletin board, Matter and Its Composition, invites students to apply what they have learned.

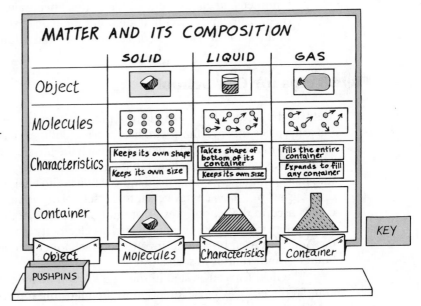

- *Sound and Light**   Divide the bulletin board into three sections, and label each *Light, Heat,* or *Sound.* Subdivide each section allowing space for children to attach pictures, and add the following subtitles: Where does it come from? How does it move? How do we use it? Provide magazines, scissors, drawing paper, and markers so children can locate or create pictures to place in each subsection.

- *Find the Forces**   Place the title "Find the Forces" across the top of the bulletin board. Have children locate magazine pictures of people actively participating in gymnastics, dancing, or sports. Each week, place one of the pictures on the bulletin board; have children attach index cards with the words *push* and *pull* near the pictures to identify where forces are acting.

- *Temperature and You**   Draw three large thermometers on the bulletin board showing the following temperatures: 0°C (32°F), 20°C (68°F), 35°C (95°F). Challenge the children to attach magazine pictures or their own drawings depicting outdoor activities that could be done at each temperature.

- *The Simple Circuit*   Create a three-dimensional bulletin board that is, in fact, a working circuit. Temporarily mount and hook up a dry cell, wires, switch, and bulb holder with bulb. Have children create a label for each item. *Safety Note:* You must use insulated wire and make sure that neither the bulb nor any bare ends of wire touch any surface. Also be sure that the circuit is switched off after each use.

- *Find the Machine*   Create a three-dimensional bulletin board to display items such as a scissors, doorknob, wood chisel, nutcracker, wood screw, clay hammer, and hand-operated egg beater. Encourage children to attach a label on or near each object that identifies the type of simple machine the item is or the name and location of a simple machine within the item.

Field Trips for City Schools

Many of the factors that make the city an interesting and exciting place to live also make it a place that overflows with field trip possibilities. There are many urban connections and field possibilities when you teach the physical sciences and technology. One place to start is in the school building itself. Consider for a moment the possibilities that abound when you consider the school as an energy user. Do you think children are aware of how energy gets into the school or the variety of ways in which energy is used in the school? A walk around the outside of the school can provide an opportunity to discover how energy, such as electricity or fuel oil, gets into the building. You may even be able to involve your school custodian or district director of buildings and grounds in such a trip.

The field trips suggested in the next section include explorations that can be done in the city. Pay close attention to the following topics to see if you can tailor them to the resources of the city in which you presently teach or study:

The Telephone Company
Force, Motion, and Machines
The Electric Company
Forces and Machines

Here are some additional ideas that should stimulate your thinking about field trips for children in city schools:

- *Shadow Study*   Children track changes in the shadows they see on a sunny day.

- *Simple Machines on the Playground*   Children locate and classify playground equipment according to the simple machines incorporated in them.

- *Temperature Here, Temperature There*   Children use thermometers to discover if the temperatures at various places on the school grounds are the same.

- *Getting from Here to There*   During a walk around the block, children gather data about the numbers of cars, trucks, buses, and bicycles observed traveling on a street. On returning to the classroom, children graph the data they have collected.

- *Count the Passengers*   After observing and gathering data about the number of people riding buses, children draw inferences regarding energy savings brought about by the use of public transportation.

- *Harbor Machines*   If your city is on an ocean, lake, or river, children can observe machines at work in the harbor.

- *Building Going Up*   From a safe distance, children can observe the machines in use at a building construction site to identify the sources of energy for the machines and the simple machines that make up the more complex machines at work.

Field Trips for All Schools

Here are starter ideas for field trips for all schools (*Note:* Asterisks indicate activities that may be particularly appropriate for young children):

- *The Telephone Company**   A trip to the local telephone company will be a memorable science lesson that has many language arts, geography, and art applications. When you make the initial contact, find out what the facility contains; repair services are often in a different location and could be considered for a separate field trip. During the actual visit, children can discover how long-distance and overseas calls are made, how records of calls are kept, the many styles of phones, and the latest advances in communication technology.

- *Force, Motion, and Machines*   The study of friction can be the basis for various field trips. Contact the showroom of a car, boat, airplane, or snowmobile dealership or the repair facility at a bus station, garage, or airport to arrange the excursion. Alert the individual who will serve as your tour guide that the children will be interested in how the design of the vehicle minimizes air and surface friction, how it's propelled, and what type of energy it uses. As a follow-up to the trip, have children draw diagrams and then build models of what they have seen. They can also invent modifications to the vehicle that would further reduce friction.

- *Energy-Conserving Home**   Look around the community for a building or home that was constructed or retrofitted to save energy. One with an active or passive solar system, windmill, off-peak power storage system, or underground design would be especially interesting. Installers of alternative energy systems and building contractors are good sources of information on energy-efficient building techniques and places to visit. After the visit, children can study the school and their homes for energy-efficient features as well as improvements needed.

Additional Physical Science Field Trip Destinations

Airport control tower
Cellular phone service provider
Chemistry or physics department at a local college
Computer repair facility
Electrical power station (hydroelectric)
Electrical power station (fossil fuel or nuclear powered)
Electronics company
Eyeglass preparation facility
Internet service provider
Oil refinery
Photographic film-processing plant
Radio station
Television station

Cooperative Learning Projects

As you consider the following starter ideas for cooperative learning projects, keep in mind the importance of stressing the three key aspects of cooperative learning (discussed in detail in Chapter 5):

1. Positive interdependence

2. Individual accountability

3. Development of group process skills

- *The Living Machine*   After doing activities or observing demonstrations related to the three types of simple machines, challenge groups to use their bodies to demonstrate each type. Various members of each group can represent resistance, fulcrum, and effort. Groups can also use their bodies to create and demonstrate a complex machine that uses all three types of simple machines. After the groups have practiced, they should present their machines and have the rest of the class identify the simple machines and locations of the resistance, fulcrum, and effort.

- *Fancy Flyers*   This project should occur over a period of days. Provide the groups with a wide assortment of materials (e.g., plastic wrap, paper of different weights, cardboard, strips of balsa wood, glue) that can be used to build model gliders. Have the groups do research to learn about various designs for gliders. After they have studied the topic, encourage each group to prepare three gliders for display and demonstration. If weather permits, have the groups display and demonstrate their gliders outdoors. If this is not possible, the gym or cafeteria might serve as an acceptable environment.

- *Density Detectives*   After discussing the concept of density (density = mass/volume), have each group develop a way to find the density of an irregular object and explain its method to the class. (***Hint:*** The volume of an irregular solid can be found by determining the volume of water it displaces when it is submerged.)

- *School Energy Survey*   Have each group evaluate how the school building loses heat to the outside environment or how heat from the outside environment enters the school. Have groups observe such things as how fast the front doors close, how airtight the windows are, and how well weather stripping seals around door jambs. After organizing their observations, groups should report the results of their studies and their recommendations for slowing down heat loss or heat gain to the class and, if appropriate, to the school principal.

Additional Ideas for Cooperative Groups

- Provide groups with flashlights, cardboard tubes, wire, "C" or "D" batteries, flashlight bulbs, and other materials, and encourage them to create their own working flashlights.
- Challenge groups to use cardboard tubes, straws, rubber bands, balloons, tape, and so forth to create air-powered rockets that will move along a length of fishing line stretched across the room.
- Challenge groups to create bridges using straws, paper, cardboard, and tape that will support one or more school books. If you use this idea, be sure that each group gets the amount of each material you provide and that the bridges must all span a fixed distance, such as 25 centimeters (about 10 inches).

Science and Children and *Science Scope*

Resource Articles for Physical Science Units, Lessons, Activities, and Demonstrations

Bracikowski, Christopher, et al. "Getting a Feel for Newton's Laws of Motion." *Science and Children* 35, no. 7 (April 1998): 26–30, 58.

Calkins, Andrew. "National Science and Technology Week." *Science Scope* 22, no. 5 (February 1999): 28.

Chiles, Melanie A. "Fearless Fliers." *Science Scope* 22, no. 4 (March 1999): 18–19.

Crawford, Barbara R. "The Poisons Project." *Science Scope* 21, no. 5 (February 1998): 18–21.

Dungey, Joan M. "Scooter Science." *Science Scope* 22, no. 4 (March 1999): 11–13.

Duthie-Fox, Christa. "The Magic of Science." *Science Scope* 22, no. 4 (March 1999): 58–59.

Guy, Mark, and Kristin Stewart. "Push-Ups and Propulsion." *Science Scope* 22, no. 4 (March 1999): 30–31.

Harris, Mary E., and Sandra Van Natta. "A Classroom of Polymer Factories." *Science and Children* 35, no. 5 (February 1998): 18–21.

Hermann, Christine K. F. "Beads + String = Atoms You Can See." *Science Scope* 21, no. 8 (May 1998): 24–26.

Hoover, Barbara G. "The Winter Olympics on Ice." *Science and Children* 35, no. 4 (January 1998): 31–33.

Ibarra, Hector. "Solar Powered Racers." *Science Scope* 22, no. 4 (March 1999): 26–29.

Ivy, Tamra, et al. "Battling Spring Fever? Try Los Remedios." *Science Scope* 21, no. 7 (April 1998): 30–33.

MacKinnon, Gregory R. "Soap and Science." *Science and Children* 35, no. 8 (February 1998): 28–31.

Newton, Diane M. " Pressure, Pressure Everywhere." *Science and Children* 36, no. 5 (February 1999): 34–37.

Ogens, Eva M. "The Method in Motion." *Science Scope* 22, no. 4 (January 1999): 30–34.

Pierce, Wendy. "Linking Learning to Labs." *Science Scope* 21, no. 4 (January 1998): 17–19.

Sapp, Lorri. "Teaching Circuits Is Child's Play." *Science Scope* 22, no. 4 (March 1999): 64–65.

Shiland, Thomas W. "Decookbook It!" *Science and Children* 35, no. 3 (November/December 1998): 14–18.

Silva, Patricia, and Paul Yamamoto. "M & M Mystery." *Science Scope* 22, no. 5 (February 1999): 26–27.

Sitzman, Daniel L., and Paul B. Kelter. "Pasta, Polymers, and Pedagogy." *Science Scope* 21, no. 6 (March 1998): 68–70.

Stewart, Gay, and Ditta Gallai. "Build Your Own Motor." *Science Scope* 22, no. 5 (February 1999): 12–16.

———. "Electrostatic Explorations." *Science Scope* 21, no. 5 (February 1998): 10–13.

The Problem Children need science experiences that range across the earth/space, life, and physical sciences. Teachers may tend to include those topics they feel most comfortable with and thus inadvertently limit the scope of the children's learning.

Assess Your Prior Knowledge and Beliefs

1. When comparing your knowledge of the physical sciences to your knowledge of the earth/space and life sciences, do you believe you have acquired more, less, or the same amount of basic science content in each?

	More	Less	Same
Earth/space sciences	_____	_____	_____
Life sciences	_____	_____	_____

2. When you were a student in grades K–8, would you say you were exposed to more, less, or the same amount of physical science content as you were to life and earth/space content?

	More	Less	Same
Earth/space sciences	_____	_____	_____
Life sciences	_____	_____	_____

3. Gravity is a common physical science topic for children. Identify five discrete items of knowledge that you now have about gravity.

   _____

   _____

   _____

   _____

   _____

4. Now identify five things about gravity that you think you should know but do not.

   _____

   _____

   _____

   _____

   _____

The Challenge You are part of a team of teachers planning a unit on gravity. You want the unit to include the discovery-learning stages of experiencing, acquiring, and applying. Give an example of a physical science activity you might include to support each of these stages.

———. "More Electrostatic Explorations." *Science Scope* 21, no. 7 (April 1998): 18–22.

———. "Pithy Problems." *Science Scope* 21, no. 8 (May 1998): 18–19.

Streitberger, H. Eric, and John Burns. "The Versatile Armchair Penny Balance." *Science Scope* 22, no. 4 (January 1999): 22–25.

Sunal, Dennis W., et al. "Semiconductive Science." *Science Scope* 22, no. 1 (September 1998): 22–26.

Taylor, Beverly A. P. "Push-N-Go: A Dynamic Energy Conversion Lesson." *Science Scope* 21, no. 4 (January 1998): 28–31.

Vasquez, Vannessa A. "Sumos and the Center of Mass." *Science Scope* 22, no. 4 (March 1999): 11–13.

Notes

1. This standard, as well as the others identified in later sections, are excerpted with permission from the National Research Council, *National Science Education Standards* (Washington, DC: National Academy Press, 1996), pp. 104–171. Note that the bracketed symbol to the right of each standard was prepared by this author. See also the list of all the K–8 content standards in the appendix of this book.

2. Note that I have related this sampling of NSE standards E, F, and G to the physical sciences.

3. This excerpt and those that follow are from *Science for All Americans, Summary/Project 2061*. Copyright © 1989 by the American Association for the Advancement of Science. Reprinted by permission of Oxford University Press. The American Association for the Advancement of Science (AAAS) grouped its Project 2061 recommendations into four categories: 1) The Scientific Endeavor, 2) The Scientific View of the World, 3) Perspective on Science, and 4) Scientific Habits of Mind. The Unit Plan Starter Ideas based on Project 2061 in Chapters 10, 13, and 16 were prepared by this author for the "Scientific View of the World" recommendations in *Science for All Americans: Summary* (Washington, DC: American Association for the Advancement of Science, 1989). I omitted three recommendations whose elementary school science implications would require a breadth of consideration beyond the scope of Chapters 10, 13, and 16. These were goals related to "consequences of cultural setting into which a person was born," "social change and conflict," and "forms of political and economic organization."

For a further specification of all the goals and the broader curriculum implications of the Project 2061 effort, see *Science for All Americans* (Washington, DC: American Association for the Advancement of Science, 1989) and *Benchmarks for Science Literacy: Project 2061, American Association for the Advancement of Science* (New York: Oxford University Press, 1993).

17A

Matter and Motion

Content

A Look Ahead

From Atoms to Rockets and Other Technological Wonders

Imagine the thrill of driving in the Indy 500. Now imagine doing so in a solar-powered car, like that shown in Figure 17A.1. In the not-too-distant future, we may all be trading in our gas-guzzling cars for newer models powered by other forms of energy, such as solar energy or electricity.

Our ability to accomplish such amazing things as faxing a document across the world or microwaving a meal in only a matter of minutes is the result of the technology available to us. We can have full-color photographs in a minute; we have drugs that can prevent or cure illnesses; we have automobiles, airplanes, unbelievable weapons of destruction, and—wonder of wonders—sonic toothbrushes. The rapid pace of technological development is a direct result of our increased knowledge of the nature of matter, our ability to release energy from it, and our ability to predict and control the motion of objects.

Matter

Silly Putty, a chicken, and pistachio ice cream all have something in common. They are all *matter*. Anything that occupies space and has weight is matter. The earth, the planets, the sun, and everything else in our universe that has weight and occupies space are composed of matter. This definition allows us to distinguish matter from energy. *Energy* is defined as the capacity to do work or to produce change. Electricity, light, sound, heat, and magnetism are all considered forms of energy. Matter and energy are related. Under very special circumstances, matter can be changed into energy, and energy can be changed into matter.

FIGURE 17A.1
This solar-powered car may seem an oddity today, but it's quite likely the car of the future.

Scientists have found that all matter in the universe exerts an attractive force on all other matter in the universe. The matter in this book is exerting an attractive force on you, and you are exerting an attractive force on the matter in the book. This attractive force is called *gravitation,* and it exists regardless of the location of the matter. The strength of the force depends on the amount of matter in both you and the book, for example, and your distance from the book. The force that the earth exerts on matter is called *weight.* The weight of an object is a measurement of the extent to which the earth pulls on the object and the object pulls on the earth.

There are many different types of matter. The earth is itself a vast storehouse of matter. Here is a list of some of the common types of matter found in the earth's crust (Next to each is the symbol that scientists use to refer to it):

	Symbol	Percent by Weight
Oxygen	O	47.3
Silicon	Si	27.7
Aluminum	Al	7.9
Iron	Fe	4.5
Calcium	Ca	3.5
Sodium	Na	2.5
Potassium	K	2.5
Magnesium	Mg	2.2
Hydrogen	H	0.2
Carbon	C	0.2
All others		1.5

The Physical Properties of Matter

We usually describe matter by its physical properties. We say various types of matter are *solids, liquids,* or *gases.* These forms of matter are known as *states,* or phases, of matter. Rocks and soils are solids. Water may be found as a solid, a liquid, or a gas. The state that matter is in can be determined by observation. A solid has a definite shape. A liquid takes the shape of its container. Both solids and liquids have a definite volume: They occupy a certain amount of space. A gas takes the shape of its container, but it also expands to fill all of the container. Thus, gases do not have a definite volume: Their volume is the volume of the container.

We can also describe matter by describing its color, how hard or soft it is, the extent to which it dissolves in liquid, and whether it is easily stretched or broken. Another specific physical property of matter is its *density.* Unlike units of weight, which represent a gravitational attraction for that matter, units of mass, such as grams and kilograms, represent the amount of matter in something. Density is commonly measured as mass per unit of volume and is expressed in grams per cubic centimeter. To find the density of something, we can simply divide its weight by its volume. Density may also be found by dividing mass by volume.

Molecular Theory

Matter can be changed from one state to another. A cold, crystal-clear icicle receives morning light from the sun and begins to change—to melt into water. A child wanting to draw a "happy face" without paper and pencil breathes on a cold mirror, creating a thin film on which to draw. All these changes in matter are physical changes. The matter has undergone a change, but the original substance remains. Some of the water in the solid icicle has changed to a liquid; the water vapor exhaled by the child has become the tiny droplets of water that formed the "canvas" for the drawing. No new substances were produced in any of these cases. They were all physical changes. This can happen, scientists have concluded, for several reasons:

1. Matter is made up of small particles called *molecules.*
2. Spaces exist among the molecules.
3. The molecules of matter are in constant motion.

Changes in the state of matter, then, can be explained by the motion of molecules. A solid has a definite shape because its molecules are arranged in a pattern. Although the molecules hold this pattern, they also vibrate. If heat is applied to a solid, the rate at which its molecules vibrate becomes so fast that they break away from one another in the pattern. If we add sufficient heat, the solid melts and becomes a liquid. If we add even more heat, the molecules in the liquid may move fast enough to escape from the surface of the liquid and enter the air. These molecules have gone from the liquid state to the gaseous state—the process known as *evaporation.*

If we reverse this process, if we take the heat from gas, its molecules may slow down sufficiently to form a liquid. If we take away more heat, the molecules may begin forming the patterns in which they exist in their solid state. These types of changes in matter are physical changes. No new matter is created.

The molecular theory of matter can be used to explain the expansion and contraction of matter. When the speed of the molecules in matter increases, they bump into one another more and tend to spread apart. *Expansion* of matter thereby occurs. If heat is removed, the molecules move more slowly and tend to come closer to one another. When this occurs, matter *contracts.*

Chemical Changes in Matter

Some types of matter are capable of uniting with one another to form very different types of matter. This characteristic is known as a chemical property of matter. A chemistry teacher holds a piece of magnesium with tongs and places it in the flame of a Bunsen burner. Bright light is produced, and the metallic magnesium changes to a white powder—magnesium oxide. Changes resulting in substances that differ from the original substance are known as chemical changes. The rusting of iron and the burning of wood or paper are other examples of matter changing and combining to produce new forms of matter.

Although we can describe these changes in many ways, to fully understand the chemical properties of matter it will be helpful to think about specific chemical changes. The roasting of a marshmallow and the phenomenon of fire are two good examples.

The Roasting of a Marshmallow

A marshmallow is made of sugar. Sugar contains carbon, hydrogen, and oxygen. You've probably noticed that when you heat a marshmallow over an open flame, the surface of the marshmallow darkens. It does so because the sugar undergoes a chemical change. The heat added to the sugar breaks the sugar into carbon, hydrogen, and oxygen. The dark material on the outside of the marshmallow is carbon. Hydrogen and oxygen leave the heated marshmallow in the form of water.

Fire

The flickering candles atop a birthday cake, the ring of blue flame on a stovetop, and a raging forest fire are all examples of matter that is undergoing a rapid chemical change that gives off both light and heat. In each case, three things are present: (1) a material that will burn (a fuel), (2) oxygen, and (3) something that heats the fuel to a temperature at which it will burn. The temperature at which a fuel will begin to burn is known as its *kindling temperature.*

All common fuels contain carbon. When these fuels burn, they undergo various chemical changes. The carbon within them combines with oxygen to form the gas carbon dioxide. If there is insufficient oxygen, however, carbon monoxide, a very dangerous gas, is released. If the fuel contains hydrogen as well as carbon, during *combustion* (another word for "burning"), oxygen in the air also combines with the hydrogen in the fuel to form water vapor. In each of these examples, matter undergoes chemical changes to become a new type of matter, and in each example, it is the presence of oxygen that allows the changes to occur quickly.

If we remove oxygen from a fire, we can prevent some chemical changes from occurring. This is what a fire extinguisher does. *Carbon dioxide extinguishers* contain liquid carbon dioxide maintained under very high pressure. When the valve of the extinguisher is opened, a stream of liquid carbon dioxide emerges and turns into carbon dioxide gas. Carbon dioxide gas is more dense than air and settles over the fire, forming a barrier between the fire and its source of oxygen—the air.

The *soda-acid extinguisher* consists of a large metallic tank filled with a solution of water and sodium bicarbonate (see Figure 17A.2, page 392). Near the top of the tank is a small container of sulfuric acid with a loose stopper. When a person turns the extinguisher upside down, the acid mixes with the sodium bicarbonate solution. The carbon dioxide gas created by the chemical changes that occur when sulfuric acid is mixed with water and sodium bicarbonate forces a spray of water and carbon dioxide out the valve and onto the fire.

These extinguishers must be used with great care, particularly if the fire has been caused by electrical wires. The metal container, the liquid sprayed on the fire,

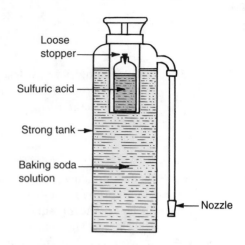

FIGURE 17A.2

A soda-acid fire extinguisher consists of a solution of baking soda and water and a container of acid. When the acid is mixed with the baking soda and water, it reacts and produces carbon dioxide.

and the liquid remaining in the tank are all excellent conductors of electricity. If active electrical wires near the fire scene touch the extinguisher or the liquids, the individual using the extinguisher risks electrocution.

Foam extinguishers are used to spray a thick, sticky foam on burning equipment. The foam blankets the burning material and deprives the fire of oxygen. *Dry chemical extinguishers* are used to spray sodium bicarbonate and other chemicals on fires. Chemical reactions release carbon dioxide to smother the flames.

Of course, there are other ways to extinguish a fire. Firefighters often use water to lower the temperature of a fuel below its kindling point. It is also possible to remove fuel—for instance, cutting down and removing trees in the path of a forest fire.

Elements, Compounds, and Mixtures

An *element* is a substance that cannot be separated into simpler substances by chemical changes. Carbon, hydrogen, and oxygen are elements and the basic building blocks of all matter. Through chemical changes, elements can be combined into *compounds*. Table salt is a compound composed of the elements sodium and chlorine. Its chemical name is *sodium chloride*. Elements and compounds can be represented as *formulas*. The formula for table salt, for example, is NaCl. This combination of symbols indicates that there is one part sodium (Na) and one part chlorine (Cl) in salt. The formula H_2O stands for a combination of two parts of hydrogen and one part of oxygen.

If we broke down a molecule of water or a molecule of salt, we would produce hydrogen and oxygen or sodium and chloride. These parts of a molecule are called *atoms*. When we write the chemical formula H_2O, we are indicating that a molecule of water contains two atoms of hydrogen and one atom of oxygen. When we write CO_2, we are saying that one molecule of carbon dioxide contains one atom of carbon and two atoms of oxygen. The number written below the line in the formula tells us how many atoms (if more than one) of the preceding element are present in the molecule.

Chemists use chemical equations to describe chemical changes in matter. Let's see how this is done. If we place a clean iron nail in a solution of copper sulfate, a chemical change will occur: The iron nail will become coated with a reddish covering, which is copper. As this occurs, the blue color of the copper-sulfate solution becomes less intense. In the chemical change that occurs, iron in the nail changes places with some of the copper in the copper sulfate. The equation that describes this reaction is as follows:

$$Fe + CuSO_4 \rightarrow FeSO_4 + Cu$$

Fe represents iron. $CuSO_4$ represents copper sulfate. The arrow means "forms" or "yields." On the right side of the arrow are the products of the chemical change: $FeSO_4$ (iron sulfate) and Cu (copper). Notice that the number of atoms on each side of the arrow is the same. No atoms are gained or lost during a chemical change.

Not all combinations of elements form compounds. The principal test is whether the various substances can be separated from one another. For example, if you were to mix a small amount of sand with a small amount of salt, no chemical change would occur. If you had patience and a strong lens, you could probably separate the two materials. It would take time, but it could be done, since the salt and sand do not chemically unite with each other. Any combination of materials that can be separated from one another is known as a *mixture*. The air we breathe is a mixture of various gases. The soil we walk on is a mixture of various rocks and minerals.

The Parts of an Atom

Scientists know a great deal about the way in which atoms interact with one another as well as the way in which they absorb and release energy. With this knowledge, scientists have constructed a model of what they believe an atom to be. Keep in mind that the protons, neutrons, and electrons that make up an atom are not really the round objects they are depicted to be in diagrams. Even so, diagrams can help us understand atomic interaction. Figure 17A.3 illustrates six different atoms. The electrons in these atoms exist in the outer rings, or shells. Electrons are negative electrical charges that orbit around the atom's nucleus. A *shell* is an energy level on which an electron exists.

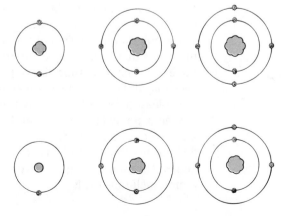

FIGURE 17A.3
Models like these are used to keep track of the number and placement of protons, neutrons, and electrons in atoms.

The center of an atom is called the *nucleus.* This is the place where *protons,* heavy particles having a positive electrical charge, and *neutrons,* heavy particles having no electrical charge, are found. It is the protons and neutrons that make up most of the atom's mass. An *electron* has only $1/1837$ the mass of a proton. Atoms are electrically neutral. That is, an atom contains as many positive charges (protons) in its nucleus as there are negative charges (electrons) around the nucleus. Some atoms do not have neutrons. The hydrogen atom, for example, has one proton and one electron but no neutrons. The helium atom consists of two protons and two neutrons in the nucleus surrounded by two orbiting electrons.

The *atomic number* of an element is the number of protons it contains. The *atomic weight* of an element is the weight of its protons plus the weight of its neutrons. An element's atomic weight is also determined in relation to the weight of a carbon atom, which is defined as 12 units. A hydrogen atom has about $1/12$ the weight of a carbon atom. Therefore, hydrogen has an atomic weight of about 1. Magnesium is about twice as heavy as carbon; its atomic weight is 24. Here are the atomic weights of some elements:

Aluminum	27.0
Carbon	12.0
Chlorine	35.5
Copper	63.5
Gold	196.9
Hydrogen	1.0
Lead	207.2
Oxygen	16.0
Silver	107.0
Sulfur	32.1

Some atoms of an element are slightly heavier than most atoms of the same element. These atoms are known as *isotopes.* For example, the most common sulfur atom has an atomic weight of 32. However, some sulfur atoms have an atomic weight of 36. Both types of atom are sulfur atoms, since they have an atomic number of 16. The average atomic weight of sulfur atoms is about 32.1. The 0.1 results from the sulfur atoms that have slightly different atomic weights. These isotopes of sulfur have the exact chemical properties of the element sulfur. Their physical properties, however, may differ from the physical properties of the predominant sulfur atoms. There are at least three isotopes of hydrogen in nature—hydrogen 1, hydrogen 2, and hydrogen 3. Study Figure 17A.4 and note that most hydrogen atoms have one proton and one electron. However, hydrogen isotopes may have one proton, one electron, and one neutron (hydrogen 2) or one proton, one electron, and two neutrons (hydrogen 3). The atomic weight of hydrogen represents the average weight of all hydrogen atoms, including the isotopes.

FIGURE 17A.4 The nuclei of these hydrogen isotopes have the same number of protons but not the same number of neutrons. Because the number of neutrons is different, each isotope has slightly different physical properties.

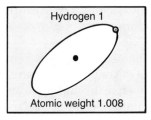

Hydrogen 1

Atomic weight 1.008

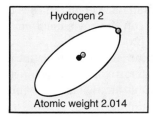

Hydrogen 2

Atomic weight 2.014

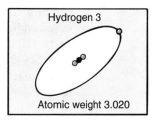

Hydrogen 3

Atomic weight 3.020

Quarks and Other More Fundamental Parts of Matter

The preceding discussion of the fundamental parts of matter is intended to provide you with background knowledge for teaching the science content commonly covered in elementary and middle school materials. Although these materials seldom carry their descriptions much further, you should be aware that there are even more fundamental particles than protons and neutrons. Scientists have hypothesized the existence of these particles as a result of experiments carried out with powerful atom-smashing devices. Two of the many laboratories involved in this type of work are the Stanford Linear Accelerator Center in California and the European Laboratory for Particle Physics in Geneva, Switzerland.

At the present time, it is believed that the most fundamental particle of matter is the *quark*. There are six kinds, or *flavors*, of quarks that are known as *up, down, strange, charm, bottom,* and *top.* Each kind of quark has three varieties, or *colors: red, blue,* and *green.* (The terms *flavor* and *color,* of course, bear no relationship to our everyday use of the words flavor and color.) Scientists believe that protons and neutrons are composed of quarks.

Obviously, a discussion of quarks is not likely to occur in elementary school. However, you should be aware of the term, as your students will undoubtedly come across it. You may want to encourage some children to pursue independent reading on this and other more advanced subjects.

Nuclear Energy

When matter undergoes chemical change, some of the electrons of the various atoms involved may be exchanged or shared. In doing this, energy is released. Energy can also be released through the nucleus of the atom. Such release of energy is brought about not by an ordinary chemical change but by a change in the nucleus of the atom. Atoms of some elements, such as radium and uranium-235, are naturally unstable: They have the potential to break up spontaneously. When they break up, they throw off some of their particles and a great amount of energy. The energy that is given off is known as *radiation*. Radioactive materials are too dangerous to be handled directly, since they may discharge rays that can damage human cells. This special property of radioactive materials is used by doctors to treat cancer patients. Focused radiation can destroy cancer cells; unfortunately, healthy cells also may be destroyed in the process.

Some uranium isotopes break down spontaneously, releasing energy and particles of matter that form radium. The nucleus of the radium atom can break down further to form a stable atom of lead. The breakdown of the nucleus of an atom is called *fission*. The amount of energy released in this process can be calculated by multiplying the amount of matter that is seemingly destroyed (actually it's converted to energy) by c (the speed of light) squared. If one gram of matter is changed directly to energy, the amount of that energy is equal to the amount produced by the burning of about 3,000 tons of coal. When scientists control these reactions, they harness great amounts of energy. A controlled flow of chain reactions occurs in nuclear power plants. In detonated atomic bombs, on the other hand, uncontrolled chain reactions take place.

Matter can also be changed by a different type of nuclear reaction—*fusion*. In this process, just as in the fission process, small amounts of matter are changed to large amounts of energy. Hydrogen bombs operate as a result of fusion. The sunlight that reaches you each day, as well as the light from the other stars in the universe, is all produced by nuclear fusion. At present, controlled fusion has been accomplished only in the laboratory.

Motion

"How long till we get there?"

This question commonly punctuates long family drives to distant destinations, regardless of the frequency of the parents' response. The driver, if he or she is patient enough, will try to give the child a response that is based on the speed of the automobile, its present location, and the location of the destination.

The *speed* of an automobile is determined by the distance it travels in a given unit of time. The units commonly used to express the speed of automobiles are *kilometers per hour* and *miles per hour*. We can use our knowledge of speed to answer the child's question about how long it will take to reach a destination fairly easily. Since speed is the distance divided by the time, we can multiply the speed of the object by the time available to find how far we will travel in that time. If you know the destination is 100 kilometers (about 60 miles) away and the average speed during the journey will be 50 kilometers (about 30 miles) per hour, you can divide the speed into the distance and remark calmly that the journey will take about 2 hours.

If you specify the speed of an object and the direction in which it is traveling, you are talking about an object's *velocity*. We call changes in velocity *acceleration*. An automobile speeding up is accelerating. The rate of acceleration is equal to the change in velocity divided by the time it took for the change. If your car stops at a red light during your trip and then gains a speed of 50 kilometers per hour (about 30 miles per hour) in 10 seconds, traveling in a straight line, the change in velocity is 50 kilometers per hour and it occurs in 10 seconds. Therefore, the rate of acceleration of the car is 5 kilometers per hour per second (about 3 miles per hour per second).

Since scientists define velocity as both speed and direction, an object that moves with constant speed yet changes direction is accelerating. For example, a racing car traveling around a track at a constant speed is accelerating because its direction is constantly changing.

With this information in mind, we can now consider objects in motion. To understand why objects in motion behave as they do, we need to understand the laws that govern them.

Newton's Laws of Motion

Have you ever blown up a balloon, held its end shut, and then released it to watch it rocket around the room? You may not have realized it, but you were demonstrating a phenomenon described about 300 years ago by Isaac Newton. Newton's observations of the motion of objects led him to reach conclusions that we now refer to as *laws of motion*. Newton's three laws of motion help us explain the motion of objects that are subjected to forces.

Newton's first law of motion, sometimes called the *law of inertia,* states that an object at rest will remain at rest and a body moving with a constant velocity in a straight line will maintain its motion unless acted upon by an unbalanced external force. This law tells us that in order to change the position of an object at rest, we must apply a force to it. Similarly, if we wish to change the velocity of an object, we must apply a force. To move a golf ball from the grass of a putting green to the hole, we apply a force with the putter. To increase the speed of an automobile, we cause the engine to increase the forces that turn the wheels. To slow down a bicycle that is moving along at a constant velocity, we apply frictional forces by using the brakes.

Newton's second law of motion states that the amount of acceleration produced by a force acting on an object varies with the magnitude of the force and the mass of the object. If the force on an object is increased and no mass is added to or taken away from the object, the object's acceleration will increase. Specifically, this law tells us that an object will accelerate in the direction in which an applied force is acting and that the acceleration will be proportional to the applied force. For example, when we begin to push or pull a child in a wagon that was stationary, the wagon moves in the direction of the push or pull and increases its acceleration as the force we apply increases.

Newton's third law of motion states that for every action, there is an equal and opposite reaction. The air escaping from the blown-up balloon mentioned earlier moves in one direction; it is the action force. The balloon moves in the opposite direction as a reaction to the action force.

Gravity and Motion

Whether you live in Beijing, China, or Paramus, New Jersey, you know that what goes up must come down and the downward path is always the same: All objects fall toward the center of the earth. After studying the behavior of falling objects, Newton concluded that the cause for the path of a falling object was the attractive force that exists between masses. This force of attraction depends on two variables: the mass of each attracting object and the distance between them.

Very precise scientific instruments have revealed that Newton was correct in his conclusion that all masses exert attractive forces. Newton's conclusion is called the *law of universal gravitation,* and it is a fundamental law of the universe. Every mass in the universe attracts every other mass with a force that varies directly with the product of the masses of the objects and inversely with the square of the distance between them. This law can be written as an equation:

$$F = G\,m_1 m_2/r^2$$

Although it may not look it, this is actually an easy equation to understand. The *m*'s represent the masses of the two objects. The *r* is the distance between the centers of the objects. The *G* is a constant. In other words, the same value of *G* is used every time the equation is solved. *F* stands for the actual force of attraction between objects. As noted earlier, the force of attraction between an object and the earth is the object's weight.

The earth's gravitational pull causes falling objects to accelerate at the rate of 9.8 meters per second per second (32 feet per second per second). This means that an object increases its speed 9.8 meters per second (32 feet per second) during each second it falls. Strictly speaking, this rate applies to objects falling through a vacuum, since the presence of air retards the acceleration of objects that have a large surface area compared with their mass.

You have seen the effect of air on acceleration if you have seen a parachutist dropped from a plane high above the earth. The parachutist does not accelerate at a constant rate because the presence of air under the large surface of the parachute resists the downward motion of the parachute. Scientists have found that as an object accelerates during a fall, the air's resistance to the downward motion increases. The parachutist stops accelerating when she or he reaches a velocity at which the upward force of air resistance exactly balances the downward attractive force of gravity. This speed, which is called *terminal velocity*, depends on a variety of factors, but the principal factor is the surface area in contact with the air.

Jet and Rocket Engines

Rockets and jet airplanes are designed to capitalize on Newton's third law of motion. Both utilize engines that discharge hot gases in one direction (an action force) so as to produce thrust (a reaction force). In both engines, chemical energy is changed to the energy of motion.

The jet engine uses kerosene fuel to heat air that is taken into the engine. The products of the combustion of kerosene reach a high temperature and pressure and leave through the rear of the engine. This produces the reaction force, or *thrust*. In the turbojet, turning compressor blades take in air through the front of the engine and force it into the combustion chamber. At this point, kerosene is sprayed into the air and ignited. The hot exhaust gases expand and move out the back of the engine, turning the turbine blades in the process. The turbine blades are connected to the compressor blades and cause them to turn and bring in more air.

The engine of a rocket is designed to operate in outer space in the absence of oxygen. To provide the fuel that is burned with the oxygen needed for burning, tanks of liquid oxygen are carried near the engine. Some rocket fuels do not require oxygen. Instead, they use a chemical known as an *oxidizer*.

Flight

"Just pull the yellow oxygen mask toward you. Now cover your mouth and breathe normally."

Each time a flight attendant says that prior to takeoff, I begin to wonder: How exactly do you breathe *normally* when an aircraft is having a serious problem that may soon give it the aerodynamic characteristics of a rock? I understand the physics of flight, but I am always astonished that masses of metal can become airborne. It is most amazing.

What causes an airplane to rise? The answer is a force called *lift*. A plane's wings are shaped so that air going across the upper surface moves at a higher velocity than the air going across the bottom surface. This causes a region of low pressure to form above the wing. The air pressure below the wing is greater than the air pressure above the wing, causing an unbalanced upward force.

The lifting force on a wing can be varied in several ways. For example, the faster a plane moves, the more lift is created. The angle that the front of the wing makes with the oncoming air also affects lift. This angle is known as the *angle of attack*. In fixed-wing aircraft, the pilot varies the angle of attack by using movable portions of the wing called *wing flaps*, or ailerons. Extending the wing flaps also increases the surface area of the wing. A larger surface produces more lift than a smaller surface.

While the forward motion, or thrust, of a jet is a reaction force to hot exhaust gases expelled from the rear of the engine, propeller-driven planes move forward because of the propeller, which is designed very much like a miniature wing. The pressure on the rear surface of the propeller pushes the plane forward. Pilots use the term *drag* to describe a force that retards the forward motion of an aircraft. It results from the friction between the air and the surfaces of the aircraft.

The direction in which an airplane moves is controlled by the pilot's use of the ailerons, elevator, and rudder (see Figure 17A.5, page 400). The *elevator* (the movable flap on the horizontal part of the tail) causes the aircraft's nose to move up or down.

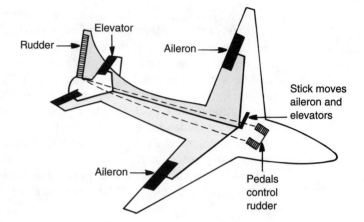

FIGURE 17A.5
Each of these controls can change an airplane's direction.

The *rudder* (the movable flap on the vertical portion of the tail) causes the nose of the aircraft to move left or right. The *ailerons* change the lift on the wing surfaces. The pilot uses all these surfaces in combination to turn the plane.

Summary Outline

I. Anything that occupies space and has weight is matter.
   A. A change in matter from one state, or phase, to another is a physical change.
   B. Molecular theory is used to explain a variety of changes in matter.
   C. A change in matter that produces a new substance is a chemical change.
   D. Matter exists as elements, compounds, and mixtures.
   E. Atoms are composed of smaller particles.
   F. Under special conditions, portions of the matter in an atomic nucleus can be converted to energy.

II. Matter can be caused to move from place to place.
   A. Newton's laws of motion describe how the motion of an object will change as a result of the application of a force.
   B. The law of universal gravitation states that all masses are attracted to all other masses by a force that varies directly with the product of the masses and inversely with the square of the distance between them.
   C. The terminal velocity of a falling object is related to the resistance of air to the downward fall of the object.
   D. The motion of jet planes and rockets can be explained by Newton's third law of motion, which states that for every action there is an equal and opposite reaction.
   E. Airplanes fly as a result of the action of two forces: lift and thrust.

17B

Matter and Motion

Attention Getters, Discovery Activities, and Demonstrations

A Look Ahead

Why Do We Need to Wear Safety Belts? [PS 2] & [SPSP 9]

MATERIALS

1 small toy wagon or truck
1 doll that can ride in or on top of toy wagon or truck
2 large rubber bands

MOTIVATING QUESTIONS

- What direction will the doll move when the wagon suddenly stops?
- If the doll were wearing a safety belt, would it still move?

DIRECTIONS

For Young Learners

1. Display the wagon or truck without the doll. Gently roll it into the wall.
2. Put the doll in the wagon, gently push the wagon, and have the children predict in what direction the doll will move when the wagon strikes the wall.
3. After they have observed the wagon striking the wall, relate the wagon and doll to a car and passenger. Discuss the likelihood of the passenger striking or going through the windshield if the car hits something or stops suddenly.
4. Use the rubber band to restrain the doll, and repeat the demonstration. Ask the children for their observations.

SCIENCE CONTENT FOR THE TEACHER

A fundamental law of motion is that an object at rest or in uniform motion tends to continue in that condition. An unrestrained passenger in a forward-moving automobile continues to move forward if the car stops, since he or she is not connected to the car.

Where Does the Water Go? [PS 1]

MATERIALS

1 sponge
Paper towels
1 clean, dry dishcloth
Bowl of water
3 dishes
Pan balance (optional)

MOTIVATING QUESTIONS

- How will the sponge (paper towel, cloth) change when we dip it in water?
- Where do you think the water goes when something dries?

DIRECTIONS
1. In this demonstration, the children will observe a sponge, paper towel, and cloth when dry and when wet. The children will already know that when they dry themselves after a bath or shower, the towels they use become wet, but they may not have connected this knowledge with the concept that some materials can absorb water.
2. Dip the sponge, paper towel, and dishcloth in the bowl of water. Have the children make observations that you record on the board.
3. After wringing out the objects, place them on plates so that further observations can be made. If a pan balance is available, the children can check changes in mass as the objects dry.

SCIENCE CONTENT FOR THE TEACHER
Many materials are capable of absorbing water. They retain this water as a liquid. The liquid that is in contact with the surrounding air evaporates and enters the air as water vapor.

Where Are Wheels? [PS 2]

MATERIALS
Easel paper
Felt-tip markers
Pack of index cards

MOTIVATING QUESTIONS
- Is it easier to pull something with wheels or something without wheels?
- Do wheels all have the same shape or size?

DIRECTIONS
1. Take the children for a walk around the school, both inside and outside the building. Challenge them to find as many wheels as they can. As they search, model how a scientist keeps track of information by writing notes about each wheeled vehicle observed on an index card. Use a different index card for each vehicle. Look for such things as automobiles, bicycles, cafeteria and custodial carts, wagons, and trucks. Don't miss the wheels under audiovisual carts and movable chalkboards or room dividers.
2. When you return to the room, prepare a three-column chart that includes a drawing of each vehicle and the number of wheels on it. Have the children discuss how wheels help move objects.

SCIENCE CONTENT FOR THE TEACHER
Friction is a force that acts against the forward-moving wagon. If the force is large enough, it can slow down or stop the wagon. Wheels reduce the friction between objects and the ground. As a wheel turns, only a small amount of it touches the ground, which reduces the friction between the object and the ground and makes the object easier to move.

Why Do Mothballs Rise and Fall? [PS 5]

MATERIALS	1 unopened 2 liter bottle of club soda 6 mothballs
MOTIVATING QUESTIONS	• Where do the bubbles in soda come from? • What is in the bubbles? • Why do the mothballs go up and down?

For Middle-Level Learners

DIRECTIONS

1. Have the children make some observations of the club soda before you open the cap.
2. Open the cap, have the children observe the bubbles that form throughout the soda, and then display the mothballs.
3. Drop the mothballs into the club soda, and have the children make observations about the motion of the mothballs.

SCIENCE CONTENT FOR THE TEACHER

Club soda is water to which carbon dioxide has been added under pressure. Mothballs have a density that is close to the density of water. Thus, they will almost but not quite float. The carbon dioxide bubbles coat the surface of the mothballs, increasing the volume of the mothballs but only minimally increasing their mass. The mothballs and attached bubbles move toward the surface of the soda. When they reach the surface, the bubbles burst and the mothballs sink. This process continues as long as carbon dioxide gas is released in the soda.

Can You Separate Sugar and Sand? [PS 4]

MATERIALS	1 empty, clear 2 liter soda bottle 1/4 cup of sand	1/4 cup of sugar 1 saucer
MOTIVATING QUESTIONS	• When you mix sugar and sand, are you making a physical or chemical change? • How could we separate the sugar and sand?	

DIRECTIONS

1. Fill the bottle half full of water, and keep it out of sight. Display the sand and sugar. Mix both together on the saucer, and challenge the children to invent a way to separate them.
2. After a discussion of alternative strategies, show the bottle containing water. Ask the children if they have any ideas on how the bottle could be used to separate the mixture.
3. Add the mixture to the bottle, and shake it vigorously. The sand will settle to the bottom, and the water will dissolve the sugar. Challenge the children to think of a way to get the sugar back.

SCIENCE CONTENT FOR THE TEACHER   Sugar, sand, and water do not chemically react to produce a new substance. The dissolving of sugar in water is a physical change, since the sugar can be recovered by evaporating the water.

What Causes Lift? [PS 5]

MATERIALS   2 textbooks of equal thickness   1 sheet of notebook paper

MOTIVATING QUESTIONS
- What do you think will happen if we blow under the paper?
- What does the movement of the paper tell us about how an airplane is able to fly?

DIRECTIONS
1. Align the books on a table top so they are about 10 centimeters (about 4 inches) apart. Lay the notebook paper across the tops of the books.
2. Ask the children to predict what will happen if you blow under the paper. Blow under the paper, and then ask the children for their observations.

SCIENCE CONTENT FOR THE TEACHER   According to Bernoulli's principle, if we cause a fluid to move, the pressure in the fluid is reduced. Think of air as a fluid. By causing the air under the paper to move, you reduce the air pressure under the paper. Because the air pressure under the paper is slightly lower than the air pressure above the paper, the paper moves down. An airplane wing has a shape that forces air to move faster across the top than across the bottom. This lowers air pressure at the top and causes the wing to rise. The unbalanced force that moves the wing up is called *lift*.

Matter and Changes[1] [PS 1]

OBJECTIVES
- The children will identify a substance as a solid or a liquid.
- The children will describe changes in the color, shape, size, and state of samples of matter.

SCIENCE PROCESSES EMPHASIZED   Observing
Communicating

MATERIALS FOR EACH CHILD OR GROUP
1 ice cube
1 cube of modeling clay 2.5 cm × 2.5 cm × 2.5 cm (about 1 inch on edge)
1 cube of butter the same size as the cube of clay
3 saucers
Paper and pencil
Source of hot water

For
Young
Learners

DISCOVERY ACTIVITIES

D
I
S
C
O
V
E
R
Y

A
C
T
I
V
I
T
I
E
S

MOTIVATION

Put an ice cube in a glass, and tell the children that you are thirsty. Pretend to drink from the glass, and ask the children why you are having trouble getting a drink. The children will indicate that the ice cube must melt before you can have water to drink. Have the children discuss whether an ice cube is really water. Suggest that ice cubes might be made of "smush," a clear solid that changes to water. After some discussion of ways in which they could check to see if there is such a thing as "smush," begin the activity.

DIRECTIONS

1. Have the children compare the size, shape, and color of the butter, clay, and ice cubes.
2. When this is done, have the children heat the plates in the hot water and then place the cube of butter on one plate, the cube of clay on another plate, and the ice cube on the third plate.
3. Have the children keep a record of the changes they observe.
4. After the butter and ice cubes have changed in form, discuss the states of matter, using the following questions to focus the children's thinking.

*KEY
DISCUSSION
QUESTIONS*

1. Which cubes were solid when you started the activity? What changes did you observe? *All three. The butter and the ice cubes started to melt.*
2. Did the color or shape of the cubes change? *The color didn't but the shape did.*
3. What would happen if we put the saucers in a freezer before the activity? How would the changes have been different? *The butter and ice cubes would not have melted as fast.*
4. What do you think caused the changes? *Heat.*

*SCIENCE
CONTENT FOR
THE TEACHER*

Matter is commonly found in one of three forms or states: solid, liquid, or gas. In this activity, three substances that display the essential observable characteristics of solids are observed as heat from the air in the room and preheated sources cause a change in state. The flow of energy from these sources causes the molecules in the substances to increase their motion. In the case of the butter cube and the ice cube, this increased energy causes the molecules to begin to flow past each other, and melting is observed. The change is a physical change because the substance remains the same but changes in form.

EXTENSIONS

Science/Art: You may wish to have some children make drawings of various changes, such as an icicle melting, water in a pond freezing, and a pond drying up during the summer.

Science/Physical Education: Some children may wish to make drawings of various sports that utilize water or ice. The children can discuss their drawings with the class and consider what would happen if the water depicted in them changed to ice or the ice changed to water.

From Gas to Liquid [PS 3]

OBJECTIVES
- The children will observe the result of water changing from gas to liquid.
- The children will infer the source of the water that condenses on the outside of a can.

SCIENCE PROCESSES EMPHASIZED
Observing
Inferring

MATERIALS FOR EACH CHILD OR GROUP
1 shiny metal can or container
Supply of crushed ice
Paper towel

MOTIVATION
Display an ice cube and a glass of water, and ask the children if they think that the ice is water. After some discussion of the possibility that water can be in a liquid form or in a solid form, explain to the children that water can be in still another form—a gas. Tell them that in this activity, they will make the invisible water in air become visible.

DIRECTIONS
1. Distribute a can and paper towel to each group, and ask the children to polish the outside of the can with the towel. Have the children describe what they observe when they examine the outside of the can.
2. Have each group add crushed ice to the can.
3. Have the children again observe the outside of the can. In a short time, a thin film of water will appear on the can.

KEY DISCUSSION QUESTIONS
1. Where do you think the water that formed on the outside of the can came from? *The air.*
2. How could we get the water that formed on the outside of the can to go back into the air? *Answers will vary. Some children will suggest that they remove the ice from the can and add hot water.*

SCIENCE CONTENT FOR THE TEACHER
Air contains water vapor, which is water in a gaseous state. The amount of water vapor that air can hold depends on various factors, including its temperature. If the temperature of air is lowered sufficiently, the water vapor in it will condense on any available surface. The temperature at which this occurs is called the *dew point*. The cold can causes air near its surface to condense and form a film of liquid water.

EXTENSION
Science/Health: Ask the children to breathe on a mirror or windowpane and observe the surface. The film of water they see on the surface results

from the condensation of the water vapor that is contained in the breath they exhale. The water is a by-product of the process by which food is converted to energy in the body.

What Is Your Squeezing Force? [PS 1]

OBJECTIVE
- The children will measure the amount of squeezing force they can apply.

SCIENCE
PROCESSES
EMPHASIZED

Measuring
Interpreting data

MATERIALS FOR
EACH CHILD
OR GROUP

1 bathroom scale thin enough for children to grip

MOTIVATION

Display the bathroom scale, and explain that it provides a measurement of the amount of pull the earth exerts on our bodies. Tell the children that they will use the scale to see how much pushing force they can exert with their hands.

DIRECTIONS

1. Divide the class into groups, and have each group member squeeze the top and bottom of a bathroom scale together. The children should use both hands. As each child concentrates on squeezing the scale, another member of the group should write down the reading on the scale's weight display.
2. Have each group make a graph that shows the name of the person and the squeezing force he or she applied.

KEY
DISCUSSION
QUESTIONS

1. Is the force you used to squeeze the scale a push or a pull? *The children should realize they are exerting two pushes with each hand. They are pushing the top of the scale down and the bottom of the scale up.*
2. When we weigh ourselves, what is pulling us down on the scale? *The earth is pulling on us.*

SCIENCE
CONTENT FOR
THE TEACHER

A bathroom scale has a spring system that reacts in response to the pull of gravity on any mass placed on the scale. Some scales include electrical devices that convert the movement of the springs to electrical information that is displayed in the form of a digital display.

EXTENSION

Science/Health: Since young children experience rather steady growth in their skeletal/muscular system, they may find it interesting to measure their squeezing force at the beginning, middle, and end of the school year and prepare a simple graph of the results.

Secret Messages and Chemical Changes [PS 1]

OBJECTIVES
- The children will observe physical and chemical changes.
- The children will describe the characteristics of physical and chemical changes.

SCIENCE PROCESSES EMPHASIZED

Observing
Communicating
Making a hypothesis

MATERIALS FOR EACH CHILD OR GROUP

Access to a small container of freshly squeezed lemon juice
Cotton swab
Sheet of white paper
Iron nail
Plastic container of water
A few sheets of paper toweling
Desk lamp with incandescent 100 watt light bulbs
Roll of masking tape
Small, clear plastic containers (such as disposable glasses) containing copper-sulfate solution. ***Safety Note:*** The containers of copper sulfate should remain under your supervision in a central location. The groups will place their iron nail in the container and simply observe the changes. At the end of the activity, you are responsible for disposing of the solutions. *At no time should the children handle copper sulfate.*

For Middle-Level Learners

MOTIVATION   This activity should be done following activities or discussion on physical changes. Ask the children to review the characteristics of a physical change with you, and discuss the possibility that some changes may result in the production of new substances. Tell the children that they will be doing some activities that may help them think about such changes.

DIRECTIONS
1. Distribute the lemon juice, cotton swabs, and paper. Have the children write secret messages on their paper, using the swabs and lemon juice.
2. Have the children allow the paper to dry. While it is drying, have them record their observations of the lemon juice patterns on the paper.
3. Under your supervision, have the children exchange messages and take turns heating them over the reading lamps.

Observing secret messages and chemical changes

4. Ask the children whether they think a physical or a chemical change has occurred.

5. Distribute an iron nail to each group. Have the children clean the nails with paper towels.

6. Tell each group to make a small identifying tag out of masking tape for its nail and affix it to the top of the nail.

7. Have each group place its nail in one of the containers of copper sulfate and make observations every few hours (if this is convenient) or every time science class begins.

8. After some changes have occurred, discuss whether the changes observed are physical changes or something else.

KEY DISCUSSION QUESTIONS

1. When the secret writing became visible, do you think that there was a physical change in the lemon juice? *No, the lemon juice changed to something else. It got darker; we probably couldn't make it turn back into lemon juice.*

2. What were some changes you observed after the iron nail was placed in the blue liquid? *The blue color of the liquid got less; red stuff started to cover the nail.*

3. Do you think you saw a physical change? *No. Some new things formed. The color of the liquid changed, and the red stuff wasn't there when we started.*

SCIENCE CONTENT FOR THE TEACHER

When matter undergoes a physical change, it changes in form but remains the same substance. Physical changes are usually easy to reverse. In contrast, this activity shows two chemical changes. In the first case, heat added to the lemon juice caused the formation of molecules that absorb light, giving the juice a dark color. In the second case, the copper that was part of the solution left the solution and accumulated on the surface of the nail as iron from the nail entered the liquid. The iron reacted with the copper sulfate to form a new substance—iron sulfate. The copper atoms that left the solution were observed in their metallic form on the surface of the nail.

EXTENSIONS

Science: You may wish to have some children observe an additional chemical change. Have them wedge some steel wool into a small glass, moisten it, and invert it in a pan of water. There should be an air space between the steel wool in the inverted glass and the water. Within a few days, the children will be able to observe the formation of rust on the steel wool—a chemical change.

Science/Language Arts: Activities such as this one can make children more sensitive to the concept of change. Recognizing changes in the environment can serve as an important first step in writing experiences that focus on change. You may wish to have the children write poetry about the changes they observe in the world around them.

Pendulums [PS 2]

Pendulums and discoveries

OBJECTIVES
- The children will predict how changing the string length and mass of a pendulum bob affect the motion of the pendulum.
- The children will measure the effect of changing the string length and mass of the bob on the motion of the pendulum.

SCIENCE PROCESSES EMPHASIZED
Observing
Predicting
Measuring

MATERIALS FOR EACH CHILD OR GROUP
Horizontal wooden support at least 1 m (about 40 in.) long
4 screw eyes fastened along the length of the support
Spool of heavy-duty twine
4 sticks of modeling clay
Stopwatch
Metric ruler

MOTIVATION
Display the materials, and ask the children to guess what they will be learning about in this activity. Tell them that they will be making some predictions and then doing an activity to check their predictions.

DIRECTIONS
1. Have one member of each group be responsible for making the pendulum bob from the clay and attaching it to string. Have another member be responsible for using the stopwatch. The children should switch roles during the activity.
2. Begin by having the children predict how changing the length of the string will affect the time it takes for the pendulum to make one complete forward-and-backward movement. Use the term *period* to represent this amount of time.
3. Explain that any object hanging from a pendulum string is call a *bob,* and ask the children to make a bob from half a stick of clay.
4. Have the children start with a 1 meter length of string and shorten it by 10 centimeters (about 4 inches) during each of the five trials. In starting the pendulum movement, always move the bob 10 centimeters (4 inches) to the left of its stationary position before releasing it.
5. The children should find the time of one back-and-forth movement by completing five such movements and then dividing by five. Once they have found the time, have them check it against their predictions.
6. Now have the children repeat this procedure using three different bobs made of one-quarter, one-half, and three-quarters of a stick of clay.

Maintain the string lengths at 1 meter (about 40 inches). Each time the bob is changed, the children should predict the period and then check their predictions against their observations.

KEY
DISCUSSION
QUESTIONS

1. Did you predict that the length of the string would affect the period of the pendulum? *Answers will vary.*
2. What did you observe when just the length of the string was changed? *The length of the string affects the period. The longer the string, the longer the period.*
3. Did you predict that the mass of the bob would affect the period of the pendulum? *Answers will vary.*
4. What did you observe when just the mass of the bob was changed? *Changing the mass of the bob does not change the period of the pendulum.*

SCIENCE
CONTENT FOR
THE TEACHER

A pendulum is a weight, or bob, suspended from a fixed point that is able to swing back and forth freely. The period of a pendulum is the time it takes for the bob to make one complete back-and-forth swing. Galileo discovered that the period of a pendulum is independent of the mass of the bob and depends only on the pendulum's length.

EXTENSIONS

Science: You may wish to ask the children if they think that the period of a pendulum depends on how far the bob is released from the point at which it is hanging straight down. They can then conduct an activity to check their ideas. (The period remains the same regardless of the position from which the bob is released.)

Science/Social Studies: This activity provides an excellent opportunity for children to become aware of Galileo. Read a brief biography of Galileo in a reference book, and then have children do some social studies activities that focus on him. For example, they can make a timeline and mark on it the time of Galileo's life as well as such events as the discovery of America, the American Revolution, the launching of the first space satellite, and the first moon walk. The children could also locate Italy on a world map and find the town of Pisa, where Galileo made his observations of the swinging pendulum.

Heat and the Fizzer [PS 3]

OBJECTIVE

• The children will experiment to discover the relationship between temperature and the speed of a chemical reaction.

SCIENCE
PROCESSES
EMPHASIZED

Experimenting

MATERIALS FOR	3 Alka Seltzer tablets
EACH CHILD	3 clear plastic cups
OR GROUP	1 ice cube
	Access to cool and hot water

MOTIVATION   Review the difference between physical and chemical changes with the children. Tell the children that in this activity, they will observe the results of a chemical change and discover how heat affects chemical changes.

DIRECTIONS
1. Distribute three cups and three tablets to each group. Provide access to ice cubes as well as to hot and cold water.
2. Tell the children that they are going to use their senses of sight and hearing to gauge the speed of the reaction of the tablet with water.
3. Have the children prepare the three cups of water and arrange them from cold (tap water plus an ice cube) to cool to hot. Tell the children to write their observations of bubble production and fizzing after they have dropped one tablet in each cup.

KEY
DISCUSSION
QUESTIONS
1. How did the temperature of the water affect the speed of each reaction? *The hotter water produced more bubbles faster.*
2. Does this experiment prove that heat speeds up a chemical reaction? *No. It only shows that more heat seems to speed up this reaction. There may be reactions that slow down if heat is added.*

SCIENCE
CONTENT FOR
THE TEACHER   One of the products of the reaction of Alka Seltzer with water is carbon dioxide gas. The rate of production of carbon dioxide bubbles is one indicator of the rate at which this reaction takes place.

EXTENSION   *Science/Health:* Have the students compare the ingredients in a variety of over-the-counter stomach upset remedies. After they have done this, have them research the common causes of an upset stomach and the preventive steps people can take to reduce their dependence on over-the-counter remedies.

For
Young
Learners

The Toy Car in the Wagon:
Pushes and Pulls [PS 2]

OBJECTIVES
- The children will identify one type of force as a push and another as a pull.
- The children will observe the tendency of an object to remain in one place or to remain in uniform motion.

DEMONSTRATIONS

D
E
M
O
N
S
T
R
A
T
I
O
N
S

SCIENCE PROCESSES EMPHASIZED	Observing Making hypotheses
MATERIALS	Child's wagon Large toy car with functioning wheels
MOTIVATION	Display the wagon, but keep the car out of sight. Tell the children that you are going to use the wagon to help them learn some interesting things about how objects move. Ask for a volunteer to assist you.

DIRECTIONS

Note: Because this demonstration requires ongoing discussion, Key Discussion Questions are included in each step.

1. Ask the children why the wagon is not floating in the air. Use their responses to help them understand that the earth is pulling the wagon downward. Explain that this pull is called a *force*. Then pick up the wagon, and ask the children if you used a force. Put the wagon down, and ask your volunteer to use a force to pull the wagon. Have the volunteer demonstrate a push. Summarize by explaining that forces can be pushes or pulls.

2. Ask the children if the wagon moves in the same direction as the force. *Yes.*

3. Place the toy car in the back of the wagon so the back of the car is touching the back of the wagon. Have the children make guesses (hypotheses) about what will happen to the wagon and car if the volunteer pulls the wagon forward at a steady but high speed. Before the volunteer demonstrates this, ask how the toy car in the wagon will move during the journey and at the stop. Have the children watch the demonstration closely. They will observe that the toy car continues to move forward after an abrupt stop. Repeat this with the toy car at the front of the wagon.

KEY DISCUSSION QUESTIONS	See Directions.
SCIENCE CONTENT FOR THE TEACHER	When the wagon is stationary, all forces acting on it balance each other. The earth's pulling force is balanced by a reacting force—the earth pushing on the cart in the opposite direction. The wagon displays forward motion if an unbalanced force acts on it. Although the term is not used, the toy car placed at the back of the wagon is used to demonstrate *inertia*. In other words, an object set in motion tends to keep moving.
EXTENSION	*Science/Physical Education:* Bring a variety of athletic equipment to class, such as a baseball, baseball bat, football, field hockey stick, field hockey ball, jump rope, and so forth. Have various children demonstrate how forces are involved in using these objects.

How Does an Earth Satellite
Get Placed in Orbit? [PS 2]

OBJECTIVES
- The children will observe a model of the launching of a rocket and the placement of a satellite in orbit.
- The children will identify the forces at work during the launching process.
- The children will infer the causes of the forces.

SCIENCE
PROCESSES
EMPHASIZED

Observing
Inferring

MATERIALS

Tennis ball
1 m (1 yd.) length of string
Magazine pictures of various satellites that have been placed in orbit
Globe
Small model rocketship

MOTIVATION

Before class, firmly attach the tennis ball to the string. When class begins, display the magazine pictures of the satellites and engage the children in a discussion of how satellites are placed in orbit. Solicit their ideas about why satellites remain in orbit after they are launched. Now display the materials, and explain to the children that you are going to use these materials to illustrate the process of launching and orbiting a satellite.

DIRECTIONS

1. Hold the rocket so the children can see it. Place it on the surface of the globe. Indicate that a satellite is usually placed in the nose cone of the rocket that will launch it into orbit. Show the satellite being launched by lifting the rocket from the earth's surface. Explain that the exhaust gases are expelled from the back of the rocket and that this causes the rocket to move forward.
2. Explain that as the rocket moves upward, it must counteract the force of gravity pulling on it. Show the rocket turning as it places the satellite in orbit.
3. Use the tennis ball on the string to show how the satellite stays in orbit. Whirl the ball around your head by the string that is attached to it, and explain that the string represents the earth's pull on the satellite. The reaction force that is produced on the forward-moving satellite acts outward and counteracts the effect of gravity. Because the inward force is counterbalanced by the outside force, the satellite is weightless.

KEY
DISCUSSION
QUESTIONS

1. Have you ever seen a satellite launch on television? What were some of the things you noticed? *Answers will vary.*
2. Does the rocket stay attached to the satellite when the satellite is put into orbit? *No. It falls to the earth, and the satellite keeps moving ahead.*

3. What keeps pulling the satellite downward? *Gravity.*

4. Why does the satellite keep moving forward? *If you start an object moving, it keeps moving unless something slows it down. In space, there are no air particles to slow the satellite down.*

SCIENCE CONTENT FOR THE TEACHER

A ball thrown in a perfect horizontal line from the top of a tall building follows a curved path as it falls to the earth. How far it travels from the building before it strikes the earth depends on how fast it was thrown and how high the building is. An object thrown forward at a speed of 7,800 meters per second (about 25,600 feet per second) at a height of 160 kilometers (about 100 miles) would not return to the earth. Instead, it would follow a curved path around the earth. Inertia would carry it forward, and the attraction of the earth's gravitational field would keep it continually bending toward the earth's surface.

Satellites remain in orbit as a result of a balance between the pull of gravity inward and a reaction force outward. The scientific names for these forces are *centripetal* (inward) and *centrifugal* (outward). The satellite orbits the earth because the inward and outward forces produce a balance.

EXTENSIONS

Science: This demonstration provides a good starting point for somewhat more extensive study of rockets and space exploration. You may wish to obtain age-appropriate books from your learning center to place in your classroom. Encourage children to look for pictures of rocket launches, actual satellites, and descriptions of each satellite's use.

Science/Social Studies: You may wish to talk to the children about the financial cost of space exploration. A class discussion could focus on whether the costs are justified when compared with the short-term and long-term benefits. Children can be made aware of the fact that a society's resources are limited and that difficult decisions must be made to ensure that they are used wisely.

DEMONSTRATIONS

For Middle-Level Learners

Teacher on Wheels: Action and Reaction Forces [PS 5]

OBJECTIVES

- The children will observe that an action force applied in one direction produces a reaction force in the opposite direction.
- The children will predict the direction and magnitude of reaction forces.

SCIENCE PROCESSES EMPHASIZED

Observing
Predicting

| MATERIALS | A pair of inline skates or a skateboard |

MATERIALS   A pair of inline skates or a skateboard
Length of board 25 cm × 3 cm × 50 cm (about 10 in. × 1 in. × 20 in.)
12 large marbles
Old textbooks of assorted sizes (or large beanbags)

MOTIVATION   Tell the children that you intend to get on inline skates or a skateboard to demonstrate action and reaction forces. That should be sufficient motivation!

DIRECTIONS
1. Place the board on the floor. Stand on the board, and have the children predict what will happen to it when you jump off one end of it. Jump and then explain to the children that although they didn't observe anything happening to the board, your action caused a reaction force to be applied to it. The board didn't move because of the friction between the floor and the board.
2. Ask the children to predict what will happen if you repeat your jump but reduce the friction between the floor and the board. Place all of the marbles under the board. Spread them out so that they support all parts of the board. Step on the board gently so that you do not disturb the marbles under it, and jump off one end. The children will see the board move in the opposite direction.
3. Put on the skates or step on the skateboard. Have a volunteer hand you some old textbooks or beanbags. Ask the children to predict what will happen if you throw a textbook or beanbag from your perch on wheels. Execute a rapid underhand throw of the textbook or beanbag to an awaiting container.
4. Vary the number of books or beanbags and the direction and speed with which they are thrown. Have children make predictions prior to each demonstration of action and reaction.

KEY DISCUSSION QUESTIONS
1. When I threw the book while I was standing on the skateboard (skates), what was the reaction and what was the action? *The action was the book being thrown. The reaction was your movement in the other direction.*
2. What happened when I threw the book faster? *You moved in the other direction faster.*
3. Jet and rocket engines work because of action and reaction. What is the action and what is the reaction when these engines operate? *The hot gases going out the back of the engine is the action. The plane or rocket moving forward is the reaction.*

SCIENCE CONTENT FOR THE TEACHER   This demonstration illustrates Newton's third law of motion, although it is unnecessary to refer to it as such. This law states that for every action, there is an equal and opposite reaction. For example, when we apply a force to the earth as we try to take a step, a reaction force pushes our body forward.

D
E
M
O
N
S
T
R
A
T
I
O
N
S

Similarly, any time we apply a force to an object, a reaction force is produced. This law of nature can be taken advantage of to produce motion in any direction. A jet engine causes an airplane to move forward as a reaction to the action force produced when hot gases are expelled from the rear of the engine.

EXTENSIONS   *Science:* You may wish to have a group of children follow up this demonstration by attempting to build a device that will launch small objects in one direction and display a reaction force in the other direction.

Many toystores sell plastic rockets that are launched as a result of the rearward movement of water out the back end. A small pump is used to fill the rocket with water. A small group of children might wish to demonstrate (under your close supervision) the launching of such a rocket on the playground.

Science/Physical Education: Some children may wish to extend their knowledge of action and reaction forces by identifying athletic events that depend on these forces. For example, the downward jump on the diving board by a diver is the action force; the reactive force is the upward propelling of the diver.

**D
E
M
O
N
S
T
R
A
T
I
O
N
S**

Note

1. This was adapted from "Change," Module 17, in *Science: A Process Approach II* (Lexington, MA: Ginn).

18A

Energies and Machines

Content

A Look Ahead

How Energy Is Transferred

"Psssst. Drop your pencil at exactly 9:15. Pass it on."

A little mischief is about to take place, and a substitute's teaching day is about to take a turn for the worse. It's an old prank, but it will work once again. At precisely 9:15, 25 pencils fall from desktops to the floor, and innocent faces gaze about, waiting for the substitute's reaction.

I'll bet that the conspirators in the old drop-the-pencils-on-the-floor routine don't realize that they are demonstrating an important scientific phenomenon—the process of energy change. Imagine that the substitute teacher outsmarted the class by not reacting to the tap, tap, tap of the pencils and the class decided to try a repeat performance. Follow the energy changes as the prank is recycled.

When you pick up the pencil from the floor and place it on your desk, you do work and use energy. Your body uses some of the energy created by the chemical breakdown of the food you eat. This energy enables you to move, grasp, and lift. It may surprise you to learn that when you pick up the pencil, some of the energy that you use increases the pencil's potential energy. The pencil resting on the desk has some potential energy. When it is lifted above the desktop, it has even more. It is higher above the earth than it was before, and if you drop it again, you will hear a sound when it hits the floor. That sound is produced when the potential energy of the falling pencil is converted to the energy of motion.

Energy of motion is called *kinetic energy*. The amount of kinetic energy of an object is equal to $1/2mv^2$ (one-half the object's mass times its velocity squared). As the pencil falls, it moves faster and faster, continually gaining kinetic energy. When it hits the floor, its acquired kinetic energy causes the floor and itself to vibrate, producing a sound wave (a vibration that moves through the air). The pencil and the floor also heat up slightly. The original potential energy of the pencil was transformed into sound energy and heat energy.

The ability of energy to change its form is the basis of the *law of conservation of energy*. This important law simply states that energy is neither created nor destroyed. Whenever we use energy, we change its form, but we do not use it up. The energy we use may be changed to a less useful form, but it still exists. In the example of the pencil being picked up, placed on a table, and dropped again, some of the sun's energy was stored in food, your digestive and cellular-respiration processes released some of this energy, and you used this energy to lift the pencil. In the process, you transferred some of this energy to the pencil in the form of heat. The pencil acquired potential energy from its new position, and as it fell, it displayed increasing kinetic energy. The kinetic energy was changed to heat and sound. It is at least theoretically possible, if difficult in practice, to recapture this heat and sound energy and reuse it. All the energy you used to pick up the pencil still exists. It has just changed to other forms of energy.

According to Albert Einstein, energy and matter are related. In fact, they can be considered one and the same, since each can be converted to the other. Einstein's equation $E = mc^2$ does not contradict the law of conservation of energy because mass can be viewed as stored energy. Scientists no longer say that energy is never used up; instead, they say that the total amount of energy and mass in the universe is never used up. The interchangeability of mass and energy has resulted in the use of a more general law than either the law of conservation of energy or the law of conservation of mass. Now it is generally agreed that we should think in terms of a *law of conservation of mass and energy.*

Electrical Energy

 The bright flash of lightning jumping across the night sky and the subdued light coming from a desk lamp are both produced by electrical energy. They are similar to each other in that the source of their energy is electrons. They are different, however, in that lightning is a form of static electricity and the light from a desk lamp is a form of current electricity.

Static Electricity

Lightning, a spark jumping from your fingertip to a metal doorknob, and the clinging together of articles of clothing when they are removed from a clothes drier are all forms of *static electricity.* In order to understand them, you will need to review your knowledge of atoms. An atom consists of protons, neutrons, and electrons. Each proton has a positive charge—one unit of positive energy. Each electron has a negative charge—one unit of negative energy. Neutrons have no charge. Because atoms normally have the same number of electrons as protons, the positive and negative charges cancel each other out. As a result, atoms usually have no charge; they are considered neutral.

If, however, an electron is removed from a neutral atom, the atom is left with a positive charge. If an electron is added to a neutral atom, the atom acquires a negative charge. When certain materials are rubbed together, electrons are transferred from one surface to the other. In other words, one surface gains electrons and acquires a negative charge. The other surface, having lost electrons, is left with a positive charge. When a surface has acquired a strong negative charge, the extra electrons may jump to a neutral or positive object. You see this jump of electrons when you see a spark. A spark is a rapid movement of a number of electrons through the air.

You may have had the exciting adolescent experience of kissing a boyfriend or girlfriend with braces and being shocked by a spark. The excitement may have come from the kiss, but the shock was the result of static electricity. Electrons were probably inadvertently rubbed from the fibers of a rug or other floor covering by the soles of the "kisser" or "kissee," giving that person's body a surplus negative charge. The extra charge was removed by the spark jumping from the negatively charged person to the neutrally charged person.

Lightning is a giant spark that sometimes occurs when clouds that have acquired a charge suddenly discharge electrons. The rapid outward movement of the air heated by the lightning causes the sound wave that reaches our ears as thunder.

Current Electricity

Sometimes, it seems that my doorbell never stops ringing, and if I am busy, I get grumpier each time it rings. If I get grumpy enough, sometimes I curse Benjamin Franklin, Thomas Edison, and my local electric company all in one breath for bringing electrical energy to my home. Even so, I know we are living at a time when electricity is a necessity, not a luxury. Occasional electrical blackouts bring activities to a grinding halt: Traffic lights don't work; elevators stop wherever they happen to be; heating and cooling equipment stops functioning; lights go out; and food in refrigerators begins to rot. Electricity has become a necessity for us because it is an excellent and convenient form of energy. It can be converted to heat, to light, and to sound. It can also be used to operate electric motors that cause objects to move.

Current electricity comes from a stream of electrons moving through a conductor. The rate at which the electrons move through the conductor is called *current*. So many electrons flow through a given point in a conductor in a short time that scientists have found it useful to have a unit to represent a large number of electrons flowing through a current. The unit for measuring electrical current is the *ampere*. It is equal to the flow of 6.25×10^{18} electrons past a point in a conductor in 1 second. Electron current that moves in just one direction is termed *direct current*. Electricity from dry cells (batteries) is direct current. Current that changes direction is known as *alternating current*. Electricity for home or industrial use is alternating current.

A *conductor* is any material that electrons can move though easily. Such a material offers little *resistance* to the flow of electrons. The amount of resistance to the flow of electrical energy is measured in *ohms*. Examples of materials that are good conductors include copper, silver, gold, and aluminum. Energy is transferred through a conductor by a process that includes high-energy electrons imparting their energy to the outermost electrons of adjacent atoms of the conductor.

Not all substances are good electrical conductors. Wood, rubber, plastic, and dry air are examples of substances that do not carry electrical energy very well. Because these materials are poor conductors, they offer high resistance to the flow of electron and are called *insulators*.

Some substances—for example, germanium, silicon, and selenium—are neither conductors nor insulators. They are *semiconductors* that can be used to make tiny electrical devices to control the flow of electrons. Semiconductors are widely used in the fabrication of computer chips.

Electrical Circuits

Figure 18A.1 illustrates a simple electrical circuit. In an electrical circuit, electrons with a great deal of energy leave a source (in this case, a dry cell), move through a conductor (a wire), lose some energy in a load or resistance (a light bulb), and return to the source. As long as the switch is closed (the wires are connected), energy is transmitted through the circuit. The light bulb—the resistance—converts some of the electrical energy to light energy.

In the type of electrical circuit illustrated in Figure 18A.1, chemical reactions in the dry cells provide the push that starts and keeps high-energy electrons flowing

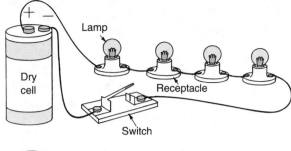

FIGURE 18A.1
In this electric circuit, the lamps are wired in series.

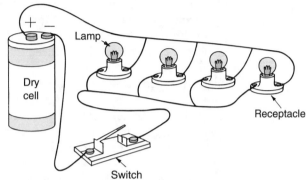

FIGURE 18A.2
When lamps are wired in parallel, as shown here, the bulbs will remain lit even if one goes out.

into the conductor. The electrons leave the negative pole, or port, and return to the dry cell at the positive pole, or port. The amount of push that causes the electrons to move through a circuit is called the *voltage*. The voltage that a dry cell can produce can be measured by determining the amount of work that the electrons do in the circuit. The unit of measurement for voltage is *volts*.

Although there are many ways to attach sources of high-energy electrons, conductors, and loads to each other, we usually concern ourselves with two basic circuits: series circuits and parallel circuits. A *series circuit* has only one path for electrons. A circuit that has more than one path for electrons is a *parallel circuit*. Figure 18A.1 shows a series circuit. Figure 18A.2 shows a parallel circuit.

Since there is only one path, the current is the same throughout a series circuit. In a parallel circuit, however, the current is divided among many paths. If one light bulb in a series circuit burns out, all the light bulbs will go out because only one path for electrons exists. If a light bulb in one branch of a parallel circuit burns out, the bulbs in the other branches will remain lit.

Magnets, Generators, and Motors

Although chemical reactions in dry cells can start a flow of electrons through a conductor, moving a conductor through a magnetic field or moving a magnet so that the lines of force in the magnetic field cut through the conductor can also start a flow of electrons. Metals that have the ability to attract iron, steel, and some other metals are said to have a property called *magnetism*. Magnetite, or lodestone, is a naturally occurring iron ore that has such magnetic properties. Alnico, a material that contains aluminum, nickel, cobalt, and iron, can be used to make a permanent magnet, even though aluminum, nickel, cobalt, and iron are not naturally magnetic. When these substances are brought near a strong magnet, they become magnetic.

All magnets have two poles—a north pole and a south pole. A bar magnet suspended at its center by a string will rotate until one end points north. The magnet end that points north is known as the *north-seeking pole.* The other end of the magnet is the *south-seeking pole.* If two **N** poles or two **S** poles are brought near each other, they will repel. When unlike poles are brought near each other, they attract. The rotation of a freely suspended bar magnet until it is oriented north and south is evidence that the earth itself is a magnet. The earth's magnetic pole attracts the pole of a magnet.

Around all magnets is a region that we call a *magnetic field.* If we move a conductor through a magnetic field so that it cuts through the lines of force in the field, an electric current will be produced in the conductor. An electrical generator produces electrical energy either by spinning a coiled conductor between the poles of a magnet or by rotating a magnet or series of magnets around a coiled conductor. Of course, a source of energy is needed to spin the coiled conductor or rotate the magnets. For commercial electrical generators that source may be moving water; fossil fuels such as coal, gas, and oil; or nuclear fission.

An electrical generator permits us to produce electricity. An electric motor permits us to put electricity to work moving objects. A simple electric motor converts electrical energy into the energy of motion by means of a coil of wire wrapped around a metal core. This wire-wrapped core is suspended between the magnetic poles of a permanent magnet. When a current flows through the coil, it becomes a magnet. The coil's **N** and **S** poles are repelled by the **N** and **S** poles of the permanent magnet. As a result of this repulsion, the coil turns. If we change the direction of flow of electricity through the coil, the location of its **N** and **S** poles will change. The coil will continue to spin as its ends are continually repelled by the poles of the permanent magnet.

Sound Energy

Sounds affect us in many different ways. The purring of a kitten brushing against your leg may make you feel wanted. The chirping of baby birds may make you feel joyful. The uproarious and chaotic sounds of sanitation workers waking up your neighborhood with an early morning symphony of bangs, crunches, screeches, and shouts may annoy you immensely. But what causes the sounds that bring you pleasure or irritation?

What Causes Sound?

All sounds, whether they come from a garbage-can orchestra or a kitten, are produced by vibrating matter. A vibrating object receives energy from a source (a kitten or a dropped garbage can) and transfers energy to a medium, such as air. The medium carries the energy away from the vibrating object. Sound travels in all directions from its source. In other words, you can hear a sound whether your ears are above it, to the side of it, or below it.

A vibrating tuning fork is a good example of a source of sound. When a tuning fork is struck, its prongs move back and forth rapidly. When a prong moves in one direction, it presses together the modules in the air ahead of it. This pressed-together air is known as a *compression.* As the tuning fork moves in the opposite direction, it causes a portion of air to pull apart. This area is known as a *rarefaction.* The movement of each prong back and forth alternately produces compression and rarefaction.

The molecules in the air disturbed by the vibration of the tuning fork during compression transfer energy to adjacent molecules before returning to their original positions during rarefaction. The newly disturbed molecules pass some of their energy on to still other molecules, and the process is repeated. If you could see the molecules being disturbed, you would see areas of compression and rarefaction, or *sound waves,* being continuously created and moving away from the source of the vibration. A full sound wave consists of one compression and one rarefaction.

Sound waves require a medium for transmission. They cannot travel through a vacuum, so if you are wondering how astronauts communicate with one another in the vacuum of space, they do so using radio transmissions. Radio waves do not require a medium. Sound waves travel most rapidly through solids and least rapidly through gases. At a temperature of 0°C, sound travels at a speed of 340 meters per second (about 1,090 feet per second) in air. In water, sound travels at about 1,420 meters a second (about 4,686 feet a second).

The *wavelength* of a sound wave is the distance between the centers of two rarefactions. The amount of energy contained in a wave is interpreted by our ears as the loudness or softness of a sound. The loudness, or *intensity,* of a sound is measured in decibels. The *pitch* of a sound—how high or low the sound is—depends on the number of complete vibrations that the vibrating object makes in one second. This rate of vibration is known as the *frequency.*

Sound Can Be Absorbed or Reflected

Sound waves that strike a surface may be so strong that they travel through the object struck. However, some surfaces absorb little sound and cause the sound wave being received to bounce off the surface, or be reflected. Reflected sound waves that can be distinguished from the original sound are known as *echoes.* Although echoes are interesting to hear, they can be distracting. Therefore, many classrooms are fitted with sound-absorbing tiles or draperies.

Some of the energy carried by a sound wave causes the surface of the object it strikes to heat up slightly. Usually, the amount of heat produced cannot be detected without the use of special instruments.

Light Energy

 Light energy, like sound energy, travels in waves, but a light wave is very different from a sound wave. Light waves travel at the speed of 300,000 kilometers per second (about 186,000 miles per second) and do not require a medium. Thus, light waves, unlike sound waves, can travel through a vacuum.

Light energy is produced from other types of energy. If we burn a substance, one of the products of combustion is light energy. The light is released as a result of the electrons in the substance changing energy levels as new compounds are formed. Electric light bulbs change electrical energy to light energy. The light energy that reaches us from the sun and other stars is the result of nuclear explosions. On stars, huge amounts of matter are converted to energy as a result of nuclear fusion. In nuclear fusion, hydrogen atoms are fused together to form helium atoms, a process accompanied by the release of light energy as well as other types of energy.

Light energy can be transformed into other forms of energy, such as heat or electricity. If you've ever had a sunburn, you've experienced both the conversion of light energy into heat (as your skin became warm) and the effect of light energy on the molecules of substances that make up your skin (as it turned red or blistered).

The Reflection and Refraction of Light

Light is able to pass through some materials, such as clear plastic or glass. A material that light can pass through is called *transparent*. Materials that light cannot pass through are called *opaque*. Materials that permit some, but not all, light to pass through are called *translucent*. Windows made of frosted glass are translucent.

As light passes from one medium to another, it is bent, or *refracted*. Light traveling through air bends as it enters water, glass, or clear plastic. This bending, or refraction, of light waves can be put to good use. A lens, for example, changes the appearance of objects because the image we see through the lens is produced by rays of light that have been bent. Eyeglasses, microscopes, hand lenses, and telescopes all provide images formed by light rays that have been refracted.

A *convex* lens is thicker in the middle than it is at its edges. Such a lens pulls light rays together. The point at which rays of light are brought together by the lens is called the *focal point*. The distance from the focal point to the center of the lens is the lens's *focal length*. When light is reflected from an object through a convex lens, the rays of light are brought together at the focal point and an image is formed. The size, position, and type of image formed depend on the distance of the object from the lens. If the object is more than one focal length from the lens, the image is inverted and formed on the opposite side of the lens. This type of image is called a *real image,* and it can be projected onto a screen. If the image is two focal lengths away, the image is the same size as the object.

If the object is less than one focal length from the lens, the image formed is magnified and rightside up. This type of image is called a *virtual image.* It is formed on the same side of the lens as the object and can be seen by looking through the lens toward the object, but it cannot be placed on a screen. When you use a convex lens as a magnifier, the image you see is a virtual image.

The refraction of light through a lens can be illustrated with a *ray diagram.* Look at the ray diagrams in Figure 18A.3. As you study them, note that the *principal axis* is an imaginary line passing perpendicular to the lens through its center. The *virtual focus* is the point on the axis at which the light would converge if you passed the light through the lens to the object, rather than from the object to the lens.

A lens that is thicker at its edges than at its center is a *concave lens*. A concave lens causes light rays to bend toward its edges. This type of lens can only produce virtual images that are smaller than the real objects (see Figure 18A.4).

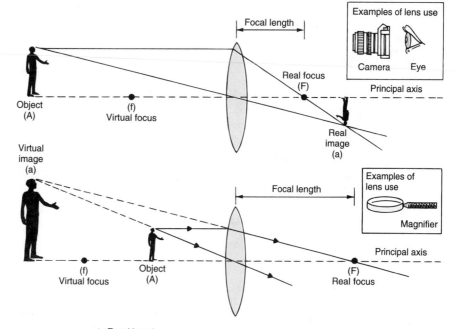

FIGURE 18A.3
These ray diagrams for convex lenses illustrate how a convex lens focuses light. Light passing through the lens converges to form an image that can be seen on a screen.

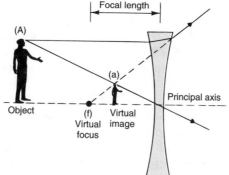

FIGURE 18A.4
As this ray diagram for a concave lens illustrates, the lens disperses light, and the image produced cannot be seen on a screen.

Light, Prisms, and Color

Have you ever been surprised to see an array of colors projected on a wall or ceiling as a result of sunlight passing through a crystal glass? This band of colors is called a *spectrum*. Some pieces of glass are made to separate sunlight or artificial light into a spectrum. A triangle-shaped piece of such glass is called a *prism*.

The colors of a spectrum represent the components of a light wave that enters a prism. As the light wave is refracted by the prism, the light is separated according to wave lengths. Each wavelength corresponds to a different color. The colors of a spectrum caused by the refraction of light by a prism are red, orange, yellow, green, blue, indigo, and violet.

The color of an object we see is a property of the wave length reflected from the object. *Pigments*—the chemical substances that we usually think of as the sources of color—actually produce their effects because they absorb some light waves and reflect others. Grass is green to our eyes because pigments in grass absorb the red, orange, yellow, blue, indigo, and violet waves and reflect the green.

427

Heat Energy

 Suppose that one hot summer afternoon, you bought a double-dip chocolate ice cream cone and decided to sit in the park while you ate it. As you walked toward the park clutching your cone, you would certainly notice the effect of heat on ice cream. Heat from the hot surrounding air will flow to the colder ice cream, causing an increase in the temperature of the ice cream, a lowering of the temperature of the surrounding air, and the immediate need for a napkin as the change in the temperature of the ice cream results in a change in the ice cream's state—from solid to liquid. The phenomenon of melting can be a good starting point for understanding heat and how it brings about change.

What Is Heat?

Heat is energy that travels from a warm substance to a cool substance. Keep in mind that all substances are made of molecules, and molecules, even in solids, are in constant motion. The motion and positions of these molecules determines the internal energy of (the energy within) a substance. If the molecules in a substance move slowly, the substance has a low level of internal energy. If the molecules move rapidly, the substance has a high level of internal energy. *Temperature* is an indication of the internal energy of a substance. The higher the temperature of a substance, the greater its internal energy and the more heat it releases to a cool substance. The temperature of a substance is measured in *degrees*. There are two temperature scales in wide use: the Celsius, or centigrade, scale and the Fahrenheit scale.

A *thermometer*, which measures temperature, consists of a narrow column of mercury or tinted alcohol sealed in a glass tube. Changes in temperature cause the liquid in a thermometer to expand or contract. Since the mercury or alcohol within the thermometer expands and contracts more than the surrounding glass with each degree of temperature change, we can see changes in the mercury or alcohol level.

Two important markings on all thermometers are the freezing and boiling points of water. The Celsius thermometer shows the temperature at which water freezes as 0° and the temperature at which water boils as 100°. The Fahrenheit scale shows the temperature at which water freezes as 32° and the boiling temperature as 212°. Wherever possible, use a Celsius thermometer and Celsius measurements in the classroom.

How Is Heat Measured?

Since it is virtually impossible to add up the individual energies possessed by the millions of individual molecules found in even a very small amount of a substance, heat energy must be measured indirectly. This is done by measuring its effect on a substance. The standard unit of heat is the *calorie*, the heat required to raise the temperature of 1 gram of water 1° Celsius. Since this is a very small amount of heat, the *kilocalorie*, which equals 1,000 calories, is a more practical unit. The energy contained in foods is expressed in kilocalories.

In the English system of measurement, the British Thermal Unit (BTU) is the standard unit of heat. This is the amount of heat required to raise the temperature of 1 pound of water 1° Fahrenheit.

How Do Changes in State Occur?

When you knock on a door or kick a tire, your hand does not go through the door and your foot does not go through the tire, even though each object is made of millions of molecules that vibrate. Therefore, there must be some force that holds the molecules together. The forces that hold molecules together are known as *cohesive forces*. By adding heat to an object, we cause the individual molecules of the object to move more freely. If we add sufficient heat, the molecules of a solid will move out of their fixed positions, and the solid will melt to form a liquid. The addition of even more heat can cause the molecules in the liquid to break free of the cohesive forces. At this point, the liquid becomes a gas. These transformations are called *changes of state*.

Machines

It is our ability to harness the various types of energy discussed in the previous sections that permits us to use machines to do work. To understand how machines operate, you need to understand what a force is. In its simplest terms, a *force* is a push or a pull. Machines enable us to increase a force, increase the speed of an object, change the direction in which a force is acting, or change the place where a force is acting. Machines work by changing one form of energy to another.

Regardless of the type of machine we study, we are always concerned with two forces—the effort and the resistance. The *effort* is the force we apply. The *resistance* is the force we overcome. We are also concerned with the amount of resistance that can be overcome by the application of a given effort. In scientific terms, this quantity is known as the *mechanical advantage*. There are various ways of calculating the mechanical advantage of a machine. In many cases, we can simply divide the resistance by the effort.

When we use a machine, we put energy into it. But not all of this energy goes into moving the resistance; some is lost to friction. The *efficiency* of a machine is a comparison of the work done by the machine (the energy put out by the machine) with the work (energy) put into it.

In Chapter 17A, Newton's Laws were discussed. You will recall that they are used to explain how forces can change the motion of objects. Humans discovered, through the invention of simple machines, that they could multiply the force they could apply to an object or change the direction in which an effort force is applied.

Simple Machines

You may not realize it, but the schoolyard seesaw is a simple machine, a *lever*. Wheelbarrows and fishing poles are also levers, as are crowbars, shovels, hammers, and oars. All levers, regardless of shape, have three parts: *a fulcrum, an effort arm,* and *a*

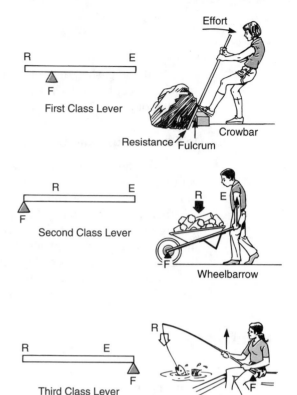

FIGURE 18A.5
There are three classes of levers. In a first-class lever, the fulcrum falls between the resistance and the effort. In a second-class lever, the fulcrum is at one end, the effort at the other end, and the resistance at some point between the two. In a third-class lever, the effort is applied between the fulcrum and the resistance.

resistance arm. As shown in Figure 18A.5, there are three types, or classes, of levers. Note the location of the effort, resistance, and fulcrum in each type. It is the position of the fulcrum that determines the type of lever.

Levers are not the only simple machines. Others are the wheel and axle, the pulley, the inclined plane, the screw, and the wedge. All other machines (which are known as *compound machines*) combine at least two simple machines.

The *wheel and axle* can be thought of as two circular objects, one larger than the other. The larger one is the wheel; the smaller one is the axle. Think of the wheel as a lever that can be moved in a complete circle around its fulcrum. The axle is the wheel's fulcrum and is at the center of the wheel. Examples of the wheel and axle are the windlass, water wheel, doorknob, pencil sharpener, screwdriver, windmill, and potter's wheel. A wheel and axle increase the effort force applied to it. When an effort force is applied to the wheel, a larger force is produced at the axle. However, the wheel moves slowly because of the resistance the effort must overcome. When effort is applied to the axle, there is less resistance, and the increased force moves the wheel more quickly. To find the ideal mechanical advantage of a wheel and axle, divide the radius of the wheel by the radius of the axle.

A *pulley* is a grooved wheel that turns loosely on an axle. The grooved wheel and axle do not have to turn together. The grooved wheel is called a *sheave*. The frame in which it rotates is called the *block*. Pulleys may be either fixed or movable. Figure 18A.6 shows examples of each. A fixed pulley does not travel with the resistance, or *load;* a movable pulley does. A block and tackle is a combination of a fixed pulley and a movable pulley. The mechanical advantage of a pulley can be calculated by dividing the effort distance (the distance the load moves) by the resistance distance (the distance the rope you pull moves) or by dividing the resistance by the effort. The ideal mechanical advantage of a pulley system can be determined simply by counting the number of supporting ropes. Figure 18A.6 shows how mechanical advantage can be achieved through an increase in the number of supporting ropes and pulleys in the system. Assuming the same effort is applied in each pulley system shown and that the pulley systems are frictionless, the three-pulley system can lift three times the weight that a single-pulley system can.

An *inclined plane* is a flat surface that is raised at one end. Ramps, slopes, and stairs are inclined planes. A resistance can be moved up an inclined plane to a desired height with less effort than it can be lifted directly to the same height. The ideal mechanical advantage of an inclined plane can be found by dividing the length of the inclined plane (the effort distance) by its height (the resistance distance).

A *screw* is a twisted or rolled-up inclined plane. Some common screws are a wood screw, a bolt, a screw jack, a brace and bit, and an auger. Screws are used to lift objects, to hold objects together, and to carry things from place to place. The rotary motion of a turning screw is changed into a straight-line motion by a lever, which is needed to turn the screw. The ideal mechanical advantage of a screw is the distance the effort moves divided by the distance the resistance moves (the distance between the threads of the screw, or its *pitch*).

A *wedge* is a double inclined plane. Some common wedges are knives, needles, axes, can openers, and cold chisels. Wedges are used to pierce, split, cut, and push apart things. Effort is needed to move the wedge into the resisting object. The ideal mechanical advantage of a wedge can be calculated by dividing its length by the thickness of its widest end.

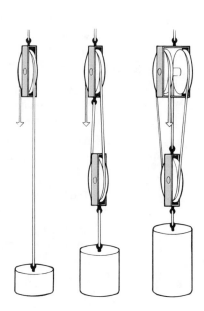

FIGURE 18A.6
A fixed pulley remains stationary, while a movable pulley travels with the object.

Friction

To work, every machine, whether simple or complex, must overcome friction. *Friction* is the resistance that an object meets when the surface of the object rubs against another surface. Friction retards motion and generates heat. It is the result of the irregularities that exist in every surface. Even surfaces that seem smooth to our touch consist of bumps and grooves. To overcome the attraction of particles of the surfaces to one another and the retardation of motion caused when a bump hits a groove, some of the energy used to move an object is changed to heat where surfaces are in contact.

There are many ways to reduce friction. Ball bearings, oils, and other lubricants permit surfaces to slide across one another more easily. If you drive a car, you should know that both the condition of bearings at the junction of the axle and wheels and the quality and quantity of lubricating oil in the engine must be checked periodically. If this is not done, the metal parts that are in contact will wear excessively or break.

Although we usually think of friction as a phenomenon that must be overcome, friction also has many positive benefits. Our ability to walk, for example, is a direct result of the friction between the bottoms of our shoes and the floor. Without friction, shoes would simply slide across floors and we would not be able to move forward.

Summary Outline

   I. Energy is never destroyed. It is changed from one form to another.

  II. Electricity is a form of energy that results from the storage or movement of electrons.
     A. Static electricity is produced by an imbalance between the positive and negative charges on the surface of an object.
     B. Current electricity is produced when electrons flow through a conductor.
        1. A source of current, a conductor, and a load (a device that converts electricity to some other form of energy) can be combined to form an electrical circuit.
        2. Generators produce electricity by moving a conductor across a magnetic field or vice versa.
        3. Motors convert electrical energy to kinetic energy.

  III. A sound wave is produced in a medium by the vibration of an object.

  IV. Light travels in waves that are refracted, or bent, as they pass from one medium to another.

   V. The heat energy contained by a substance is the total kinetic energy possessed by the atoms or molecules of the substance.

  VI. Machines are devices that enable us to increase a force, increase the speed of an object, change the direction of a force, or change the location of a force.

18B

Energies and Machines

Attention Getters, Discovery Activities, and Demonstrations

A Look Ahead

How Do Instruments Make Sounds? [PS 2]

MATERIALS	1 ruler Cymbals, bells, small drum, triangle, guitar, clarinet, or other instruments
MOTIVATING QUESTIONS	Point to each instrument and ask: • Do you think this instrument will make a high or low sound? • What part of this instrument does the musician vibrate?

DIRECTIONS

1. Ask the children what happens when you tap on your desk. Walk around the room tapping on various objects.
2. Indicate that tapping on an object causes it to move back and forth very quickly, or vibrate. Explain that there are many ways to make things vibrate.
3. Display each instrument, and have the children suggest what parts vibrate.

For Young Learners

SCIENCE CONTENT FOR THE TEACHER

All sounds are the result of vibrating objects. High-pitched sounds come from objects that vibrate very fast. Each musical instrument produces a sound because the musician causes some part of it to vibrate.

Do Magnets Pull on All Objects? [PS 3]

MATERIALS	Assortment of objects such as a rubber band, a metal tack, a piece of chalk, paper clips Magnet
MOTIVATING QUESTIONS	• Which of these objects do you think will be pulled toward the magnet? • How are the objects that are pulled to the magnet different from objects that are not pulled?

DIRECTIONS

1. Write the names of the objects on the board.
2. Display the magnet, and have the children predict which objects will be pulled toward it. Note their predictions under the names of the objects you have written on the board.
3. Have the children touch each object with the magnet. Record the results in another row on the chart, and explain that the objects that are attracted are those that contain iron (steel).

SCIENCE CONTENT FOR THE TEACHER

A magnet has the ability to attract objects that contain iron, nickel, cobalt, and their alloys. Most common objects that are attracted to a magnet contain iron in the form of steel.

ATTENTION GETTERS

Why Do Some Machines Need Oil? [PS 2]

MATERIALS

1 ice cube   Sandpaper
1 saucer   1/4 cup of sand
1 wooden block   1 can of motor oil

MOTIVATING
QUESTIONS

- Which will move more easily—the ice cube on the plate or the block on the sandpaper?
- Why do you think a car needs oil?

DIRECTIONS

1. Show the children how easily the ice cube slides across the plate, and then show them how difficult it is to move the wooden block across the sandpaper. Explain that it is difficult for car tires to stop or move forward on roads that are covered with snow or ice.
2. Ask the children for ideas about what could be done to make it easier for tires to start and stop in ice and snow.
3. Demonstrate how friction can be increased by sprinkling some sand on the plate and sliding the ice cube across the sand. Display the can of oil, and discuss its use as a liquid that permits the metal parts of an engine to slide over one another easily.

SCIENCE
CONTENT FOR
THE TEACHER

The ice cube on the plate melts slightly, producing a layer of water that reduces the friction between the ice cube and the plate. Reducing the friction makes it easier to move one surface over another surface. The presence of friction converts some of the energy used to operate a machine into heat. Oil is frequently used to reduce this energy loss. The oil fills in some of the roughness on the metal surfaces so the parts ride on an oil film.

Can Sound Travel through a Solid Object? [PS 6]

For Middle-
Level
Learners

MATERIALS FOR
EACH GROUP

Meterstick

MOTIVATING
QUESTIONS

- Have you ever heard sounds while you were swimming underwater?
- Have you ever heard sounds through a wall?
- Do you think sound can travel through a meterstick?

DIRECTIONS

1. Have the children work in pairs. One child will stand, and one child, the listener, will be seated. The child standing will hold one end of the meterstick, and the listener will hold the other. The meterstick should be parallel to the floor and 50 centimeters (about 20 inches) away from the listener's ear.
2. Have the child who is standing gently scratch his or her end of the meterstick. The listener should say whether he or she heard the scratches.

3. Repeat the procedure with the meterstick 25 centimeters (about 10 inches) away from the listener's ear.
4. Finally, have the listener position the meterstick so that it is gently touching the jawbone joint in front of his or her ear, and have the standing student gently scratch the meterstick. The listener should hear the sounds clearly.

SCIENCE CONTENT FOR THE TEACHER   Sound waves are disturbances that move through a medium. The medium may be a solid, liquid, or gas. A dense solid, such as the hardwood in a meterstick, carries sound waves very well. When the standing child scratches the meterstick, the sound waves travel through the meterstick and into the tissues and bones near the listener's ear, eventually reaching his or her eardrum.

What Type of Cup Loses Heat the Fastest? [PS 6]

MATERIALS   Plastic cup
Styrofoam cup
Ceramic cup
Metal cup or empty soup can with label removed
Source of hot water

MOTIVATING QUESTIONS
• If you were going to have a cup of hot chocolate on a cold day, which of these cups do you think would keep it hot for the longest time?
• If you were going to have a cup of cold chocolate milk on a hot day, which of these cups would keep it cold for the longest time?

DIRECTIONS
1. Display the cups, and have the children make predictions about their heat-retaining abilities. You may wish to have the children arrange the cups in order of their ability to retain heat.
2. Fill each cup half full of hot water. **Safety Note:** Alert the children to the dangers of working with hot water.
3. Have the children gently touch the outside of each cup as soon as the water is added and then gently touch the cup again after 1 minute and after 2 minutes.
4. Have the children discuss how their predictions matched or differed from their experiences.

SCIENCE CONTENT FOR THE TEACHER   All solids conduct heat; however, some conduct heat better than others. Metals tend to be good conductors of heat. Thus, a cup made of metal will permit heat to pass through it easily, resulting in the cooling down of the liquid within the cup. Ceramic materials, on the other hand, are good insulators, so most china cups will retain heat. The Styrofoam cup is an excellent insulator because bubbles of air are part of the materials that make up the cup.

ATTENTION GETTERS

Can You Move a Stream of Water without Touching It? [PS 4]

MATERIALS	Access to a water faucet Inflated balloon Plastic or hard rubber comb Piece of wool fabric

MOTIVATING QUESTION

- Do you think it is possible to move a stream of water without touching it or blowing on it?

DIRECTIONS

1. Keep the comb and balloon out of sight as you begin this activity. Turn the water faucet on so that it produces a thin stream of water, and ask the children how the stream could be moved without touching it.
2. Display the comb and the balloon. Run the comb through your hair or over the wool fabric a few times, and then move it near the stream of water. The water will bend toward the comb.
3. Repeat the demonstration using the balloon rubbed across the wool fabric.

SCIENCE CONTENT FOR THE TEACHER

The water has a neutral charge. The comb picks up a negative charge after it has been run through hair or over a sweater. When the comb is positioned near the water, negative ends of neutral water molecules move away from the negatively charged comb, leaving the positive ends on the portion of the molecules closest to the comb. These ends are attracted to the comb, causing the stream to bend. The same phenomenon can be observed if you use a charged balloon in place of the comb.

Move Those Loads: Making and Using a Simple Lever [PS 2]

OBJECTIVES

- The children will identify the effort force, load, and fulcrum of a lever.
- The children will construct a lever and make and test hypotheses about the effect of changing the fulcrum's position.

SCIENCE PROCESSES EMPHASIZED

Making hypotheses
Experimenting

MATERIALS FOR EACH CHILD OR GROUP

30 cm (12 in.) wooden ruler
Flat-sided pencil
2 paper cups
Masking tape
8 to 10 objects of equal mass, such as washers
Small objects to serve as loads: chalk sticks, boxes
   of paper clips, chunks of clay
Marking pen

For Young Learners

DISCOVERY ACTIVITIES

MOTIVATION On the day of the activity, take to class a block of wood with a nail partially embedded in it and a claw hammer. Before beginning the activity, demonstrate how to remove the nail using the claw end of the hammer. Tell the children that the hammer is a lever. Without pointing to the apparatus, review the meaning of effort force, load, and fulcrum (turning point). Then ask if they can locate the effort force, load, and fulcrum. Leave this as an open question, and begin the activity.

DIRECTIONS 1. Distribute the cups, rulers, tape, flat-sided pencil, washers, and objects used as loads to each group.
2. Have the children make one label reading *Effort Force* and attach it to one cup. Have them make another label reading *Load* and attach it to the second cup. Have them tape a cup to each end of the ruler.
3. Tell the children to place a load in the Load cup and center the ruler on the flat-sided pencil. Have them determine how much effort force is needed to move the load by adding washers to the Effort Force cup.
4. Have the children make and test hypotheses about the effect of moving the fulcrum closer to or further from the load.

KEY DISCUSSION QUESTIONS 1. Where is the load, fulcrum, and effort force in your lever? *The load is the weight of the objects in the Load cup, the fulcrum is the top of the pencil, and the effort force is the weight of the washers in the Effort Force cup.*
2. When did you use the least amount of force to move the load? The most? *The least force was needed when the fulcrum was near the Load cup. The most was needed when the fulcrum was close to the Effort Force cup.*
3. When you moved the load with a small force, what moved the greatest distance—the load or the effort force? *The effort force.*

SCIENCE CONTENT FOR THE TEACHER The lever constructed by the children is a lever of the first class. This lever multiplies the effect of an effort force. A small effort force moving a large distance can move a large load a small distance.

EXTENSION *Science/Art:* Some children may enjoy discovering that mobiles are really levers. The children can use thread, plastic straws, paper cutouts of birds, or other objects to assemble mobiles consisting of various horizontal arms (lever arms) made of plastic straws.

Can You Build a No-Frills Telephone? [S&T 1]

OBJECTIVES • The children will construct a telephonelike device that allows them to communicate with one another.
• From their experimentation, the children will infer that a vibration moving through a thread is the basis for how their devices work.

SCIENCE	Communicating
PROCESSES	Inferring
EMPHASIZED	

MATERIALS FOR
EACH CHILD
OR GROUP

2 paper cups
2 m (about 7 ft.) or longer length of strong sewing thread or dental floss
2 toothpicks or buttons
Additional thread, buttons, and cups for those children who wish to
  invent more complicated phone circuits

MOTIVATION

Display the materials. Ask the children if they can guess what they will be making with them. After they have made some guesses, tell them that they will be making telephones that will actually work.

DIRECTIONS

1. Before distributing the cups, punch a small hole in the center of the bottom of each one. You can use scissors or a pencil to make the holes.
2. Distribute two toothpicks or buttons, two cups, and a length of thread to each group. Have the children thread the string through the prepunched hole in the bottom of the cup and knot one end of the thread around the center of the toothpick or through the button. You may need to assist some children with this. They should then do the same with the other cup.
3. When the thread between the cups is stretched, the toothpick will keep the thread end in the cup. If the thread is taut, the sound of one child speaking directly into a cup will be transmitted along the thread to the cup held to a listener's ear.
4. Encourage the children to try their telephones. Some groups may want to construct more complicated telephone circuits.

KEY
DISCUSSION
QUESTIONS

1. Which cup is used like the bottom part of a telephone? *The speaker's cup.*
2. Which cup is used like the top part of a telephone? *The listener's cup.*
3. How could you make a telephone that will let one person speak and two people listen? *Answers will vary. Have children try an experiment to test out their ideas. Some will find that tying a second cup somewhere along the string will permit the second listener to hear the sounds made by the speaker.*

SCIENCE
CONTENT FOR
THE TEACHER

When we speak, our vocal cords vibrate and produce sound waves that travel through the air. When the children use their string telephones, sound waves vibrate the bottom of the speaker's cup. These vibrations move through the string and cause the bottom of the listener's cup to vibrate and reproduce the sound waves in the air inside the listener's cup. These sound waves strike the listener's eardrum and cause it to vibrate. In a real telephone, the vibrations produced by the speaker are converted to variations in electrical impulses that travel through wires.

DISCOVERY ACTIVITIES

EXTENSION   *Science/Art:* Have the children design and then draw various arrangements of thread and cups for more complex telephone systems prior to further experimentation.

Simple Circuits [S&T 4]

For Middle-Level Learners

OBJECTIVES
- The children will assemble a simple series circuit and a simple parallel circuit.
- The children will describe the similarities and differences between a series circuit and a parallel circuit.

SCIENCE PROCESSES EMPHASIZED
Observing
Experimenting
Communicating

MATERIALS FOR EACH CHILD OR GROUP
3 bulbs
3 bulb sockets
2 dry cells, size "D"
Switch
8 pieces of insulated bell wire, each 2.5 cm (about 1 in.) long and stripped at the ends

MOTIVATION   This activity should follow a class discussion about the nature of simple circuits and the functions of various circuit components. Display the materials, and make schematic drawings on the chalkboard of a three-lamp series circuit and a three-lamp parallel circuit (like the ones shown on the facing page). Have a general discussion of how the circuit diagrams are alike and different. Keep the discussion open ended, and begin the activity at an appropriate point in the discussion.

DIRECTIONS
1. You may wish to have half of the groups construct series circuits and the other half construct parallel circuits. If you happen to have double the amount of equipment listed, each group can construct both circuits.
2. Have the children light the bulbs to demonstrate how their circuits operate. Suggest that they make observations of what occurs when one bulb is removed from each type of circuit.
3. Allow the children time to make observations, and then have a class discussion about how the circuits are the same and different.

KEY DISCUSSION QUESTIONS
1. What do the symbols in the circuit diagrams stand for? *(See figures on page 441.)*
2. How is the path of the electrons different in the two circuits? *In the series circuit, all the electrons go through all the bulbs. In the parallel circuit, they split up: Some go to each bulb.*

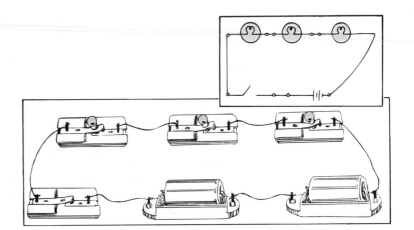

A series circuit

A parallel circuit

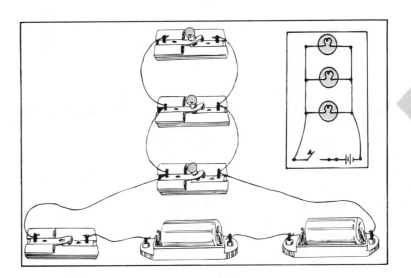

3. What happened when you took one lamp out of each type of circuit? Why? *In the series circuit, the other bulbs went out. In the parallel circuit, the other bulbs got a little brighter. The series circuit bulbs went out because there was a gap (a break) in the circuit, so the current stopped. In the parallel circuit, the electrons stopped going through one path and joined the electrons going through the other paths. The bulbs got brighter because they had extra current going through them.*

SCIENCE CONTENT FOR THE TEACHER Circuits can be represented by diagrams and symbols like those shown above. In a series circuit, all the electrons go through all the bulbs (or other resistances) in the circuit. A gap, or break, at any place in the circuit will stop the flow of current through the entire circuit. A defective bulb, a loose connection, or a break in the wire will stop the flow of current. If the voltage is large enough, electrons may jump across gaps in the circuit, a phenomenon evidenced as a spark. In a parallel circuit, the current divides. Some of it flows through each resistance. If a resistance is removed from a parallel circuit, the current that would normally have flowed through it is distributed to the remaining resistances.

EXTENSIONS   *Science:* If you have access to a small electric motor, you may wish to have a group substitute it for a bulb in the series circuit and in the parallel circuit to determine the effect of a running motor on the brightness of the bulbs.

You may wish to challenge one or two groups to combine their resources and make a circuit that is partly parallel and partly series.

Science/Social Studies: Some children might enjoy studying one of the bulbs more closely to see if they can find the path that the electrons take. This could be the beginning of some library research on the scientist who invented the incandescent bulb—Thomas Edison. Have the children focus their attention on how everyday life has been affected by Edison's many inventions.

Electrical Conductors and Nonconductors [S&T 4]

OBJECTIVES   • The children will distinguish between materials that conduct electricity and materials that do not.
• The children will make hypotheses about characteristics of conductors.

SCIENCE   Experimenting
PROCESSES   Making hypotheses
EMPHASIZED

MATERIALS FOR   Dry cell, size "D"
EACH CHILD   Dry-cell holder
OR GROUP   Flashlight bulb
                   Flashlight-bulb holder
                   Strips of aluminum foil
                   3 pieces of insulated bell wire, each about 25 cm (10 in.) long
                       and stripped at the ends
                   Assortment of 2.5 cm (1 in.) lengths of bell wire of various thicknesses
                   Box of paper clips
                   Sharpened pencils
                   Box of toothpicks
                   Box of crayons
                   Box of steel nails

MOTIVATION   This activity should follow activities or class discussions about the characteristics of simple circuits. Ask the children to describe the function of the wire used in circuits. They will indicate that the wire serves as the path for electrons. Then display the materials, and indicate that the children will be finding out whether the electrons can pass through them.

DIRECTIONS   1. Have each child or group assemble a simple circuit using two of the pieces of wire, a dry cell, and a bulb. After the bulb lights, detach the wire attached to the negative end of the battery and attach the third wire in its place. The exposed ends of the two wires (one from the dry cell and one from the bulb holder) will serve as probes to be touched to the materials tested.

2. Ask the children to check that their testers work by briefly touching the exposed ends together. If the dry cell is fresh, the bulb is in working condition, and all the connections have been properly made, the bulb will light.

3. When all the circuits are working, have the children test the various materials by touching both exposed wires to the materials at the same time. If the material is a conductor, the circuit will be completed and the bulb will light. Have the children note which materials are good conductors of electricity. They should manipulate each material to see if those that are conductors share similar characteristics.

4. When this has been accomplished, have the children make hypotheses that distinguish electrical conductors from nonconductors.

KEY
DISCUSSION
QUESTIONS
1. Which of the materials were good conductors of electricity? *Aluminum foil, paper clips, wire pieces.*
2. Which of the materials did not conduct electricity? *Toothpicks, crayons.*
3. Was there anything that conducted electricity but conducted it poorly? *The lead (graphite) in the pencil.*
4. What are some hypotheses that you made? *Metals conduct electricity.*
5. What other activities could you do to test your hypotheses? *Answers will vary.*

SCIENCE
CONTENT FOR
THE TEACHER
Substances that allow the movement of electrons with relatively little resistance are known as conductors. Materials that do not allow electrons to pass through them are insulators. There are no perfect conductors, since all materials offer some resistance to the flow of charges. Metals are better conductors than nonmetals. Metals differ in conductivity. The following metals are arranged from highest to lowest conductivity:

Silver	Platinum
Copper	Tin
Aluminum	Steel
Tungsten	Lead

D
I
S
C
O
V
E
R
Y

A
C
T
I
V
I
T
I
E
S

EXTENSIONS   *Science:* Some children may wish to invent activities that will reveal whether good electrical conductors are also good conductors of heat. Others may wish to modify their tester circuit so that the entire apparatus can be packaged in a small cardboard box. The tester should have two probes extending from the side and the light bulb extending from the top.

Science/Social Studies: Some children may be interested in discovering what areas of the world are sources of the various metals used in this activity. To identify these regions, the children can use an encyclopedia and look under headings such as "Copper" and "Aluminum."

The Ink-Lined Plane [PS 6]

OBJECTIVES
- The children will construct a simple device that can be used to measure forces.
- The children will use their force measurer to find how an inclined plane makes work easier.

SCIENCE PROCESSES EMPHASIZED
Experimenting
Measuring

MATERIALS FOR EACH CHILD OR GROUP
Piece of cardboard 25 × 12 cm (about 10 × 5 in.)
3 paper clips
Rubber band
1 m (40 in.) length of board
String
Small box of paper clips, crayons, or chalk
5 books
Wood wax and cloth for polishing the board

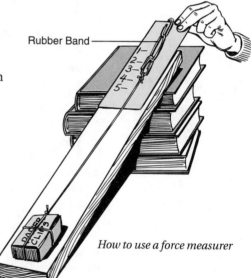

Rubber Band

How to use a force measurer

MOTIVATION   Start this activity with some humorous word play. Do not display any of the materials. Tell the children that today they are going to work with an "ink-lined plane." When you say the phrase, space the words as shown and do not write the words on the chalkboard. Tell the children that one year you had a student who thought you wanted him to build an "ink-lined plane" (say it exactly as you said it before). The children should be a little puzzled. Now show the children what the imaginary child built by making a paper airplane and drawing some lines across it. Explain that the child was really confused until you wrote the phrase on the chalkboard. Ask the children to guess what you wrote on the board.

When they have done this, write the words *inclined plane* on the chalkboard, bring out the materials, and discuss the characteristics of an inclined plane. Tell the children that in this activity, they are going to make a device that measures forces and then use it to see how an inclined plane makes work easier.

DIRECTIONS

1. Have each child or group of children make a force measurer by clipping one paper clip to the cardboard, attaching a rubber band to the paper clip, and clipping another paper clip to the end of the rubber band. Now have the children make their own scale divisions on the cardboard. The scale divisions shown in the illustration on page 444 are arbitrary, but the first division should began at the bottom of the rubber band.
2. Tell the children to assemble the inclined plane by elevating one end of the board and placing three books under it. The children should wax the board until its surface is smooth.
3. Have the children determine how much force is needed to lift the box of paper clips from the tabletop straight up to the high end of the board using their force measurers. To do this, they will need to tie a string around the box and attach the string to the paper clip hanging from the bottom of the rubber band on the force measurer. Have them note the amount of force required.
4. Now have them measure the force needed to move the paper-clip box to the same height by means of the inclined plane. They should pull the box up the length of the board, parallel to the surface of the board.
5. Have the children compare the amounts of force required and experiment with various loads and inclined-plane heights. Then hold a class discussion of the results.

KEY DISCUSSION QUESTIONS

1. Which required less force, pulling the load straight up or moving it along the sloping board? *Moving it along the board.*
2. Why do you think people use inclined planes? *You can move heavy objects up without applying a lot of force.*
3. Show the children that the distance the load moves vertically is the load distance, or resistance distance, and that the distance along the sloping board is the effort distance. Now ask the children how the effort distance compares with the load distance. *The effort distance is longer.* (This question helps the children see that inclined planes require that the small effort force moves over a long distance.)

SCIENCE CONTENT FOR THE TEACHER

The inclined plane is a simple machine used to move heavy objects to heights. Ramps used to load boxes on a truck and roads that slope upward are inclined planes. An inclined plane multiplies force at the expense of distance, since the effort force must move farther than the distance the load is raised. Steep inclined planes require more effort force than less steep planes.

EXTENSIONS   *Science:* You may wish to have two or three groups of children assemble inclined planes of various slopes and move the same load up all of them to observe the increased force needed on the steeper machines. If possible, secure a toy truck with wheels that roll easily and have the groups compare the effort forces required to move it up the various slopes.

Science/Math: You may wish to have some children measure the effort distance and load distance of an inclined plane and compare them. Then have the children make the inclined plane steeper and repeat their measurements of effort and load distance. They can then repeat their measurements with the inclined plane in more steep and less steep positions.

How Does Heating and Cooling Change a Balloon? [PS 3]

OBJECTIVE
- The children will predict and then observe how balloons are affected by heating and cooling.

SCIENCE
PROCESSES
EMPHASIZED

Observing
Predicting
Communicating

MATERIALS

2 or 3 round balloons
Hot plate
Saucepan 1/4 full of water
Access to a refrigerator

DEMONSTRATIONS

For Young Learners

MOTIVATION   Display the balloons. Then inflate each one to about one-half its capacity and tie a knot in the neck. If the balloons are new, stretch them a few times before inflating to make them more elastic. Ask the children to predict what will happen to the sizes of the balloons as they are heated and cooled.

DIRECTIONS
1. Have a volunteer draw the balloons at their exact sizes on the chalkboard.
2. Place one balloon on the saucepan so it is held above the surface of the water by the sides of the pan. Have another volunteer take the other balloon to the school kitchen to be stored in a refrigerator. Turn on the hot plate, and set the heat indicator to low or warm.
3. Have the children note changes in each balloon every half hour for the next 2 hours. After they have made their observations, have them try to explain what caused the changes.

KEY
DISCUSSION
QUESTIONS

1. Why do you think the heated balloon became larger? *The molecules of the gases in the air in the heated balloon started to move faster. They started to bounce into each other and the sides of the balloon more.*
2. Why do you think the cooled balloon became smaller? *It lost energy. The molecules of the gas slowed down and didn't bounce into each other or the sides as much. They moved closer together.*

SCIENCE
CONTENT FOR
THE TEACHER

The heat energy of an object is the total energy of motion of all atoms the object has. An object gains energy if it is placed in an environment that has more heat energy than it and loses heat energy if it is placed in an environment that has less heat energy than it.

EXTENSION

Science/Health: You may want to discuss how the loss of heat from an object can be diminished. This will offer the children an opportunity to talk about the need to wear particular types of clothing to decrease or increase heat loss.

Tuning Forks Feed Food for Thought [PS 1]

OBJECTIVES

- The children will observe that the source of the sound produced by a tuning fork is the vibration of the tines.
- The children will predict various effects that will occur when the tuning fork is struck vigorously.

SCIENCE
PROCESSES
EMPHASIZED

Observing
Predicting

MATERIALS

2 tuning forks that produce sounds of different pitches
Rubber striker (rubber tuning fork hammer)

MOTIVATION

Display the tuning forks, and ask the children if they have ever seen any objects like them before. Ask the children if they have any ideas about what these objects are used for.

DIRECTIONS

1. Without striking the fork, have the children sit quietly and listen to the natural sounds of the classroom and school. After a minute or two, gently strike one of the forks with the rubber hammer and have the children listen to the sound produced. Ask volunteers to touch, very gently, one of the tines after you have struck the fork. Have them tell the class what they feel.
2. Strike the tuning fork harder, and have the children listen to the change in the sound.

3. Ask the children to predict how the sounds produced by the two forks will differ. Strike one fork, stop its vibration, strike the other fork, and ask the children how correct their predictions were. If you happen to have a larger selection of tuning forks available, ask the children to place them in order from the highest pitch to lowest pitch. Check the children's ideas by striking each fork in turn.

KEY DISCUSSION QUESTIONS

1. Can you guess why the tuning fork is called a *fork? Answers will vary. Some children will note the resemblance between a tuning fork and a fork used for eating.*
2. How do you think the sound will change if I hit the tuning fork harder? *Answers will vary. Some children will say that the sound will be louder.*

SCIENCE CONTENT FOR THE TEACHER

When you strike a tuning fork, the tines vibrate back and forth. This vibration produces sound waves in the air. Although tuning forks are used for experimentations with sound, they are also used by piano tuners and others who need to hear sounds at exact pitches.

EXTENSION

Science/Music: Some children may be interested in how musical instruments amplify sounds. Display various musical instruments, and for each, have the children identify the part that vibrates and the part or parts that make sounds louder—for example, the wooden structure of the guitar amplifies the sound of the vibrating string.

You Could Hear a Pin Drop: The Conduction of Heat[1] [PS 6]

OBJECTIVES

- The children will observe the ability of various materials to conduct heat.
- The children will make a hypothesis concerning the nature of objects that conduct heat.
- The children will predict which of three objects will conduct heat the fastest.

SCIENCE PROCESSES EMPHASIZED

Observing
Making hypotheses
Predicting

For Middle-Level Learners

The apparatus for measuring the conduction of heat

DEMONSTRATIONS

MATERIALS	Candle
	Safety matches
	Container of water to extinguish matches
	5 steel pins
	Glass, steel, and brass (or aluminum) rods of equal thickness
	Chalk stick
	Old metal fork
	Long, narrow chip of pottery
	Support stamp and burette clamp (see illustration on page 448)
	Watch with second hand

MOTIVATION

This demonstration should follow a class discussion about energy and heat as a form of energy. **Safety Note:** The demonstration requires the lighting of a candle by you and manipulation of the candle flame by you. Appropriate safety measures should be observed.

Display all the materials, and indicate that you are going to do a demonstration that will help the children discover how well various materials conduct heat. Explain that you are going to attach a pin near one end of each rod with a dab of wax, heat the end of each rod, and measure the time for the wax to melt and the pin to fall. Select a responsible child to measure the length of time it takes the wax to melt.

DIRECTIONS

1. Fasten a steel pin to a dab of wax placed 4 centimeters (about 1.5 inches) from the end of each of the three rods. Do this by lighting the candle, allowing it to burn for 2 minutes, and then rolling the rod in the pool of wax beneath the candle flame. Briefly heat the head of a pin in the flame and press it into the wax. Repeat this procedure for the fork, the piece of pottery, and the chalk.
2. Place one of the rods in the burette clamp, and lower the clamp so that the end of the rod is about 1 centimeter from the tip of the flame (see illustration).
3. Ask your assistant to time how long it takes for the pin to drop.
4. Repeat steps 2 and 3 for the other two rods, and ask the class to make a hypothesis about the type of material that is a good conductor of heat.
5. Display the test objects, and have the children use their hypothesis to predict which will be the best heat conductor. Repeat steps 2 and 3 with each object.

KEY DISCUSSION QUESTIONS

1. Which rod was the poorest conductor? *Glass.*
2. What conclusion can you make about heat conducting? *Metals are good conductors of heat.*
3. What are some objects that are good conductors of heat? *Pots and pans.*
4. What test object did you predict to be the best conductor of heat? *The metal fork.*

D
E
M
O
N
S
T
R
A
T
I
O
N
S

SCIENCE
CONTENT FOR
THE TEACHER

The carrying of heat by a solid is called *conduction*. Heat energy is transferred through a conductor as a result of the increased movement of molecules at the point on the object where heat is applied. The increased motion of these molecules causes adjacent molecules to increase their energy.

In this activity, the glass rod will be the poorest conductor. The best heat conductor among the metal rods will be the aluminum one, followed by the brass, and then the steel.

EXTENSIONS

Science: You may wish to have some children find out how the transfer of heat takes place in air. They should focus their investigation on the term *convection.*

You may wish to have some children bring in samples of kitchen utensils that are both conductors and insulators (e.g., a stirring spoon with a metal end and a wooden handle).

Science/Math: You can extend this demonstration by fastening pins at regular intervals along each rod. The children can time how long it takes the heat to travel down the rods to release each pin. This data can then be graphed, with "Time for Pin to Drop" on the vertical axis and "Distance from Heat Source" on the horizontal axis.

Making Work Easier:
Using Fixed and Movable Pulleys [S&T 4]

OBJECTIVES

- The children will predict how a fixed pulley and a movable pulley can be used to make work easier.
- The children will observe the effect of using various pulley arrangements to move loads.
- The children will compare the required effort force and the direction of the effort force used in various pulley arrangements.

SCIENCE
PROCESSES
EMPHASIZED

Observing
Measuring
Predicting

MATERIALS

Spring scale
String
Rock that has about 100 grams of mass
Single fixed pulley
Single movable pulley
2 screw hooks
Supported horizontal wooden board

MOTIVATION   Prior to the demonstration, insert the screw hooks into the wooden support. Display the pulleys, and ask the children if they have ever seen one being used. Discuss various uses of pulleys, and then display the rock. Tell the children that pulleys make work easier and that they will observe this during the demonstration. Have a volunteer come forward to assist you.

DIRECTIONS

1. Have your assistant weigh the rock by tying a piece of string around it and attaching it to the spring scale. Write the weight on the board. Be sure that the children understand that the rock is the load to be moved with the pulleys. Attach the fixed pulley to the screw hook on the horizontal board, tie one end of a piece of string around the rock, and run the string through the pulley.
2. Ask the children to predict what the effect of using a fixed pulley will be. Have your volunteer carry out the demonstration, and ask the children to compare their predictions with the actual result.
3. Attach a string to the other screw hook, run one end of it through the pulley, and attach the rock to the pulley with another piece of string. Have your volunteer carry out the demonstration.
4. Now use the fixed pulley and the movable pulley together. Attach the string to the eye of the fixed pulley, and run the string through the bottom of the sheave of the movable pulley and up through the top of the sheave of the fixed pulley. Have your assistant repeat the demonstration.
5. Have the children compare the distance moved by the effort in step 4 with the distance moved by the load.

KEY
DISCUSSION
QUESTIONS

1. How does using a fixed pulley make work easier? *You can apply the effort force in a different location.*
2. How does using a movable pulley make work easier? *You use less force to move the load.*
3. About how much less effort do you need to raise a load with a movable pulley? Why? *You need about half as much. The load is held up by the hook and by the person holding the other end of the string.*
4. How does using a movable pulley and a fixed pulley together make work easier? *You use less force than the load's weight. The fixed pulley lets you change the direction of the effort force.*

SCIENCE
CONTENT FOR
THE TEACHER
Pulleys are simple machines that enable us to multiply the effect of an effort force or change the direction in which the effort force is applied. A fixed pulley performs the latter function. For example, a fixed pulley at the top of a flagpole makes it possible to move a flag upward by pulling down on the rope attached to the flag. A movable pulley attached to a load can ideally halve the effort needed to move the load. Friction, of course, diminishes the pulley's efficiency. When a movable pulley is used to lift a load, the effort force must move farther than the distance the load is lifted.

EXTENSIONS   *Science:* If you can acquire additional pulleys, some children may enjoy assembling more elaborate machines. A movable-and-fixed pulley arrangement (block and tackle) can be used to show how loads can be moved by quite small effort forces.

Science/Math: You can help children understand the amount of energy lost to overcoming of friction by comparing the actual mechanical advantage of the pulley (found by dividing the load by the effort) with the ideal mechanical advantage (found by dividing the load by the number of strands supporting the movable pulley).

Note

1. This demonstration is an adaptation of a portion of "Conduction and Non-Conduction," Module 70, *Science: A Process Approach II* (Lexington, MA: Ginn).

For
the Teacher's
Desk

Your Classroom Enrichment Handbook

Keeping Living Things . . . Alive   Living Materials in the Classroom   Tells you what to do to keep those green plants green and those animals happy and healthy.

   The Plant Picker   Would you like to have a classroom that is green year round with or without sunny windows? Here is a list of plants for sunny and not-so-sunny indoor locations.

Safety Management Helper   A checklist to use as you plan science experiences that meet the safety guidelines developed by the National Science Teachers Association.

Materials to Keep in Your Science Closet   A list of items you should have to give you flexibility when planning a unit or lesson and when *changing* one after it has started.

The Metric Helper   Confused by the metric system? Here are key pieces of metric information you will need to help children use it with their discovery activities.

Content Coverage Checklists   How will you decide whether CD-ROM software, optical disk software, elementary science textbooks, school curriculum guides, and other instructional materials attend to the basic concepts of the earth/space, life, and physical sciences? These checklists will give you an easy way to make comparisons.

Your Science Survival Bookshelf   The Bookshelf   Books to keep in your personal library as sources of easy-to-do, hands-on activities for children.

   The Magazine Rack   Help can arrive in your mailbox every month if you subscribe to one or more of these magazines.

Your Science Source Address Book

Free and Inexpensive Materials   Addresses of agencies and businesses that provide free or inexpensive materials to help you teach children science.

The "Wish Book" Companies   These companies produce or distribute a wide variety of teaching materials to help you create a discovery-based classroom. If your school provides funds for materials or if you have a benefactor, contact these companies to peruse their products.

Bilingual Child Resources   Are you teaching in a school where some or most of the children do not speak English as their primary language? If so, contact the agency near you and ask them to send you resources.

Special-Needs Resources   A list of addresses of agencies that provide materials to help you teach children with special needs.

Science Teachers Associations   Two heads are better than one, and thousands are better than two. Join one of these professional associations of educators who share ideas, projects, and activities.

NASA Teacher Resource Centers   If your children are "taking up space" under your guidance, here is a list of resource centers that each have an abundance of free or inexpensive materials about space exploration.

Keeping Living Things . . . Alive

Living Materials in the Classroom*

Animals

Before introducing animals into the classroom, check the policy of your local school district. When animals are in the classroom, care should be taken to ensure that neither the students nor the animals are harmed. Mammals protect themselves and their young by biting, scratching, and kicking. Pets such as cats, dogs, rabbits, and guinea pigs should be handled properly and should not be disturbed when eating. Consider the following guidelines for possible adoption in your science classroom.

1. Do not allow students to bring live or deceased wild animals, snapping turtles, snakes, insects, or arachnids (ticks, mites) into the classroom, as they are capable of carrying disease.
2. Provide proper living quarters. Animals are to be kept clean and free from contamination. They must remain in a securely closed cage. Provision for their care during weekends and holidays must be made.
3. Obtain all animals from a reputable supply house. Fish should be purchased from tanks in which all fish appear healthy.
4. Discourage students from bringing personal pets into school. If pets are brought into the classroom, they should be handled only by their owners. Provision should be made for their care during the day—give them plenty of fresh water and a place to rest.
5. When observing unfamiliar animals, students should avoid picking them up or touching them.
6. Caution students never to tease animals or insert fingers, pens, or pencils into wire mesh cages. Report animal bites and scratches to the school's medical authority immediately. Provide basic first aid.
7. Rats, rabbits, hamsters, and mice are best picked up by the scruff of the neck, with a hand placed under the body for support. If young are to be handled, the mother should be removed to another cage—by nature she will be fiercely protective.
8. Use heavy gloves for handling animals; have students wash their hands before and after they handle animals.
9. Personnel at the local humane society or zoo can help teachers create a wholesome animal environment in the classroom.

Plants

Create a classroom environment where there are plants for students to observe, compare, and possibly classify as a part of their understanding of the plant world.

*From *Science Scope* 13, no. 3 (November/December 1989), p. 517. Used with permission of the National Science Teachers Association.

Plants that are used for such purposes should be well-known to you. Plants that produce harmful substances should not be used.

Since many plants have not been thoroughly researched for their toxicity, it is important for students and teachers to keep in mind some common-sense rules:

1. Never place any part of a plant in your mouth. (*Note:* Emphasize the distinction between nonedible plants and edible plants, fruits, and vegetables.)
2. Never allow any sap or fruit juice to set into your skin.
3. Never inhale or expose your skin or eyes to the smoke of any burning plant.
4. Never pick any unfamiliar wildflowers, seeds, berries, or cultivated plants.
5. Never eat food after handling plants without first scrubbing your hands.

The reason for these precautions is that any part of a plant can be relatively toxic, even to the point of fatality. Following is a list of some specific examples of toxic plants. This list is only partial; include additional poisonous (toxic) plants for your specific geographical area.

A. Plants that are poisonous to the touch due to exuded oils are:

Poison ivy (often found on school grounds)	Poison oak
Poison sumac	(other)

B. Plants that are poisonous when eaten include:

Many fungi	Belladonna	Pokeweed	Indian tobacco
(mushrooms)	Wake robin	Tansy	Jimson weed
Aconite	Henbane	Foxglove	(other)

C. The saps of the following plants are toxic:

Oleander	Trumpet vine	Poinsettia	(other)

Note: Also be aware that many common houseplants are toxic.

The Plant Picker

Plants That Will Survive with Little Sunlight

African Violet	Corn Plant	Peperomia	Spider Plant
Asparagus Fern	English Ivy	Philodendron	Spiderwort
Begonia	Ficus	Piggyback (Tolmeia)	(Tradescantia)
Boston Fern	Hen and Chickens	Snake Plant	Staghorn Fern
Chinese Evergreen	Parlor Palm		

Plants That Need a Great Deal of Sunlight

Agave	Echeveria	Mimosa (Acacia)	Spirea
Aloe	Geranium	Oxalis	Swedish Ivy
Blood Leaf	Hibiscus	Sedum	(filtered sunlight)
Cactus	Jade Plant		Yucca
Coleus	(filtered sunlight)		

Safety Management Helper

Safety Checklist*

The following general safety practices should be followed in your science teaching situation:

_____ Obtain a copy of the federal, state, and local regulations which relate to school safety, as well as a copy of your school district's policies and procedures. Pay special attention to guidelines for overcrowding, goggle legislation and "right to know" legislation.

_____ Know your school's policy and procedure in case of accidents.

_____ Check your classroom on a regular basis to insure that all possible safety precautions are being taken. Equipment and materials should be properly stored; hazardous materials should not be left exposed in the classroom.

_____ Before handling equipment and materials, familiarize yourself with their possible hazards.

_____ Be extra cautious when dealing with fire, and instruct your students to take appropriate precautions. Be certain fire extinguishers and fire blankets are nearby.

_____ Be familiar with your school's fire regulations, evacuation procedures, and the location and use of fire-fighting equipment.

_____ At the start of each science activity, instruct students regarding potential hazards and the precautions to be taken.

_____ The group size of students working on an experiment should be limited to a number that can safely perform the experiment without confusion and accidents.

_____ Plan enough time for students to perform the experiments, then clean up and properly store the equipment and materials.

_____ Students should be instructed never to taste or touch substances in the science classroom without first obtaining specific instructions from the teacher.

_____ Instruct students that all accidents or injuries—no matter how small—should be reported to you immediately.

_____ Instruct students that it is unsafe to touch their faces, mouths, eyes, and other parts of their bodies while they are working with plants, animals, or chemical substances and afterwards, until they have washed their hands and cleaned their nails.

When working with chemicals:

_____ Teach students that chemicals must not be mixed just to see what happens.

_____ Students should be instructed never to taste chemicals and to wash their hands after using chemicals.

*Reprinted with permission from *Safety in the Elementary Science Classroom*. Copyright © 1978, 1993 by the National Science Teachers Association, 1840 Wilson Boulevard, Arlington, VA 22201-3000.

_____ Elementary school students should not be allowed to mix acid and water.

_____ Keep combustible materials in a metal cabinet equipped with a lock.

_____ Chemicals should be stored under separate lock in a cool, dry place, but not in a refrigerator.

_____ Only minimum amounts of chemicals should be stored in the classroom. Any materials not used in a given period should be carefully discarded, particularly if they could become unstable.

Glassware is dangerous. Whenever possible, plastic should be substituted. However, when glassware is used, follow these precautions:

_____ Hard glass test tubes should not be heated from the bottom. They should be tipped slightly, but not in the direction of another student.

_____ Sharp edges on mirrors or glassware should be reported to the teacher. A whisk broom and dustpan should be available for sweeping up pieces of broken glass.

_____ Warn students not to drink from glassware used for science experiments.

_____ Thermometers for use in the elementary classroom should be filled with alcohol, not mercury.

Teachers and students should be constantly alert to the following safety precautions while working with electricity:

_____ Students should be taught to use electricity safely in everyday situations.

_____ At the start of any unit on electricity, students should be told not to experiment with the electric current of home circuits.

_____ Check your school building code about temporary wiring for devices to be used continuously in one location.

_____ Electrical cords should be short, in good condition, and plugged in at the nearest outlet.

_____ Tap water is a conductor of electricity. Students' hands should be dry when touching electrical cords, switches, or appliances.

Materials to Keep in Your Science Closet

Primary Grades

Depending on the maturity of your students, you may wish to keep some or most of these items in a secure location in the room:

aluminum foil
aluminum foil pie plates
aquarium
baking soda
balance and standard
    masses
basic rock and mineral
    collection
beans, lima
camera and supplies
cardboard tubes from
    paper towel rolls
clipboard
cooking oil
corks
dishes, paper

dishes, plastic
egg cartons
feathers
first aid kit
flashlight
food coloring
globe
hand lenses
hot plate
iron filings
latex gloves
lemon juice
lunch bags, paper
magnets, various sizes
    and shapes
masking tape

measuring cups
measuring spoons
meterstick
microscope
mirrors
modeling clay
peas, dried
plastic bucket
plastic jugs
plastic spoons
plastic wrap
potholder
potting soil
rain gauge
rubber balls of various
    sizes

salt
sandwich bags, plastic
scales and masses
seeds, assorted
shell collection
shoe boxes
small plastic animals
small plastic trays
sponges
string
sugar
tape measure
terrarium
vinegar
yeast, dry

Middle Grades

Depending on the maturity of your students, you may wish to keep some or most of these items in a secure location in the room:

aluminum foil
assorted nuts and bolts
balance and standard
    masses
balloons
barometer
batteries
beakers
binoculars
cafeteria trays
calculator
candles
cans, clean, assorted,
    empty
cellophane, various
    colors
chart of regional birds
chart of regional rocks
    and minerals
clothespins, spring-
    variety

compass, directional
compass, drawing
desk lamp
extensive rock and
    mineral collection
eyedroppers
first aid kit
flashlight
flashlight bulbs
forceps or tweezers
glass jars
graduated cylinders
graph paper
hammer
hand lenses
hot glue gun*
hot plate*
hydrogen peroxide (3%)*
incubator
iron filings
isopropyl alcohol*

latex gloves
lenses
litmus paper
map of region, with
    contour lines
map of country, with
    climate regions
map of world
marbles
microscope slides and
    coverslips
mirrors
net for scooping mater-
    ial from streams
    and/or ponds
petroleum jelly
plastic bucket
plastic containers, wide-
    mouth, 1 and 2 L
plastic straws
plastic tubing

plastic wrap
pliers
prisms
pulleys
safety goggles
screwdriver
seeds, assorted vegetable
sponge, natural
steel wool
stop watch
sugar cubes
switches for circuits
tape, electrical
telescope
test tubes (Pyrex or
    equivalent)
thermometers
toothpicks
washers, assorted
wire for making circuits
wood scraps

*Keep these items in a locked closet.

The Metric Helper

Length

1 centimeter (cm) = 10 millimeters (mm)
1 decimeter (dm) = 10 centimeters
1 meter (m) = 10 decimeters
1 kilometer (km) = 1,000 meters

Liquid Volume

1,000 (mL) = 1 liter (L)

Dry Volume

1,000 cubic millimeters (mm^3) = 1 cubic centimeter (cm^3)

Mass

1,000 milligrams (mg) = 1 gram (g)
1,000 grams (g) = 1 kilogram (kg)

Some Important Metric Prefixes

kilo = one thousand
deci = one-tenth
centi = one-hundredth
milli = one-thousandth
micro = one-millionth

Temperature

Water freezes at 0° Celsius
Normal body temperature is 37° Celsius
Water boils at 100° Celsius

Approximate Sizes

millimeter = diameter of the wire in a paper clip
centimeter = slightly more than the width of a paper clip at its narrowest point
meter = slightly more than 1 yard
kilometer = slightly more than ½ mile
gram = slightly more than the mass of a paper clip
kilogram = slightly more than 2 pounds
milliliter = 5 milliters equal 1 teaspoon
liter = slightly more than 1 quart

Content Coverage Checklists

The following content checklists can be used to evaluate various elementary science textbooks, curriculum materials, audiovisual materials, software packages, and other resource materials for use in your classroom. Obviously, these lists do not include every concept, but they will provide a framework for analysis.

The Earth/Space Sciences and Technology

_____ The universe is 8 to 20 billion years old.

_____ The earth is about 5 billion years old.

_____ The earth is composed of rocks and minerals.

_____ Evidence of the many physical changes that have occurred over the earth's history is found in rocks and rock layers.

_____ The study of fossils can tell us a great deal about the life forms that have existed on the earth.

_____ Many species of animals and plants have become extinct.

_____ Our knowledge of earlier life forms comes from the study of fossils.

_____ Such forces as weathering, erosion, volcanic upheavals, and the shifting of crustal plates, as well as human activity, change the earth's surface.

_____ Natural phenomena and human activity also affect the earth's atmosphere and oceans.

_____ The climate of the earth has changed many times over its history.

_____ _Weather_ is a description of the conditions of our atmosphere at any given time.

_____ The energy we receive from the sun affects our weather.

_____ The water cycle, a continuous change in the form and location of water, affects the weather and life on our planet.

_____ Weather instruments are used to assess and predict the weather.

_____ The natural resources of our planet are limited.

_____ The quality of the earth's water, air, and soil is affected by human activity.

_____ Water, air, and soil must be conserved, or life as we know it will not be able to continue on the earth.

_____ The responsibility for preserving the environment rests with individuals, governments, and industries.

_____ Our solar system includes the sun, the moon, and nine planets.

_____ The sun is one of many billions of stars in the Milky Way galaxy.

_____ Rockets, artificial satellites, and space shuttles are devices that enable humans to explore the characteristics of planets in our solar system.

_____ Data gathered about the earth, oceans, atmosphere, solar system, and universe may be expressed in the form of words, numbers, charts, or graphs.

Life Sciences and Technology

_____ Living things are different from nonliving things.

_____ Plants and animals are living things.

_____ Living things can be classified according to their unique characteristics.

_____ The basic structural unit of all living things is the cell.

_____ All living things proceed through stages of development and maturation.

_____ Living things reproduce in a number of different ways.

_____ Animals and plants inherit and transmit the characteristics of their ancestors.

_____ Species of living things adapt and change over long periods of time or become extinct.

_____ Living things depend upon the earth, its atmosphere, and the sun for their existence.

_____ Living things affect their environment, and their environment affects living things.

_____ Different areas of the earth support different life forms, which are adapted to the unique characteristics of the area in which they live.

_____ Animals and plants affect one another.

_____ Plants are food producers.

_____ Animals are food consumers.

_____ Animals get their food by eating plants or other animals that eat plants.

_____ The human body consists of groups of organs (systems) that work together to perform a particular function.

_____ The human body can be affected by a variety of diseases, including sexually transmitted diseases.

_____ Human life processes are affected by food, exercise, drugs, air quality, and water quality.

_____ Medical technologies can be used to enhance the functioning of the human body and to diagnose, monitor, and treat diseases.

Physical Sciences and Technology

_____ _Matter_ is anything that takes up space and has weight.

_____ Matter is found in three forms: solid, liquid, and gas.

_____ All matter in the universe attracts all other matter in the universe with a force that depends on the mass of the objects and the distance between them.

_____ Matter can be classified on the basis of readily observable characteristics, such as color, odor, taste, and solubility. These characteristics are known as _physical properties of matter._

_____ Matter can undergo chemical change to form new substances.

_____ Substances consist of small particles known as *molecules.*

_____ Molecules are made of smaller particles known as *atoms.*

_____ Atoms are composed of three smaller particles called *protons, neutrons,* and *electrons.* (Protons and neutrons are composed of yet smaller particles known as *quarks.*)

_____ Atoms differ from one another in the number of protons, neutrons, and electrons they have.

_____ Some substances are composed of only one type of atom. These substances are known as *elements.*

_____ In chemical reactions between substances, matter is neither created nor destroyed but only changed in form. This is the law of conservation of matter.

_____ An object at rest or moving at a constant speed will remain in that state unless acted upon by an unbalanced external force.

_____ *Acceleration* is the rate at which an object's velocity changes.

_____ The amount of acceleration that an object displays varies with the force acting on the object and its mass.

_____ Whenever a force acts on an object, an equal and opposite reacting force occurs.

_____ The flight of an airplane results from the interaction of four forces: weight, lift, thrust, and drag.

_____ *Energy*—the capacity to do work—manifests itself in a variety of forms, including light, heat, sound, electricity, motion, and nuclear energy.

_____ Energy may be stored in matter by virtue of an object's position or condition. Such energy is known as *potential energy.*

_____ Under ordinary circumstances, energy can neither be created nor destroyed. This is the law of conservation of energy.

_____ The law of conservation of matter and the law of conservation of energy have been combined to form the law of conservation of matter plus energy, which states that under certain conditions, matter can be changed into energy and energy can be changed into matter.

_____ The basic concepts of matter, energy, force, and motion can be used to explain natural phenomena in the life, earth/space, and physical sciences.

_____ The diminishing supply of fossil fuels may be compensated for by the increased utilization of alternate energy sources, including wind, water, and synthetic fuels, and by energy conservation measures.

Your Science Survival Bookshelf

The Bookshelf

Abruscato, Joseph. *Whizbangers and Wonderments: Science Activities for Young People.* Boston: Allyn and Bacon, 2000.

Abruscato, Joseph, and Jack Hassard. *The Whole Cosmos Catalog of Science Activities.* Glenview, IL: Scott Foresman/Goodyear Publishers, 1991.

Blough, Glenn, and Julius Schwartz. *Elementary School Science and How to Teach It.* Fort Worth, TX: Holt Rinehart & Winston, 1990.

Carin, Arthur A. *Teaching Science through Discovery.* Columbus, OH: Merrill, 1996.

Esler, William K., and Mary K. Esler. *Teaching Elementary School Science.* Belmont, CA: Wadsworth, 1996.

Friedl, Alfred E. *Teaching Science to Children.* New York: Random House, 1991.

Hapai, Marlene Nachbar, and Leon H. Burton. *BugPlay: Activities with Insects for Young Children.* Menlo Park, CA: Addison-Wesley, 1990.

Hassard, Jack. *Science Experiences: Cooperative Learning and the Teaching of Science.* Menlo Park, CA: Addison-Wesley, 1990.

Jacobson, Willard J., and Abby B. Bergman. *Science for Children.* Englewood Cliffs, NJ: Prentice-Hall, 1991.

Lorbeer, George C., and Leslie W. Nelson. *Science Activities for Children.* Dubuque, IA: W. C. Brown, 1996.

Neuman, Donald B. *Experiencing Elementary Science.* Belmont, CA: Wadsworth, 1993.

Tolman, Marvin H., and Gary R. Hardy. *Discovering Elementary Science.* Boston: Allyn and Bacon, 1999.

Van Cleave, Janice Pratt. *Chemistry for Every Kid.* New York: Wiley, 1989.

Victor, Edward, and Richard E. Kellough. *Science for the Elementary School.* New York: Macmillan, 1997.

Weisgerber, Robert A. *Science Success for Students with Disabilities.* Menlo Park, CA: Addison-Wesley, 1993.

The Magazine Rack

For Teachers

Audubon Magazine
National Audubon Society
1130 Fifth Avenue
New York, NY 10028

Natural History
The American Museum of Natural History
Central Park West at Seventy-Ninth Street
New York, NY 10024

Science Activities
Heldref Publications
1319 Eighteenth Street, NW
Washington, DC 20036

Science and Children
National Science Teachers Association
1840 Wilson Boulevard
Arlington, VA 22201-3000

Science News Letter
Science Service Inc.
1719 North Street, NW
Washington, DC 20036

Science Scope
National Science Teachers Association
1840 Wilson Boulevard
Arlington, VA 22201-3000

Science Teacher
National Science Teachers Association
National Education Association
1742 Connecticut Avenue, NW
Washington, DC 20088-0154

Technology and Learning
Peter Li, Inc.
330 Progress Road
Dayton, OH 45449

For Children

Chickadee
Young Naturalist Foundation
P.O. Box 11314
Des Moines, IA 50340

The Curious Naturalist
Massachusetts Audubon Society
208 South Great Road
South Lincoln, MA 01773

Current Science
Xerox Education Publications
5555 Parkcenter Circle Suite 300
Dublin, OH 43017

Discover
Family Media, Inc.
3 Park Avenue
New York, NY 10016

Geotimes
American Geological Institute
1515 Massachusetts Avenue, NW
Washington, DC 20075

Junior Astronomer
Benjamin Adelman
4211 Colie Drive
Silver Springs, MD 20906

Junior Natural History
American Museum of Natural History
Central Park West at Seventy-Ninth Street
New York, NY 10024

Ladybug
Cricket Country Lane
Box 50284
Boulder, CO 80321-0284

National Geographic World
National Geographic Society
Seventeenth and M Streets, NW
Washington, DC 20036

Odyssey
Kalmbach Publishing Company
1027 North Seventh Street
Milwaukee, WI 53233

Owl
Young Naturalist Foundation
P.O. Box 11314
Des Moines, IA 50304

Ranger Rick
National Wildlife Federation
1412 Sixteenth Street, NW
Washington, DC 20036-2266

Science Weekly
Subscription Department
P.O. Box 70154
Washington, DC 20088-0154

Science World
Scholastic Magazines, Inc.
50 West Forty-Fourth Street
New York, NY 10036

Scienceland
Scienceland, Inc.
501 Fifth Avenue
New York, NY 10017

SuperScience
Scholastic Magazines, Inc.
50 West Forty-Fourth Street
New York, NY 10036

3-2-1 Contact
Children's Television Workshop
One Lincoln Plaza
New York, NY 10023

WonderScience
American Chemical Society
1155 Sixteenth Street, NW
Washington, DC 20036

Free and Inexpensive Materials

American Solar Energy Society
2400 Central Avenue, Suite G–1
Boulder, CO 80301

American Wind Energy Association
777 North Capitol Street, NE, Suite 805
Washington, DC 20002

The Energy Learning Center
1776 I Street, NW, Suite 400
Washington, DC 20006

Environmental Protection Agency Public
    Information Center and Library
401 M Street, SW
Washington, DC 20460

Environmental Sciences Services Administration
Office of Public Information
Washington Science Center, Building 5
Rockville, MD 20852

Fish and Wildlife Service
U.S. Department of the Interior
1849 C Street, NW
Mail Stop 304 Web Building
Washington, DC 20240

Jet Propulsion Laboratory (JPL)
Teacher Resource Center
4900 Oak Grove Drive
Mail Stop CS–530
Pasadena, CA 91109

National Aeronautics and Space Administration
    (NASA)
NASA Education Division
NASA Headquarters
300 E Street, SW
Washington, DC 20546

National Park Service
U.S. Department of the Interior
1849 C Street, NW
Washington, DC 20240

National Science Foundation
Division of Pre-College Education
1800 G Street, NW
Washington, DC 20550

National Wildlife Federation
8925 Leesburg Pike
Vienna, VA 22184-0001

Superintendent of Documents
U.S. Government Printing Office
732 North Capital Street, NW
Washington, D.C. 20401

U.S. Bureau of Mines
Office of Mineral Information
U.S. Department of the Interior
1849 C Street, NW
Washington, DC 20240

U.S. Department of Education
555 New Jersey Avenue, NW
Washington, DC 20208

U.S. Department of Energy
Conservation and Renewable Energy Inquiry and
    Referral Service
P.O. Box 8900
Silver Spring, MD 20907

U.S. Department of the Interior
Earth Science Information Center
1849 C Street, NW, Room 2650
Washington, DC 20240

U.S. Forest Service
Division of Information and Education
Fourteenth Street and Independence Avenue, SW
Washington, DC 20250

U.S. Geological Survey
Public Inquiries Office
U.S. Department of the Interior
Eighteenth and F Streets, NW
Washington, DC 20240

U.S. Public Health Service
Department of Health and Human Services
66 Canal Center Plaza, Suite 200
Alexandria, VA 22314

The "Wish Book" Companies

Accent Science
P.O. Box 144
Saginaw, MI 48605

AIMS Education Foundation
P.O. Box 7766
Fresno, CA 93747

Carolina Biological Supply Co.
2700 York Road
Burlington, NC 27215

Central Scientific Company (CENCO)
3300 CENCO Parkway
Franklin, Park, IL 60131

Connecticut Valley Biological Supply Co., Inc.
82 Valley Road
Southhampton, MA 01073

Delta Education, Inc.
P.O. Box 915
Hudson, NH 03051-0915

Exploratorium Store
3601 Lyon Street
San Francisco, CA 94123

Flinn Scientific, Inc.
131 Flinn Street
P.O. Box 291
Batavia, IL 60510

Frey Scientific
905 Hickory Lane
Mansfield, OH 44905

Hubbard Scientific
3101 Iris Avenue, Suite 215
Boulder, CO 80301

Learning Alternatives, Inc.
2370 West 89A, Suite 5
Sedona, AZ 86336

Learning Spectrum
1390 Westridge Drive
Portola Valley, CA 94025

Learning Things, Inc.
68A Broadway
P.O. Box 436
Arlington, MA 02174

LEGO Systems, Inc.
555 Taylor Road
Enfield, CT 06802

NASCO West, Inc.
P.O. Box 3837
Modesto, CA 95352

Ohaus Scale Corp.
29 Hanover Road
Florham Park, NJ 07932

Science Kit and Boreal Labs
777 East Park Drive
Tonawanda, NY 14150

The Science Man Co.
A Division of TSM Marketing, Inc.
4738 North Harlem Avenue
Hardwood Heights, IL 60656

Teacher's Laboratory, Inc.
P.O. Box 6480
Brattleboro, VT 05302

Ward's Natural Science Establishment, Inc.
5100 West Henrietta Road
P.O. Box 92912
Rochester, NY 14692

Wind and Weather
P.O. Box 2320-ST
Mendocino, CA 95460

Young Naturalist Co.
614 East Fifth Street
Newton, KN 67114

Bilingual Child Resources

Alabama, Florida, Georgia, Kentucky, Mississippi, South Carolina, Tennessee

Bilingual Education South Eastern Support Center [BESES]
Florida International University
Tamiami Campus, TRM03
Miami, FL 33199

Alaska, Idaho, Montana, Oregon, Washington, Wyoming

Interface Education Network
7080 SW Fir Loop, Suite 200
Portland, OR 97223

American Samoa, Hawaii

Hawaii/American Samoa Multifunctional Support Center
1150 South King Street, #203
Honolulu, HI 97814

Arizona, California (Imperial, Orange, Riverside, San Bernardino, San Diego Counties)

SDSU-Multifunctional Support Center
6363 Alvarado Court, Suite 200
San Diego, CA 92120

Arkansas, Louisiana, Oklahoma, Texas Education Service Regions V–XIX

Bilingual Education Training and Technical Assistance Network [BETTA]
University of Texas at El Paso
College of Education
El Paso, TX 79968

California (all counties north of and including San Luis Obispo, Kern, and Inyo), Nevada

Bilingual Education Multifunctional Support Center
National Hispanic University
255 East Fourteenth Street
Oakland, CA 94606

California (Los Angeles, Santa Barbara, Ventura Counties), Nevada

Bilingual Education Multifunctional Support Center
California State University at Los Angeles
School of Education
5151 State University Drive
Los Angeles, CA 90032

Colorado, Kansas, Nebraska, New Mexico, Utah

BUENO Bilingual Education Multifunctional Support Center
University of Colorado
Bueno Center of Multicultural Education
Campus Box 249
Boulder, CO 80309

Commonwealth of Northern Mariana Islands, Guam, Trust Territory of the Pacific Islands

Project BEAM [Bilingual Education Assistance in Micronesia]
University of Guam
College of Education
UOG Station,
Mangilao, GU 96923

Commonwealth of Puerto Rico, Virgin Islands

Bilingual Education Multifunctional Support Center
Colegio Universitario Metropolitano
P.O. Box CUM
Rio Piedras, PR 00928

Connecticut, Maine, Massachusetts, New Hampshire, Rhode Island, Vermont

New England Bilingual Education Multifunctional Center
Brown University, Weld Building
345 Blackstone Boulevard
Providence, RI 02906

Delaware, District of Columbia, Maryland, New Jersey, North Carolina, Ohio, Pennsylvania, Virginia, West Virginia

Georgetown University Bilingual Education Service Center
Georgetown University
2139 Wisconsin Avenue, NW, Suite 100
Washington, DC 20007

Illinois, Indiana, Iowa, Michigan, Minnesota, Missouri, North Dakota, South Dakota, Wisconsin

Midwest Bilingual Educational Multifunctional Resource Center
2360 East Devon Avenue, Suite 3011
Campus Box 136
Des Plaines, IL 60018

New York

New York State Bilingual Education Multifunctional Support Center
Hunter College of CUNY
695 Park Avenue, Box 367
New York, NY 10021

*Texas Education Service Center, Regions
I through IV, XX*

Region Multifunctional Support Center
Texas A&I University
Kingsville, TX 78363

Native American Programs

*Alaska, Arizona, California, Michigan,
Minnesota, Montana, New Mexico,
North Carolina, Oklahoma, South Dakota,
Utah, Washington, Wyoming*

National Indian Bilingual Center
Arizona State University
Community Services Building
Tempe, AZ 85287

Special-Needs Resources

Alexander Graham Bell Association for the Deaf
3417 Volta Place, NW
Washington, D.C. 20007

American Foundation for the Blind
15 West Sixteenth Street
New York, NY 10011

American Printing House for the Blind
1839 Frankforth Avenue, Box A
Louisville, KY 40206

American Speech, Language, and Hearing
Association
10801 Rockville Pike
Rockville, MD 20852

Center for Multisensory Learning
University of California at Berkeley
Lawrence Hall of Science
Berkeley, CA 94720

Council for Exceptional Children
1920 Association Drive
Reston, VA 22091

ERIC Clearinghouse on Handicapped and
Gifted Children
1920 Association Drive
Reston, VA 22091

The Lighthouse for the Blind and Visually Impaired
1155 Mission Street
San Francisco, CA 94103

National Technical Institute for the Deaf
One Lomb Memorial Drive
Rochester, NY 14623

The Project on the Handicapped in Science
American Association for the Advancement
of Science
1776 Massachusetts Avenue, NW
Washington, DC 20036

Recording for the Blind
20 Roszel Road
Princeton, NJ 08540

Science for the Handicapped Association
University of Wisconsin–Eau Claire
Eau Claire, WI 54701

Sensory Aids Foundation
399 Sherman Avenue
Palo Alto, CA 94304

Science Teachers Associations

The major association for teachers with an interest in science is the National Science Teachers Association (NSTA). Joining this association provides you with a choice of periodicals, related support materials, and opportunities to participate in regional and national meetings. For information on membership, write to the following address:

National Science Teachers Association (NSTA)
1840 Wilson Boulevard
Arlington, VA 22201-3000

The following affiliated organizations may be reached through the NSTA address:

Association for the Education of Teachers in Science (AETS)
Council for Elementary Science International (CESI)
National Association for Research in Science Teaching (NARST)

If you teach the middle grades and have a special interest *and* a strong content background in the biological, earth, or physical sciences, you may wish to consider joining one of these groups:

National Association of Biology Teachers
1420 N Street, NW
Washington, DC 20005

American Chemical Society
1155 Sixteenth Street, NW
Washington, DC 20006

National Association of Geology Teachers
P.O. Box 368
Lawrence, Kansas 66044

American Association of Physics Teachers
c/o American Institute of Physics
335 E. 45th Street
New York, NY 10017

This association is for teachers interested in science or mathematics or both:

School Science and Mathematics Association
P.O. Box 1614
Indiana University of Pensylvania
Indiana, PA 15704

NASA Teacher Resource Centers

NASA Teacher Resource Centers provide teachers with NASA-related materials for use in classrooms. Contact the center that serves your state for materials or additional information.

Alabama, Arkansas, Iowa, Louisiana, Missouri, Tennessee

NASA Marshall Space Flight Center
Teacher Resource Center at the U.S. Space and
   Rocket Center
P.O. Box 070015
Huntsville, AL 35807

Alaska, Arizona, California, Hawaii, Idaho, Montana, Nevada, Oregon, Utah, Washington, Wyoming

NASA Ames Research Center
Teacher Resource Center
Mail Stop 253-2
Moffett Field, CA 94035

California (cities near Dryden Flight Research Facility)

NASA Dryden Flight Research Facility
Teacher Resource Center
Lancaster, CA 93535

Colorado, Kansas, Nebraska, New Mexico, North Dakota, Oklahoma, South Dakota, Texas

NASA Johnson Space Center
Education Resource Center
1601 NASA Road #1
Houston, TX 77058

Connecticut, Delaware, District of Columbia, Maine, Maryland, Massachusetts, New Hampshire, New Jersey, New York, Pennsylvania, Rhode Island, Vermont

NASA Goddard Space Flight Center
Teacher Resource Laboratory
Mail Code 130.3
Greenbelt, MD 20771

Florida, Georgia, Puerto Rico, Virgin Islands

NASA Kennedy Space Center
Educators Resource Laboratory
Mail Code ERL
Kennedy Space Center, FL 32899

Kentucky, North Carolina, South Carolina, Virginia, West Virginia

NASA Langley Research Center
Teacher Resource Center at the Virginia Air and
   Space Center
600 Settlers Landing Road
Hampton, VA 23669

Illinois, Indiana, Michigan, Minnesota, Ohio, Wisconsin

NASA Lewis Research Center
Teacher Resource Center
21000 Brookpark Road
Mail Stop 8-1
Cleveland, OH 44135

Mississippi

NASA Stennis Space Center
Teacher Resource Center
Building 1200
Stennis Space Center, MS 39529-6000

Virginia and Maryland Eastern Shore

NASA Wallops Flight Facility
Education Complex-Visitor Center
Building J-17
Wallops Island, VA 23337

General inquiries related to space science and planetary exploration may be addressed to:

Jet Propulsion Laboratory
NASA Teacher Resource Center
Attn: JPL Educational Outreach
Mail Stop CS-530
Pasadena, CA 91109

For catalogue and order forms for audiovisual material, send request on school letterhead to:

NASA CORE
Lorain County Joint Vocational School
15181 Route 58 South
Oberlin, OH 44074

Appendix

The National Science Education (NSE) Content Standards, Grades K–8

Unifying Concepts and Processes

Standard: As a result of activities in grades K–12, all students should develop understandings and abilities aligned with the following concepts and processes.

Systems, order, and organization
Evidence, models, and explanation
Constancy, change, and measurement
Evolution and equilibrium
Form and function

Content Standards: Grades K–4

Science as Inquiry*
Content Standard A: As a result of activities in grades K–4, all students should develop

- Abilities necessary to do scientific inquiry
- Understanding about scientific inquiry

Physical Science [PS]
Content Standard B: As a result of the activities in grades K–4, all students should develop an understanding of

- Properties of objects and materials [PS 1]
- Position and motion of objects [PS 2]
- Light, heat, electricity, and magnetism [PS 3]

Source: National Research Council, *National Science Education Standards* (Washington, DC: National Academy Press, 1996), pp. 104–171. Used with permission. Note that the bracketed symbol to the right of each standard was prepared by this author.

*This general standard is the foundation all the NSE standards. Since it is emphasized in all *Teaching Children Science* projects and activities, it is not identified for each experience.

Life Science [LS]

Content Standard C: As a result of the activities in grades K–4, all students should develop an understanding of

- The characteristics of organisms [LS 1]
- Life cycles of organisms [LS 2]
- Organisms and environments [LS 3]

Earth and Space Sciences [ESS]

Content Standard D: As a result of the activities in grades K–4, all students should develop an understanding of

- Properties of earth materials [ESS 1]
- Objects in the sky [ESS 2]
- Changes in earth and sky [ESS 3]

Science and Technology [S&T]

Content Standard E: As a result of the activities in grades K–4, all students should develop an understanding of

- Abilities of technological design [S&T 1]
- Understanding about science and technology [S&T 2]
- Ability to distinguish between natural objects and objects made by humans [S&T 3]

Science in Personal and Social Perspectives [SPSP]

Content Standard F: As a result of the activities in grades K–4, all students should develop an understanding of

- Personal health [SPSP 1]
- Characteristics and changes in populations [SPSP 2]
- Types of resources [SPSP 3]
- Changes in environments [SPSP 4]
- Science and technology in local challenges [SPSP 5]

History and Nature of Science [HNS]

Content Standard G: As a result of the activities in grades K–4, all students should develop an understanding of

- Science as a human endeavor [HNS 1]

Content Standards: Grades 5–8

Science as Inquiry

Content Standard A: As a result of their activities in grades 5–8, all students should develop

- Abilities necessary to do scientific inquiry
- Understanding about scientific inquiry

Physical Science [PS]

Content Standard B: As a result of their activities in grades 5–8, all students should develop an understanding of

- Properties and changes of properties in matter [PS 4]
- Motion and forces [PS 5]
- Transfer of energy [PS 6]

Life Science [LS]

Content Standard C: As a result of their activities in grades 5–8, all students should develop an understanding of

- Structure and function in living systems [LS 4]
- Reproduction and heredity [LS 5]
- Regulation and behavior [LS 6]
- Population and ecosystems [LS 7]
- Diversity and adaptations of organisms [LS 8]

Earth and Space Sciences [ESS]

Content Standard D: As a result of their activities in grades 5–8, all students should develop an understanding of

- Structure of the earth system [ESS 4]
- Earth's history [ESS 5]
- Earth in the solar system [ESS 6]

Science and Technology [S&T]

Content Standard E: As a result of the activities in grades 5–8, all students should develop an understanding of

- Abilities of technological design [S&T 4]
- Understanding about science and technologyy [S&T 5]

Science in Personal and Social Perspectives [SPSP]

Content Standard F: As a result of the activities in grades 5–8, all students should develop an understanding of

- Personal health [SPSP 6]
- Populations, resources, and environments [SPSP 7]
- Natural hazards [SPSP 8]
- Risks and benefits [SPSP 9]
- Changes in environments [SPSP 10]
- Science and technology in society [SPSP 11]

History and Nature of Science [HNS]

Content Standard G: As a result of the activities in grades 5–8, all students should develop an understanding of

- Science as a human endeavor [HNS 2]
- Nature of science [HNS 3]
- History of science [HNS 4]

Index

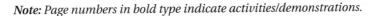

Note: Page numbers in bold type indicate activities/demonstrations.

Photo, Figure, and Text Credits

p. 198, Figure 11A.8, photo by Joseph Abruscato.

p. 223, illustration from J. Abruscato and J. Hassard, *The Whole Cosmos Catalog of Science Activities,* 2nd ed. (Glenview, IL: Scott, Foresman and Co., 1991). Used with permission.

pp. 232 and 234, Figures 12A.1 and 12A.2, photos courtesy of NASA.

p. 236, Figure 12A.4, adapted from "Charting the Planets," *Educational Brief,* EB-111, a publication of NASA.

p. 237, Figure 12A.5, photo by NASA TV (AP/Wide World Photos).

pp. 238, 241, 242, and 243, Figures 12A.6, 12A.7, 12A.8, and 12A.9, photos courtesy of NASA.

p. 245, Figure 12A.10, photo by Marshall Space Flight Center/NASA/Science Photo Library (Photo Researchers).

p. 262, Figure 12B.1, photo courtesy of NASA.

p. 299, Figure 14A.1, photo by Mitch Reardon (Photo Researchers).

pp. 304 and 307, Figures 14A.3 and 14A.4, based on Charles Tanzer, *Biology and Human Progress,* 7th ed. (Englewood Cliffs, NJ: Prentice-Hall, 1986).

p. 309, Figure 14A.5, photo courtesy of Dr. Ester R. Angert.

p. 316, illustration from J. Abruscato and J. Hassard, *The Whole Cosmos Catalog of Science Activities,* 2nd ed. (Glenview, IL: Scott, Foresman and Co., 1991). Used with permission.

pp. 337, 341, 342, and 343, Figures 15A.2, 15A.3, 15A.4, and 15A.5, from *Biology: The Living Science,* by Miller and Levine. © 1998 by Prentice Hall, Simon & Schuster Education Group. Used by permission.

p. 351, illustration from *Science: A Process Approach II,* American Association for the Advancement of Science. Used with permission.

pp. 360 and 361, illustrations from J. Abruscato and J. Hassard, *The Whole Cosmos Catalog of Science Activities,* 2nd ed. (Glenview, IL: Scott, Foresman and Co., 1991). Used with permission.

p. 388, Figure 17A.1, photo by Jean-Marie Blase (AP/Wide World Photos).

p. 409, illustration from *Science: A Process Approach II,* American Association for the Advancement of Science. Used with permission.

p. 411, illustration from J. Abruscato and J. Hassard, *The Whole Cosmos Catalog of Science Activities,* 2nd ed. (Glenview, IL: Scott, Foresman and Co., 1991). Used with permission.

pp. 441 and 448, illustrations from *Science: A Process Approach II,* American Association for the Advancement of Science. Used with permission.

pp. 455–456, "Living Materials in the Classroom," from *Science Scope* 13, no. 3 (November/December 1989), p. 517. Used with permission of the National Science Teachers Association.

pp. 457–458, "Safety Checklist," reprinted with permission from *Safety in the Elementary Science Classroom.* © 1978, 1993 by the National Science Teachers Association, 1840 Wilson Boulevard, Arlington, VA 22201-3000.

pp. 473–476, from National Research Council, *National Science Education Standards* (Washington, DC: National Academy Press, 1996), pp. 104–171. Used with permission.